IRANIAN CLASSICAL MUSIC

*To Navid, who arrived close to the start of this journey;
and to Kayvon, who came of age just as it reached its end.*

Iranian Classical Music
The Discourses and Practice of Creativity

LAUDAN NOOSHIN
City University London, UK

ASHGATE

Published by
Ashgate Publishing Limited
Wey Court East
Union Road
Farnham
Surrey, GU9 7PT
England

Ashgate Publishing Company
110 Cherry Street
Suite 3-1
Burlington, VT 05401-4405
USA

www.ashgate.com

British Library Cataloguing in Publication Data
A catalogue record for this book is available from the British Library

Library of Congress Cataloging-in-Publication Data
Nooshin, Laudan.
  Iranian classical music : the discourses and practice of creativity / by Laudan Nooshin.
    pages cm. – (SOAS musicology series)
  Includes bibliographical references and index.
  ISBN 978-0-7546-0703-8 (hardcover : alk. paper) 1. Music– Iran– History and criticism. I. Title.
  ML344.N66 2014
  780.955– dc23

2014012040

ISBN 9780754607038 (hbk)

Bach musicological font developed by © Yo Tomita

MIX
Paper from
responsible sources
FSC
www.fsc.org FSC® C013985

Printed in the United Kingdom by Henry Ling Limited,
at the Dorset Press, Dorchester, DT1 1HD

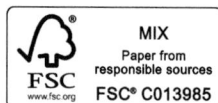

Contents

List of Figures

Examples on the Accompanying CD

Note: Except for Tracks 9–11, the pieces on the accompanying CD are not covered by international copyright legislation. Full details of Tracks 1–8 are given in Appendix A.

Track 1: *darāmad* of *Segāh*, Nur Ali Borumand (*tār*), *radif* 1 (Figure 4.1) (23″)

Track 2: *darāmad* of *Segāh*, Pashang Kamkar (*santur*) and Jamshid Andalibi (*nei*), performance 15 (Figure 4.2) (4′12″)

Track 3: *zābol*, Mahmud Karimi (voice), *radif* 2 (Figure 4.3) (1′24″)

Track 4: *zābol*, Farhang Sharif (*tār*), performance 13 (Figure 4.4) (1′09″)

Track 5: *mokhālef*, Nur Ali Borumand (*tār*), *radif* 1 (Figure 4.5) (2′07″)

Track 6: *mokhālef*, Lotfollah Majd (*tār*), performance 10 (Figure 4.6) (2′59″)

Track 7: *maqlub*, Mahmud Karimi (voice), *radif* 2 (Figure 4.7) (43″)

Track 8: *maqlub*, Parviz Meshkatian (*santur*), performance 16 (Figure 4.8) (37″)

Track 9: '*Zakhmeh*' ('Strum'). Track 3 (first 3 minutes) from *All of You* (Hermes Records HER-059, 2010). Used with permission

Track 10: '*Khiyāl*' ('Illusion'). Track 6 (first 2 minutes) from *All of You* (Hermes Records HER-059, 2010). Used with permission

Track 11: '*Golrizoon*' ('Flower Scatter'). Track 9 (first 4 minutes) from *All of You* (Hermes Records HER-059, 2010). Used with permission

Note on Transliteration

Several systems are in current use for transliterating Persian words from Arabic to Roman script, and each has its limitations. In this book I have chosen to privilege the sonic by seeking to convey the pronunciation of words in standard spoken Persian to an English-language readership. I have therefore avoided some of the more widely-accepted transliteration conventions by which Persian words are rendered with Arabic pronunciation (Hafiz, rather than Hafez, for instance).

Where there are standard spellings for names of people and places, technical musical terms, names of instruments and so on, these are used, although it should be noted that there is much inconsistency both in the literature and in the spelling of musicians' names on recordings and programme notes.

Since the aim is to convey the sound of spoken Persian as closely as possible, I make no distinction between different spellings with the same pronunciation, for example *ghayn* and *ghāf* (which are distinguishable in some regional accents, but not in standard Persian) nor between the several alphabet characters used for the sounds 's', 't', 'z' and so on. To do so would lead to inconsistencies in the Roman script and possible confusion for an English-speaking readership. Similarly, I do not indicate the letter *ayn* with an apostrophe, as is often done, since the distinction in spoken Persian is not significant as it is in Arabic (hence, *elmi* rather than *'elmi*). The only exception is where a glottal stop occurs in the middle of a word, where it is indicated with an apostrophe.

In quoting from other authors, I maintain their original spellings.

Dastgāh names use upper case (as in *Segāh*); *gusheh* names, lower case (*darāmad*).

It should be noted that many of the quotations from interviews with musicians use colloquial language. In transliterating these I have maintained this style rather than 'correcting' the Persian to more literary prose.

Transliterations

'oo'   As in c<u>oo</u>l. 'oo' is used in preference to 'u' to avoid confusion with the short 'u' in English. However, in cases where the 'oo' sound is conventionally transliterated with 'u' (e.g. *santur, musiqi, gusheh, sorud*), I follow the latter.

'i'   As in f<u>ee</u>l. For example *asil*. Again, there are instances where a different spelling is conventionally used (e.g. *hazeen*).

'q'   Indicates the sound of the letters *ghayn* and *ghāf*.

'ay'   As in s<u>ay</u>. For example, *pa<u>y</u>dā*. However, conventional spelling is followed for *feyli*, even though the pronunciation is closer to '*fa<u>y</u>li*'.

'kh'   As in Ba<u>ch</u>. For example *mokhālef*.

The only diacritic used is a macron 'ā' to indicate a long vowel (as in 'f<u>a</u>r'). Diacritics are not used for proper nouns other than the names of institutions, concert halls and government departments, and also titles of books, albums and music groups when transliterated from Persian.

The silent final '*h*' of words is written, for example *gusheh*.

The *ezāfeh* is written as *-e* after consonants and *-ye* after vowels (and a silent final *h*), for example *naghmeh-ye maqlub*.

The *tashdid* is represented by doubling the letter, for example *sonnati*.

In general, plurals are indicated by adding an 's' (rather than the Persian suffix *-hā* or *-ān*), for instance *gusheh*s. However, the Persian suffix is used when transliterating spoken interviews.

Preface

This book is a study of creativity, and specifically an attempt to understand the processes by which Iranian classical music comes into being. It is also an exploration of the discourses through which ideas about musical creativity are constructed, exchanged and negotiated within this tradition. The book started life as a doctoral thesis, but has undergone much revision. For one thing, my post-doctoral encounter with critical theory and postcolonial studies caused me to revisit much of the material in the light of ideas relating most pertinently to questions of power and ideology. The original thesis was based primarily on research carried out between 1987 and 1990, and the emergence of the New Musicology in the US (and later Critical Musicology in the UK) largely passed me by as I focused on wrapping up a project which had extended well beyond its original limits. When I discovered the work of scholars such as Susan McClary, Richard Taruskin and Stuart Hall in the mid-1990s, the shock of recognition that this is what I had been searching for was akin to my first encounter with ethnomusicology almost 10 years earlier. I had long felt uneasy about some of the central narratives of creativity in writings on 'improvised' musics, but did not yet possess the scholarly tools with which to theorize the problem. This book is in part an attempt to redress this, and I therefore begin with a critique of the discourses of ethno/musicology, which continue to be heavily dependent on binary thinking and notions of difference – between written and oral/aural, between art and folk, between 'authentic' and (consequently) 'inauthentic', between 'West' and 'East', 'First World' and 'Third World', 'us' and 'them', and so on – and which have been immensely influential on the ways in which Iranian musicians think and talk about their music. From the earliest years of my research, I found the ease with which scholars invoked such pairings troubling, and this ultimately led to an interrogation of one particular dualism: between composition and improvisation.

The book is in three main parts: Part I, Chapter 1 discusses the ways in which musicologists, folk music scholars and ethnomusicologists have approached questions of creativity, and the embedding of this in discursive and conceptual disciplinary paradigms. In Part II, we move to the world of Iranian classical music. Chapter 2 examines the place of creative performance in this tradition, and the ways in which musicians and others have written and talked about creativity, as well as how local concepts and practice have been impacted by profound social, cultural and political changes since the late nineteenth century. Chapter 3 focuses on the canonic repertoire known as *radif*. I discuss the history of the *radif*, its role as a starting point for creative performance, and the processes by which it is transmitted from one generation of musicians to the next. I also consider its ideological aspects, including the iconic status which the *radif* has acquired in recent decades, hand-in-hand with newly arrived ideas about 'authenticity'. Finally, Part III discusses the music 'itself'. Chapter 4 focuses primarily on the modal system known as *dastgāh Segāh* (with some reference to *Māhur*), examining its sectional and modal organization in a number of performances and *radif*s, the ways in which individual *gusheh*s are varied, and the compositional strategies used by musicians to generate new material. At the heart of the analysis is an attempt to understand the underlying creative processes, and in particular the relationship between learnt *radif* and the performances based on it. Chapter 5 explores recent developments in creative practice, charting some of the most significant changes to the tradition over the past 30 years, including an increasingly diverse musical voice in line with the recent emergence in Iran of a civil society discourse, and new ideas about performance practice that go beyond traditional deference to the *radif*.

As with any book, many people have helped along the way, influenced me in ways which they may well be unaware of, and provided invaluable support. From the earliest days of my musical training I have been blessed with teachers, colleagues and fellow travellers without whom I would never have reached the point where writing this book was possible. Without the inspired teaching of Diane White, I might never have studied music at university; without Peter Franklin I might never have survived undergraduate study, let alone proceeded to postgraduate; without Owen Wright I might never have thought this material worthy of publication. Of the many people whose valued help, advice and feedback has kept me going, I would particularly like to thank John Baily, Martin Stokes and Derek Scott. Derek gave me my first full-time opportunity in academic teaching and has continued to be supportive in his inimitable way ever since. The writing of this book was facilitated by two periods of research leave, funded by Brunel University and the Arts and Humanities Research Board (2003–4) and City University London (2010). My thanks to the SOAS Musicology Series Editorial Board and to staff at Ashgate for bearing with me all these years, and to the latter in particular for their wonderful work in seeing the book through to publication. To all the friends, colleagues and musicians, some of whom are sadly no longer with us, who have given their time to talk and correspond with me over the past 25 years, I am most indebted – to Hossein Alizadeh, Shahram Nazeri, Kayhan Kalhor, Parviz Meshkatian, Faramarz Payvar, Asghar Bahari, Mohammad Reza Lotfi, Dariush Talai, Amir Eslami, Hooshyar Khayam, Sasan Fatemi, Hooman Asadi, and Ramin Sedighi at Hermes Records. To Bruno Nettl for spending time with me in the early stages of this research and so generously giving me free rein in his archive in Urbana. To my former student, James Gardner, for his painstaking work setting the musical examples. To Jane Lewisohn for help with musicians' dates and other matters. To Rick Campion for his assistance with the audio examples. To Sally Pomme Clayton for allowing me to use her re-retelling of the nightingale story. To my father, Hoshyar Nooshin, for his knowledge of Persian and his help with transliteration. Of course, the greatest debt is to my family for their love, support and patience.

Laudan Nooshin
November 2014

PART I
Musicological Narratives of Creativity

Chapter 1
Approaching the Study of Musical Creativity: Musicologies, Discourses and Others

In the Beginning: Creativity and Its Myths

> In the darkness, something was happening at last. A voice had begun to sing … it was, beyond comparison, the most beautiful noise he had ever heard. It was so beautiful he could hardly bear it … Polly was finding the song more and more interesting because she thought she was beginning to see the connection between the music and the things that were happening. When a line of dark firs sprang up on a ridge about a hundred yards away she felt that they were connected with a series of deep, prolonged notes which the Lion had sung a second before. And when he burst into a rapid series of lighter notes she was not surprised to see primroses suddenly appearing in every direction. Thus, with an unspeakable thrill, she felt quite certain that all the things were coming (as she said) 'out of the Lion's head'. (C.S. Lewis 1989 [1955]:93, 99)

> … the musical creator is a being comparable to the gods, and music itself the supreme mystery of the science of man, a mystery that all the various disciplines come up against and which holds the key to their progress. (Lévi-Strauss 1969:18)

The passage describing the creation of the land of Narnia in C.S. Lewis' *Chronicles of Narnia* draws its symbolic power from a deep-rooted seam of signification in which music and creation are intimately bound together. Here, the song of Aslan the Lion serves as the prime agent of creation and Lewis traces a direct correlation between the song and the forms created through it. The extent to which the creative power of music serves as a rich source of mythic narrative is evidenced by the many creation stories which invoke music in some way. Claude Lévi-Strauss, that great scholar of myth, noted 'the great number of myths that bear on musical creativity and [by] the veneration accorded to compositions and composers in many societies' (in Blum 2001:186, who cites several examples of such myths).[1]

The creative process is perhaps one of the most enduring mysteries of humankind. On the one hand, it has been argued that it is the ability to create that distinguishes us from other living beings, the essence of what it means to be human. On the other, as indicated by Lévi-Strauss, creativity has across various times and places been regarded as a symbol, and often a preserve, of the divine. In the highly influential book *The Courage to Create*, psychologist Rollo May suggests that the creative impulse can be understood as an aspiration to the condition of divinity and a challenge to mortality:

> Creativity is a yearning for immortality. We human beings know that we must die. We have, strangely enough, a word for death. We know that each of us must develop the courage to confront death. Yet we must also rebel and struggle against it. Creativity comes from this struggle – out of this rebellion the creative act is born. (1975:27)

Of all the arenas of human creativity, perhaps none has been more shrouded in mythology than music, which with its intangible and invisible presence has proved 'the supreme mystery of the science of man'. From the Ancient Greek muses to the nineteenth-century divinely inspired genius, the ineffable connection between music and the other-worldly is found everywhere. In part, this has rendered taboo attempts at explanation,

---

[1] As Bohlman observes, 'The panoply of origin theories reflects a remarkable range of concepts about folk music … The broadest conceptualization of origins attempts to explain the very existence of music. Myth, for example, often contains a variety of explanations of music, often as a salient component of creation itself' (1988:3).

as though delving too deeply may destroy music's essence. No doubt the absence of physical materiality has contributed to this, and more generally to the attribution of supernatural and magical powers to music. To quote again from Lewis, when the Lion's adversary, the Witch, hears the song, she 'felt that this whole world was filled with a Magic different from hers and stronger' (1989:95).[2]

From a scholarly perspective, the mythical and often sacred qualities associated with creativity have long deflected attention away from questions such as how one defines creativity (or creativities?), whether the concept has universal significance, who is permitted to create, whether creativity is valued, and so on, as well as obscuring the relations of power inscribed in the creative process. General literature on the subject has tended to reflect a philosophical rift: between the idea of creativity as a mark of (divine) genius possessed by a few; and creativity as inherent to the human condition. Such positions reflect deep-rooted cultural paradigms which have also pervaded ethno/musicological discourse, as will be discussed. Following earlier advances in psychology and understanding of human cognitive processes, the 1950s and '60s was a watershed period in scholarly attention to creativity.[3] Whilst a detailed consideration of writings on the broad topic of creativity, including debates around definition, lies outside the scope of this book, the significance of this early work was two-fold: first, it began the process of demystifying what had long been regarded as sacrosanct; and, as a result, scholars began to question certain long-held assumptions and to situate creativity within the realms of the social and the everyday. A useful summary of the early literature is provided by Abt and Rosner (1970) who consider creativity in a range of scientific and artistic fields and draw interesting conclusions regarding similarities between creative processes in quite different arenas. With increased interest and research across a range of disciplines, many began to challenge the idea of creativity as the preserve of the few. Particularly influential was the theory of generative linguistics, first proposed by Noam Chomsky in *Syntactic Structures* in 1957, and which argued that the ability to use spoken language depends on a highly developed creative faculty.[4] Following on by just a few years, one of the most comprehensive general publications on creativity, *The Act of Creation* by Arthur Koestler (1964), similarly argued that creativity is innate to *all* humans. Also significant was a later publication by Robert Weisberg, *Creativity and Other Myths* (1986), who suggested that the cognitive processes involved in producing works of artistic and scientific 'genius' are not fundamentally different from those of 'every-day' activities such as problem-solving and speech. I will return to some of these ideas in due course.

This study seeks to explore creative processes in one particular musical tradition – focusing on musicians' cognition, their verbal discourses, and their musical practice. It is both about understanding the creative process, and how the creative process is itself understood. However, this book is not just a study of Iranian classical music, but also a reflective critique of the conceptual and discursive frameworks which underpin ethno/musicological approaches to and understandings of creativity, and which operate dialectically in relation to lay concepts and discourses. As Cook observes, 'both music and musicology are ways of creating meaning rather than just of representing it' (1998:125–6) and Clayton goes further, 'musicological discourse does not only comment on practice and experience … It also influences that very practice and experience … the work of musicology is not to describe musical facts but to be implicated in a wider discursive field' (2003:59). The aim of this opening chapter is to explore the ways in which musical creativity has been historically approached and discussed within different areas of music study. Whilst it may seem curious to

---

[2]   Note the religious overtones of Lewis's narrative: Aslan represents a Christ-figure whose creative power parallels that of God; and the creation of Narnia an analogy to Genesis. Music plays a similarly generative role in J.R.R. Tolkien's *The Silmarillion* (published posthumously in 1977) where it is the first thing created from the void by the God-figure Ilúvatar. Tolkien and Lewis were friends from the mid-1930s.

[3]   The reader is referred to the seminal work of Guildford (1950; his presidential address to the American Psychological Association, 5 September 1950) and others, mainly psychologists, working in this field in the 1950s and '60s: Ghiselm (1952), Lowenfield (1952), Smith (1959), Taylor (1959), Heinze and Stein (1960) and Summerfield and Thatcher (1964). Later publications include Abt and Rosner (1970), Vernon (1970), May (1975), Mansfield and Busse (1981), Weisberg (1986), Csikszentmihalyi (1988), Sternberg (1988), Boden (1990) and Ingold and Hallam (2007).

[4]   Chomsky's work in this area spans several decades and his original ideas were subject to significant revision. However, the basic principle of an innate creative linguistic faculty remains unchanged. See 1957, 1965, 1972, 1980 and 1986 for his most significant writings on language. I return to the ideas of Chomsky in Chapter 4.

begin a book on Iranian classical music with a chapter focused primarily on 'Western' discourses, from the earliest period of my research I was aware of the significant impact of such discourses, both academic and lay, on creative practice in Iran, and particularly the role of binary thinking in relation to ideas about musical difference.[5] Moreover, I am very mindful of the ways in which my own work has been shaped by such ideas, ideas which have remained largely unassailed through one of the most turbulent and self-questioning periods in the history of musicology. Thus, the specific discussion of Iranian classical music and local concepts of creativity is deferred until Chapter 2, and the reader is instead invited to consider how creative processes might be better understood by first interrogating our own terminologies and ideologies. I begin with the concepts and discourses of creativity within 'mainstream'[6] musicology and folk music studies, both of which impacted significantly on ethnomusicology in its formative years, before proceeding to examine how ethnomusicologists have approached questions of creativity. I then consider how these issues have shaped my own work, specifically the ways in which difference is imagined in relation to creative process in the Iranian tradition. Whilst the various approaches to creativity described briefly above differed in significant ways, they shared a relative inattention to questions of ideology and power, in which respect they were very much of their time. As I hope to show, such questions are fundamental to an understanding of musical creativity as social practice; indeed, the theme of power will continue in the chapters that follow as I examine relations of authority and alterity. Given the thrust of the discussion which follows, it seems pertinent to start with issues of power.

Difference, Alterity and Power: Ethno/musicology Meets Postcolonialism

> And now we are at the heart of the great quarrel that, more than anything else, divides the folklorists and will continue to divide them for a good while to come: the problem of creation remains the theme of their liveliest, and sometimes most confused, argument … whatever the manner in which they express themselves, do the folk possess creative gifts, yes or no? (Brăiloiu 1984 [1949]:5–6)

Among the many insights that studying the musics of the world has offered ethnomusicologists and others working in cognate areas such as folklore studies, one of the most exciting has been a recognition of the creative nature of all music-making. And yet, as the above quotation from Romanian musicologist Constantin Brăiloiu testifies, it took some time for this recognition to emerge. Writing in the late 1940s on the eve of ethnomusicology's birth, Brăiloiu sums up a debate which had exercised the minds and pens of folklorists for decades. For many nineteenth- and early twentieth-century European and American folksong collectors, what most distinguished 'art' from 'folk' music was in the creative process. Brăiloiu ends his polemic with a question addressed to folklorists, but which could as easily have been directed to scholars of 'non-Western' music. And therein lies one of the central themes of this chapter: the extent to which musical creativity has been historically mobilized as a marker of difference. I will return to Brăiloiu and the folklorists below.

This chapter examines the ways in which ethnomusicologists and others have approached questions of musical creativity, focusing on the underlying narratives which have shaped discourses in this area. I use the term 'discourse' in its Foucauldian sense to indicate the ways in which language produces a particular kind of knowledge, a knowledge which represents and constitutes its subjects in specific ways. The idea that discourse and knowledge are deeply implicated in the exercise of power is one of the most enduring legacies

---

[5] The terms 'West'/'Western' are clearly problematic in reinforcing the very Orientalist and dualistic positioning which this volume sets out to critique. For one thing, 'Western' implies the equally problematic 'non-Western'. At the same time, one is inevitably bound by inherited discourses with their historical trajectories and contemporary currency. As Born and Hesmondhalgh observe, 'We accept that writing even a self-critical account focused on the West might lead one to reproduce the very hegemony, the very binary oppositions, it sets out to deconstruct' (2000b:47). They suggest (note 1, p.47) that perhaps the most acceptable alternative is 'Euro-American', but even that doesn't reflect the complexities of current global configurations. For the moment, then, I retain 'Western' whilst also signalling that its use should by no means be taken as uncritical or naturalized.

[6] By 'mainstream' musicology, I refer to the area of music studies dealing with 'Western art music' broadly defined, thus following general current UK usage. I am not concerned with divisions between fields such as 'historical musicology' and 'music theory', for instance, as found in the United States.

of post-structuralist theorists such as Foucault and Derrida, and the convergence of these ideas in the writings of Edward Said arguably one of the most influential scholarly watersheds of the late twentieth century. Few academic publications can have had so profound an impact in such a range of disciplinary areas in the arts, humanities and social sciences as *Orientalism* did when it was published in 1978. Of course, Said was not the first to present a critique of Orientalist scholarship (see Halliday 1993:148), but his incisive commentary on its ideological implications proved both timely and explosive. Above all:

> *Orientalism* exposed the intellectual and interpretive certainties of an earlier age for what they were: not the disinterested objective studies that scholars supposed, but a kind of political discourse that both grew out of and helped to constitute global relations of power. As a result, we are all conscious now that the pursuit of knowledge has political implications, as a form of domination, control and even subjugation. Knowledge and power are inextricably linked. (Donnan and Stokes 2002:6)

In the case of mainstream musicology, it was almost a decade before the radical changes of the mid-to-late 1980s created an environment in which scholars could respond to the challenge of *Orientalism* and the broad area of what became known as postcolonial studies. From the early 1990s, a number of musicologists began to explore both the Orientalist implications of their subject of study and of the discipline itself, as well as offering fresh critiques of Said's work from a musicological perspective.[7] In contrast, few ethnomusicologists at this time paid much attention to Said or indeed to issues of ideology and power generally, focusing instead on the task of ethnography.[8] There were exceptions, of course, but in general ethnomusicologists in the 1980s and early '90s were largely unreceptive to ideas emerging from the broad area of postcolonial studies, cultural studies and critical theory, and even from anthropological critiques of structuralism.[9]

There is an extensive literature on the work of Said and it is not my intention to revisit the arguments here.[10] However, certain strands of the debate are pertinent to the current discussion, for example the charge that Said allows little space for agency on the part of 'Others' represented by European writers, and that he fails to examine the often implicated role of those represented. In general, many have called for a more nuanced understanding of the relationship between 'representer' and 'represented' and a move away from the very essentializing discourses which Said himself criticized, by acknowledging different kinds of Orientalism (Stokes 2000:214) and even the possibility of a 'benign Orientalism' (Stokes 2002:168).[11] Notwithstanding such critiques (and Said's later refinements), the significance of the central ideas remain. Above all, *Orientalism* was a wake-up call to the inescapably ideological nature of scholarly processes. The ideas explored in this

---

[7]   For example, Locke (1991, 1993), McClary (1992) and Taruskin (1992). There is now a substantial literature on Orientalism in Western music; see, among others, Bellman (1998), Hayward (1999), Head (2000), several of the chapters in Born and Hesmondhalgh (2000a), Clayton and Zon (2007), Downes (2007) and Locke (2011).

[8]   See Nooshin (2009a) for further discussion.

[9]   Including, in the area of Middle Eastern anthropology, scholars such as Dale Eikelman, Michael Gilsenan, Kenneth L. Brown, Talal Asad, Lila Abu-Lughod, Charles Hirschkind, Walter Armbrust and Ted Swedenburg; much of this scholarship is also indebted to the writings of Pierre Bourdieu.

[10]   Among the vast critical literature, the reader is referred to Donnan and Stokes (2002) for a comprehensive overview. Other useful sources include Porter (1983), Halliday (1993) and Ahmad (1992). Among those discussing the significance of Said's work (and postcolonial studies and critical theory more generally) for music, see Born and Hesmondhalgh (2000b), and several of the chapters in that volume (including Stokes (2000)), Everist (1996), Qureshi (1999) and Solomon (2012). Stokes (2001, 2003) considers the broad impact of postcolonial thought on ethnomusicology and popular music studies in the late 1980s and early 1990s. From a slightly different perspective, Stokes (2002) traces the various strands of Orientalist discourse in writings on Middle Eastern musics and the disciplinary connections between musicology and Orientalist scholarship.

[11]   Postcolonial theorist Gayatri Chakravorty Spivak, for instance, has questioned simplistic binaries of hegemony and resistance, and has also written about the 'combined destructive *and productive* impacts of imperialism in the concept of an "enabling violence"' (Born and Hesmondhalgh 2000b:5; emphasis mine).

book have been profoundly shaped by writers in a number of fields but it is to Said that I am most indebted, both in his own work and in the many ensuing debates and critiques.[12]

One of the central questions to emerge from the writings of Said and others was how to theorize difference, clearly of great relevance to ethnomusicology as a field of study largely built on difference. Within musicology, an interest in difference first emerged in the early 1990s, initially focused on issues of gender and resulting in several ground-breaking publications, including *Feminine Endings* (McClary 1991), *Musicology and Difference: Gender and Sexuality in Musical Scholarship* (ed. Solie, 1993) and *Queering the Pitch: The New Gay and Lesbian Musicology* (ed. Brett, Wood and Thomas, 1994). Of particular significance was the introduction to Solie's volume in which she positions music unequivocally within a postcolonial framework and explores the ideological implications of difference, particularly as embodied in essentialized and dualistic discourses. Already at this time there was a growing awareness within music studies of the intersection of dichotomies of 'self' and Other[13] with a whole series of dualities, and in particular correlations between gender and racial 'othering'. Writing in the same volume, Treitler invokes earlier parallels drawn by Said between male/female and Europe/Orient, but suggests going 'one step further: the two are not only of the same sort, they are the same myth, differently peopled' (1993:30). The role of dualities in musicological discourse will be explored below.

For ethnomusicologists and their comparative musicologist predecessors, the debate over what musics share (for instance, in so-called 'universals', a topic of interest both to comparative musicologists and later to ethnomusicologists of the 1960s and '70s) and what sets them apart, has a long history. Yet, despite a growing interest in Orientalism in the 1990s, and increasing reflexivity regarding ethnomusicologists' relationships with their 'otherly' subjects of study, scholars were surprisingly slow to engage with difference as a theoretical concept.[14] Over the last decade and more, however, an emerging body of work has led the way. One of the first books to examine the ways in which music serves as a marker of racial difference was *Music and the Racial Imagination* (ed. Radano and Bohlman, 2000). Difference also forms the focus of another volume published in the same year: *Western Music and Its Others: Difference, Representation and Appropriation in Music* (ed. Born and Hesmondhalgh, 2000a) which with its strong tenor of interdisciplinarity includes several chapters by ethnomusicologists. It is not insignificant that both volumes appeared in the same millennial year at a time when questions of difference were increasingly coming to the fore. The work of Philip V. Bohlman and Kofi Agawu stands out in this respect. Specifically, Agawu's charge that ethnomusicologists have tended to seek out difference rather than explore similarities points to a central problematic: how to recognize and write about difference without essentializing it. Since this problematic lies at the heart of the ideas explored in this chapter, I'd like to pause briefly on this issue.

As well as its defining role for ethnomusicology, difference is central to structuralist ideas (following Saussure) about the creation of meaning in language. Thus, 'Meaning arises in the relations of similarity and difference which words have to other words within the language code' (Hall 1992:288). Clearly, we need difference. The issue, 'therefore, is not whether but *how* to construct difference' (Agawu 2003:165). Radano and Bohlman trace the historical linking of concepts of 'race' and musical difference from the fourteenth-century writings of Ibn Khaldun through to the present day. For eighteenth-century Enlightenment writers such as Rousseau, 'Music's differences became as evident as those of color and the other human distinctions of a racialized world' (Radano and Bohlman 2000:10) and things had changed little by the late nineteenth and early twentieth centuries when ethnographers and folklorists continued to 'exalt difference' (ibid.:21). Tenzer also draws attention to the ways in which our habitual discourses are informed by 'The politics of

---

[12]   Several writers have noted the irony that despite Said's strong interest in music, his writings on the subject rarely bring to bear a postcolonial perspective but rather reinforce the normative hegemony of the Euro-American canon (see in particular *Musical Elaborations*, 1991). There are a few exceptions, such as the essay on Aida in *Culture and Imperialism* (1993:133–59, 'The Empire at Work: Verdi's *Aida*'). *Musical Elaborations* also includes a passage describing Said's interest in Arab music (and culture) later in life (1991:98), but the point of comparison remains Western art music (Born and Hesmondhalgh 2000b:50–51).

[13]   I use these terms as a binary whilst also recognizing the mutually constitutive and fluid nature of the relationship between them.

[14]   Mention should be made of two pioneering articles: Grenier (1989) and Grenier and Guilbault (1990).

irreducible difference' (2000:435), citing, among other examples, the tendency of writers on Balinese music to use oppositional concepts of time in which Balinese cyclical structures (often represented as trance-like and static) are contrasted with the more directed and apparent progressive linearity of much Western music: 'The linkage is an orientalism: another trope of the "timeless" East, recalling also Geertz's characterization of Balinese time as a "vectorless now" (1973:404)' (2000:375). Similarly, using examples from Africanist ethnomusicology, Agawu argues that a presumption of (often essentialized) difference has historically been privileged. In challenging a whole series of 'normalized' modes of representation, he argues that such writing has often followed a quasi-imperialist agenda (no doubt partly subliminal, but nevertheless persuasive) in which differences are emphasized and distilled into stereotypical essences. In calling for greater demystification of 'other' musics, writers such as Tenzer and Agawu have pointed to the imperative of exploring what traditions share as well as what distinguishes them, and of discussing difference in ways that are not reliant upon Orientalist stereotyping.

The work of Agawu is important in drawing attention to the 'inescapably ideological nature of writing' (1992:256) and the 'confluence of difference, knowledge and power' (2003:155) within scholarly discourse. However, as someone who sets out to empower the Other through questioning presumptions of difference, he rarely explores the ways in which many (postcolonial) Others have used their peripherality as a means of empowerment *through difference* in the form of 'strategic essentialism'.[15] To argue for 'sameness' in a context where difference may be the only means to combat discrimination or hegemonic forces would seem naive.[16] We therefore need to ask on whose terms a concept of sameness might be constructed. Notions of 'universalism' may be no less ideologically-implicated than those of 'difference', as Born and Hesmondhalgh argue of postmodernism's 'discursive universalism' through which, 'The global art music network [thus] risks "aesthetic (as opposed to epistemic) violence" through the tyrannies and closure of its universalizing discourses' (2000b:21).

The common thread running through these various debates is not so much difference *per se*, but rather the ways in which difference becomes imbued with power. 'Politically, then, difference is about power', asserts Solie (1993:6), quoting from Martha Minow:

> When we identify one thing as like the others, we are not merely classifying the world; we are investing particular classifications with consequences and positioning ourselves in relation to those meanings. When we identify one thing as unlike the others, we are dividing the world; we use our language to exclude, to distinguish – to discriminate. (1990:3, in Solie 1993:2)

Thus, language represents a site where difference and power become entwined, not least through the binary oppositions so central to the creation of linguistic meaning:

> ... *difference* in an encompassing sense has been at the center of one arena of linguistic study ever since structuralism proposed the notion that difference creates meaning. From this origin emerges the proposition that Western thought has been ... dominated by a series of tightly interconnected binary dualisms: good/evil, male/female, culture/nature, reason/emotion, self/other, and so forth .... These linked pairings create long chains of associations, virtuosic in their ready applicability, that exercise a strong and virtually subliminal influence on the ways we position and interpret groups of people, their behaviour, and their works. (1993:11)

As Derrida argues, such oppositions are rarely neutral, 'we are not dealing with ... peaceful coexistence ... but rather with a violent hierarchy. One of the two terms governs ... or has the upper hand' (1972:41). From the mid-1990s, music scholars began to explore the implications of binary thinking and attendant questions of power, calling attention for the first time to the constructed nature of difference and the profound impact

---

[15]   See Born and Hesmondhalgh (2000b:42).

[16]   I am reminded of Stokes' observation that 'The critique of Orientalism thus has a way of reproducing the very voicelessness that the critique itself diagnoses' (2000:215).

of notions of alterity on musicological thought and discourse. According to Lawrence Kramer, one of the foremost thinkers on this topic:

> Music has been closely tied to the logic of alterity since the mid-eighteenth century at the latest ... Not all dualities are automatically or consistently oppressive ... Nonetheless, binary thinking must clearly be understood as a historical, not just a conceptual, phenomenon, the consequences of which have too often been inhumane or worse. ... we risk allying ourselves with the cultural agenda of domination whenever we embrace a duality, however abstract or depoliticized, that repeats the logic of alterity. The energies of valuation have high voltage; a duality is a treacherous instrument to ply. (1995:35, 38–9, 41)[17]

Questions of alterity are central to the ideas explored in this chapter: specifically, how discourses of musical creativity have been invoked in the construction of self/Other boundaries, thereby serving an agenda of essentialized difference; and the implications of this for an understanding of creative practice in Iranian music.

Musical Creativity from a Postcolonial Perspective: The Ghosts of Others

How, then, might a postcolonial perspective be applied to the study of musical creativity? Examining ethno/musicological discourses on creativity through the prism of postcolonial studies reveals a great deal about relationships of power. Even a cursory foray into the literature shows the extent to which, from the earliest colonial encounters through to the work of nineteenth-century folklorists and later musicologists of various kinds, writings on musical creativity represented a highly politicized domain, simultaneously presented as normative and ideologically-free. For many years, conventional wisdom maintained that the central difference between (mainstream) musicology and ethnomusicology was that ethnomusicologists dealt primarily with 'non-Western' musics, and musicologists didn't. There were exceptions of course, but examining the general trend of scholarship prior to the 1990s one might suppose that musicology and the music of exotic (and other) Others had little to do with one another. Nothing could be further from the truth. Just as the European encounter with other peoples was (and continues to be) crucial to the shaping of European identities, so musicological thought could only emerge in the context of 'the dialectic of identities' (Hall 1992:307), a direct result of the colonial encounter. Radano and Bohlman chart the impact of such encounters on European conceptions of music, particularly from second half of the eighteenth century:

> From the beginning of any historiography of music and race, Europe is there, and its interactions with those it imagines as Others secures its place in that historiography ... With the escalation of imperialism, missionaries and colonial officials encountered music in the spaces of Otherness, that is the music of 'races' other than their own, and with this music they were able to imagine for the first time in European history a truly global music ... One might even argue that the modern comprehension of 'music' as such would not have come about without the emergence of a relational circumstance that positioned a European practice above and beyond the more authentic, yet ultimately lesser, forms of 'emerging' peoples. (2000:11, 16–17)

Acknowledged or not, the ghosts of Others have lurked in the spaces between what was made explicit in musicological writings.[18] To some extent, the very existence of ethnomusicology enabled the study of such musics to be conveniently delegated elsewhere. And the representation of Western art music as being above such issues made it possible to elevate 'a particular local musical culture (that of eighteenth- and nineteenth-century Vienna) to the status of a universal and autonomous aesthetic code' (Stokes 2002:169). What better example to illustrate the more general point that 'we may have something to learn about the circuitry of power within [a] discipline by reflecting on what disciplines select for attention and what they repress' (Donnan and

---

[17] See Kramer (1995:260–61) for a comprehensive listing of relevant work in this area. Discussion of the broader implications of a postmodernist musicology and a critique of Kramer can be found in Williams (2001).

[18] To borrow a powerful metaphor from the opening of *Music and the Racial Imagination*: 'A spectre lurks in the house of music, and it goes by the name of race' (Radano and Bohlman 2000:1).

Stokes 2002:4). Once one accepts that 'knowledge is a social construction serving complex political ends', it becomes possible to understand how musicology has maintained its 'particular regimes of truth' (ibid.:4).

One of the most naturalized self/Other dichotomies in relation to creative practice is the division between 'composition' and 'improvisation', the ideological dimensions of which I have written about elsewhere. This discursive binary is of particular relevance to the chapters that follow, since Iranian classical music is usually understood to be 'improvised'. In an earlier article (Nooshin 2003), I suggested that changing musicological discourses of creativity over several decades have both reflected disciplinary shifts and specific agendas, and in particular that the composition/improvisation binary has served to mark purportedly essential differences between Western art and Other musics. Of course, improvisation played a significant role in European music for several centuries and many composers were also skilled improvisers.[19] However, by 1938 when Ernst Ferand's now classic study of improvisation in European music was published, improvisational practice had lost its earlier centrality, although it remained in certain forms such as piano preluding, concerto cadenzas and organ playing. I have argued that whilst the term 'improvisation' in the context of Other musics was often valenced negatively prior to the 1960s, the later emergence of a more celebratory discourse of improvisation as a symbol of freedom was no less Orientalizing than earlier ones (Nooshin 2003:250–51). One of the central arguments of this chapter is that the composition/improvisation binary was not an isolated phenomenon, but part of a wider process of alterity-construction. Thus, in the context of Radano and Bohlman's claim that music has long played an important role in the 'imagination of difference' (2000:11), the discussion below will explore 'the shifting matrix of ideological constructions of difference associated with [creative processes in music] that have emerged as part of the network discourse of modernity' (ibid.:5) by examining some of the broad narratives which have dominated scholarly thought and writings on musical creativity over the past century or so – both within musicological studies of Western art music, and in the work of folklorists. I then consider their impact on ethnomusicology as an emerging and distinct field of study, before returning in the final section to further consideration of the composition/improvisation binary and looking towards new paradigms for understanding musical creativity.

Musicological Narratives of Creativity in Western Art Music

In Europe, it was the Romantic movement of the nineteenth century which canonized the image of the creator of music, primarily the (male) composer, as a solitary inspired genius, often misunderstood by his contemporaries and heroically defending his art for audiences of the future.[20] The creation of music through 'inspiration' seemed to render superfluous, even sacrilegious, any investigation of compositional processes. McClary notes that, 'the word [composition] has been mystified since the nineteenth century, such that it summons up the figure of a semidivine being, struck by holy inspiration, and delivering forth ineffable delphic utterances' (1985:156)[21] and Kivy discusses this 'ideology ... which might well be described as "composer worship" ... the composer of the past has become, in our time, a kind of musical oracle' (1995:278, 284). For some, such as Heinrich Schenker, the composer was a mouthpiece for a 'higher Author' (Cook 1998:32) and Levin discusses how contemporary performers 'have been trained to try piously to observe the written

---

[19]   Taruskin describes improvisation as 'nine-tenths of the Renaissance and Baroque musical icebergs' (1995:61). For further discussion of improvisation in European art music, see Kivy (1995:273–7, on the performance of Mozart piano concerto cadenzas), Bohlman (1988:74), Goertzen (1998), and a growing body of research over the past decade including Sherman (2003), Treitler (2007, particularly Chapter 2), Berkowitz (2010), and several of the chapters in Solis and Nettl (2009): Levin (2009), Mattax Moersch (2009), Hatten (2009), Kinderman (2009) and Temperley (2009).

[20]   This account of the rise of the 'autonomous' Euro-American composer is necessarily cursory, and is intended to explore the impact of largely nineteenth-century discourses on twentieth-century canon formation and on ethnomusicology. The modern notion of the composer is rooted much further back in the Renaissance. For a detailed survey of the emergence and development of 'the composer' and 'composition' as modern concepts, see Blum (2001); Chanan also provides a useful account of the changing position of the European (and later North American) composer from the early eighteenth to the late twentieth centuries (1999).

[21]   In her 'Afterword' to Jacques Attali's *Noise* (1985), and commenting on his revisionist use of the term 'composition'.

testament of the composer' (2009:144). Similarly, Cook presents the 'image of the inspired composer ... whose vision – a term whose biblical resonances are entirely pertinent – encompasses every detail of the music's unfolding. This is an image of authorship that borders on the divine; indeed it echoes theological accounts of the moment of Creation' (1998:64–5). The terms are striking – divine, semidivine, holy, biblical, delphic; and the invoking of quasi-religious, mystical qualities return us to some of the ideas at the start of this chapter. This 'cult' of the genius, God-like composer was sustained by an underlying narrative which set him apart from others and from the broader socio-political context:

> These composers simply stood outside time, and the particularities of the societies in which they were rooted. Their transcendent aesthetic qualities were to be studied and imitated textually, and the task of a positivistic musicology was to make the texts available in their purest and most original form. (Stokes 2002:169)

Cook and Toynbee have both written about the ways in which such discourses still permeate our thinking, both academic and lay. Cook discusses how the figure of Beethoven, particularly posthumous representations of the composer and his work, helped to fuel such myth-making and the resulting Romantic discourse which, 'asserts that music comes from within and is a direct product of the psyche of the creator ... it treats creation as a mystical process, and creators as a select band of individual geniuses' (Toynbee 2003:103–4). Above all, 'Romanticism ignores the profoundly social nature of authorship in all forms of culture, including music' (ibid.:104), as noted also by Bigenho:

> ... the romantic individualized view of artistic production, [with its] principles of constant innovation, and the idea of creators as the proprietors of their works. This is the founding myth of modern concepts of authorship and copyright ... [and] the presumed division between art created by individuals and culture created by collectivities. (2002:20)

Emerging towards the end of the nineteenth century, the new discipline of musicology was profoundly informed by such paradigms and for most of the following century tended to privilege creativity conforming to a narrative in which the composer (usually male and using notation to record his cerebral inspirations) is accorded almost total creative license, in contrast to the more limited agency of performers and the mostly passive consumption of audiences. Cook observes, 'the idea that the performer's role is to reproduce what the composer has created builds an authoritarian power structure into musical culture' (1998:265); and in relation to the role of audiences, 'Romanticism, [is] the strongest account we have of creativity as a factor of production' as opposed to reception (Toynbee 2003:103).

Granted, the above presents a rather broad brushstroke: identifying trends inevitably means glossing over complexities and exceptions. In general, however, it is the case that 'the composer' has been central to Euro-American conceptions of music for several centuries and that discourses of creativity in European art music since the early nineteenth century have depended on a hierarchy with a named 'creator' (composer) at the top and the generally anonymous 'consumers' at the bottom. Moreover, within this, a few composers and their works became singled out to form a central canon which effectively serves to 'discipline' music studies.[22] Of course, the creative role of the performer, often the composer himself, has long been acknowledged, but performance *per se* is only rarely admitted into the canon, primarily due to the nature of the work concept, another legacy of the nineteenth century, and its dependence on the score. As Goehr observes, 'By 1800, when composition was defined as involving the predetermination of as many structural elements as possible, the notion of extemporization acquired its modern understanding. For the first time, it was seen to stand in strict opposition to composition "proper"' (1992:234).[23] Cook argues that the new work concept was intimately

---

22   The history, nature, role and ideological implications of the musicological canon has come under scrutiny in recent years. See, for instance, Bergeron and Bohlman's (1992) ground-breaking volume. On canon-formation in 'folk music', see Bohlman (1988, Chapter 7).

23   Whilst Goehr identifies Beethoven as an important watershed in the conceptual separation of composition from improvisation in European art music, Kinderman has shown how 'even after Beethoven retired from concert life, he continued to incorporate aspects of his improvisational style into his composed pieces' (Solis 2009:14). Hatten

tied to the emergence of capitalist economic structures and the increasing commodity value of printed music before the age of sound recording (1998:15–16).[24] As well as defining the particular 'relationships of authority which permeate [the western classical] musical culture' (ibid.:24), the pre-eminent position of the composer has had significant ramifications, including a fetisthistic preoccupation with 'original meaning' (usually taken to indicate the composer's 'intentions') which has remained within musicology long after such ideas have been challenged elsewhere and even discarded in favour of more nuanced understandings of how 'receivers' create meanings across time and space.

My aim in drawing attention to some of the broad narratives which have dominated musicological thought in this area is not to critique musicology *per se*. I acknowledge the profound changes within music studies over the last quarter century and the emergence of a more reflexive musicology. Rather, such narratives are of interest here for two main reasons: first, from a historical perspective, because of their influence on ideas about creativity within ethnomusicology; and second, because of what they reveal of the deeply implicated and ideological nature of musicological discourse. Was it by chance, for instance, that the rise in the iconic status and symbolic power of the autonomous male composer should have coincided with the height of European colonialism? To what extent can such changes be understood in terms of Europe's relationship with its Others? I return to these questions below. With the emergence of a mediated popular music industry in the twentieth century, initially in Europe and the United States, Romantic discourses slid easily into the domain of popular music, increasingly applied to the performer as the nature of the 'text' changed. Here again, discourses are shaped by economics, and by a 'capitalist ideology built on insecurity and the profit motive [which] suppresses the social nature of the creative process … industry strives to reduce uncertainty of demand by marketing a few big stars' (Toynbee 2003:111). There is thus at root a 'contradiction between Romantic ideology and the reality of social authorship' (ibid.), and the fact that anything new 'is woven from voices that already exist' (ibid.:105).

Notwithstanding recent critiques of some of the central tenets of musicology, including the notions of work concept, canon and composerly authority, still, perusing the titles of books and the pages of scholarly journals today shows that the musicological universe still largely revolves around the figure of 'the composer'.[25] By and large, scholars still tend to specialize in the work of a composer or group of composers. Challenges to prevailing notions of authorship as informed by debates within critical theory and elsewhere, have yet to make much of an impact. Within musicology, the autonomous composer is still king. Charles Wilson has explored the enduring currency of the 'rhetoric of autonomy', the 'familiar Romantic image of the autonomous artist – the myth of the "uncreated creator" [biblical inferences again], floating free of social or institutional allegiances' (2004:6). Writing about Hungarian composer György Ligeti's presentation of self, Wilson shows how Ligeti's ' [own] public statements … through the uniquely authoritative status accorded them by scholars, have played an essential role in propping up this image of the heroically independent creator' (ibid.). Once again, capitalism emerges as an important factor, such discourses providing a means of 'differentiating them [composers] from other creators and proclaiming the uniqueness of their work in a competitive market of symbolic goods' (ibid.). I will consider the impact of such discourses within ethnomusicology below.

---

makes similar observations with reference to the piano music of Chopin: 'ironically, just when the "work concept" was becoming increasingly entrenched for both composers and performers – improvisation and its values continued to be implied by composers in works that were completely notated. With Chopin we have compelling evidence for "composed-in" improvisation, as inferred from his notated works conceived for performance in intimate salon settings' (2009:284). See also Rink (2001).

24   Note that such changes were taking place at the same time as radical shifts in patronage structures. The implications of commodification clearly became even more heightened with the arrival of sound recording. For further discussion of the work concept see Attali (1985), McClary (1985), Kivy (1995:260–65), Boorman (1999) and Blum (2001:197–8).

25   I am also keenly aware that compositional developments since the early twentieth century, including various kind of electronic and electro-acoustic music, aleatoric music, live performance art and so on, have complicated both the notion of the musical 'text' as discussed here, and in some cases the authorial power of the composer. However, the general point about the central symbolic role of the composer remains.

Folk Music and the Creative Individual

Among other areas of scholarship which impacted on the early development of paradigms within ethnomusicology, folklore studies presents an interesting point of contrast with musicology: despite the long tradition among folk song collectors and scholars of recognizing and naming individual singers and other musicians, as seen in the earlier quotation from Brăiloiu the question of creative agency was widely contested. It is instructive to examine such writings, both for the various debates over creativity and for the prominence of dualistic thinking. These two points are not unrelated, as I will discuss.

Another legacy of the nineteenth century, European interest in its own 'folk' revolved around a paradox. The emergence of modern nation states and the increasing appeal to nationalist discourses in the nineteenth century required a source of 'authenticity' for which the 'folk' conveniently came to embody the purest essence of nationhood. Porter describes how Cecil Sharp presented English folk music as 'the pure and crystalline musical expression of an English "peasant class"' (1991:113). Such a position, however, depended on maintaining a static and romanticized view of the 'folk' and required that their traditions, including music, be preserved in pristine form[26] for the national patrimony. Much late nineteenth- and early twentieth-century folksong collecting in Europe was concerned with preservation, something which was given added impetus by the arrival of sound recording. At the same time as embracing the 'folk' as the essence of nation, however, it was also necessary for the predominantly middle- and upper-class collectors to maintain the 'folk's Otherness, just as comparative musicologists at this time invoked 'primitive', 'exotic' or 'savage' Others. Moreover, from the creation of a separate category of 'folk music' flowed a series of binaries which depended on essentialized difference: art/folk, complex/simple, notated/oral and so on. Nowhere was this essentializing more apparent than in the arena of creativity.

Unlike their comparative musicologist contemporaries, early folklore scholars generally recorded and published details of musicians' names (and sometimes biographical information), as well as dates of recording and other information. To this extent, there was an acknowledgement of the individual, most often a singer. However, their exact role was less clear and it was here in the debate around one central question, which for decades divided scholars, that the deep-rooted othering became manifest: were the 'folk' capable of creation, or only embellishment or (accidental) variation? A.L. Lloyd identified the 'heart of the problem' in his 1967 book *Folk Song in England*:

> How is a folk song made up? The question is the most captivating, most bothersome in all folklore, and we do well to approach it with the humility of ignorance. Is the folk song created in the first instance by a single talented individual like any other poem or musical work? Or is it the product of a collective, a community? … Or is it the fact, as the Germans Hoffman-Kreyer and Hans Naumann suggested, that the lower classes are imaginatively so sterile that they can create nothing for themselves but merely take over the songs of the upper classes after the gentry have finished with them. (1967:53)

Lloyd considers a range of positions on this issue. Referring to the work of Béla Bartók, he quotes one of the best known and most often cited statements on the topic, published in 1931:

> Whether peasants are individually capable of inventing quite new tunes is open to doubt. We have no data to go on. And the way in which the peasant's musical instinct asserts itself encourages no such view. (in Lloyd 1967:62)

Similarly, Bohlman reports on linguist and collector of folktales Joseph Grimm's curious assertion that 'a folk song composes and transmits itself' (1988:7, citing Danckert 1966:9), firmly according agency to the song rather than the performer.[27] Setting aside for the moment the question of agency, it becomes clear that these

---

[26] Or at least presented as such. For the debate around Sharp's alleged selectivity in collecting practices, a debate largely fuelled by Dave Harker's 1972 article 'Cecil Sharp in Somerset: Some Conclusions', see Porter (1991) and Bearman (2002).

[27] In his 1988 book, Bohlman challenges 'The long-standing failure of folk music scholarship to take account of individual creativity' (69) and instead 'persistently call[s] attention to the importance of the individual folk musician as an agent of change and creativity' (ix).

various positions cannot be disengaged from scholars' personal ideological views. Thus, Lloyd considers the apparent contradiction between Bartók's statement and his approach to folk music elsewhere in his work, as well as his close relationship with the people he studied (he was often 'attacked by middle-class Hungarian critics for his "infatuation" with the despised peasantry' [1967:62]). He asks, 'Can it be that the ghost of some haughty old Hapsburg prejudice still lurked even in so sympathetic and daring a mind as Bartók's?' (ibid.:62). By the same token, Lloyd would doubtless have been the first to acknowledge his own insistence on the creative abilities of the 'folk' as being shaped in part by his Marxist leanings and desire to empower the peasantry and working classes.

Among early twentieth-century collectors, one of the first to consider the creativity of folk musicians was Percy Grainger. As early as 1915 (and a good few years before Bartók), he wrote:

> The primitive musician unhesitatingly alters the traditional material he has inherited from thousands of unknown talents and geniuses before him to suit his own voice or instruments, or to make it conform to his purely personal taste for rhythm and general style. There is no written original to confront him with, no universally accepted standard to criticize him by. He is at once an executive and creative artist, for he not only remoulds old ditties, but also weaves together fresh combinations of more or less familiar phrases, which he calls 'making new songs'. (cited by Balough 1982:69; in Blacking 1987:45–6)

In the original *Musical Quarterly* article from which this quotation is taken, 'Grainger emphasized the creative work of individual singers and musicians' (Blacking 1987:45); in this, as in other respects, he was ahead of his time. For instance, Grainger's interest in the people whose music he studied was evidenced in the detailed life stories which he documented alongside the songs.[28] Moreover, he collected material not just from the rural 'folk', but also from the urban poor. Another significant voice in this debate was folksong scholar Phillips Barry, who wanted it to be 'cried from the house tops that the folk singer is a personality, an individual, and most of all a creative artist' (1961:76).

The issue of agency relates to another strand of the debate, that concerning so-called 'communal creation'. Long accepted by many as the source of folk music, the supposedly communal nature of creation became a determinant in defining boundaries, a 'factor of difference' expressed through the paradigm of the individual/ named composer (of art music) versus the communal/anonymous (of folk). By recognizing individuals, writers such as Grainger and Phillips called into question the idea of communal composition, and by extension that which separated 'folk' from 'art'. Among the most vociferous on this issue was Brăiloiu. In his essay 'Reflections on Collective Musical Creation' (published shortly after his death in 1958 [1984:102–9]), he attempts to deconstruct the notion of communal creation by examining the ways in which musicians continually draw from communal traditions which are in themselves the accumulation of countless individual creations over generations. Expressing similar views, Lloyd quotes from Van Gennep, describing 'folk creation' as:

> 'the act of a single individual whose product is subsequently modified by other individuals who come into contact with it'. It is a collective art displayed by individuals. A single person expresses an idea acceptable by his community, and the community, in the form of a sequence of individuals joins in re-creating and adapting the work over the years and across the counties. (1967:69)

Examining the creativity debate among folklorists reveals that each strand of the argument is bound up with one or more dualistic paradigms. Consider the issue of notation, which by the late nineteenth century had come to occupy a central position within European art music. Not only was the fact that a great deal of compositional activity took place in performance largely ignored, but notation itself became both a fetish and a signifier of difference. Thus emerged the familiar dualism between notated music (as the norm) and so-called 'oral' tradition, which in turn suggested other essential differences, including in the nature of the creative process itself. Whilst the notated/oral dualism has held strong sway in musicological discourse, as with the communal/individual debate a number of writers have challenged it, observing that *all* musics depend

---

[28]   See Porter (1991:114). Grainger was also among the first to collect English folk songs on wax cylinders (Porter 1991:113, 119), an activity initially met with scepticism by the folk music establishment of the time.

on oral-aural knowledge. Clearly, prescriptive notation is selective in what it records, and even in a tradition as notation-bound as Euro-American art music, the ability to compose and to interpret a written score depends on acquired aural knowledge: 'In the first place, (music) writing can be learned only by oral-aural techniques; in the second, no conventional music writing can be read without them' (Seeger 1977:154).

Whether in relation to individual agency, the role of notation, or the alleged 'simplicity' of folk music, the paradigmatic dualisms have positioned folk music in a relationship of alterity to art music. But many of the same scholars who wrote about creative individuals also came to recognize the problems with dualistic thinking and the difficulty of differentiating between 'folk' and 'art' music on the basis of creative processes, as in the following from composer and folklorist Zoltán Kodály, writing in 1941:

> In folk music, a new transcription, a variation, is produced by the singer on each occasion. An essential trait of folk song is this power of unconditional ownership; but this used to exist also in high art – Shakespeare, Bach, Handel. At first it seems that the mode of production is entirely different: .... But let us look closer at musical history. Do compositions of such individual character, showing no likeness to anything already in existence, spring from the heads of composers like Minerva from the head of Jupiter? The early works of the great masters are often mere imitations, scarcely different from the compositions of their predecessors; only gradually do individual tones develop. A new type of folk song develops from existing forms by slow variation, but hardly at slower pace than that discernible in art music. (quoted in Lloyd 1967:68)

Lloyd continues:

> Deep at the root, there is no essential difference between folk music and art music; they are varied blossoms from the same stock, grown to serve a similar purpose, if destined for different tables. Originally they spring from the same area of man's mind; their divergence is a matter of history, of social and cultural stratification. (1967:17)

Just two years after Lloyd, Blacking expressed similar views: 'The only useful distinction which the terms "folk" and "art" might express are differences of process,[29] of the ways in which the experiences of individuals in society may be expressed. The terms are certainly not accurate indications of *musical* difference' (1969:64). He goes further in later writings, arguing that 'musical composition in all cultures is a process of the same order' (in Nettl 1995:viii).

Through this foray into the creativity debate within folk music studies, I hope to have highlighted a number of points. First, the pivotal role of a series of dualistic pairings and their attendant discourses: primitive/ advanced, simple/complex, communal/individual, oral/notated, natural/art(ifice), and so on. Second, these dualisms provide a platform for perpetuating and naturalizing ideas about essentialized difference. In the context of this discussion, folk music scholarship is interesting not only because the field itself is defined through a dualism (folk/art), but its discourses are saturated with relationships of alterity. Individuals such as Kodály, Lloyd and Brăiloiu struggled to varying degrees with these discourses, but were unable to go beyond a general questioning and pinpoint their role in validating particular relations of power. Thus, within the broad areas of both musicology and folk music scholarship, each in its own way, creativity was conceptualized, talked and written about in ways that served a discourse of difference, and this impacted profoundly on ethnomusicology as it emerged as a field of study in its own right in the 1950s.

Ethnomusicology, Creative Processes and the Individual

In what ways, then, did ethnomusicology inherit the dominant discourses of creativity described above? In one key respect – the recognition of the individual – the narratives were diametrically opposed for decades. In contrast to musicological pre-occupation with individual composers and folklorists' naming of performers, comparative musicologists and early ethnomusicologists rarely acknowledged, let alone named, individuals.

---

[29] 'Process' here does not refer to compositional processes but, as Blacking explains, indicates the social contexts in which music is experienced.

Instead, they described anonymous 'traditions' in which individuals were largely invisible. Whether stemming from a rejection of musicological 'norms', or whether recognition of individuals was deemed unnecessary in writing about 'ethnic' Others, the result was almost complete silence on the subject of creativity.[30] To some extent, this can be accounted for historically by examining general trends over the past century or so. The comparative musicologists were primarily concerned with historical and general comparative matters, and although some of the most prominent scholars had backgrounds in psychology (Carl Stumpf, Erich von Hornbostel and Otto Abraham, for example, were based at the Psychological Institute of Berlin University), this did not translate into an interest in aspects of cognition.[31] Hornbostel's vision was of a comparative musicology which would identify 'deep similarities and differences among *types* (repertoires, music cultures?), and would not be concerned with the detail of individual *instances* (performances?)' (Clayton 2003:65).[32] The later emergence in North America of an ethnomusicology closely allied to the social sciences led to an interest in social context; just as anthropologists at this time were concerned with identifying social norms, so ethnomusicologists tended to seek out the norms of musical systems rather than their individual expression.

Notwithstanding the above, the earliest ethnomusicological studies of creativity do date from this period. An important publication was Alan P. Merriam's *The Anthropology of Music* (1964) which includes a chapter on 'The Process of Composition' (165–84). That such an anthropologically-oriented scholar should have chosen to write about this topic is interesting (granted, the chapter includes little in the way of musical detail). Whilst Merriam was not the first ethnomusicologist to write about creative process, his work reflected a growing interest in this area and represented a significant landmark in affirming the creativity of 'nonliterate peoples', and which depended on a critical shift which had begun during the previous decade, as evidenced in the writings of Bruno Nettl, Denison Nash (1961) (to both of whom Merriam refers) and Constantin Brăiloiu. For the first time in ethnomusicology, there was an emerging recognition of creative individuals, usually performers of 'oral-aural' traditions. Thus, Merriam begins his chapter by referring to Nettl's 1954 article 'Notes on Musical Composition in Primitive Culture', which argues that, 'any item of music, a song, an instrumental piece, or a series of pieces, is the product, originally, of the creation of an individual or a group of *individuals*' (1954:81). Challenging earlier notions of communal composition, Merriam and Nettl both set out to explore 'different kinds of composition' (ibid.:81) and 'composition as a process – how new songs are brought into being' (Merriam 1964:175). Merriam draws both on his own work and accounts by others, presenting examples from a range of traditions (but characteristically dominated by North American 'native' music) in which 'not only is composition recognized by the society but [that] individuals are expected to be able to compose and thus contribute to the music corpus of a culture' (ibid.:167). Focusing on ethnographic descriptions, including how musicians themselves discuss compositional processes, Merriam asks:

> What are the sources from which music is drawn? Is music composed only through the agency of superhuman assistance and sanction, or is it a purely human phenomenon? How do new songs come into existence? If the composer has a recognised status in the society, how does he compose and what does he say, if anything about the process of composition? (ibid.:47)

This recognition of individual agency represented a significant break with the past.[33] But there were also continuities. When Merriam considers 'the identity of the composer' (ibid.:175), the discussion remains

---

[30]   Writing in 1983 Nettl notes, 'There is a curious disparity. While ethnomusicologists experience a great deal of face-to-face contact with individual informants or teachers in the field and specialize in concentration on a particular person, the literature of the field provides surprisingly little information about the individual in music … ethnomusicologists tend, with a few notable exceptions, to be drawn to the anonymous' (279).

[31]   Personal communication with Christian Kaden, Philip V. Bohlman, John Baily and Dieter Chistensen (May 2004), to whom my thanks for their various thoughts on this issue. See also Christensen (1991) and Baily (1992) for discussion of the early comparative musicologists in Berlin.

[32]   Among the few who showed an interest in such matters, most were influenced by the paradigms of folk music scholarship, as in the following from George Herzog: 'The creative process is not one begun and finished by a single individual; it is spread over many individuals and generations, and it never comes to an end as long as the tradition is alive' (1950:1034).

[33]   See also the work of David Rycroft (1961/2) and Gerhard Kubik (for instance, 1994).

general and individuals are not named. Similarly, in writing about the 'actual techniques used in composing a new song' (ibid.:175), there are no illustrative examples; instead, Merriam quotes at length from other authors to describe techniques such as 'taking parts of old songs and putting them together to make new ones' (ibid.:177), 'improvisation and communal re-creation' (ibid.:179), 'transposition' (ibid.:179), and 'creation arising out of emotion' (ibid.:179). This work is interesting for what it reveals both of the continuities and the discontinuities which have shaped ethnomusicological thought on this topic. On the one hand, recognizing the creative individual (composer or performer) was an important first step towards more detailed studies of creative practice. On the other, the relative absence of named individuals continued the anonymity of comparative musicology. In fact, a few individual musicians, usually performers, were named at this time. Berliner cites the work of Andrew Tracey who, as early as 1961 wrote about the playing styles of (named) *mbira* players in Zimbabwe (then Rhodesia; 1978:152). However, this was certainly not the norm.

Such writing also reveals a growing awareness at this time of the tension between sameness and difference in ethnomusicological discourse. Merriam was among the first to discuss specific compositional techniques, leading him to conclude that 'Composition seems ... not to differ radically between literate and nonliterate peoples save in the question of writing' (1964:184), sentiments which resonate with the above-cited views of Kodály, Lloyd and Blacking. Whilst surface differences are recognized (Merriam gives many examples), there is no 'presumption of difference' (Agawu 2003:181) in underlying processes. Furthermore, it is significant that the compositional techniques listed are found both in performance (what Merriam calls 'composition in performance') and in (oral-aural) composition away from the performance context (as found, for instance, in several 'native' American traditions). The fact that Merriam makes no distinction between these, but includes creative performance within the category of 'composition', is noteworthy.

During the late 1960s and early 1970s, the work of one ethnomusicologist stood out in its uncompromising critique of some of the accepted paradigms relating to creativity. John Blacking was arguably the first ethnomusicologist to position the socially-situated creative individual at the heart of his work. Proposing that 'All societies and cultures are the results of individuals' attempts to express their inner experience and to transmit them and share them with others', he continues, 'all musical expression comes from within each individual, either in solitude or in community' (1969:69–70). Thus, 'In the African context, the rhythm expresses the perfect co-operation of two performers who nevertheless preserve their individuality by maintaining different main beats' (1970:18). Blacking invokes the paradigmatic differences between musicological and ethnomusicological approaches to creativity, observing, 'Music has been studied as the product of societies or of individuals, but rarely as the product of individuals in society' (1969:34–5). Questions of creativity are central to Blacking's writings and his best-known work, *How Musical Is Man?* (1973), is effectively a manifesto of the 'fundamental musicality of the species' (Kippen 1990:264). Blacking's writings on compositional processes in the music of the Venda people of South Africa (1970, 1973) – and specifically his attempt to identify underlying 'rules' of composition in this music – were particularly influenced by his encounter in the early 1970s with transformational linguistics and the work of Chomsky (Howard 1991:71).

Still, there is a central paradox in Blacking's early work: while insisting that '*all* music is composed by individuals, even in tribal societies' (1969:35), like Merriam he continued to invoke the anonymous, except when writing about Western composers. In *How Musical Is Man?* Blacking focuses on the experience and value of music and questions many accepted notions of difference, particularly the mapping of 'complex'/'simple' onto 'Western'/'non-Western'. Yet the privilege of naming is reserved for the great (male) composers of Western art music: Britten, Mahler, Gibbons, Tchaikovsky, Beethoven. The Venda musicians remain anonymous. Not until much later did Blacking name individuals and critique his earlier approach, as in the following from an article published in 1989:[34]

---

[34] This article was 'based on a lecture scheduled for 1989, but cancelled at the last minute because of John's deteriorating health' (Nettl 1995:viii). Blacking died in January 1990.

> In the performing arts at least, the anthropological convention of anonymity of informants should not apply, as I was reminded by a Venda critic who objected to my failure to give people's names in the captions to the photographs for *How Musical is Man?* (17)[35]

He then proceeds to consider a piece by (named) composer Ida Sakala, and to discuss the circumstances of its first two performances.

Blacking was among several scholars in the 1970s and '80s arguing for greater consideration of the individual within ethnomusicology;[36] and increasingly, individuals were named, as in *The Soul of Mbira* where Berliner discusses specific musicians and gives detailed biographies (1978:207–33), and even co-authored texts, as in Sorrell and Narayan's study of performance practice in North Indian music (1980). Elsewhere, however, the tradition of anonymity continued. Nettl's many publications on Iranian classical music are particularly interesting, presenting a disjuncture between the reverential respect for his (named) teacher, Nur Ali Borumand, and the anonymity of others. In the 1972 study of the *darāmad* of *Chāhārgāh* (with Foltin), incidentally, dedicated to Borumand, Nettl provides 'Brief Sketches of the Musicians' (43–45) in a table at the end, offering short 'clues' such as age, teachers and so on, explaining, 'in order to avoid embarrassment due to critical statements, performers are referred to by number, not name' (ibid.:21). For those familiar with the tradition, however, the musicians are not difficult to identify. Even in a chapter discussing the very issue of studying individuals (1983, Chapter 21, 'I am the Greatest'), Nettl is again selective: Borumand is named but none of the Blackfoot singers are. Whatever the reasons in 1972 and 1983, the scholarly climate had clearly changed sufficiently by 1987 that in his book *The Radif of Persian Music* Nettl openly names musicians. At the heart of Rice's proposal for a 'Remodelling of Ethnomusicology', published in the same year, is the idea that ethnomusicology should seek to explain 'formative processes' by asking 'how do people historically construct, socially maintain and individually create and experience music?' (1987:473).[37] Not only does this resonate with the interweaving of the social and individual advocated by Blacking, but reflects the history of the discipline:

> If interest in the individual and individual experience continues to grow, then eventually the history of ethnomusicology might be interpreted as having moved successfully through the three stages of this model from a concern with historical and evolutionary questions in its early 'comparative musicology' stage to a concern for music in social life after *The Anthropology of Music*, to a concern for the individual in history and society in the most recent or next phase. (ibid.:476)

Returning to creative processes, that this new focus on the individual (the 'ethnomusicology of the person' [Nettl 1983:288]) should have led to an increased interest in creative processes seems unsurprising. Yet, whilst there were examples of composition which conformed more or less to the Euro-American 'work concept' (whether preserved orally or in notation), much of the creativity encountered by ethnomusicologists took place in performance, often within groups. However, since ethnomusicologists still depended on the discourses and categories inherited from musicology, such creativity could not easily be admitted into the category of 'composition'. With the notable exception of Merriam, few prior to the 1980s positioned creative performance as a form of 'composition', or sought to deconstruct the inherited categories. Nettl, in particular, made a significant contribution to the understanding of creative performance, most notably with regard to Iranian classical music. In the 1983 edition of *The Study of Ethnomusicology*, he provides a summary of ethnomusicological studies of creativity up to the early 1980s in a chapter entitled 'Divine Inspiration and Tonal Gymnastics' (26–35). Drawing on his work on Iranian music and on Plains Indian music, and positioned early in the book, this chapter (second out of a total 27), heralds a burgeoning interest in creative processes,

---

[35]   Interestingly, this (unnamed) Venda critic did not object to the anonymity of musicians in the main text.

[36]   See also Harwood (1976), Koskoff (1982), Wachsmann (1982), Nettl (1983:278–89) and Feld (1984). The lack of attention to the individual seems curious given that many of the traditions studied by ethnomusicologists, particularly the art musics of Asia, recognize and value individual (often well-known) musicians.

[37]   A formulation derived from Geertz's proposition that 'symbolic systems are ... historically constructed, socially maintained and individually applied' (1973:363–4).

as well as being perhaps the first attempt to theorize a general approach to creativity within ethnomusicology.[38] Writing just a few years before the new postcolonial consciousness impacted on ethnomusicology, Nettl's work is still largely couched in dualistic terms. However, like others, Nettl had been grappling with this problem for several years and had started to use the idea of a continuum as a way of circumventing dualistic categories. From the early 1970s he published a series of articles and monographs questioning the widely accepted oppositional positioning of composition vs improvisation (and also improvisation vs performance from notation).[39] The use of continua by several scholars at this time no doubt reflected a growing unease with binary categories, but Nettl was the first to apply this to the arena of creativity. However, whilst some were ready to question alterity *per se*, few were yet in a position to engage with the wider ideological implications of these discourses.

Creativity as an Icon of Difference[40]

My aim has been to trace broad trends. The changes described above happened over many decades, and not always in a linear fashion. Certainly, however, one can say that from the 1980s, named musicians appeared more regularly in the writings of ethnomusicologists, and this included explicitly biographical studies – for example, Erlmann (1996), Stock (1996), Danielson (1997), Loza (1999) – as well as ethnographically-rich accounts of creative processes by Berliner, Tenzer and others. Moving away from earlier paradigms, this strongly 'subject-centred musical ethnography' (Rice 2003:156) foregrounds the 'personal, the idiosyncratic and the exceptional' (Stock 2001:15).[41] In some cases, such writings arguably move too far towards an individualistic understanding of creativity, to the extent of overlooking the fact that 'agency is never solely individual; existing social structures empower individuals differently, according to their place in a configuration of social hierarchies and institutional organizations' (Monson 2009:24). The interplay between individuals and the broader social network of actors and circumstances within which they operate is complex;[42] and certainly, the growing focus on mediated (in particular, popular) musics has drawn attention to different kinds of 'authors' and the role of a range of individuals – listeners, producers, arrangers, sound engineers and so on – in the creation of music and musical meaning.

Clearly, much has changed in recent decades, both in ethnomusicologists' understanding of socially-situated creative processes and in an increasingly reflexive approach to discourse. And these two intersect in interesting ways: creativity is now firmly on the ethnomusicological agenda; and there is more awareness than ever of the inevitably loaded nature of scholarly language. We may indeed be our own discourses (to paraphrase Agawu 1992:266), but we also need discourse in order to communicate. As Helen Myers observed in the early 1990s:

---

[38] Drawing on ideas which Nettl had set out in his earlier writings; see for example 1972 (with Foltin) and 1974c.

[39] His 1974 *Musical Quarterly* article was particularly significant.

[40] Paraphrased from Tenzer, who uses this expression to describe the othering of Bali by Western writers (2000:435). Whilst much of the current discussion addresses ways in which music serves as a marker of difference, Born presents a rather different perspective in describing music as a 'medium that destabilizes some of our most cherished dualisms concerning the separation not only of subject from object, but present from past, individual from collectivity, the authentic from the artificial, and production from reception' (2005:8). I suggest that music's power lies partly in its capacity to be invoked both to construct and challenge alterities of various kinds.

[41] This article appears in a special issue of the journal *World of Music* on 'Ethnomusicology and the Individual'.

[42] A good example is the distinction, described by Fossum, in Turkmen instrumental music between *halk saz*, 'a piece authored by "the people"', and *öz döreden saz* or *kompozitorski saz*, 'an original work, "created by oneself"' (2010:129–30). In the former, 'composition is a collective effort' in that 'One musician may create a germ that will grow into a masterwork in the hands of the Ahal School as a whole' (2010:132). Notions of creativity thus depend less on 'a concern with authoring "original" material than with participating in a collective effort. The first to compose a melody is no more a composer of the *halk saz* than future performers who enrich the piece' (2010:186–7).

... the conscientious ethnomusicologist is often at a loss for descriptive words to explain his [sic] enterprise, having been stripped during the last several decades of his working vocabulary of vivid colourful terms. In the kingdom of exiled words live the labels condemned as pejorative: the old-timers, 'savage', 'primitive', 'exotic', 'Oriental', 'Far Eastern'; some newcomers, 'folk', 'non-Western', 'non-literate', 'pre-literate'; and recently 'world'. 'Traditional' survived the trial of the 1970s, leaving ethnomusicologists with an important concept that refers, in the world of music, to everything and therefore nothing. (1992:11)

Terms which as recently as the 1970s were the staple of ethnomusicological discourse make us cringe today. In light of the earlier discussion, it will come as no surprise that many of the now-'exiled' words depend on a dualistic imagining of the world: explicitly or not, they invoke an Other, for instance, 'non-Western' or 'pre-literate' which define a music in relation to what it is not or a stage of development not yet reached. Other terms heading towards likely exile include 'acculturation', 'hybrid', 'race' and even 'culture', the latter critiqued by anthropologist Adam Kuper both for its associations with cultural determinism and its contemporary overuse as a politically-correct substitute for 'race' (1999). Having learnt to 'speak properly' (Agawu 1992:247), we no longer write about anonymous 'primitive' musicians. But one might ask how much has really changed. To what extent does the rhetoric of disciplinary development, often expressed as a series of 'paradigm shifts' (Seeger 1991:342) and which Seeger suggests 'provide ethnomusicology with direction and coherence' (ibid.), hide the many continuities. Specifically in relation to creativity, to what extent do recent discursive shifts mask the fact that our discourses continue to depend on and perpetuate the same markers of difference found in earlier writings? Arguably, the terminological discomfort which has dogged ethnomusicologists as one set of words replaced another has rarely been accompanied by the kind of conceptual questioning necessary to address the underlying issues.

Comparing the various approaches to creativity in different areas of music study, it becomes increasingly evident that the question of agency is a central linchpin around which this discursive universe revolves. Perhaps no other single issue has impacted so widely on approaches to creativity as that of the identity and role of the individual. But how to explain the disproportionate musicological focus on the individual (composer), compared with the relative inattention to the individual in ethnomusicology before the 1970s? Similarly, since folklorists readily acknowledged individual performers, why did it take so long to recognize their creativity? I suggest that the answer lies in the discursive role of creativity within music studies as a means of marking Otherness: the former in relation to an ethnic/racial Other; the latter in relation to an internal Other defined primarily in terms of class.[43] In both cases, the discourses serve to perpetuate the idea of fundamental and essential differences between Western art music and the musics of Others, whether so-called 'non-Western' or 'folk', which for many decades shared a peripherality. Thus, whilst ethnomusicology's subject matter, approaches and methodologies have ostensibly set it apart from musicology and folk music studies, a closer examination of the underlying assumptions about, approaches to, and discourses around creativity reveals surprising continuities.

Towards New Paradigms: Improvisation and Its Others

What are the implications of the above discussion for the central focus of this book: the ways in which creativity is thought about, discussed and practised in Iranian classical music, a tradition in which the performer plays a central creative role and which is therefore most often described as 'improvised'? As will be discussed in Chapter 2, equivalent local concepts and terminology emerged in Iran during the twentieth century and are today used largely unproblematically by musicians and others. Among the many binary constructs mentioned above, most relevant to the discussion of Chapters 2 to 5 are those which present 'improvisation' as a discursive Other, whether in relation to notated composition or to 'interpretive' performance. I'm particularly interested in how these dualisms effectively reify certain aspects of music-making, and the impact of such (originally)

---

[43]   It is also worth noting that within Western art music, creativity has been used as a marker of gender difference. Taylor-Jay discusses the highly gendered and sexualized discourses of German composer and writer Hans Pfitzner and his late nineteenth- and early twentieth-century contemporaries, when writing about musical (and other) creativity (2009).

Western discourses on local understandings and practice. I should make clear, however, that there is no attempt here to define improvisation, nor to survey writings on the topic, for a number of reasons, some of which I have discussed elsewhere (Nooshin 2003). For one thing, my focus is not on improvisation *per se* but on the specific ways in which the discourses separate (and connect) creative practices; second, there is a considerable literature, almost all of which seeks in some way to define the term.[44] Indeed, the extent to which this area is marked by definitional anxiety highlights the fetish-like pre-occupation with essentializing improvisation: treating it as one particular kind of music usually defined by its relationship with, and distinction from, composition. Whilst most acknowledge the difficulties with definition, few diagnose the problem as rooted in an essentialized binary construct which developed in the context of one specific music tradition (European art music) at a particular historical moment, in response to particular musical needs. In the case of Iran, whilst such binaries saturate the literature, and more recently the discourses of musicians, musical analysis reveals just how problematic these (now) dominant paradigms are. I am therefore increasingly of the view that this reification of 'improvisation' as a category separate from other forms of creative practice needs to be rethought.

As will be discussed in later chapters, the discourses of Iranian musicians are heavily dependent on dualisms, most obviously the improvisation/composition divide, but also in the positioning of tradition vs modernity, East vs West, authentic/pure vs hybrid, oral vs notated, unscientific vs scientific, Iranian vs non-Iranian, urban vs rural, and so on. Through these pairings, musical and broader social binaries reinforce one another such that ideas of tradition, nationhood, authenticity and so on, become indexically linked. Like many other countries in the so-called 'developing world' in the first half of the twentieth century, Iran's encounter with modernizing forces was tied up with (quasi)-colonial relations of prestige and power. In promoting the idea of tradition and modernity as antithetical, the ruling elites created a powerful binary that continues to infuse all areas of social life, and which was arguably the fountain from which many others flowed. There are interesting parallels with the case of Iran elsewhere. In her book *Singing the Classical, Voicing the Modern* (2006), an incisive analysis of the postcolonial politics of sound in South India, Amanda Weidman suggests that much binary thinking emerged in relation to the clear dichotomy set up between modernity and tradition, itself largely constructed through the West's colonial encounters. Following the work of Timothy J. Mitchell (2000), she argues:

> Modernity is thus not a purely Western or European project; on the contrary, it is constituted in and by the colonial encounter ... modernity can be seen as a discursive formation which has naturalized particular ways of thinking dependent on a series of familiar binaries: secular vs. sacred, content vs. form, rational vs. nonrational, mind vs. body, public vs. private, and, not least, tradition vs. modernity. Indeed, one of the most powerful ways in which the project of modernity operates is by defining itself as representative of rationality, progress, change, and universality, in opposition to 'tradition', a category which comes to stand for all that is irrational or emotional, stagnant, ancient, and local (Bauman and Briggs 2003). Such oppositions gain currency, of course, by being mapped as the difference between the west and the non-west. (Weidman 2006:6–7)

Weidman considers how such colonizing binaries were used to 'orchestrate the ways in which Western classical music and Indian classical music, defined by their mutual opposition, are allowed to meet' (2006:5). For Karnatic music, local discourses promoted the centrality of the voice and oral tradition, which were:

> ... used to oppose Karnatic music to a generalized idea of Western music: whereas Western music is instrumental, Karnatic is vocal; whereas Western music is 'technologically' superior, Karnatic is more 'spiritual'; whereas Western music can be played just by looking at written music (or so the stereotype goes), Karnatic is passed

---

[44]   This is a vast topic and it is not possible to provide a comprehensive list here. Arguably the most significant early writer is Ernst Ferand (1938, 1961), and within ethnomusicology important publications appeared from the 1970s, including Nettl with Foltin (1972), Nettl (1974c), Hood (1975), Sorrell and Narayan (1980), Lortat-Jacob (1987a), Nettl (1991), Berliner (1994), Monson (1996), Blum (1998), Nettl with Russell (1998) and Solis and Nettl (2009). Outside ethnomusicology, notable publications include Sudnow (1978), Bailey (1980), Pressing (1988), Benson (2003) and Berkowitz (2010). Much of the early literature on improvisation was focused on jazz and the art musics of Asia, a pattern which continues. For more recent work on improvisation in Western art music, see footnote 19.

on through gurukulavsam, a centuries-long oral tradition and a system of teaching that technology cannot duplicate. (ibid.:246)

The central focus of Weidman's study is how 'the vocal nature of Indian music and its ties to oral tradition – came to stand for [this] essential difference between South Indian classical music and western music', in much the same way that for many of the writers discussed earlier individual vs communal creation became the most significant axis of differentiation between folk and art music. It is thus important to understand how discourses of difference come to frame musical practices, aligning them or distinguishing them in particular ways. In the case of Iran, it wasn't the voice/instrument divide that acquired significance; rather, the mapping of difference was played out through discourses around creative practice that emphasized the oral, ephemeral and improvised nature of Iranian music against something more planned and structured as represented by Western notions of composition.

Returning to musicological discourses, I have argued elsewhere (2003) that a central problem with the composition/improvisation divide is that it depends on notions of essentialized difference: no matter how natural the categories of improvisation and composition may seem, nor how obvious the differences between them, they are ultimately constructions which depend on the privileging of certain criteria – *viz.* context, temporality and product – over others. Here, the fault line effectively separates musical creativity taking place away from performance – often over an extended time period, usually resulting in notation and requiring further creative acts to be realized – and that taking place in the course of performance and which doesn't result in a physical product (other than perhaps a recording, which differs from notation in following rather than preceding performance). But one might reasonably question the significance of drawing the boundary along this axis rather than another; indeed, does this boundary reflect essential differences, or deflect attention from what musics on either side share? As Blum observes:

> Despite the fact that people in many parts of the world have felt inclined, even obliged, to define their acts as musicians with reference to this set of three categories [composition, improvisation, performance], the contrasts implicit in the system are not always the most pertinent ones for understanding what musicians do ... To the extent that the restricted senses of composition and performance became normative, people were increasingly inclined to describe too many alternatives as 'improvisation'. (2009:240)

Moreover, as many have observed, what is normatively understood to define improvisation – performer spontaneity, freedom, risk-taking, interaction between musicians and with a responsive audience,[45] and so on – is both relative and found to varying extents in 'non-improvised' practice. Focusing for a moment on the differences between performance from notation (memorized or not) and that without, whilst the latter is often taken to indicate greater freedom, this is clearly not necessarily the case: musicians spend many years memorizing oral repertoires which function in much the same way as a score. Since all performance involves some degree of performer creativity, where the dividing line between the reified categories of 'improvised' and 'non-improvised' performance lies is not at all clear. The latter is as much about re-creating music on the basis of social conventions, past experiences, and personal taste and feelings, as Charles Seeger observes:

> European musicians, musicologists, and the general public have distinguished three types of individuals: composers, performers, and listeners ... In the Western world composers alone are supposed to create; performers, to re-create. But in direct proportion to expertness, performers create 'what is between or outside of the notes'; and in direct proportion to their recognition of the potentialities of the continuity and variance of a tradition, composers re-create it. In the non-Western world, within specifications of raga, maqam, pathet, and

---

[45]   Whilst the creation of music in performance arguably allows a quality of interaction between improviser and audience which is not possible for a (notation-based) composer, this depends on the specific tradition or context. It is true that composers tend to interact less directly with audiences; however, they will often assess reception and critical appraisal from one composition, or performance, to the next. For group improvising musicians, interaction with others clearly plays a key role in the creative process. Monson (1996) provides one of the most detailed studies of 'the musical and social frameworks in which interactive improvisation takes place' (7).

the like, creativity is mostly or entirely in performance, the composer, as a separate individual, being often as not nonexistent or merely a name in the annals of the tradition. (1977:153–4)

There are two main lines of thought. On the one hand, there is the idea that 'To some extent every performance involves elements of improvisation, though its degree varies according to period and place' (Sadie 1980:32, see below); for example, in performing J.S. Bach's *Das Wohltemperirte Klavier*, András Schiff adds ornaments which he describes as 'improvisations on the spur of the moment, according to the style and the composer ... consciously and carefully studied beforehand' (in Kertész Wilkinson 1989:10). Thus, different renditions of a notated piece are regarded as 're-creations' in much the same way as 'improvised' performances. On the other is the view that performing from notation is qualitatively different from interpreting a less well-defined model or framework. During distinguishes between interpretation ('*exécution*') and improvisation, on the basis that the former requires only an ability to play music, whilst the latter demands 'the assimilation and integration of the very principles of the music' (1987b:36). As with the composition-improvisation divide, detailed analysis reveals that these categories ('improvising performer', 'non-improvising performer') fail to account for the extent to which all performance brings to bear traditional or pre-determined elements (notated or otherwise), and new elements, and for the blurring between 'creation' and 're-creation'.

Without doubt, recent work has moved the field on substantially, including a gradual acceptance of improvisation as a form of composition. The entry on 'Improvisation' in the 1980 edition of *The New Grove Dictionary of Music and Musicians* presents the improviser as someone combining the roles of performer and composer:

> The creation of a musical work, or the final form of a musical work, as it is being performed. It may involve the work's immediate composition by its performers, or the elaboration or adjustment of an existing framework, or anything in between ... To some extent every performance involves elements of improvisation, though its degree varies according to period and place; and to some extent every improvisation rests upon a series of conventions or implicit rules .... (Sadie 1980:31–2)[46]

Even more interesting is the transition between the respective entries on 'Composition' in the 1980 edition of *The New Grove* – a fairly short contribution by musicologist Mark Lindley – and the more extensive 2001 entry by ethnomusicologist Stephen Blum. Whilst the earlier definition positions notation at the forefront: 'A term usually referring to a piece of music embodied in a written form or the process by which composers create such pieces' (Lindley 1980:599), in 2001 the first five sections discuss compositional processes in a range of traditions, and not until section 6 ('Counterpoint') is the role of notation directly broached. Indeed, Blum more or less dispenses with the idea of composition as an activity separate from improvisation, writing instead of 'composition during performance' to refer both to the act of interpreting a score and to improvisation as normatively understood (2001:187, 188). Above all, European concepts of composition are situated historically and culturally: notation is not assumed, nor presented as a norm.[47] This marks a new phase in which the perennial question of whether a piece is 'really' improvised becomes immaterial, since 'improvisational' and 'compositional' elements are always present. From this perspective, the 'composer' is as much an 'improviser' (on paper or in the mind) as the improvising musician is a 'composer': both create within the conventions of a system, drawing on past experience and extant models, which might include a score.

---

[46]   This entry can be usefully contrasted with its 1954 predecessor (by H.C. Colles) in the 5th edition of *Grove's Dictionary of Music and Musicians*, see Nooshin (2003:249–50). The 2001 edition of *The New Grove* repeats the 1980 definition virtually unchanged (slightly shortened). The article itself, however, is expanded, with a significantly longer section on Western Art Music (by various authors), and a new section on Jazz (by Barry Kernfeld). However, the earlier 1980 section on 'Asian Art Music' is replaced by a more general opening 'I. Concepts and Practices' (by Bruno Nettl), which references a range of traditions; several Asian art musics form the focus of the final sub-section. '4. A Sampling of Genres'.

[47]   Similarly, see the definition of 'composer' recently adopted by the UK-based organization Sound and Music, as a 'creator of original new music or sound'. In the same item, Sound and Music Chief Executive Susanna Eastburn asks whether there is a better term than 'composer' to describe the work of those creating contemporary music. http://soundandmusic.org/node/7526?utm_campaign=blog&utm_medium=email&utm_source=J13&utm_content=&utm_term= (accessed 6.6.2013).

Even the notion of a continuum comes into question, since it takes the reified categories as starting points. Of course, the idea of an integral relationship between improvisation and composition has not been entirely absent from musicological discourse. Fifty years before Nettl's seminal 1974 *Musical Quarterly* article, Heinrich Schenker wrote about this relationship in his 1925 essay 'Die Kunst der Improvisation'. Rink notes Schenker's insightful awareness of the improvisatory nature of composition and the 'frequency and conviction with which Schenker uses the term to describe the act of composition and to define musical structure' (1993:2). Such ideas, however, have been largely sidelined by the vigour of the dominant discourses and the tenacious categories which continue to shape our thinking about music.

In light of the above discussion, and if we accept that all music is improvisational in some way, one might reasonably ask whether the concept serves a useful purpose any longer.[48] If, as Blum suggests 'Usage of the term *improvisation* continues to be motivated by desires to discuss *differences* that people perceive and experience in our ways of making and interpreting music' (2009:241), what exactly do the wide variety of genres, traditions and practices normatively understood as 'improvised' have in common; and what distinguishes them from other modes of creative practice? Is there, in the idea that all 'improvised' musics share something essential, a risk of essentializing sameness?[49] Back in 1998, Nettl observed that 'we will increasingly have to look at improvisation as a group of perhaps very different phenomena' (1998:16),[50] and, later, in the Introduction to the 2009 volume edited with Nettl, Solis also questions the very basis of the book:

> Are the jazz musician from 1927 who ornately elaborated and ornamented a melody, the free improviser of today who creates collective sound spaces, the Baroque keyboardist of the 17th century or today who preludes, and the sitarist who plays an alap really all doing the same thing? All create new music using models known and in some way agreed upon beforehand, but the nature of the models, the degree of departure, the context for interpretation, the interactive frameworks, and the meaning those creations take on among the musicians and audience are all distinct. (Solis 2009:3)

Solis predicts that eventually, 'this book [will] ensure its own obsolescence ... the study of improvisation will ultimately melt into the basic paradigms of musical study, so that there may no longer be a rationale for studying it as distinct from the rest of music making' (2009:9). Continuing these thoughts in a 2012 conference paper, Nettl also asks whether 'all the things we include under the rubric of improvisation [and he expands significantly on the list above] have enough in common to justify a collective term', at the same time acknowledging the irony that just as improvisation is starting to gain some visibility within music studies, we should be questioning its validity as a category: 'I know I'm swimming upstream as music researchers finally get some recognition for this neglected art' (2012). Likewise, I would argue that there are 'plenty of reasons for replacing this system with better sets of categories' (Blum 2009:240) which more closely reflect musical practice and allow us to understand 'musical creation holistically' (Nettl 2012).

It is instructive to trace changing definitions as presented in key publications such as *The New Grove* for what they reveal of shifts in musicological thinking over several decades. Certainly, this has been evident

---

[48]   See also Benson (2003).

[49]   Indeed, it might be argued that publications which focus on the theme of improvisation, bringing together writings on different traditions – for example Bailey (1980), Lortat-Jacob (1987a), Nettl (1991), Nettl with Russell (1998), Solis and Nettl (2009) – reinforce this reification of improvisation as a particular 'type' of music.

[50]   Several writers have in fact sought to distinguish different types of improvisation, rather than viewing it in the singular. In his now-classic book, Bailey (1980) coined the term 'non-idiomatic improvisation' to indicate improvisation which has no connection with, and hence no allegiance to the conventions of, a particular genre or style. Goehr has recently suggested a similar distinction between what she terms 'improvisation impromptu' (which aligns closely with Bailey's 'non-idiomatic' improvisation) and 'improvisation extempore', which occurs within pre-established parameters (2012). Turino (2009) offers a more radical approach, distinguishing between 'formulaic' and 'improvised' performing, thereby implicitly negating the formulaic nature of much of what is often understood as 'improvised'. Considering the specific context of group participatory music-making, Turino discusses the different states of mind achieved by musicians, arguing that the risk-taking and elements of surprise characteristic of 'improvised' (as opposed to 'formulaic') performance can disrupt the sense of 'flow' (as used by Csikszentmihalyi 1990) so valued by musicians. Turino's observations are specific to group situations and less relevant to the kinds of solo performance found in Iran.

in the growing body of research reporting on an increasingly diverse range of creative practice, including group and collaborative projects of various kinds; detailed studies of compositional processes, including the interpenetration of the compositional and the improvisational; the role of technology in the changing nature of creative practice; the boundaries between tangible and virtual, between human and machine, and between 'popular' and 'art' musics; the creative role of listeners; as well as perspectives from music psychology, music education, music therapy; and so on.[51] Whilst this is clearly a vast area, there are some points of relevance to the current discussion. Perhaps the two most significant factors to have impacted on creative processes in the past half-century or so have been the possibilities opened up by new, particularly digital, technologies, and the emergence of creative group work, often based around interactional relationships between composers and performers (normatively understood), with the collaborative development of pieces, often in workshop situations.[52] These new practices strain existing taxonomies and boundaries between creative actors, particularly in relation to the locus of creative agency. In her 2005 article 'On Musical Mediation: Ontology, Technology and Creativity', Georgina Born argues that these changes demand not just new methodological tools but a 'radically revised conception of music's ontology' (2005:10), particularly in relation to the work concept. Drawing on Alfred Gell's work on the anthropology of art, she explores:

> ... the distribution of creative agency between different producers, as in collaborative forms of musical authorship; and between subjects and objects, human and non-human agents ... [and] the way that electronic and digital technologies afford and enhance a dispersed and collaborative creativity. (2005:25)

Focusing on three case studies – the digital circulation of South Asian diasporic music; live electronic art music; and the piece *Voyager* by African-American musician George E. Lewis – Born considers the ways in which 'Digital music media ... afford entirely new modes of collaborative authorship ... Distributed across space, time and persons, music can become an object of recurrent decomposition, composition and re-composition by a series of creative agents' (2005:26). Proposing the term 'relayed creativity' to describe this process, she discusses the fluidity and malleability of digital sound worlds, which 'yield[ing] a provisional musical work which both retains and blurs the traces and boundaries of individual and collective authorship' (ibid.:30). For Born, the provisional work represents this new ontology, which she suggests was 'anticipated in jazz' (ibid.:30) and which contrasts with the old ontology of the work concept.

Born's work is important in drawing attention to these new forms of creative practice. Yet the article is surprisingly uncritical of some of the associated discourses, and in particular the disjuncture between discourse and practice – despite her own critique in her earlier work on the electronic music centre IRCAM (*Institut de Recherche et Coordination Acoustique/Musique*), of the 'gap between the discourse of invention and its actuality', the latter being 'IRCAM-modernism's remarkable capacity to stay the same' (ibid.:15). Similarly, here there is no allowance for the gap between the dominant discourses of the work concept and musical practice itself. Whilst the new digitality undoubtedly makes possible new forms of authorship, in contrasting the 'vertical hierarchy of mediations characteristic of the work concept' (ibid.:26) with the 'lateral and processual' nature of jazz (ibid.:27), Born establishes a binary which arguably underestimates continuities with earlier practices. Moreover, according to this view, jazz (as a broad category) with its 'distinctive ontology' (ibid.:28) becomes symbolic of a new world/musical order in which there is 'no hierarchy between composer as Creator and performer as interpreter of the Word' (ibid.:27) and 'no final, untouchable work' (ibid.:27). Discursive tropes aside, it is not difficult to find counter-examples to these characterizations. Born's discussion of the (European) work concept ontology is also problematic in failing to position it as emerging at a specific historical juncture, and only loosely applicable to earlier periods. Thus, much of the description

---

[51]   To mention just one example, the 2012 volume *The Act of Musical Composition*, edited by Dave Collins, covers a range of compositional practice and positions improvisation within the purview of composition, although only one chapter focuses explicitly on improvisation: 'Improvisation as Real-Time Composition' by Simon Rose and Raymond MacDonald explores the role of improvisation within the compositional process, drawing on interviews with improvisers.

[52]   Although, of course, such interactions are by no means new. Group improvisation has a long history in European art music, stretching back to the sixteenth century and earlier. See also Butt (2002:90–91, 93–4) for discussion of the relationship between composers and performers in eighteenth-century Europe.

of relayed creativity and 'Innovative practices of re-composition' exemplified according to Born by various African-American musics (ibid.:26), could be equally applied to European compositional practices of the Baroque and earlier, as well as many other music traditions.[53] And there are further examples of discourse accepted at face value, for instance the suggestion that in experimental electronic music, there is 'no building of an aesthetic language ... the emphasis is on open process and unpredictability in performance', and it is this which 'point[s] to a refusal of the telos of the finished work' (ibid.:31); that the discourses claim an absence of aesthetic language does not mean that there isn't one. Similarly, Lewis's description of his piece as 'a non-hierarchical interactive musical environment that privileges improvisation' (ibid.:32) is linked uncritically to the idea of improvisation as essentially 'anti-authoritarian' (ibid.:33, Lewis's term). In general, the article offers a celebratory view of improvisation; and even a statement as seemingly innocuous as jazz being 'grounded in an aesthetics of collaborative improvisation' (ibid.:27) needs unpicking in order to understand in what specific contexts truly collaborative improvisation might be possible. Even more surprising perhaps, given the focus of the article and Born's own caution 'to resist the equation of mediation simply with mobility or progressive change' (ibid.:30), is the idea of cyberspace as a democratic space operating outside power, as in the description of music created in the digital domain:

> This is a music in process, predicated on the suspension of any master discourse – an aesthetics of mutual encounter, of bridging and negotiation, not an aesthetics of appropriation and subsumption of an other. It augurs a relational aesthetics, one with roots in the movement between performance and reified object and the dialogical music-socialities of jazz. (ibid.:30)

I have discussed Born's article in some detail because it offers a good example of scholarship which significantly pushes forward our understanding of new forms of creative practice, yet remains heavily reliant on existing discourses, and particularly the binary positioning of composition and improvisation: the former aligned with the 'vertical hierarchy' of the work concept, the latter with the familiar romanticized trope of improvisation as a place beyond power, here represented by the lateral, dialogic space of jazz. Thus, even in a piece of writing which explicitly sets out to destabilize existing ontologies, many of the underpinning paradigms remain unchallenged. And this brings me to a central point: that despite the many new insights and approaches offered by recent work, improvisation continues its life as a 'marked term' (Blum 2009:239) and 'everyday usage ... continues to favour the restricted senses in which composition and performance are understood to exclude improvisation unless otherwise specified' (ibid.).[54] Further, the burgeoning scholarly interest in improvisation (within music studies and beyond) has arguably led to a heightened reification of improvisation as a separate and essentialized form of musical practice as described. This can be seen in the emergence of a discrete field of Improvisation Studies and the establishment of organizations such as the International Society for Improvised Music (founded 2006) and recently-formed special interest groups within the Society for Ethnomusicology and the Society for Music Theory, as well as dedicated conferences

---

[53]   See the discussion above of Kodály and Lloyd's work, and the quotation from Van Gennep describing processes of 'folk creation'. A useful discussion of the open-ended nature of compositional processes in European art music well into the nineteenth century can be found in Butt (2002), particularly Chapter 4 which considers the fluid relationship between composition, notation and performance. Interestingly, Butt uses almost the same wording as Born to suggest (in relation to early polyphonic church repertoire) that the notated 'product was by no means a finished, immutable [Born uses 'untouchable'] piece' (116). The historical evidence thus problematizes Born's ascribing of a distinctive ontological status to jazz. Similarly, in the Editorial of the journal issue in which Born's article appears, Robert Adlington and Sophie Fuller comment on Leta Miller's article on American composer Lou Harrison, specifically his extensive use of 'revision, alteration and self-borrowing' which 'presents a situation analogous to Born's account of digital music, in which "there is no original and no copy, only rapidly proliferating, variant versions" (p.28) – in Harrison's case the creative relay is conducted introspectively as much as socially' (2005:4), thus questioning the extent to which processes of relayed creativity described by Born are radically new and specific to the digital age.

[54]   For example, whilst some contemporary composers have used 'improvised' elements in their compositions, there remains a clear conceptual division between these two creative modes.

and conference panels[55] and several significant publications, including an issue of the *Journal of Music Theory* (2005) focused on improvisation[56] and the forthcoming two-volume *Oxford Handbook of Critical Improvisation Studies* (edited by George E. Lewis and Benjamin Piekut).[57] In particular, increased attention to the historical place of improvisation in Western art music has resulted in a number of publications, conference panels and even dedicated conservatoire courses.[58] The impetus for this has no doubt partly come from the growing interest in performance studies generally within musicology since the 1990s, and recent research projects and centres such as (in the UK) the Arts and Humanities Research Council funded Research Centre for Musical Performance as Creative Practice, established in 2009.[59]

*   *   *

Looking ahead to the remaining chapters of this volume, the issues discussed above have profoundly shaped my work on Iranian classical music over many years as I have grappled with the dominant discourses – both of my disciplinary home and of the music culture that I study – and sought to understand the ways in which European paradigms have impacted on local discourses, social meanings and musical practice. The aim of this preliminary chapter has been to set out what I see as the central problematics and to argue for an understanding of musical creativity as a domain of knowledge which both shapes and is shaped by specific musicological discourses. Much of the discussion has focused on the ways in which discourses of creativity have been mobilized as a marker of musical difference, particularly in relation to the locus of creative agency. Such discourses cannot be understood in isolation, but form part of a network of mutually reinforcing ideas which ultimately service alterity-construction. Similarly, as noted and as will be discussed in later chapters, whilst local discourse and most writings on Iranian classical music frame creativity in performance primarily in terms of improvisation – understood as a reified category distinct from (notated) composition, largely using ideas derived (originally) from European taxonomies – such imaginings of difference are mediated through a series of other, related binaries, including East/West, oral/notated, traditional/modern, unscientific/scientific and so on.

This study is ultimately about understanding musical creativity as a meaningful social practice. Questions of power remain central as I consider the relations of authority, hierarchy and alterity embedded in the creative processes, their attendant discourses, and the central *radif* repertoire. One of the questions I ask is whether there can be a place beyond alterity, or is our understanding of the world inexorably tied to the kinds of structural oppositions discussed in this chapter? What would an approach to creative practice in Iranian classical music that went beyond the arguably unhelpful improvisation/composition paradigm look like? This is precisely what I have sought to do in my earlier work, and in the current volume such ideas are explored further in Chapters 4 and 5. In considering the kinds of compositional principles and strategies deployed in performance, one finds a highly structured and formulaic practice, also suggestive of parallels with other areas of human creativity such as language. Regardless of whether the concept of improvisation has real explanatory power for this music, however, the discourse of improvisation is now so deeply embedded that attempting to 'undo the logic of alterity' (Kramer 1995:49) is not easy when set against the weight of

---

[55]   To give just two examples, 'Perspectives on Musical Improvisation', held at the University of Oxford, UK, September 2012 (http://www.music.ox.ac.uk/pomi/welcome.html) and 'Perspectives on Musical Improvisation II' (University of Oxford, September 2014), and a joint AMS/SEM/SMT panel 'Improvisation: Object of Study and Critical Paradigm', held at the joint meeting of the American Musicological Society, the Society for Ethnomusicology and the Society for Music Theory, New Orleans, November 2012.

[56]   All of the contributions are in fact about improvisation in jazz, including one article (by Steve Larson) on the improvisation/composition divide (2005).

[57]   The increasingly interdisciplinary thrust of these trends is evidenced, for instance, in the establishment of a new cross-disciplinary journal (in 2004), *Critical Studies in Improvisation*. http://www.criticalimprov.com/index (accessed 13.7.2012).

[58]   In the UK, for example, the Centre for Classical Improvisation and Creative Performance at the Guildhall School of Music and Drama was established in 2006 http://www.gsmd.ac.uk/music/staff/teaching_staff/centre_for_classical_improvisation_and_creative_performance/ (accessed 12.5.2014).

[59]   See http://www.cmpcp.ac.uk (accessed 21.8.2014) and 'Perspectives on Musical Improvisation II' (University of Oxford, September 2014).

normalization which one is somehow 'historically fated to reproduce' (ibid.). Whilst 'such binary oppositions and the alterity on which they depend cannot readily be eradicated except by sophisticated theoretical means … by coming to understand how the structuring of othering works, interpreters will then at least be in a position to envisage musical subjectivities more porous to the imaginary' (Williams 2000:391). And indeed there is evidence that a more porous understanding of creative practice is emerging among some (mainly younger) musicians in Iran who, as I will discuss in Chapter 5, are moving beyond the dominant discourses of opposition, and imagining – and articulating – a more integral relationship between the compositional and the improvisational. The chapters that follow chart the discourses and practice of creativity in Iranian classical music, and the complex relationship between them, bringing to bear a perspective which aims to transcend traditional binaries and offer a more holistic understanding of musical creativity.

PART II
Creativity in the Iranian Context:
Discourses and Structures

Chapter 2
Discourses of Creativity in Iranian Classical Music

Introduction: Issues, Positions, Terminologies

The Story of the Nightingale

It was the seventh day. God had finished making the world and at last he could rest. But then he realised that there was one job left to do: he had to paint the birds, because they were all a dusty brown colour, like the earth from which they had been made. So God took out his paints and announced, 'Calling all birds! If you want to be painted, come to heaven now!' The air was filled with the whirring of wings. All the birds came to be painted. God painted the robins rosy red; he gave swans snow-white wings and shiny black feet; he painted peacocks turquoise and gold; and made ravens black as night. God painted the birds all day. But as the sun was setting, a little bird appeared. 'Sorry I'm late', she cried 'I only just got the message. I'd like to be pink!' 'Sorry', said God 'The pink has been used up. I gave it to the Flamingos'. 'Green then'. 'That went to the Parrots and the Woodpeckers'. 'I'll be any colour', said the little bird. 'I'm afraid all the paint has been used up'. God looked at the paint pots and brushes, and on the tip of the smallest brush was a tiny speck of gold paint. 'I have an idea! This might be a speck of paint, but where I'm going to paint it, it will be worth all the colours of the rainbow put together. Open your beak little bird'. God painted the tip of the bird's tongue gold. And the bird flew back down to earth. It landed in a tree, opened its beak and began to sing. The song was so sweet that people came out of their houses and listened. 'That bird has a golden tongue!', they cried. The bird was the nightingale. It is still a dusty brown colour, but its golden tongue is worth all the colours of the rainbow put together.
(Sally Pomme Clayton, based on a Middle Eastern folktale)

Creative performance lies at the heart of Iranian classical music.[1] The centrality of individual creative expression is commonly symbolized by the nightingale, a bird regularly encountered in the literary and visual arts of the Middle East and said to possess the most beautiful voice on earth. According to popular belief, the nightingale never repeats itself (Nettl 1983:208) and this paradigm of an aesthetic universe which revolves around ever-changing expression is often invoked by teachers as an ideal to which their pupils, particularly singers, should aspire. Such expression, however, is always understood as operating within a defined framework, primarily that of the repertoire known as *radif*. I begin this chapter with the iconic image of the nightingale because it illustrates nicely some of the tensions which inhere around debates relating to individual agency in Iranian music. Following some preliminary issues and considerations, I will explore the place of creative practice in Iranian classical music and consider how discourse and practice in this area have been impacted by the significant social, cultural and political changes which Iran has undergone since the late nineteenth century.[2] Whilst Chapter 1 was concerned primarily with the central discourses and underlying assumptions of musicology in relation to creativity, these clearly follow their own historical trajectories, in the process accruing specific meanings in particular contexts. However problematic the term 'improvisation', it is generally used unproblematically in the literature on Iranian music, and equivalent Persian terms have emerged over the last several decades and are now readily accepted by musicians and others: not only is there

---

[1]   Known variously in Iran as *musiqi-ye asil* ('pure' or 'noble' music), *musiqi-ye sonnati* ('traditional music'), *musiqi-ye radifi* ('music of the *radif*'), *musiqi-ye dastgāhi* ('*dastgāh* music') or *musiqi-ye kelāssik-e Irani* ('Iranian classical music'). These terms are discussed below.

[2]   As well as information from the literature, much of the material in this and the following chapters is based on interviews, informal discussion (some during lessons) and correspondence with musicians, mainly during the period 1987–1990 when the bulk of the research was undertaken, but with additional material from the 1990s and 2000s. These were conducted in Persian and translated into English by the current author, and are referenced with the relevant date. Translations from books and articles originally in Persian or French are also by the author.

no satisfactory alternative to the inherited dualistic terms, but they have become deeply embedded in local discourse. Since this chapter reports on discourses within the tradition, active deconstruction of terminology is deferred to later chapters. Whilst detailed discussion of the recent social history of Iranian classical music lies outside the scope of this book, I provide a summary here in order to contextualize the discussion that follows, particularly in relation to processes of modernization and westernization which have impacted profoundly on concepts of creativity.[3]

Refined and contemplative, the aesthetic beauty of Iranian classical music lies in the intricate nuances of the usually unmetered solo melody line known as *āvāz*, which in its ornamental detail has been compared with the complex patterns of Iran's visual arts (miniature painting, tilework, carpets, calligraphy and so on). Developed under royal patronage over several hundred years, the sparse documentary record dates this music to before the Arab invasion of the seventh century CE. Later treatises written during the golden age of Middle Eastern scholarship by theorists such as Abu Nasr Farabi (872–950), Abolfaraj Esfahani (896–966), Abu Ali Ebn-e Sina (Avicenna, 980–1037) and Safiaddin Ormavi (d.1294) include the names of pieces still performed today, although the extent to which the music has changed over time is unclear. Before the twentieth century, this music was largely heard in courtly settings, but with the declining influence of the monarchy, and particularly with the seismic changes following the 1906 Constitutional Revolution, found new patronage in the homes of musicians, cultured amateurs and aristocratic patrons. Although still very much a private and elite affair, this marked the first stage of a 'democratization' of the classical music which continued through the first half of the twentieth century, gaining momentum with the arrival of sound recording, broadcasting, public concerts (from the first decade of the twentieth century, but more regularly from the 1930s), and the institutionalization of music education.[4] As discussed below, each of these impacted in various ways on notions of creativity, the role of tradition and the social status of musicians. Many of these changes were a result of the modernizing and pro-Western policies of the Pahlavi monarchy,[5] first under Reza Shah (r.1925–41), a high-ranking army commander who assumed power in a *coup d'état* in 1921 and later became king, and his son, Mohammad Reza Pahlavi (r.1941–79). It was partly the speed with which the latter sought to transform Iran from a traditional, still strongly tribal, society to a modern, cosmopolitan, capitalist nation with a centralized state apparatus, partly the top-down nature of the changes, which depended both on suppressing aspects of traditional culture – most notably religion – and any political dissent, as well as promoting an oil-rich Western-oriented elite, and partly his perceived control by Western powers which led to the Revolution of

---

[3]   The extant European-language literature on Iranian classical music includes a number of introductory texts: Caron and Safvate (1966), Sadeghi (1971), Zonis (1973), During (1984a) and Farhat (1980b, 1990). Discussion of the *radif* can be found both in these and other general publications such as Khatschi (1962), Nettl with Foltin (1972), Tsuge (1974) and Babiracki and Nettl (1987; also published in slightly revised form in Nettl 1987), as well as writings concerned primarily with the *radif*, such as Modir (1986b), Nettl (1987), During (1991a, the introduction to the transcription of Borumand's *radif*, given in Persian and English as well as the original French) and Talai (1997, 2000). Other writings include Gerson-Kiwi (1963), Zonis (1965), Khatschi (1967), Wilkens (1967), Massoudieh (1968, 1973), Battesti (1969), Jones (1971), Nettl (1972, 1974a, 1974b, 1975, 1978, 1980, 1981), During (1975, 1977, 1984b, 1987c, 1989, 1991a, 1991b, 1994), Beeman (1976), Lotfi (1976), Ayako (1980), Zolfonoun (1980), Caton (1983), Modir (1986a), Ogger (1987), Miller (1999), Azadehfar (2006), Wright (2009) and Simms and Koushkani (2012a, 2012b). Publications in Persian include: Sha'bani (1973), Mansuri and Shirvani (1977), Massoudieh (1989[1978]), general introduction preceding the transcription of Karimi's *radif*, also in French), Joneydi (1982), Khaleqi (1982, 1983a, 1983b, 1983c), Kiani (1987), Sepanta (1987), Behroozi (1988), Darvishi (1995) and Zolfonoun (2001).

[4]   In encouraging modern (versus traditional) sensibilities, Talai discusses the particular significance of broadcasting in bringing music to a nationwide audience for the first time. Especially influential in the early days were broadcasts by the female singer Qamar ol-Molouk Vaziri (1905–1959; often accompanied by Morteza Ney-Davud (c.1900–1990) on *tār*), singing the *tasnifs* (songs) of writers such as Aref Qazvini (1882–1934) and Amir Jahed (1895–1977) (in Shahrnazdar 2004a:15–16).

[5]   Although such processes had begun during the Qajar period (1794–1925) with increased contact between Iran and Europe, they were not central to government policies and discourses as they became under the Pahlavis. I have discussed (in Chapter 1) the problematics of using essentialized terms such as 'Western' or 'the West', and have explained the caveats under which I use them. At the same time, it should be noted that essentialized notions of '*qarb*' ('West'; referring to the political 'West' – Europe, North America, Australia and so on) and '*qarbi*' ('Western') are an important part of local discourse in Iran and are often invoked in debates on music, particularly in relation to questions of national belonging and identity.

February 1979 and his overthrow.[6] As I (and others) have discussed, the Revolution was akin to a national independence struggle, in this case against neo-colonial control, effected by a populist uprising which brought together nationalists, religious groups and a wide spectrum of political organizations. Only after the Shah fled Iran in January 1979, and the subsequent return of Ayatollah Khomeini from exile, did the religious factions gain the upper hand, leading to the declaration of the Islamic Republic on 1 April 1979. The nationalist nature of the Revolution had profound implications for Iranian classical music which, despite the restrictions that took effect almost immediately, experienced an extraordinary grass roots renaissance. In contrast to the pre-1979 period, prominent singer Shahram Nazeri recalls:

> It was as if a nation that had been asleep for centuries had woken; as if a fire had been lit in a reed-bed and each
> of these reeds, since they are burning, was obliged to think about itself, its society, its history. People gradually
> became interested in their own culture, because for many years in Iran, there was a long period of loss of
> identity [*bihoviyyat*]. (interview 21.8.99)

I return to questions of identity, and specifically their intersection with notions of 'authenticity' in Chapter 3.

Having secured an increasingly public profile from the 1930s onwards, with the rapid pace of westernization and modernization from the early 1950s, there was a sense in which traditional music became somewhat distanced from the mainstream of social change. There was certainly an audience for this music, which was available via radio broadcasts, television programmes, commercial recordings and public concerts, but it increasingly became a minority interest. Fortuitously, the establishment of both the Music Department at the University of Tehran and the Markaz-e Hefz-o Eshāeh-ye Musiqi-ye Irāni (Centre for the Preservation and Propagation of Iranian Music) in 1969 and 1970 respectively, created the conditions for the emergence of a new generation of musicians who rose to the challenge of the post-1979 period and took forward the ensuing musical renaissance. Further aspects of musical development, both before and after 1979, will be discussed below and in later chapters as they relate specifically to issues of creative performance and its interface with the traditional repertoire.

It is instructive to consider the impact of historical and political events on the trajectory of a particular field of study. Much of the European-language musicological literature on Iranian classical music was published in the 1960s and '70s at a time when scholarship in this area was dominated by the structuralist approaches and the dualistic composition-improvisation paradigm. Not until the 1980s did ethnomusicologists become interested in generative aspects of music-making, by which time the 1979 Revolution had effectively cut short the growing interest in this music outside Iran. As a result, most post-1979 studies of performance practice in Iranian music follow the predominantly structuralist and positivist approach of the 1960s and '70s. An important exception is Bruno Nettl, who has arguably done more than anyone to challenge dominant discourses on musical creativity. It is not coincidental that the very period when he was developing his ideas on this (as crystallized in the landmark 1974 article 'Thoughts on Improvisation: A Comparative Approach') was also the time when Nettl was working on material collected in Iran during the late 1960s. After 1979, with international relations in tatters, scholars outside Iran either turned elsewhere or (re)published earlier work (for instance, Nettl 1987, Farhat 1990), the main exception being Jean During who, through local connections, was able to continue working in Iran. Over the last decade or so, research in this area has regained momentum, but with a noticeable shift in focus from classical towards Iranian popular music, previously much neglected within ethnomusicology. Also noteworthy has been the growing musicological presence in Iran, spearheaded by a number of individuals at the various (mainly Tehran-based) universities, several of whom have doctorates gained outside Iran. This growing, and still relatively young, community of scholars was given impetus by the establishment of two Persian-language scholarly music journals in the late 1990s, most notably *Mahoor Music Quarterly*, which publishes both local research and translations of key English-language articles previously published elsewhere. Although there are a few Iranian sociologists and cultural theorists working on music, by and large Iranian ethnomusicology can be characterized as operating within the structuralist paradigms

---

[6]   For further discussion of the background to and events of the 1979 Iranian Revolution, the reader is referred to Keddie (1981), Katouzian (2003), Parsa (1989), Chehabi (1990), Farhi (1990), Halliday (1996:42–75), Martin (2000) and Ansari (2003), among others.

inherited from the 1960s and '70s, and from the 'father' of Iranian (ethno)musicology, Mohammad Taghi Massoudieh (see footnote 22), and, further, is focused almost exclusively on the music of Iran (and parts of Central Asia). Thus, the Revolution had a significant impact on Iranian music research, not only in largely bringing to a halt work by scholars outside Iran, but in creating a hiatus in such research at a critical time when scholarly paradigms were being rethought.[7] A further observation concerns the wide availability of published interview and (auto)biographical material compared with the late 1980s when this research started. From the late 1990s, there has been a steady increase in material presenting musicians' views 'in their own words', often unmediated, both in scholarly journals and books and lay music magazines such as *Honar-e Musiqi* (*The Art of Music*). This relatively recent phenomenon seems indicative both of a growing interest among the public to read the views of musicians, and the rising social status and educational level of musicians over the past half century. Such publications, which were previously unavailable, have proved an invaluable source of information, views and discursive positions.

It seems pertinent before proceeding further to consider the question of nomenclature. Outside Iran, this music is generally referred to in English-language writings as 'Persian (or Iranian) classical music', and the equivalent *persische Kunstmusik* in German (but, interestingly, more often *musique traditionelle Iranienne* in French). Exactly when the English 'classical' was first applied to this music is unclear, but it seems that its courtly origins and continued high-art associations were determining factors. In her discussion of the 'classicization' of Hindustani music, Schofield (2010) explores the complex web of meanings associated with the terms 'classical' and 'art' in relation to music and discusses the work of scholars who have argued that certain kinds of north Indian music became 'refashioned' as 'classical' as part of the colonial legacy. In contrast, Schofield suggests that processes which could be understood as classicization had been ongoing for several centuries and were not 'inherently Eurocentric' (2010:487).[8] Whilst the dynamics of (neo) colonial intervention were very different in Iran, from the second quarter of the twentieth century, with the push towards a new envisioning of Iran as a modern nation state, Iranian classical music took on symbolic associations to which existing notions of high-art prestige remained central, but which also included new ideas about 'authenticity' (in the sense of fidelity to an imagined past), centred on a body of music which parallels in certain ways the European 'work concept'. Notwithstanding Powers' assertion (1980a) that 'no Middle Eastern music c.1980 qualified [as classical], despite the colonial-period classicizing efforts of nationalist modernizers, whereas earlier traditions of the pre-colonial Ottoman and Qajar courts did qualify' (quoted in Schofield 2010:486), a view which depended on an understanding of 'classical' defined by specialist performers, connoisseur audiences and an established 'tradition', if one takes a more literal understanding of the term as first used in Europe in the late eighteenth and early nineteenth centuries, and following Schofield's argument that '*classicization processes*, in which past cultural artefacts are preserved, revived, or invented to serve the remodelling and political positioning of their present-day counterparts, have been widespread in human societies historically and cross-culturally, regardless of what they have been called' (ibid.:490), then this music c.1980 arguably merited the label 'classical' *more than* that of the late nineteenth- and early twentieth-century Qajar courts. I return to questions of tradition and discourses of 'authenticity' in Chapter 3.

Local terminologies have been no less convoluted and contested. Whilst *musiqi-ye asil* or *musiqi-ye sonnati* were most commonly used before the 1980s, the more recent *musiqi-ye dastgāhi* or *musiqi-ye radifi* point to the increasingly central role of the *radif*. The ongoing debate on appropriate terminologies (and not just

---

[7]   As well as the impact of political events on broad areas of study, one might also consider their effect on individual scholars. There was perhaps no worse time to embark on a project researching Iranian music than the mid-1980s, a period of extreme hardship in Iran when the war with Iraq was at its peak. As such, securing a British Academy doctoral award in 1987, a time when travel to Iran was difficult and access to musicians restricted to the few individuals (Firuz Berenjian, Taghi Tafazoli) based in the UK and the rare visits by musicians from Iran, was something of a mixed blessing. This clearly shaped the direction of the research, and particularly the necessity to focus on extant recordings and on what the musical material 'itself' reveals about creative processes.

[8]   See also Weidman (2006), who discusses the tensions in early twentieth-century fashioning of Karnatic music as 'classical', a construct that emerged 'in the crucible of colonial modernity, nationalist ideology and South Indian regional politics' and for which the music needed to be 'modeled on Western classical music, with its system of notation, composers, compositions, conservatoires and concerts. At the same time, it needed to remain distinctively Indian.' There are clear parallels with Iran, as will be discussed.

for 'art' music) – and reflecting other tensions within the music culture – has been aired publicly in the music press and published interviews in recent years. Particularly interesting is a pair of items in *Mahoor Music Quarterly* (Issues 1 and 4, Shahrnazdar 1998/99) in which a group of prominent musicians and scholars – Mohammad Reza Darvishi, Dariush Talai, Farhad Fakhroldini, Majid Kiani, Hossein Alizadeh, Shahin Farhat and Davud Ganjei – were invited to give their views on current terms (and suggest alternatives). The responses reveal some interesting positions and divergences. Most agreed that the term *sonnati* emerged in the 1960s, initially used by Western musicologists or Iranians trained abroad as a direct translation of the English/French 'traditional/*traditionelle*',[9] some claiming that the pace of social change at this time necessitated a (new) distinction between 'traditional' and other musics. Whilst *sonnati* is widely used today, several contributors questioned its usefulness, since the term could potentially be extended to other kinds of Iranian music (rural or 'traditional' urban popular musics, for example). Alizadeh expressed the following concern:

> When the term *sonnat* is discussed in our society, it is interpreted as something not in relation to its cultural roots but as a kind of backwardness [*aqab māndegi*], worshipping outdated things [*kohneh parasti*] and tied to the past [*vābastegi be gozashteh*], which generally is not connected to the present or future. (Shahrnazdar 1998/99, no. 4:148)

According to both Talai and Ganjei, the 1960s was also the period when the term *asil* ('pure', 'noble') gained wide currency and both quote from Nur Ali Borumand (1906–1978),[10] a musician who became closely associated with discourses of 'purity' (*esālat*). Indeed, it was largely through such discourses that the two terms (*asil* and *sonnati*) eventually became largely synonymous when used in relation to music (traditional = pure). Several contributors felt that these should be more clearly distinguished and even questioned the usefulness of *asil*. Ganjei defines *musiqi-ye asil* as 'possessing roots and identity' and for which it can be clearly discerned 'when, where and how it has come into being' (Shahrnazdar 1998/99, no. 4:152), an idea I return to in due course. Several observed that *musiqi-ye dastgāhi* provides a more factual description of the music, and is therefore perhaps preferable to the more 'evaluative' (*arzyābi*) labels *asil* and *sonnati*. As an alternative, Kiani suggested *musiqi-ye farhangi* ('cultural music') and Talai and Ganjei mentioned *musiqi-ye kelāssik*, a term previously reserved for Western art music.[11] Such discussions have become quite common among musicians and often feature in published interviews, revealing a certain anxiety around issues of terminology. Within society at large, however, the terms *sonnati* and *asil* remain the most current, and are used more or less interchangeably.[12]

Moving through the first and into the second decade of the twenty-first century, it seems that '*musiqi-ye kelāssik*' is gaining some currency, particularly among music scholars (but less so, for example, on CD covers, tutor books or concert posters), some of whom are keen to promote the term, as evidenced in books and articles as well as in discussion and published interviews. In an article published more than a decade after those above, musicologists Hooman Asadi and Sassan Fatemi, and sociologist Mohammad Reza Fayaz consider the term

---

[9]   The same view was expressed by several musicians that I talked to, including Nazeri (23.4.10). Given the patchy historical record, it is unclear whether this now widely circulated 'folk myth' has any basis; nevertheless, the fact remains that many musicians believe it to be true. See also During (1994:37–65) for discussion of various terminologies and attendant meanings, drawing on interviews with master musicians.

[10]   Dates of musicians are given at the first mention only.

[11]   Although Fayaz cites some limited use of this term in the 1970s and earlier (Khazrai 2009:164), it was not commonly used before the 1990s to indicate Iranian classical music.

[12]   Note also that since the mid-1980s, the Ministry of Culture and Islamic Guidance (Vezārat-e Farhang va Ershād-e Eslāmi) has operated a permit system for commercial cassette, and later CD, releases, such that approved albums are allocated a permit number which is displayed on the product. This is preceded by a letter indicating musical style: S for *sonnati*; T for *taqir-kardeh* ('changed', referring broadly to musical 'fusions'); P for pop music; J for *jadid* ('new' music); M for 'moderne', usually orchestral music by Iranian composers; and N for *navāhi* (regional folk music). The logic of such labelling is often hard to fathom; for instance, I have recordings of classical music from the early 1980s which are classified as 'T' for no obvious reason, and very similar film music, some of which is labelled 'T' and others 'J'. The letter is followed by a number, from 1 to 4, purportedly indicating the 'quality' of the music, although again the criteria for such assessments are entirely unclear.

musiqi-ye kelāssik-e Irani in a group interview, again published in *Mahoor Music Quarterly* (Khazrai 2009). An interesting aspect of this article is how the debate over terminology, at least among scholars, appears to be shaped in part by their perception of how these terms are used and understood abroad. Opening the discussion, Asadi argues for the term *kelāssik* to be widely adopted because this is how the music is known outside Iran, and he even refers to Ella Zonis' (1973) text to support his argument (Khazrai 2009:163).[13] Whilst he later qualifies this by setting out the 'inherent' criteria by which the music merits the label 'classical' (originally the music of ruling classes, possessing a developed theoretical system, featuring a body of professional practitioners and so on), there is a strong sense of what Stokes describes as 'East looks at West looking at East' (2000:213), and yet another example of the strong influence of Western musical thought in Iran. As Fayaz observes, 'we need to understand how the ways in which we look at ourselves is influenced by how Westerners look at us' (Khazrai 2009:164). Whether the adoption of the term *kelāssik* is motivated by a genuine desire to facilitate dialogue across musical borders, or rather to draw on the symbolic capital associated with Euro-American art music, such debates indicate a broad awareness among musicians and scholars of how Iranian music is received, written about and labelled outside Iran. Beyond this, one is reminded of the extent to which discussion around a range of issues in Iranian music is underpinned by historically-rooted and continuing anxieties over Iran's neo-colonial past and its relationship with the contemporary 'West': specifically, how to operate and move forward in a postcolonial, globalizing world without simply imitating the metropolitan power centres; and how to maintain one's traditions without fossilizing them.

Another area of terminological contestation (primarily outside Iran) concerns 'Iranian' and 'Persian', both of which are used adjectivally to refer to Iran's art music outside Iran. This debate has spawned a vast commentary, both scholarly and lay. On one level, the distinction between the two is clear: Iran is the nation state and 'Iranian' indicates national affiliation. Iran has a long history of plurality, as home to a range of cultural/ethnic/linguistic and religious groups, of which the Persian-speakers (*fārs-zabān*) are the largest and most dominant (although it should be noted that there is considerable regional diversity even among Persian speakers; and members of other 'ethnic' groups also speak Persian as the *lingua franca*). For centuries, Europeans referred to Iran as 'Persia', following the Greek Pérsis (Πέρσις), a Hellenized form of Old Persian Parsa. Today, Fars is the southern province of which the main city, Shiraz, was an important trading centre for centuries and capital of Iran under the eighteenth-century Zand dynasty, and before that briefly under the Safavids. In 1935, Reza Shah Pahlavi requested that the international community recognize and adopt the local name for the country, 'Iran'. This was part of a broader process of fashioning a modern, forward-looking national identity, disconnected from the preceding Qajar regime, which was represented as backward and regressive; processes similar to those happening in neighbouring Turkey in the 1930s, as Atatürk attempted to purge Turkish culture of Ottoman associations.[14] What the Shah could not have foreseen was that a name used to promote the image of a modernizing nation state could acquire such different associations after 1979 and the establishment of Iran as an Islamic Republic. For the post-revolutionary regime, 'Iran' conveniently severed the country from 'Persia' and its monarchic heritage in the international imaginary. Thus, many Iranian expatriates, particularly in North America, prefer to call themselves 'Persian', a term which they consider re-connects them with their ancient, pre-Islamic (or at least pre-1979) past.[15] However, one of the (many) problems of conflating 'Persian' and 'Iranian' to denote national identity is that it denies a space to the many Iranians who do not identify themselves as being of Persian heritage (Kurds, Armenians, Jewish-Iranians, Arab- or Turkish-speaking Iranians and so on).

---

[13]   As further evidence, he invokes the use of 'classical' to refer to Indian art music (Khazrai 2009:164).

[14]   The change of name was also motivated by Reza Shah's desire to highlight Iran's Aryan heritage, partly in line with his pro-Nazi sympathies. Kashani-Sabet (1999) provides a detailed account of the shaping of Iran as a nation between 1804 and 1946, and also charts the debates and reasonings around the 'official' change of name internationally (216–26).

[15]   Indeed, the use of 'Persian' (rather than 'Iranian') has become a political statement by some supporters of the pre-1979 regime, somewhat ironic given that it was a Pahlavi monarch who promoted the name Iran abroad. For an amusing commentary on expatriate, particularly North American, insistence on 'Persian', see hip-hop music video 'Kind of Persian' http://www.youtube.com/watch?v=OxBfJffCoAs (accessed 27.7.12), music by Nima M., video by Ahmad Kiarostami, based on a song by Arash Tebbi.

Returning to music, the point is that there is no direct equivalent to the English 'Persian' as used, for example, to describe carpets, cats or indeed music. The term *Fārsi* refers specifically to the Persian language. In other words, the English 'Persian Classical Music' has no local counterpart, or rather the counterpart uses the adjectival *Irāni*, 'Iranian'. Whilst the music has strong Persian cultural associations (and is almost invariably set to Persian poetry), the current repertoire was in fact consolidated at the courts of the Turkic Qajar monarchs (r.1794–1925), and as discussed below, includes pieces which in their titles and melodies suggest diverse regional origins. As I hope to have indicated, 'Iranian/Persian' and 'classical' each have their own trajectories and (ideological) associations; for the purposes of this book, whilst recognizing the complexities and interests vested in any terminology, I use 'Iranian classical music' as perhaps the best English-language compromise in what is often a terminological minefield.

Concepts of Creativity in Iranian Music

Bedāheh-navāzi: Historical and Contemporary Perspectives

The Persian term for creativity, *khalāqiat* (also *khalq*, 'to create'; *khalāq*, 'creative'), is regularly invoked in relation to Iranian classical music, both in discussion with musicians and in the literature. Another term, *noāvari*, tends to indicate more experimental practices which are less bound to traditional structures. The idea of creative performance has a long history in the courtly traditions. Blum discusses this with reference to descriptions of performance practice in Near Eastern writings from the tenth century CE onwards, and in particular the expectation that musicians should be responsive to audiences and to the performance setting (1998:28–36). The constraints within which musicians worked, the extent to which performances were prepared in advance, and how much license was allowed or expected (ibid.:32), is not entirely clear; however, creative performance was evidently the norm and highly valued.[16] Whilst the figure of the composer (as distinct from performer: *navāzandeh*, 'instrumentalist'; *khānandeh*, 'singer') was not unknown before the twentieth century, by the early eighteenth century named composers had disappeared from the historical record (Wright 2009; in contrast to neighbouring Ottoman, and later Turkish, traditions).[17] However, from the mid-nineteenth century, increased contact with European music and concepts of creativity, and in particular the introduction of notation, led to changes in concepts about the creative roles of musicians and specifically the emergence of a new figure, the 'composer' (*āhangsāz*, lit: 'songmaker'), who used notation and whose status was enhanced by association with Western culture. Darvish Khan (1872–1926) and Ali Naqi Vaziri (1887–1979) were among several musicians who travelled and studied abroad, and who began to compose notated pieces, often in the form of genres such as *tasnif* (accompanied song) or *pishdarāmad* (instrumental prelude), some of which became appended to more traditional teaching materials. By the mid-twentieth century, the conceptual division between composition and improvisation was widely accepted, and with it the idea that Iranian classical music is predominantly improvised.

The gradual acceptance of improvisation as a concept has not been uncontested. Some older musicians resisted the trend towards a normative acceptance of these new categories, as During notes, 'When H. Gholi (d.1915) was asked why he did not "compose" fixed pieces like his pupils, he replied haughtily: "what I compose is what I play"' (1987b:34). One finds similar views among younger musicians, for example,

---

[16]   According to Blum, the term *badihe* was in use by the twelfth century, but seems to have referred primarily to the poetry set rather than to the music (1998:29).

[17]   Wright observes 'The last major Safavid song text collection, dating from c1700 ... records pieces by named composers, thus providing a striking contrast with the earliest modern equivalent, the *bohur al-alhan* of 1904, which contains no pre-composed pieces at all, but rather a selection of texts deemed suitable for singing such-and-such a modal configuration ... A similar trajectory towards anonymity and an increasing lack of composed pieces may be detected in the Eastern Arab world (but not in the Ottoman tradition). A possible explanation in terms of socio-economic factors (especially a decline or even absence of court patronage) might be deduced for, say, Baghdad, but would seem less persuasive for Iran, although given the conflicts and upheavals that marked the final years of the Safavid period and those following, some similar rupture may well have occurred' (2009:27).

'Whenever a master of *dotār* plays his instrument, he creates [*khalq*] a work [*āsāri*] and makes new music' (Talai in Shahrnazdar 2004a:35).[18] Nettl and Foltin suggest that as recently as the early 1970s, 'Those who had been in contact with Western musicians and with Western ways of thinking about music were familiar with the concept [of improvisation] and accepted it readily. Others, however, were somewhat baffled by it' (1972:12). Specifically, there was a perception among some that improvisation gave musicians licence to transgress traditional limits, evidently based on a certain understanding of the term at a time when 'improvisation as freedom' was the dominant discourse in Europe and North America, and which appeared to contradict the ethos of discipline and training so central to Iranian classical music. Invoking notions of purity, authenticity and even national identity (in the face of encroaching westernization), and underpinned by a strongly moralistic tone, musicians such as Borumand expressed strong views on the matter:

> Improvisation has (also) been a problem to Persian music, in the sense that (some) musicians have been thinking and saying that you can play whatever you feel like playing; and this is what they have done all along. As a result, we now have musicians who call themselves improvisers, and who do actually improvise. But when we really pay attention to their performances, we find them to be far removed from genuine traditional music … they should realize that, in order to develop the subject properly, the work of an improviser must have a basic structure, and every phrase should be appropriately related to the one that precedes it. (in During 1991b:204–5).[19]

As will be discussed in Chapter 3, it is interesting to note how the debate over improvisation and the extent of performers' freedom became an avenue for negotiating ideas about the place of a centuries-old tradition in a rapidly modernizing society. From this emerged a discourse of authenticity quite new to this music.[20]

Whilst *bedāheh-navāzi* (also *fel-bedāheh, bedāheh-sarāi, bedāheh-sāzi, bedāheh-khāni, bedāheh-pardāzi*) is the closest Persian equivalent to the English 'improvisation', the history of its use in relation to music is uncertain. *Bedāheh-sarāi* is said to have referred originally to the extempore recitation of poetry at the courts of the pre-Islamic Sassanian kings (r.224–637 CE; During 1991b:154). Precisely when the term came to be applied to music is uncertain (most likely in the 1960s), but it is today accepted and widely used by musicians, most of whom are familiar with a range of musics and aware of both the word and concept of 'improvisation' outside Iran. It is therefore interesting that the only non-Iranian scholar of Iranian classical music to mention the term is During (1984a:202), whilst adding the caveat that *bedāheh-navāzi*[21] differs from the general understanding of 'improvisation' in the West (implying a consensus on this). Others simply use the English (or French) 'improvisation' without mentioning local terminology. Nettl is the only author to question the applicability of the term in the Iranian context. Researching in the 1960s, he reported that most musicians tended to think not in terms of 'improvisation', but simply of 'performance', accepting the differences between renditions as a normal part of the music (Nettl with Foltin 1972:11–12). Nettl may well have been influenced by the ambivalence of his teacher, Nur Ali Borumand, towards improvisation. The latter's views are endorsed by Talai, who concurs that the term was not used in the past; comparing the musical performer to a reciter of poetry such as the epic *Shāhnāmeh*, he suggests that it would be better to refer to 'performance' (*ejrā*) or 'interpretation' (*ravāyat*), rather than *bedāheh-navāzi* (in Shahrnazdar 2004a:96). Other than the work of Nettl and Blum (the latter primarily historical), most of the literature published outside Iran takes the composition-

---

[18]   Later in this publication, Talai cites the improvisational work of Bach and Chopin to illustrate the permeable relationship between 'composition' and 'improvisation', and to understand 'improvisation' as a form of 'composition' (Shahrnazdar 2004a:97). This is the only example I have come across where a musician of Talai's generation (the first generation of graduate musicians in Iran) has sought to articulate the problematics of the composition/improvisation divide. The fact that he studied in France for many years may well explain Talai's broad awareness of the role of improvisation in Western art music.

[19]   This statement probably dates from the 1970s. Sha'bani (writing in 1973) expresses similar concerns, listing five 'problems' with improvisation, particularly when practised by less experienced musicians (32). See also Talai in Shahrnazdar (2004a:96).

[20]   Fayaz (1998) also examines the role of European musicologists in promoting notions of 'authenticity' during the 1960s. The role and extent of creative performance continues to be debated at a time when the *radif* has become central to quasi-ideological discourses of canonical control and authority. See also Ghader (1999).

[21]   During transliterates as *bedai navazi*.

improvisation binary as a given. All acknowledge the importance of creative performance, but few examine the associated discourses, how they emerged and developed, and their cultural and ideological significance. Zonis describes 'compositional procedures' when writing about improvisation (1973:98) but composition (in notation) is regarded as something else altogether and like many others she includes a separate section entitled 'Composed Persian Music', meaning notated pieces by named composers (ibid.:139–47). Sadeghi, on the other hand, shows some awareness of the problem: as well as a section on 'Composed Pieces' (1971:65–9), he discusses a separate category of 'Improvised-Composed Pieces' (ibid.:69–74), explaining: 'Some of the composed forms have gone through an improvised stage before they became a fixed written composition.'

As Zonis observes, in contrast to literature published outside Iran one finds no mention of improvisation in Persian-language writings before the 1970s. After this, as the concept gained acceptance, writers started to use the term but there is no discussion of improvisational techniques (by examining specific performances, for instance). Joneydi's 1982 introductory book *Zamineh-ye Shenākht-e Musiqi-ye Irāni* (*The Basis for Understanding Iranian Music*) is fairly typical in an almost deliberate avoidance of discussion of the music 'itself'. In a short chapter entitled '*Bedāheh-navāzi dar Musiqi-ye Irāni*' ('Improvisation in Iranian Music'), he writes surprisingly little about Iranian music, instead quoting at length from the French musicologist Lavignac on improvisation in European art music, and briefly discussing improvisation in Persian poetry (1982:185–93). The absence of detailed musical commentary may well reflect the fact that musicological scholarship was still relatively young in Iran at that time, but is also possibly symptomatic of a reluctance to delve into the quasi-sacred mysteries of creativity, as discussed in Chapter 1. Indeed, most books and articles published in Iran prior to the 2000s are either general introductory texts, commentaries accompanying different versions of the *radif*, or other didactic materials.[22]

The establishment of formal higher education in music in the late 1960s was significant in encouraging greater reflexivity in relation to creative performance and a wider acceptance of improvisation as a concept. Improvisation now has a tangible presence: referred to in programme and album liner notes, some teachers even discuss aspects of improvisation with pupils, something which rarely happened in the past. All of the musicians whom the author interviewed or corresponded with used the term *bedāheh-navāzi* (or just 'improvisation') readily. The discourses emphasize at one and the same time the absolute rigour of the training process and a rather idealized mystique of the creative performer. Moreover, some even talk about Iranian classical music as linked in some way to other 'improvised' traditions, many citing jazz and Indian classical music.[23] Of particular interest is the way in which the *idea* of improvisation has, over the last 30 years or so, encouraged musicians to think of their music in a broader global context; indeed, its current popularity can perhaps be explained both through what it appears to represent in terms of creative licence,[24] and in providing a point of connection with musics outside Iran. To some extent, the latter also offers a sense of validation, even empowerment, to younger, more experimental musicians. Regardless of how the concept of improvisation entered the tradition (or how accurately it describes the music), then, this idea has taken on a life of its own,

---

[22]   An important exception is the work of Mohammad Taghi Massoudieh (1927–1999) who studied in France and Germany in the 1950s and '60s before returning to Iran in the 1970s. After his initial interest in Iranian classical music, Massoudieh spent much of the post-1979 period writing about regional rural traditions, as well as teaching at the University of Tehran in the 1980s during the brief periods when the Music Department was open. He was a significant influence on an emerging generation of Iranian musicologists in the 1980s and 1990s.

[23]   For example, Talai describes his interest in 'musics which are close to the culture of Iranian music such as Indian music, Arabic music, Turkish music and even jazz' (in Shahrnazdar 2004a:133). Some classical musicians have even worked with non-Iranian 'improvising' musicians, for example *kamāncheh* virtuoso Kayhan Kalhor's longstanding collaboration with Shujaat Khan in the Ghazal Project which has to date resulted in four albums, see http://www.kayhankalhor.net/ (accessed 18.11.14). Hossein Alizadeh (and percussionist Madjid Khaladj) also worked with Indian musicians Swapan Chaudhuri (*tablā*) and Rajiv Taranath (*sarod*), presenting concerts in the United States and Europe in the autumn of 1997.

[24]   In some cases becoming a trope of social and individual (as well as musical) freedom, not unlike the situation of modal jazz from the mid-1960s as described by Monson (1998:162–3). An interesting parallel example from a gender perspective is discussed by Weidman for Karnatic music where one particular form of improvisation, *swara kalpana*, is equated with sexual freedom and excess, and therefore considered unsuitable for performance by respectable women. As such, Weidman was advised to restrict herself to playing the *raga alapana*, a purer and more chaste practice which her teacher likened to one's mother (2006:134–5).

adapted to meet the needs of a complex musico-cultural web, and acquiring heightened resonance in an increasingly globalized world. It should also be noted that with changing patterns of music education and the emergence of a body of university-educated musicians with a cosmopolitan and internationalist outlook, the line between 'performer' and 'composer' has once again become blurred as many performers also compose (using notation) away from the performance context. Of the many who could be cited, Hossein Alizadeh (b.1951) and Kayhan Kalhor (b.1963) have both composed orchestral pieces (including film scores), the latter including work with Yo Yo Ma's Silk Road Project.[25] Nevertheless, they are clearly regarded as '(improvising) performer' in the one context and 'composer' in the other.

Among contemporary musicians, then, improvisation has come to occupy a central position and exploring the ways in which they talk about improvisation can be revealing. For Shahram Nazeri (b.1951) improvisation is both a starting point and 'the ultimate destination of the musical journey [*ākhar-e khat-e musiqi*], something amazing or astonishing [*shegeft āvar*] and a kind of inspiration [*ayn ol elhām*] which is about the internal relationship of a person with him/herself [*bā hasti*]' (interview 23.4.10). According to Alizadeh:

> Improvisation, in the connection of human characteristics in it, comprises the basis [*asl*] of art. All the techniques of art are directed towards the artist reaching improvisation. When you fix [*sābet*] this improvisation, a work of art [*asr-e honar*] has been created. (in Shahrnazdar 2004b:33)

For Talai, 'improvisation gives our music spirit [*ruh*] and soul [*jān*] and transmits the state of the present into it' (in Shahrnazdar 2004a:97). Nazeri suggests that whilst the ability to improvise is partly inherited, it also requires a deep musical knowledge as well as other personal qualities, extending to the philosophical and the existential:

> Such a person should know literature, history and have an understanding of the world; they should know their country; and they should have a knowledge of themselves and of the nature of being [*khod-shenāsi va hasti-shenāsi too vojoodesh bāsheh*]. They should also be familiar with a broad spectrum of the arts, as well as issues of the world [*tayfhā-ye mokhtalef-e honari va masāel-e jahān*]. Someone who can look at everything from above, like an eagle who with one glance can see the mountains and the plains and the sea. (interview 23.4.10)

I will return to musicians' discourses on improvisation, and their various themes, below.

Interlude: Binary Thinking and the Imagination of Musical Difference

As can be seen from the above discussion, the emergence of binary thinking in relation to creative practice in Iranian music, in particular the conceptual division between the act of composition and improvisation and the figure of composer (using notation) and performer, was part of broader processes of social change taking place during the twentieth century. This is not to suggest that aspects of binary thought were not previously part of the tradition – dualistic constructions are found widely in Iran, seen for instance in the polarity between a largely undifferentiated 'West' (*qarb*) and a similarly essentialized 'East' (*sharq*) – but that increased contact with Euro-American music, its terminologies and concepts encouraged particular ways of thinking about musical difference. Two factors are relevant here. First, from the early twentieth century, and with increased momentum during the Pahlavi period, the social arena was dominated by a struggle between proponents of modernization and more traditional factions.[26] Second, the association of notated composition with the cerebral was significant in a society where the dualism of mind and body has a long history, further serving to elevate the status of the composer (*āhangsāz*) using notation.[27] One of the most disturbing indicators of this

---

25   See http://www.silkroadproject.org/MusicArtists/TheSilkRoadEnsemble/PerformersComposersTabbed/Kayhan Kalhor/tabid/251/Default.aspx (accessed 10.06.13).

26   For a useful summary of the main issues in relation to music, see Wright (2009:9–17).

27   Many Iranian composers were (and still are) trained in 'Western' techniques and styles of composition and have composed for Western instrumental forces, usually orchestral, some having studied in Europe or North America. Nettl

'discourse of difference' was the way in which Western (art) music came to be labelled as 'scientific' (*elmi*) and Iranian music its unscientific (*qayr-e elmi*) 'Other'. Alizadeh suggests two main reasons for the use of these terms in the context of national teaching institutions: first, the generally low level of public musical education when the terms were first used in the 1930s; and second, the fact that Western music was regarded as having a more developed theory, notation in particular being a clear index of the 'scientific' (in Shahrnazdar 2004b:75). A similar trope can be found in Mansuri and Shirvani's writing on Iranian composers in which they distinguish between composers of 'traditional music' (*musiqi-ye sonnati*; compositions rooted in Iranian tradition) and 'developed music' (*musiqi-ye tahavvol-yāfteh*), the latter mainly by younger composers trained abroad and composing in a Western style or for Western instruments (1977:157). The semantic oppositions between scientific/unscientific, developed/un(der)developed are evident. Whilst this particular discursive formation has been critiqued and is encountered less frequently today, one does still come across it. A normative understanding of 'scientific music' as Western, and specifically Western art music, represents a clear form of 'self-othering' in which Western music and culture become something to emulate.[28]

In the discussion that follows, I'm particularly interested in the myriad ways in which binary thinking entered the Iranian musical tradition during the Pahlavi period, largely influenced by broader social changes, and increasingly seen in the various discourses of difference underpinning musical thought: East/West, tradition/modernity, improvised/composed, unscientific/scientific, oral/notated and so on. In part, such discourses represented a desire by musicians to respond to Western and westernizing discourses. Indeed, some of this binary thinking can be traced directly to the habitual European musical and musicological discourses discussed in Chapter 1, and to which Iranians had been increasingly exposed since the first musicians arrived from Europe in the mid-nineteenth century, and later as Iranian musicians travelled abroad. But it also reflected the broader social milieu of the Pahlavi period in which tradition and modernity were often presented as incompatible, and modernity was positively valenced within the dominant discourses. Among the many binaries, that relating specifically to the creative process arguably served as the most important marker of difference between Western music (or Western-style compositions by Iranians) which was composed, notated, scientific and so on, and its traditional 'Other'. What is interesting is that Iranian musicians today continue to depend on some of these inherited discourses whilst deconstructing others, as discussed below.

Thematic Strands in the Discourses of Creativity

Risheh dar Gozashteh; Rooted in the Past …

> The improviser, let us hypothesize, always has something given to work from – certain things that are at the base of the performance, that he uses as the ground on which he builds. We may call it his model. In some cultures specific theoretical terms are used to designate the model …. (Nettl 1974c:11)

As many authors have noted, previous knowledge of a musical system is a prerequisite to creative license, 'Composition and improvisation demand … the assimilation and integration of the very principles of the music' (Nettl 1987:36), although the extent to which such models are explicitly theorized varies widely. Indeed, the most valued improvisers are often those who can exercise creativity within the closest confines. In the case of Iran, the idea of improvisation as something *grounded*, and specifically underpinned by knowledge of the *radif*, emerges strongly in discussion, and is a constant theme in the literature. In one of the earliest introductory books on Iranian music to be published outside Iran (in France), Caron and Safvate explain that

---

discusses the work of Ali Reza Mashayekhi and Dariush Dolatshahi (1987:125; see also Mansuri and Shirvani 1977:158–72) and Shelemay profiles Reza Vali's 1998 Flute Concerto (2001:251–6). A similar situation is found elsewhere in Asia, of course. For instance, Tenzer discusses the emergence of Indonesian *musik kontemporer* in the 1970s (2000:436–9).

[28]   The positioning of Iranian music as 'unscientific' is particularly surprising given how central the idea of the 'science of music' (*elm-e musiqi*) is in earlier theoretical writings going back several centuries before the advent of Western influence in Iran.

the music 'gives a large place to improvisation, but in the framework of strict rules' (1966:19).[29] Whilst such improvisation is 'partly innate ... [it] cannot be developed without many years of hard work' (ibid.:129), an idea echoed time and again, as for instance in the following from prominent santurist Faramarz Payvar:

> For someone to be creative [*khalāq*] requires taste and ability [*zoq va estedād*]. Without these, you can't be creative. Taste and ability are god-given [*khodādādi*] and you can't increase or decrease them, but you can develop them with education [*tahsilāt*]. (interview 8.11.90)

Creativity may be 'god-given', but it can only be nurtured and developed through the discipline of learning the *radif*: 'The improviser should know the traditional music and its interpretation and application by memory in order to be able to *improvise properly*' (Sadeghi 1971:21; my emphases). Describing how only musicians who have studied the *radif* for many years are able to improvise correctly, Berenjian used the word *pokhteh* ('cooked', 'ripe') to indicate this state of maturity and readiness. That there are correct (and thereby incorrect or less correct) ways of improvising confirms that 'free' improvisation has no place in this tradition: 'far-flung inventiveness may play a smaller part than does the importance of showing that one has a thorough control of the *radif*' (Nettl 1987:64).

A number of musicians have eloquently expressed the relationship between tradition, as embodied in the *radif*, and creativity, some drawing parallels with poetry:

> The form is the prerequisite of every creation. If you have an idea ... but you know nothing about the rules of poetry, you cannot compose a poem ... If you really wish to write poetry, you must know the forms called *qālebs* or molds. In the same way, the *radif* is truly a mine of forms and molds for music. (Safvate, in During 1991b:215)

> In reality, the *radifs* came about so that a musician could place their foot on a firm basis [*bastar*] from which to fly. Like an architect who wants to construct a building needs a firm foundation [*pāyeh*] on which to build ... it's a mould [*qāleb*] for learning and for moving in the right direction; like a light that guides you ... and it allows you to fly in this very secure and dependable light, so you can be free to express things. Someone who isn't standing on a firm foundation but on loose or shaky ground, they can't fly. They can't travel in a proper and exact way, or with precise vision. (Nazeri, 23.4.10)

One important thematic strand in the discourses around creativity in Iranian classical music, then, is the importance of training and knowledge, as represented by the repertoire of the *radif*. This idea will be explored further in Chapter 3.[30]

Nākhodāgāh; Unconscious ...

Another recurrent trope is that of improvisation as something 'intuitive', 'innate' or 'natural':

> Iranian musicians do not isolate this branch of theory, and they do not teach it formally. In fact, in the literature improvisation is hardly mentioned ... most of the theory of practice comes to an Iranian intuitively ... the student simply absorbs the compositional procedures without being aware of them as such. For this reason, a musician is often unable to explain precisely what he is doing during his improvisation. Likewise, Persian music theorists, considering this aspect of music to be an intuitive procedure, do not discuss it in their writings.

---

[29]   Dariouche Safvate (b.1927) is a respected musician, and founder and first director of the Centre for the Preservation and Propagation of Iranian Music. He studied in France in the 1960s, which is when he co-authored this book with Nelly Caron.

[30]   Whilst creative performance and the structures upon which it is based are so interdependent that one can only be understood in relation to the other, detailed discussion of the *radif* has been deferred until Chapter 3, since it necessitates a chapter in its own right.

Therefore … the foreign musicologist has little indigenous methodology or terminology on which to base a study of improvisation. (Zonis 1973:98–9, 125)

Similarly, Sadeghi suggests that some skills can be learnt whilst others are 'intuitive', but (paradoxically perhaps) gained only by a great deal of practice (1971:120). And in response to a question about the use of certain compositional techniques, Payvar used the terms *hesi* ('intuitive') and *tabi'i* ('naturally'):

This is really something intuitive. The musician has experienced and felt [*hes*] it and it comes naturally. It is not worked out [consciously] [*hesāb nemikoneh*]. It is intuitive, but based on what a musician has already heard. He doesn't think about it – 'now I'll go up one pitch, now I'll come down again' [in the case of sequence] – it just happens like that. (8.11.90)

Indeed, *santur* master Parviz Meshkatian claimed that 'When you are performing, if you think about what comes next, the music will go wrong [*kharāb misheh*]' (20.7.92). A related idea is that musicians who are infused with the *radif* cannot but help improvise within its structures:

When you have played the *radif* for many years, and the *gusheh*s are 'in your ears', you can't play anything else; whatever you play will be near the *radif* … As a result of [*dar asar-e*] playing different *radif*s, there are certain movements which in are the musician's hands [*dar panjeh-ash*]. (Berenjian 10.11.89)

Such comments point to the importance of motor memory, which develops over many years and is able to 'take over', allowing for performance with a minimum of prior planning, sometimes in a transcendental state.

Perhaps the most commonly encountered Persian term in this context is *nākhodāgāh*, which denotes a lack of awareness of self and is usually translated into English as 'unconscious'. Regularly invoked by musicians, this term is often used to explain what many believe to be a quasi-mystical process: 'improvisation has a close relationship with the unconscious, a relationship from outside oneself, like an inspiration [*elhām*]. But it doesn't come about for everyone' (Nazeri, 23.4.10). There is also the notion of losing oneself, relinquishing conscious control during performance, as in the following passage where Alizadeh describes his 'Concert-e Nava',[31] as 'completely improvised' in the sense of involving no prior planning unlike some of his other works:

In improvisation if you have feeling [*hes*] and concentration [*tamarkoz*] the choice of direction [*masir*] is not very much up to you; it's the feeling that takes you forward. Now, if these feelings are blended [*tarkib*] with those of other musicians, the result is something magical. (in Shahrnazdar 2004b:126)

The quotations in this and the following chapter indicate that whilst Iranian musicians can be highly articulate when discussing performance, they tend to focus on large-scale structuring, perhaps due to the relative dearth of technical terminology with which to discuss finer musical details, particularly as they take shape during performance. To quote again from Zonis, 'a musician is often unable to explain precisely what he is doing during his improvisation … [there is] little indigenous methodology or terminology on which to base a study of improvisation' (1973:98–9). Despite a greater awareness of improvisation since the time when Zonis was writing, there is still 'little indigenous methodology or terminology' with which to discuss creative practice. Thus, unlike aspects of the music such as the ordering of *gusheh*s (pieces) in a *dastgāh* or the hierarchy of pitches in a mode, for which a relatively rich body of terminology exists, aspects such as compositional techniques (sequencing, varied and extended repetition, and so on) are acknowledged by musicians when pointed out but seldom discussed voluntarily. The scholarly assumption has therefore tended to be that these operate below the level of awareness, in what During terms the 'deep memory'.[32] However, there is evidence

---

[31]   Recording of a landmark concert given in 1976: *Dastgah-e Nava*, Mahoor Institute of Culture and Art, Tehran, CD015 (published October 1993), Hossein Alizadeh (*tār*), Majid Khaladj (*tombak*).

[32]   In contrast to the 'immediate memory' (During 1987b:41). These terms seem particularly suitable substitutes for words such as 'conscious', 'preconscious' and 'subconscious', which can be problematic when taken outside the context of

of an increasing awareness of such aspects of the music and some teachers have even started to discuss them with pupils (see Chapter 3).

Dar Lahzeh; In the Moment ...

The question of prior planning is an interesting one. Whilst it is acknowledged that a certain amount of advance preparation is necessary, particularly in points of overall structural organization in the case of group renditions, for instance, there remains an ideal that performances should be unprepared and 'spontaneous'. Whilst there is of course general consensus that the *radif* needs to be played and memorized, the music does not generally demand long hours of practice in order to develop physical technique. Rather, it is the 'soul' (*hāl*) of the music which is important; indeed, During reports that some older musicians consider that 'too much work harms musicality' (1984a:35), perhaps because extensive practice focuses attention on the physical rather than the spiritual. However, During also cites the example of court musician Aqa Hossein Qoli (c.1851–1915), the most renowned *tār* player of his time, who reputedly practised the *radif* for many hours each every. Certainly, nowadays the idea of intensive practice is more common, possibly due to the greater value attached to virtuosity. In his study of *dastgāh Chāhārgāh*, Nettl found many regularities which led him to conclude that 'preparation and planning play a substantial role' (1987:64; see also Nettl and Riddle's 1973 analysis of performance by Lebanese musician Ali Jihad Racy). Clearly, even an 'unprepared' performance will include musicians' idiosyncrasies and habitual patterns of playing developed over many years. Zonis attributes preparation to the time limits imposed by changing performance contexts and in particular the shift from the traditional, informal *majles* setting, where performances were apparently 'truly extemporaneous' (1973:102) and sometimes lasted several hours, to public concerts and recording studios; in the latter, where 'a recording remains as an example [*namāyandeh*] of the work of that musician' (Payvar, 8.11.90), the pressure to prepare is even greater. During even suggests that 'Rather than assume the risks involved in creative inspiration, it is standard [for the performer] to prepare his solos, implicitly presenting his arrangements or compositions as spontaneous creations' (1987c:140). Meshkatian corroborated some of these points, but said that his improvisations are created at the time of performance, regardless of context:

> The improviser does not practise improvisation [beforehand]. If I have a concert, I prepare by playing studies [*études*] to warm up and relax. The music must be the expression of that moment [*hamoon lahzeh*]. (20.7.92)

However, he did concede that group performances require some prior agreement, for instance on the order of *gusheh*s and inclusion of pre-composed pieces.[33] Thus, there are larger-scale decisions which may be made in advance, and finer details which are expected to be 'expressions of the moment'. Nazeri describes the process as follows:

> When you're alone, you create something through improvisation [*be soorat-e bedāheh*]; I mean, the inspiration happens in a moment and this melody [*āhang*] comes into being [*be vojood āmadeh*]. But when you work with a group, you bring your ideas either in notation or orally [*be soorat-e gooshi*] and you rehearse in the group. Any melody that is beautiful and that will remain has definitely come into being through inspiration, but because a group is playing it, it needs to be co-ordinated [*hamāhang*] and arranged. It starts with improvisation but in order to work together and move together, you have to agree on some points. (23.4.10)

---

psychology (and when dissociated from concepts of repression). See Walker (1962:127–48) for an interesting discussion of the role of the 'musical unconscious' in the creative processes of Western composers.

[33]   It should be noted that even in group performances, traditional improvisational practice remains essentially solo: instrumentalists take turns at playing on their own (or shadowing the voice) rather than simultaneously (other than in pre-composed, measured, and usually whole ensemble pieces such as *tasnif*s or *pishdarāmad*s).

Sometimes, if the conditions are right, a group performance can be more spontaneous:

> It depends on the relationships between the group members. If they have worked together before, are friends, are familiar with each other's state of mind [*roohiyeh*], it has happened that a beautiful piece [*qeteh-ye zibāi*] has been created at that moment [*hamoon lahzeh*]. (ibid.)

The impact of changing performance contexts on the concepts and practice of creativity will be discussed below.

Degrees of Improvisation

Having established that all creative performance in Iranian classical music takes place in relation to the *radif*, here I consider how musicians and others have discussed this relationship. Notwithstanding that musicians differ in the extent to which they vary the material of the *radif* in performance, most seek a balance between some level of creative freedom, but without digressing so far as to be criticized for not knowing the repertoire. Nettl has discussed the link between status and licence, suggesting that an established master musician may depart significantly from the *radif*, whilst a similar performance by a less advanced player might indicate a lack of knowledge or disregard for the tradition (1987:157). In any case, the more experienced a musician, the more comfortable they are likely to be in exploring and extending the material.

Based partly on the writings of Caron and Safvate (1966:128), During identifies several 'levels of interpretation' (*niveaux d'interprétation*), which depart progressively from the learnt repertoire until the musician becomes 'liberated from the formality of the *radif*' (1984a:202). He refers to this as '*la grande improvisation*' (most likely derived from Caron and Safvate 1966:129 but not acknowledged) as opposed to '*la petite improvisation*' in which the *radif* is simply modified. In a later publication, During suggests four types of improvisation based on similar criteria (1987c:137–8). Neither During nor Caron and Safvate say whether such levels are discussed by musicians and none mention Persian terms for '*grande*' and '*petite*' improvisation.[34] Caron and Safvate consider the most advanced level of improvisation to be *morakkab-khāni* (or *morakkab-navāzi*, the movement from one *dastgāh* to another using shared *gusheh*s as bridges; 1966:128), a practice not commonly heard today. During also includes *morakkab-khāni* as part of his third level of improvisation (1984a:202; again possibly derived from Caron and Safvate), as well as the performance of measured pieces such as *chāhārmezrāb* and *reng*. However, where one level ends and the next begins is unclear, suggesting that it might be more useful to think of these as a continuum. Also unclear is how these levels relate to During's categories of 'strategic' and 'creative' improvisation (1987a:23), in the first of which musicians choose between alternative possibilities without creating any 'new' musical material, which happens in the second type.

Rather than levels of improvisation, musicians' discourses tend to focus on whether a performer is *radif-navāz* ('*radif* player') or *bedāheh-navāz* ('improviser'); in practice this is (once again) a continuum rather than a binary. The following is fairly typical:

> Some musicians are *radif-navāz*, some are *bedāheh-navāz*, some are both. These are all relative. Some musicians are not creative enough [to improvise]. (Meshkatian 20.7.92)

This apparently simple statement belies an intense debate which has taken on quasi-ideological dimensions over the last 40 years or so, as will be discussed in Chapter 3. The distinction between musicians who purportedly perform the *radif* without variation and those who use it as a basis for creative performance has become a well-established part of the discourse. But there are other things to consider. Creativity in Iranian classical music depends on the interaction between a musician's knowledge of the *radif*, individual idiosyncrasies, past experiences and instrument morphology on the one hand,[35] and on the other a certain

---

[34]   I have not come across equivalent terms in Persian.

[35]   Taken together these comprise a kind of 'schema', described by Dyson as, 'an abstract framework ... that both structures and is structured by experience' (2006:9). See Chapter 4.

degree of spontaneity. The former always provides a backdrop for the latter. However, one cannot judge the degree of spontaneity by simply comparing a performance with the *radif*. Beyond the challenge of identifying a specific model on which any one performance is based, certain elements may be prepared beforehand (or drawn from a musician's store of cognitive or motor patterns): these elements are not spontaneous but neither are they taken (directly) from the *radif*. In other words, whilst a performance which remains close to the *radif* can be recognized as such (by those who know the repertoire), beyond this, judging the degree of creativity is tricky because an improvisation can only be assessed in relation to the specific model on which it is based. The difficulties involved in identifying such a model will be considered in Chapter 3.

Changing Concepts and Practice of Creativity

As noted, Iran has experienced profound socio-cultural changes since the late nineteenth century, many of which have had far-reaching consequences for music, whether in relation to changing performance contexts and audiences; the institutionalization of music education; the introduction of notation; the arrival of sound recording and broadcasting, leading to the rise of the mass media and commodification of music; the increasing importance of instrumental music; and so on. The final section of this chapter will consider each of these specifically in relation to their impact on the concepts and practice of musical creativity.[36]

Musical Notation, Sound Recording, Performance Contexts and Audiences

The gradual introduction of notation, sound recording and broadcasting in the early decades of the twentieth century had a significant bearing on the dynamics of the tradition and on musicians' perceptions of creativity. Given how deeply embedded the concept of individual variation is, there has been much speculation on the impact of 'fixing' the music in recording or on paper, in making possible an authoritative and relatively stable version of the taught repertoire (the 'work'?) and definitive renditions of it. Certainly, as will be discussed in Chapter 3, the *radif* has grown in significance since the mid-twentieth century, with an unprecedented late twentieth/early twenty-first-century proliferation in published versions. At the same time, the idea of the one definitive *radif* (that of Mirza Abdollah) is also well established. It has been suggested that sound recording (and later broadcasting) may have encouraged standardization through opportunities afforded to repeatedly hear the same version of a piece, unlike earlier generations where musicians' musical experiences would have comprised a kaleidoscope of continually varying interpretations. However, it could equally be argued that access to a wider range of performance practice has enabled musicians to hear a *larger* number of variants. Certainly increased access to many different kinds of music (Iranian and other) has led to a widening of experiences, with likely impact on creative practice.

   In the early years of its introduction, the use of notation as a learning tool was strongly contested by some teachers who felt that it contravened basic tenets of the music. Today, however, notation is widely accepted – both staff notation and specialized notations developed for certain instruments, particularly percussion – and most musicians are musically literate. Since it has been used in fairly specialized contexts (and not usually in performance), notation has arguably had less of an impact than sound recording. However, it is worth noting the symbolic value and prestige accorded to notation; for the nationalist modernizers of the first half of the twentieth century in particular, and those who wished to elevate the status of Iranian music, it was a source of pride that the *radif* could be notated, just like Western music (Nettl 1987:119, 136).[37] The use of notation in the teaching context is discussed further in Chapter 3.

---

   [36]   For discussion of the social history of music in Iran since the early twentieth century see the work of Nettl (for example 1978 and 1985). Chehabi (1999) discusses the mobilization of music, particularly nationalistic anthems (*sorud*) which were introduced into the school system in the 1930s and used to promote the polices of Reza Shah; Klitz and Cherlin (1971) examine musical change in the early 1970s, particularly within music education; and Beeman (1976) considers various aspects of musical change, including the impact of an expanding mass media on the musical culture in the 1970s.

   [37]   As discussed earlier, for many in the 1920s and '30s notation was an indicator of a modern, 'developed' and 'scientific' musical culture. In particular, notation was the ultimate means of preserving the music, a view which largely

As described earlier, Iranian classical music developed as a courtly tradition over many centuries, but was also heard in informal gatherings (*majles*) of musicians and music-lovers in homes and gardens. Until the early twentieth century, the audience for this music was relatively restricted and comprised musically-educated (or at least informed) members of the aristocratic elite. Such settings were in part necessitated by religious proscriptions on public music-making, but were also fortuitously well suited to the music, allowing performers to respond directly to an intimate audience of initiates, and affording considerable freedom, not least in the length of performances. During (1987a:18) suggests that improvisation flourishes best in informal situations and many musicians that I talked to recalled with nostalgia these traditional settings as being highly conducive to improvisation:

> The best place to play is the *majles*. There is more improvisation. Everyone is relaxed and seated comfortably. (Payvar 8.11.90)

> The smaller the venue, and the fewer the numbers of listeners, the music has more of an effect. That's why private concerts have more presence and spirit [*hāl o havāyi*]. The larger the concert, the harder it is to make a connection with the audience. (Nazeri 23.4.10)

Nazeri also discussed the impact of large performance groups on improvisational practice:

> The smaller the group, the more the opportunity for improvisation. If you only have two performers, it can all be improvised. But if you have a few people and include some rhythmic [metered] pieces or a *tasnif*, you need to work on it; although naturally each time you perform, it will be different. (ibid.)

With the notable exception of court musicians, the most respected performers prior to the early twentieth century were amateurs;[38] indeed, it appears that the musical freedom of the amateur was closely associated with the *majles* and contrasted sharply with the rather low status, at that time, of professional musicians playing for events such as weddings, and who were usually answerable to the event patron (see Nettl 1978:152–3, 1987:119–20, 143–4). As classical music became more professionalized in the mid-twentieth century, it was largely within state organizations that musicians found employment (Zonis 1973:198); the new patronage of the state effectively replaced the court patronage of the Qajar period.[39] Yet whilst state employment afforded some degree of respectability, many still preferred to retain their amateur status, working in other professions and playing music in their leisure time.

With the establishment of public concerts in the early twentieth century, classical music emerged from seclusion and informality, and musicians were required to adjust to the length of a concert with a pre-arranged programme, and to play to larger, more distant and less knowledgeable audiences.[40] Sound recording and

---

disregarded the central role of oral knowledge in interpreting notation. There are interesting parallels (but also important divergences) with South India, where 'The desire to "fix" compositions in notation at the turn of the twentieth century was ... part of the project of showing that Karnatic music obeyed a system of conventions and rules, that there was a structure beneath, or within, the music ... notation was thought to represent an authoritative version of a composition, a version that could stand apart from various future renderings' (Weidman 2006:241–2). Weidman devotes a chapter to the various debates around notation, both Western and local, in Karnatic music from the mid-1880s (192–244).

[38] This is similar to the case of Afghanistan (see Baily 1988:101–2, 118–20) and also North India, where Neuman (quoting from Gaisberg 1942:57) reports that some of the earliest musicians recorded by the Gramophone Company insisted that 'the word "amateur" should be printed on the record label' (1990:216), particularly female musicians who wished to distance themselves from the traditional association of women performers and prostitution. As in Iran, the situation in North India has changed somewhat since the early twentieth century.

[39] Although until 1979, some royal support was still provided.

[40] Khaleqi (1983b:83) gives 1906 as the date of the first public concert in Iran, at a time when prohibitions on public gatherings were lifted following the Constitutional Revolution (see also Zonis 1973:144, Nettl 1978:151–2); however, such events did not become a regular feature of musical life until the 1930s. Lucas (2014) describes the early transition from court to civic arena, and in particular the role of the Okhovat Society (Anjoman-e Okhovat, established in 1899 by Qajar court official Zahir al-Dowleh, originally as a secret 'society of brotherhood' with strong Sufi connections) in organizing

broadcasting presented similar constraints; musicians recording in a studio faced the unprecedented prospect of performing without an audience. The Gramophone Company was recording in Iran from the early twentieth century,[41] followed later by other companies, and some musicians also travelled abroad to record (see Chapter 3). Those accustomed to playing for several hours were now required to perform a *dastgāh* to fit one or two sides of a 78rpm disc – just a few minutes of music. The absence of a responsive audience and the time limits must surely have affected these early recording musicians. During notes, 'Without the traditional responses of the public, the artist can no longer evaluate the impact of his performance and the feed-back mechanism is blocked' (1987a:21). Moreover, a sound recording remains for posterity, potentially available to millions of listeners. As noted, it seems that the shift from informal to formal contexts may have worked against the improvisation ethos, making it more likely for performances to be prepared beforehand, both to meet time requirements and in order to present more polished performances.[42] Similar issues applied to broadcasting. Radio Tehran was established in 1939 and musicians were again required to perform within tight time limits: music programmes were initially 15 minutes, later lengthened to 30. Even after the arrival of television, radio retained its prime position as the most popular medium for music listening (the two later merged to form the national radio and television organization, Radio Television-e Melli-e Iran).[43]

Recording times have obviously lengthened considerably since the days of wax cylinders and the 78rpm disc, and studio performance has become commonplace for musicians, but still many prefer informal gatherings. On one such occasion attended by the author, the solo *nei* player (Mohammad Mousavi) commented that each listener was contributing to the music by their very presence. Nazeri described the connection between musicians and audience as a wave (*mowj*):

> It's a wave and this wave is passed back and forth [*rad-o-badal misheh*]. Sometimes you see that the wave gets cut off [*qat shod*] or that it is a negative wave [*mowj-e manfi*]. Or that you just can't connect [*aslan nemitooni ertebāt barqarār koni*]. These all have a bad effect. It needs to be a good situation [*sharāyet*] from all these points of view. (23.4.10)

---

the earliest public music events. Mansuri and Shirvani (1977:134ff) give details of a number of public concerts in Tehran from the late 1920s to the early 1940s, as well as concerts in Tehran's main hall, the Rudaki Hall (re-named Tālār-e Vahdat [Unity Hall] after 1979) between 1965 and 1975 (ibid.:174–9).

[41]   According to Gronow, over 14,000 recordings were made by the Gramophone Company in Asia and North Africa between 1900 and 1910, of which 221 were from Iran (1981:255). Some of these recordings have been re-released by the Mahoor Institute of Culture and Art in Tehran as part of a series called 'Persian Music Heritage', see www.mahoor. com/cdcategory/Persian-Music-Heritage-24.aspx (accessed 31.7.14). See also Mohammadi (2011) for discussion of early recordings made in Iran by the German Lindström Company.

[42]   See also Simms and Koushkani (2012b:21). Similar observations are made by El-Shawan regarding the impact of changing performance contexts on the improvised Egyptian genres *taqsim* and *layali* (1987:154–5). See Weidman (2006:245–85) for a detailed discussion of the impact of sound recording in South India. She describes how recording artists in the early twentieth century would be assisted by 'hired music "tutors", often musicians themselves' who would help them tailor performances to the short time span available (262–3), 'the idea being to carefully plan one's spontaneity' (322). According to Weidman, the reduced time led to 'improvised passages … [that] seem more like a pouring out of ideas than a gradual drawing out of ideas' as musicians had to 'keep a tight rein on a process that would normally have required considerable repetition and listening to oneself in the very act' (263). The implications of developments in recording technology and studio recording for jazz musicians are also discussed by Berliner (1994:473–84).

[43]   In the first decade after the 1979 Revolution, when musicians faced severe restrictions on public performance, particularly during the Iran-Iraq war (1980–1988), concerts in private residences were common, sometimes accommodating several hundred people. It should be noted that assessing the level of musical activity on the basis of public concerts alone is particularly problematic in Iran. Not only does much music-making still take place in private, but media such as broadcasting and sound recording are extremely popular, particularly the audio cassette, which arrived in Iran in the 1960s and despite the later availability of CDs remains the most common sound recording medium. Simms discusses the emergence of a 'cassette culture' in Iran and the significant impact of this medium on musical style and aesthetics (Simms and Koushkani 2012b:18–22). For discussion of the rise of the mass media in Iran, see Sepanta (1987). Also useful are Klitz and Cherlin (1971), Beeman (1976) and Nettl (1978:154–6).

Wright notes that sound recording:

> … presents us with a paradox: it allows us to recreate in the intimacy of a domestic environment a reflex of what has become an institutionalized separation of music from the milieu in which it had previously been lodged, a separation that results in the inevitable dilution of the relaxed yet charged atmosphere of shared connoisseurship within which *musiqi-ye sonnati* would occupy, together with poetry, intellectual conversation and conviviality, a recognized zone of cultural refinement among the educated urban elite. (2009:39)[44]

A number of commentators have described the impact of changing audience identity – from the kinds of connoisseurs described by Wright to a less elite audience – on expectations in relation to creative performance. Modir, for example, suggests that the musical knowledge of an audience may directly affect the degree to which a performer adheres to the *radif*. Based on interviews with a single musician, Mahmoud Zolfonoun, he suggests that if the audience comprises connoisseurs with knowledge of the *radif* (as in the traditional *majles* setting), musicians are less likely to adhere strictly to the model but use the opportunity to demonstrate their creative skills. On the other hand, he suggests that performing to an audience unfamiliar with the repertoire, a musician might remain close to the *radif* and outline the basic structure (Modir 1986b:67). Conversely, however, musicians performing to such an audience may feel less compelled to adhere to the tradition, particularly in the case of less experienced performers. Either way, there is a subtle communication between musician and audience, the latter nowadays potentially ranging from one with little or no knowledge of the *radif* (for instance, a performance outside Iran comprised largely of non-Iranians) to a highly informed local audience (of Iranian musicians). Modir thus posits the identity of the audience, correlated with their expectations and responses as an important variable in the performance process. This is certainly true for some musicians. For instance, Simms reports that master vocalist Shajarian 'feels that the quality and knowledge of the audience is absolutely crucial to him performing well' (Simms and Koushkani 2012b:32). In contrast, both Payvar and Meshkatian claimed that whilst the mood and response of the audience affected their performances, audience identity and knowledge did not; indeed, both considered that this might compromise the integrity of their work.[45] Whilst most Iranian listeners are familiar with the sound and ethos of the classical music, detailed knowledge of the repertoire remains a relatively specialized domain. Few non-musicians can identify specific sections of the *radif* let alone judge the degree of adherence to it. This raises a number of largely unexplored questions concerning listener experience; almost all of the scholarship on Iranian classical music has been written from the perspective of *production* and issues of reception have been largely neglected. However, During usefully suggests that one might distinguish between an 'expressive' model in the minds of lay audiences, and a 'formal' model of trained musicians or informed listeners (1987a:22).

Greater or Lesser Freedom?

Whilst scholarly sources and musicians are in broad agreement that factors such as those described above have impacted on Iranian classical music over the past century or so, there is less agreement on how this has been manifested in practice. Thus, the topic on which I found most divergence was whether the trend over the last century had been towards greater or lesser performance in freedom. Many of the opinions expressed, often quite strongly, were speculative, but interesting nevertheless for what they reveal of musicians' broader views of the tradition and the role of the *radif*. On the one hand I found a strong 'discourse of decline' according to which, since many performers no longer had a thorough knowledge of traditional models, performances lacked structure and direction. Such assertions seemed largely predicated on invoking a 'golden age' sometime in the late nineteenth and early twentieth centuries when musicians knew the models well and how to improvise on them. Writing in 1971, for instance, Sadeghi claims:

---

[44] Wright also discusses the broader impact of increased availability of sound recording, both in the dissemination of music beyond Tehran, and in the canonization of certain performers and recordings (2009:5).

[45] For useful work in this area outside the realm of Iranian music, see Berliner, who provides an account of the effect of audience identity and reception on jazz musicians, particularly in relation to audience knowledge of the style or idiom being played (1994:455–73).

> In this century Persian musicians [improvise] ... more freely than before. Therefore, their connection with the traditional music is breaking apart, and their knowledge of the *radif* is diminishing. Each generation develops its own repertory which suits its own specific idea of improvisation. (1971:148)

Payvar also considered musicians to be 'freer' relative to their predecessors, not necessarily through want of knowledge, but simply due to fewer restrictions; however, he dated the start of this trend much earlier, to the first half of the twentieth century:

> Yes, I think that there is more improvisation today than in the past. They were stricter at that time ... until the time of Darvish Khan and Vaziri, when musicians found a little more freedom. (8.11.90)

If this is indeed the case, it is possible that the freedom to which Payvar refers came about through familiarity with improvisational practices outside Iran. Others have suggested that the shift from traditional to modern lifestyles has reduced the number of years of study, the extent of immersion in the tradition, and changed the intimate relationship between master and pupil, all of which have decreased respect for the traditional repertoire. Certainly, this seems to have prompted the concerns of Borumand (quoted earlier), for whom knowledge of the *radif* was paramount (Nettl 1987:145). According to Nettl, Borumand claimed that the *radif* was traditionally performed with little variation. Concurring with Payvar's comments, he suggested that it was musicians of the first half of the twentieth century who began the process of diversification, which he saw himself as resisting:

> The relationship of the *radif* to performance did not interest him greatly. He asserted that in earlier times, musicians performed the *radif* itself in public, deviating very little; and that the notion of improvisation was a more recent development. But on the other hand, he agreed that each person performed the *radif* in his own way, and that its structure and character depended on the mood of the occasion. (Nettl 1987:143)

Whilst detailed comparison of historical recordings and more recent performances remains to be undertaken, the available recordings (many of them published quite recently by the Mahoor Institute of Culture and Art) suggest that performances by the old masters tend to be closer to the *radif* than those of later musicians.[46] However, very little is known about the recording situations. For one thing, since recording times were limited, musicians may have simply decided to outline a particular *dastgāh* as found in the *radif*. And since many of these recordings were made outside Iran, musicians would have been performing in unfamiliar environments and may even have been asked to present the basic repertoire without elaboration. Either way, we simply do not know whether these recordings represent what would have been typically performed in an early twentieth-century *majles*.

   In contrast to the views above, there is also evidence of a trend towards *less* freedom in performance:

> Since the older musicians tend to deviate more from a norm, or to exhibit more variety in performance style and thematic content, one might wish to assume that there is now less variety in the range of performances ... than was the case in the past. (Nettl with Foltin 1972:36)

Certainly, performances by musicians such as Ahmad Ebadi (1907–1994), Jalil Shahnaz (b.1921), Hassan Kassai (1928–2012), Asghar Bahari (1905–1995) and Faramarz Payvar (1932–2009) analysed for this study (mainly recorded in the 1950s and '60s) were generally less predictable and more varied than those of younger musicians, particularly students of Borumand. Writing in 1987, Nettl suggested that even in the preceding 20 years there had been a decrease in improvisational freedom (1987:158). Both in the literature and in conversation with musicians, one encounters the view that the ability to improvise is being lost, something which may be a manifestation of the 'respect for standardization in modernized society' (Nettl 1987:15); moreover, access to sound recordings arguably enables, even encourages, a culture of imitation. Writing

---

46   Personal communication, Amir Eslami and Hooshyar Khayam (26.11.10).

in 1986 (but citing the earlier work of Caron and Safvate [1966:193], thus pointing to a trend which began in the 1960s and possibly earlier), Modir attributed diminishing improvisational skills to the use of notation:

> Since the method of Western notation for teaching the *radif* has developed, the free unrestricted sense of improvisation characteristic of early masters' performance styles has been regressing. (1986b:65)

Talking in 2010, Nazeri expressed strong views, citing among the great improvisers of the past Aqa Hossein Qoli (c.1851–1915), Soma Hozur (1852–1917), Darvish Khan, Ali Naqi Vaziri, Morteza Khan Mahjubi (1900–1965), Habib-e Somai (1901–1946), and in the subsequent generation the musicians listed above. Nazeri claimed that since the 1970s, whilst there have been some very good performers, improvisational skills had suffered due both to the passing of older masters from whom younger musicians could no longer learn, and broader issues relating to the institutionalization of music education. He suggested that many students today are encouraged to copy their teachers, 'the same style [*sabk*], the same tone [*lahn*], the same form', and therefore aren't able to find their own voice. He proceeded to invoke again (as in the earlier quotation) the metaphor of flight: 'like a bird whose wings are cut from birth; well, it can't fly!' (23.4.10). Performances have therefore become very similar and include a great deal of '*shabi khāni*' or '*shabi navāzi*' ('similar singing', 'similar playing') and even '*photocopy kāri*' ('photocopy work').[47] Mentioning the few contemporary musicians who can improvise well, Nazeri cited *nei* player Mohammad Mousavi in particular.

Discussing a recent series of concerts on consecutive nights by a highly respected performer, in which the first half was billed as '*bedāheh-navāzi dar dastgāh-e Māhur*', one musician that I spoke to, who had attended all three performances, noted that they were almost identical. Rather than interpret this as a lack of musical skill, however, he took it as an indication that the material had been worked on, rather in the manner of a composition:

> It is improvisation, but improvisation that has been worked on beforehand; it has a structure. He wants to play something new. It isn't *radif* but he has worked on the basis of *radif* and he plays that all three nights. The person who attends the concert once accepts that [as improvisation]; but when I go to all three, I see that he has played the same thing.

These seemingly contradictory views regarding the level of creative freedom compared with 'the past' generally share a central claim that knowledge of the *radif* is declining (and, according to the views reported, has been for decades). As a result, musicians either rely on their own creative fantasies; or, conversely, remain close to the *radif*, since they do not know it well enough to depart from it. In fact, whilst it is not easy to ascertain how the repertoire and its realization have changed since the late nineteenth century, comparison of earlier and more recent performances suggest a range of practice with both of these trends in evidence. Finally, beyond the specific claims and counterclaims, the level of anxiety that the topic generates among musicians is itself interesting. This will be discussed further in Chapter 3.

The Rise of Instrumental Music

A final area relevant to this discussion is the changing relationship between voice and instrument. As in much of the Middle East, vocal music has traditionally enjoyed a higher status than instrumental music in Iran, partly due to the pre-eminence of poetry which has not experienced the kind of antipathy from Islamic orthodoxy that music has. The presence of poetry may have lent the classical music respectability, particularly since the lyrics are most often from highly regarded medieval poets such as Sa'di (1184–1291), Mowlana Jalal-ed Din-e Rumi (1207–1273) and Hafez (1325–1389). Moreover, religious proscriptions have tended to be directed at instrumental music, with its secular associations, and a clear division formerly held between singing and chanting (*khāndan*, 'to read'), and instrumental music (without voice, *musiqi*). *Khāndan* is acceptable through association with the written or spoken word; indeed, the only 'sonic art' found in mainstream religious settings

---

47 Beale makes a similar observation regarding increased formalization in the teaching of jazz in recent years, which he suggests has led to a decline in stylistic diversity (2005).

in Iran is unaccompanied voice.[48] It would seem that before the twentieth century, Iranian classical music was predominantly vocal (Nettl 1987:134) – notwithstanding that the most important court musicians were players of long-necked lutes – the instrumentalist's role generally being to shadow the voice and play between lines of poetry. Whilst there may have been some space for elaboration, instrumentalists were generally expected to imitate the vocal line. Indeed, the old masters apparently attached great importance to this technique, known as *javāb āvāz* ('answering the voice'; Caron and Safvate 1966:192–3), which formed the most advanced stage of learning. Indicative of the central position of the voice is that the main unmeasured sections of performances are referred to as *āvāz* ('song', 'voice'), even when played by instrumentalists. The lower status of instrumental music is also seen in religious sensitivities over the visible presence of instruments in public spaces, to the extent that carrying an instrument in public was problematic in the past, particularly on religious holidays.[49] The situation has changed somewhat in recent decades, as music and musicians have secured greater social acceptance, but vestiges can still be seen, for example, in the contestation over showing musical instruments on television.[50]

In the course of the twentieth century, solo or group instrumental performance (without a singer) became increasingly common, and nowadays it is not unusual to dispense with a vocalist altogether (although audiences still generally expect there to be one). Nettl suggests that this change may have resulted from Western influence, reflecting the relative importance of instrumental music in Euro-American art music (1987).[51] It may also be a factor of the higher status enjoyed by music as an art, no longer dependent on poetry for respectability. Thus, *javāb āvāz* is rarely mentioned in the literature after Caron and Safvate as being part of a musician's training (incidentally, they do not give the Persian name, but translate into French and describe the technique).[52] Certainly, the generation most active in the early to mid-twentieth century, including musicians such as Ahmad Ebadi (*setār*) and Asghar Bahari (*kamāncheh*), played an important role in promoting solo instrumental music:

> With Ebadi, the *setār* came out from being a hidden [*lāqabāi*][53] instrument to one that can be held forward. Naturally, it takes time for this to become accepted. The generations had to pass until someone like Alizadeh *really* took the *setār* to that place where it is today. (Khayam 26.11.10)

Perhaps more than any other contemporary musician, Hossein Alizadeh has worked towards 'emancipating' instrumental music, maintaining that the 'sheltering of music behind words inevitably resulted in the potential of the voice and poetry affecting the music' (Sarkoohi 1989:37), most notably in terms of rhythm which he maintains is limited by the prosody of poetry. His groundbreaking *Torkaman* (1986) was the first album of entirely solo instrumental music published in Iran. Describing another of his pieces, he says:

---

[48]   The main exceptions are the use of instruments (mainly frame drums) by Sufi groups; and in the religious *ta'ziyeh* (passion play, usually presented as a form of street theatre) which re-enact the martyrdom of Imams Hassan and Hossein during the holy month of Moharram. See Caron and Safvate (1966:204–6), Darvishi (1995:130–55) and the comprehensive study by Massoudieh (1988).

[49]   Stories circulate about small *setār*s designed to be carried unobtrusively under a cloak (*abā*) (see Alizadeh in Sarkoohi 1989:37). Kalhor recounted how in the early 1980s, living in the Kurdish town of Kermanshah, he carried his instrument in a sack so as not to attract attention (4.8.99).

[50]   Still prohibited at the time of writing in 2014, even though instruments can be seen openly in public, in concerts or in music shops. Indeed, somewhat ironically, the main area for music shops in Tehran, around Baharestan Avenue, is located directly opposite the Iranian parliament building.

[51]   However, these changes have not been accompanied by the kinds of local discourses which emerged in Karnatic music in the late nineteenth century by which Western music came to be viewed primarily as instrumental, and 'the voice came to stand for authenticity and Indianness' (Weidman 2006).

[52]   Shajarian has complained that instrumentalists can no longer perform *javāb āvāz* properly, suggesting that it is now below their dignity to follow the voice. *Javāb āvāz* is still part of the university curriculum for those studying Iranian classical music.

[53]   Literally, 'under the *abā*'; see footnote 49.

> The basis of this work was the relationships between the instrumentalists ... and the voice was just where it should be, like another instrument and not more [important]. (ibid.:38)

This can be heard on the 1998 album *Rāz-e No* (*A New Mystery*, Mahoor Institute of Culture and Art, M.CD-38) in which the three voices (two female and one male: Afsaneh Rasayi, Homa Niknam and Mohsen Keramati) are used 'instrumentally', blending with and responding to the instruments of the ensemble. Describing instrumental music as having found its 'independence', Alizadeh suggests that this can 'lead to a whole series of other experiences' and that meanings can emerge which have hitherto been suppressed because listeners mainly focus on the poetry (in Shahrnazdar 2004b:103). It remains to be seen whether, as musicians explore the characteristics of their instrument independent of the voice, more distinct instrumental styles will emerge. As will be discussed in Chapter 3, there is already a clear distinction between *radif-e āvāzi* (vocal *radif*) and *radif-e sāzi* (instrumental *radif*). Nettl suggests that some of the features of the *radif* which make it the basis for creativity are more developed in the instrumental *radif*s, relating this to the consolidation of the repertoire at a time when instruments were starting to gain importance (1987:134–5). It is certainly the case that the *radif* considered the most authoritative is intended primarily for long-necked lutes, since the most prominent Qajar court musicians were *tār* and *setār* players. Nonetheless, the continued significance of the voice in the broader culture is evidenced by the fact that when a singer is present, they invariably form the central focus. Moreover, gifted vocalists often gain wider popularity among the general public than instrumentalists.[54]

Alongside the increasing centrality of instrumental music, some commentators have noted a greater preoccupation with technical expertise in recent decades.[55] The *santur*, an instrument on which the layout of strings allows leaps, rapid scalar passages and arpeggios (none of which are 'traditional' musical features), and whose relatively loud volume makes it suitable for large performance venues, experienced a significant rise in popularity in the second half of the twentieth century. As noted above, displays of virtuosity are somewhat contrary to traditional concepts of musicality, which instead emphasize the ability to communicate the spirit (*hāl*) of the music. Traditionally, there were no technical exercises, the *radif* being said to contain all that pupils needed to know in order to perform. Indeed, the idea that once the essence is understood, technique will follow still persists (During 1984a:35), reflecting the continuing strength of spiritual aspects.

The processes described here, of a gradual 'decoupling' of instrumental music from the voice, are relatively recent; however, one increasingly comes across musicians working without singers (or, like Alizadeh, using voices as instruments), thus enabling them to explore the potential of their instruments away from the specific demands of the voice to which the music has been tied for centuries. Whilst it is too soon to assess the long-term impact, the work of musicians like Alizadeh and others to be discussed in Chapter 5 suggest that this could have far-reaching consequences for both the concepts and practice of creativity.

*   *   *

Creativity in performance is central to the ways in which Iranian classical music is imagined and discussed, both by practitioners and those who experience it as listeners. And yet, more than any other topic, it generates intense anxiety and debate. On the one hand, there is the imperative to be creative, to aspire to the ideal of the nightingale; on the other, seemingly at odds with the first, the imperative to work within the bounds of tradition. How musicians negotiate these is significant in revealing some of the deepest fault lines in Iranian classical music today, most obviously in relation to the role and extent of individual performer agency. Whilst agency is fundamental, it has to operate in a dialectical relationship with the taught repertoire. In the following chapter, I introduce the *radif*, its history, role, ideologies and contestations, and discuss how it functions and is understood as a basis for creative practice. I also explore the social dimensions of this repertoire, including its now iconic status and mobilization in debates about tradition, 'authenticity' and the intersection between music and nationhood.

---

[54]   See also Simms (in Simms and Koushkani 2012b:23) on the growing importance of instrumental music and Alizadeh's role in this.

[55]   For discussion of similar changes within Hindustani music, see Kippen (1988b:95–6) and Neuman (1990:217). El-Shawan notes the increased focus on virtuosity in Egyptian music (1987:157).

Chapter 3
Disciplining Creativity:
The *Radif* of Iranian Classical Music

Introduction

Musical creativity always takes place in relation to the conventions of a musical system, most often in the context of an organizing structure – a model or framework, a pre-composed piece, a memorized repertoire, a chord sequence – or simply the stylistics of a genre. Pressing refers to such conventions as a 'referent' (1998:52) and Nettl uses the expression '"points of departure" (POD)' (2009:185).[1] Having explored concepts of creativity in Iranian classical music in Chapter 2, I now consider the repertoire which underpins it: the *radif* (lit. 'row', 'series'), a collection of several hundred pieces (*gusheh*, 'corner') distinguished by mode and by characteristic melodies and motifs, arranged into the 12 *dastgāh*.[2] Each *dastgāh* and *gusheh* is individually named, some referencing regions or towns of Iran (and beyond), others alluding to a sentiment or quality of character; many of the names are shared with neighbouring Arab and Turkic traditions. But the *radif* is much more than a repertoire. As a concept it is imbued with great symbolic power, simultaneously indexing canonicity, 'authenticity', authority and even nationhood. In order to explore both the musical and symbolic significance of the *radif*, I start with a summary of its history, followed by discussion of the ways in which it can be understood as a musical model, and the processes of transmission from teacher to pupil. The final section examines the increasing importance of the *radif* since the 1960s, in particular how it has come to embody notions of authenticity.

Fundamental to an understanding of creative practice in this music is the relationship between the learnt *radif* and performances based on it. However, relatively few writers have examined this in detail. Exceptions include studies by Nettl of the opening of *dastgāh Chāhārgāh* (with Foltin 1972) and other sections of repertoire (1987, in collaboration with several authors); Tsuge tackles similar issues in his study of vocal music (1974), and Massoudieh (1968) compares different *radif* versions and one performance of *dastgāh Shur*. It is notable that earlier writers, including Khatschi, Massoudieh, and Caron and Safvate, mention the *radif* only in passing. Nettl suggests that this may be because the concept did not correspond with ideas of Middle Eastern musical practice already developed by Euro-American scholars (1987:4). However, the fact that several of these writers were themselves Iranian suggests another explanation: that in the course of the twentieth century the *radif* gained in importance. This will be discussed below.

Radif in Historical Perspective

Whilst the history of the *radif* is somewhat speculative, what evidence there is suggests that for many generations (possibly hundreds of years), a master (*ostād*) would have taught his individual repertoire of pieces – but related to those of other teachers – developed and refined over many years. This idea is found in the literature and in discussion with musicians. Despite the paucity of evidence, it is probable that before the

---

[1] These include 'many sorts of musical phenomena – abstracted features of musical style such as collections of tones and rhythmic modes; brief motifs; sequences of harmonies; themes; compositions thoroughly worked out; general conceptions of soundscapes; or very specific models for elaboration such as forms (e.g., fugues, 12-bar blues)' (Nettl 2009:185).

[2] Several authors translate *dastgāh* as 'system' (Zonis 1973:65, During 1984a:107, Farhat 1990:20). The number of *gusheh*s varies from one *radif* to another; similarly, there are differences of opinion regarding the number of *dastgāh* (12 being the most widely accepted). Such differences are well documented in the literature and are not significant for the current discussion.

mid-nineteenth century there would have been a good deal of variation, both regionally and between different masters and schools. Several musicians suggested that such repertoires were rooted in improvisational practice: according to Payvar, musicians would select pieces from their performing repertoires, which would become 'fixed' (*sābet*) to form a teaching repertoire or *radif* (8.11.90). This is turn would become the basis for performance and teaching by the subsequent generation. The trends of musical practice since the mid-nineteenth century suggest that many of these repertoires have been lost (Nettl 1987:6), but the patchy historical record, and the fact that surviving accounts record only the names of pieces, makes it difficult to determine whether any of the material may have survived in modern-day *radif*s.

Whilst the *radif* is specific to Iranian classical music, the idea of a modal core which forms the basis for improvisation is shared with neighbouring traditions. Powers (1980b, 1989) discusses the semantic field of 'mode' at length, distinguishing between mode as 'tonal category' (a hierarchy of pitches) and as 'melody type', and suggesting ways in which useful comparisons might be drawn between the various modal entities of the region. The *gusheh* is the basic modal unit of the *radif*, and the *dastgāh* comprise a series of *gusheh*s in different (usually related) modes. It is likely that prior to the development of the *radif*, Iranian practice was closer to the present-day *maqām* system found elsewhere in the Middle East and Central Asia, with performances including both improvised and pre-composed sections in a single *maqām*.[3] Speculating on why these became grouped into the multi-modal entity of the *dastgāh*, Farhat attributes this to the 'general decline of musical scholarship in Persia, from the sixteenth to the twentieth century' (1990:19):

> As musical scholarship suffered and performance ability, based on theoretical know-how, was eroded, it became increasingly difficult to present a performance of a respectable length with the use of a single *maqām* … Consequently, performers resorted to the device of progressing, or modulating, from one *maqām* to another, usually not too remote in its modal structure. In some cases, eventually, this stringing of *maqām*s led to more distant modes. (Farhat 1980a:5)

Whilst the linking of modally-related pieces most likely dates from the sixteenth century –according to Asadi, the term *dastgāh* first appeared in the late Safavid period (1501–1722) to refer to what he calls a 'multi-modal cycle' (2004) – During suggests that the development of the *dastgāh* concept can be linked to similar constructs in the music of Azerbaijan which found their way into Iran through Qajar influence and later rule (r.1794–1925), particularly after the arrival of Azeri musicians at the Qajar court in the new capital of Tehran (1991a:63). Whatever the reason, at some point in the mid-nineteenth century, the teaching repertoires of individual musicians acquired the name of *radif*, and it was around this time that Ali Akbar Farahani (1810–1855), court musician and master of *tār*, began to codify the *gusheh*s of his teaching repertoire into the 12 *dastgāh*s of the *radif*, doubtless using much material inherited from a long line of masters and from the wider musical tradition.[4] However, it was two of his sons, Mirza Abdollah (1843–1918) and Aqa Hossein Qoli

---

3   Sumits, for example, posits the *chahār shadd* tradition of modal suite performance found in Central Asia from the late sixteenth century as a possible precursor for the Iranian *dastgāh* (2011:116), although lack of nineteenth-century treatises in Iran makes it difficult to establish the relationship for certain (139). For further discussion on antecedents to the *radif* system, see Wright (1978), Farhat (1980a), Feldman (1996), Asadi (2001, 2004), Mohammadi (2001 [a response to Asadi 2001], 2006) and Olley (2010). Several scholars of Ottoman music have suggested that prior to the Safavid period, Ottoman and Iranian practices were part of a shared 'musical *lingua franca*, tolerant of local variation but evolving in a fairly uniform fashion' (Wright 2001:797) and that the processes of differentiation which began in the sixteenth century were largely due to very different socio-political conditions, and which in the Ottoman case led to a move away from earlier improvisational practice and to a greater focus on composition. In the twentieth century, musical reforms initiated during the Republican period continued this trend by 'emphasising the role of group performance, composition and modal theory … While improvisation still serves as a cultural symbol and a vital component of the Turkish tradition, it is profoundly influenced by compositional and theoretical models' (Olley 2010:30).

4   The formalization of the *radif* marked an important departure from earlier teaching practices which shared a great deal with neighbouring traditions, for example Arabic music where 'Before the coming of the modern conservatory system … there were no standard teaching materials, and individual teachers probably had their own ways of imparting materials – for example, the typical or required content of a maqam, such as scales and motifs' (Nettl 2009:189–90). Elsewhere one finds interesting parallels with the formalization of teaching repertoires in Iran: for instance, I have been particularly struck by the discussion around eighteenth- and nineteenth-century European piano preluding, by Temperley

(c.1851–1915), and his nephew Aqa Qolam Hossein (dates unavailable), who were largely responsible for the transmission of Farahani's *radif* (Khaleqi 1983b:110). Although Farahani had many pupils, little information survives about them, and the most important line of transmission is generally considered to be through his sons and nephew.[5]

The historical record is far from complete and twentieth-century historiography of Iranian classical music of the nineteenth century is largely based on a small number of anecdotal and personal sources, the details of which are often hard to verify but which have been multiply cited for so long that they are now generally accepted as fact. According to Ruhollah Khaleqi's *Sargozasht-e Musiqi-ye Irān* (*A History of Iranian Music*[6]), perhaps the most widely-cited account of the history of Iranian music from the late nineteenth to the mid-twentieth century, and which provides a wealth of information on the lives of the most prominent musicians at this time, following the death of Farahani, Qolam Hossein assumed the education of his cousins, apparently with some reluctance (1983b:110). Mirza Abdollah was 12 years old when Farahani died, and there is some doubt as to whether he studied with his father at all; his main teachers were his cousin and older brother, Mirza Hassan (who died young), both of whom were in receipt of Farahani's repertoire. Mirza Abdollah played *tār* and *setār* but was particularly known for the latter; and unlike many musicians of the day who guarded their knowledge closely, he was aware of the importance of transmitting this knowledge to his pupils. However, his most enduring legacy was the completion of the organization of the *radif* into 12 *dastgāhs* begun by his father. Of Mirza Abdollah's four children (all proficient *setār* players), the youngest, Ahmad Ebadi (1907–1994), became the most highly regarded performer of *setār* of the twentieth century. Ebadi was still a child when his father died and, as the narrative goes, learnt the *radif* mainly from his older sister, Mowlood (precise dates unavailable), who reputedly had a good knowledge of the repertoire.[7]

Farahani's youngest son, Hossein Qoli, learnt *tār* initially with his brother and then with his cousin, Qolam Hossein. He was also an important teacher, but unlike Mirza Abdollah who directed his energies towards teaching and consolidating the *radif*, Hossein Qoli spent many hours each day practising and perfecting his technique, and is now remembered as the most highly regarded *tār* player of his time. One of his sons, Ali Akbar Shahnazi (1898–1985), became a prominent teacher and performer of *tār*. Like Mirza Abdollah, Hossein Qoli was a court musician to Nasereddin Shah (r.1848–1896), arguably the most influential Qajar monarch in relation to musical developments. Regardless of the finer details of the narrative, it is clear that Farahani and his descendants played a significant role in the development of the *radif* and the history of Iranian classical music in the nineteenth and twentieth centuries.

The arrangement of the repertoire into the 12 *dastgāhs* coincided with increased contact with Europe. Nasereddin Shah himself travelled to Europe, and indeed it was his encounter with military music in France that led to the establishment of the first formal music school in Iran (Zonis 1973:39, 186, Talai in Shahrnazdar 2004a:69; see below). In addition, between c.1909 and 1915, a number of musicians including Mirza Abdollah, Hossein Qoli and Darvish Khan (1872–1926) travelled abroad to give concerts and make recordings for the Gramophone Company (Lucas 2014).[8] The itinerary for the first tour included Baku,

---

and others, where originally improvised preludes were later published for teaching purposes. The published preludes of the virtuoso pianist and improviser Johann Nepomuk Hummel (1778–1837), for instance, were intended 'to provide models for students' (Temperley 2009:332). In this way, improvised preluding was transformed 'into a form of premeditated composition that became a model for others' (ibid.:339). The parallels with Iran are clear.

⁵ Another important court musician whose name appears in the historical record is Mohammad Sadeq Khan (also known as Soroor al-Molook [precise dates unknown] and mentioned by several writers including Caron and Safvate 1966:15, and Talai in Shahrnazdar 2004a:88), but little has survived from his line of transmission.

⁶ First published in 1954 (Volume 1) and 1956 (Volume 2). Much of the information in this and the following paragraph is taken from Khaleqi. The reader is also referred to Massoudieh (1973) for an historical overview of Iranian music in the nineteenth century.

⁷ See also interview with Ebadi, http://www.youtube.com/watch?v=7W2G9GeH858&feature=relmfu (accessed 19.11.12). Mowlood is just one of the 'hidden' women musicians – mothers, sisters and so on – who played a role in the transmission of the repertoire. Their names occasionally surface in historical accounts and some appear in the iconographic record, but they are generally absent from official narratives. See also Simms and Koushkani (2012a:123–6).

⁸ For more information on these early recording and concert trips see Khaleqi (1983b:133–4), Zonis (1973:192) and Kinnear (2000). Not only did Iranian musicians travel to Europe, but from the early twentieth century, European and North

Constantinople, Vienna, Paris and London, with later trips to Tiflis (1912 and 1915). Speculating on reasons for the emergence of the *radif*, Nettl (1987:6) suggests that Mirza Abdollah may have been influenced by these various contacts and what he learnt of European music theory, and wanted to develop a similar unified theory for Iranian music. By the mid-nineteenth century, the 'golden age' of medieval scholarship was long past and, as suggested earlier, Iran had experienced a decline in musical learning, due primarily to socio-political-religious factors. Greater contact with Europe in the nineteenth century certainly fostered the idea of Western music as more theoretically-grounded, and thus more 'advanced'. Endeavouring to present Iranian music as similarly 'scientific' may, as Nettl argues, have been part of an attempt to elevate the social status of music at this time; also suggesting that Mirza Abdollah represented something of a synthesis between the inherited tradition and the new concepts filtering into Iran from Europe.[9] Other reasons have also been proposed for the emergence of the *radif*, including the special attention paid to music by the Qajar monarchs in comparison with their predecessors. According to contemporary singer Shahram Nazeri:

> From a historical point of view, everything has a time. It seems that the time had come for this. Bearing in mind the history of social and artistic change in Iran, and the problems that music had from Safavid times, things had reached a point that this had to happen. If Mirza Abdollah hadn't done it, someone else would have. These musicians brought together [*tadvin*] these pieces so that they could be used as a model [*olgoo*] for teaching and learning. (23.4.10)

Asked whether the *radif* might have emerged in response to the rise of nationalist sentiment and the desire to create a distinctly Iranian repertoire, Nazeri conceded:

> We can say that many social factors played a part. The *radif*s themselves were responsible for other foreign [*khāreji*] musics not mixing with ours. The linking of these melodies created a web-like chain [*bāft-e zanjireyi*] which didn't allow other music – Arabic, Turkish – to infiltrate [*nofooz*]. (ibid.)

The connection between the *radif* and notions of nationhood will be discussed below.

One *Radif*, Many *Radif*s

Whilst historical evidence points to a certain diversity among teaching repertoires prior to Farahani (see also During 1991a:63), from the early years of the twentieth century it was his *radif*, as consolidated and transmitted by Mirza Abdollah which became increasingly central. This was likely due to a number of factors: not only did Mirza Abdollah and Hossein Qoli enjoy relatively favoured positions at court, their pupils also played a key role in disseminating this *radif*. Moreover, Farahani's comprehensive ordering of pieces seems to have emerged at a time when musicians were starting to feel the need for a focal repertoire, perhaps as suggested due to increased contact with European ideas. Ultimately, the combined effects of the growing political and cultural dominance of the relatively new capital, and the fact that the most prominent musicians of the twentieth century emerged from this line of teaching, served to establish the *radif* of Mirza

---

American companies started to expand their operations, as they became aware of the vast potential markets worldwide. In 1906, the Gramophone Company received its first royal warrant from the Shah of Persia, and in the same year, the Persian branch of the Gramophone Company was opened, but closed in 1908. For most of the period between 1900 and 1910, Iran was supplied by the Tiflis (now Tbilisi, at that time under Russian control) office of the Russian subsidiary of the Gramophone Company, A.O. Grammophon, and Iranian musicians also travelled there to make recordings. Indeed, Russia was Iran's main supplier of gramophone machines and records until 1917. For further information, see Gronow (1981), Sepanta (1987, the first extended study tracing the history of sound recording in Iran), Tabar (2005) and Mohammadi (2011).

[9]   See Baily (1988:162) for an analogous situation in Afghanistan, where the adoption of Indian music theory was partly motivated by a desire to secure a more respectable position for music and musicians. There are also interesting parallels with the kinds of 'classicizing' processes in North India discussed by Schofield (2010). Some Iranian scholars have contested Nettl's idea, pointing to the long tradition of organized collections of modally-related pieces in the musics of the region (see Mohammadi 2001).

Abdollah as *the radif* of Iranian music, and the particular style of these musicians came to dominate. As formal institutions started to replace traditional teaching contexts from the second quarter of the century, and as music education became more centralized and standardized in line with the trends of the early Pahlavi period, it was this *radif* which came to be regarded as the most prestigious and 'authentic' version of the repertoire. The fact that most classical musicians born after c.1940 were educated at such institutions has been a major factor in this.[10] However, there is no definitive version of the *radif* of Mirza Abdollah. The original was never recorded, although it was of course transmitted through numerous students, some of whom began the process of recording, initially in notation and later in sound. One of the earliest notations was made in the early twentieth century by Medhi Qoli Hedayat from the playing of Dr Mehdi Montazem al-Hokama (also known as Mehdi Solhi), reputed to be one of Mirza Abdollah's best pupils.[11] Another transcription, by Ali Naqi Vaziri, who studied with both Hossein Qoli and Mirza Abdollah, and said to have been verified by the masters themselves, appears to have been lost (During 1991a:32, 128), although apparently not before Mussa Ma'rufi had a chance to study it (see below; details of early versions of Mirza Abdollah's *radif* are given in During 1984a:127–9, 1991a:62–3, Nettl 1987:5–7). Consistent with earlier practices according to which a master would compile his individual repertoire, there developed several versions of this *radif*, some of which were published. Thus, we have 'the *radif* of *ostād* Saba' or 'the *radif* of *ostād* Karimi', whilst acknowledging their derivation from Mirza Abdollah. Indeed, most *radif*s in circulation today can be traced back to Farahani and Mirza Abdollah. The complex of teacher-pupil relations has resulted in close connections between these versions, which Nettl has likened to European folksong 'tune families' (1987:5); similarly, Talai draws parallels between different *radif*s and variants of epic poems such as 'Leili and Majooon' or Ferdowsi's *Shāhnāmeh* (in Shahrnazdar 2004a:94–5). On the one hand, then, is the idea of many closely related *radif*s (of individual musicians); on the other, the original 'authentic' *radif*: that of Mirza Abdollah.

Whilst Mirza Abdollah's *radif* has become the central repertoire, others outside the Farahani line were transmitted, particularly in the provinces, as Zonis observed in the early 1970s, 'the radif of Mirza Abdullah ... does not represent the entire maqam tradition in Iran but merely one of its major branches' (1973:67). Tsuge (1974:29–30) lists four main sources: the *radif* taught by Mirza Abdollah and Hossein Qoli; the *santur radif* of Soma Hozur and his son, legendary santurist Habib Somai; the *radif* used by ta'ziyeh (religious 'passion plays') singers; and the 'Esfahan School', Esfahan being renowned for its *nei* (end-blown flute) players and which was the Safavid capital during a period of intense artistic flourishing (see Sepanta 1964:29, Massoudieh 1989:16, During 1984a:25).[12] Of these, the second has not survived in print or recording[13] and the latter two are poorly documented.[14] It should be noted that not until the Qajar period (1794–1925) did Tehran, as the new capital, become a centre of musical activity. Writing in 1964, Sepanta mentions traditions in Kerman and Shiraz and expresses concern that the increasing dominance of Mirza Abdollah's *radif* has led to the marginalization of other, equally valuable, repertoires (1964:29). Massoudieh briefly describes *maktabs* ('schools') in Qazvin and Shiraz, as well as Esfahan and Tehran (1989:16), and

---

[10]   The promotion of this particular *radif* at the University of Tehran by Borumand was significant; see below. The University of Tehran continues to teach only the *radif* of Mirza Abdollah; whereas the syllabus of the University of Art (in Karaj, near Tehran) is more flexible, allowing students to study 'One of the established/trusted *radif*s' (*'yeki az radifhā-ye motabar'*), whether that of Karimi, Davami, Payvar and so on (Amir Eslami, personal communication, November 2010).

[11]   The *dastgāh*s and *gusheh*s in this *radif* are listed in Hedayat (1928); and During (1984a:128) mentions that the notation was deposited at the Honarestān-e Melli in Tehran. It has only recently been prepared for publication, by Amir Eslami and due to be published by the University of Art. This version of the *radif* was apparently verified by Mirza Abdollah (Eslami, personal communication, November 2010).

[12]   There are contradictory accounts of how music fared under Safavid rule. Visual arts and architecture certainly flourished, but this was also a period of increased religiosity as Shieh Islam became the state religion, and many claim that this impacted negatively on music (see Farhat 1980a:5 and Caton 1983:39). On the other hand, extant iconography suggests some musical activity at court, as also reported by Caton (1983:41; see also Olley 2010:4). According to Eslami, it was through the performance of *ta'ziyeh*, which developed at this time, that much of the repertoire of Iranian music was preserved under the Safavids (26.11.10).

[13]   Some of this repertoire may have survived through assimilation into the *radif* of Saba, who studied with Habib Somai.

[14]   The first recording of a *radif* representing the tradition of Esfahan, played by Hassan Kassai on *nei*, was published in 2010 by the cultural organization of the Tehran municipality (Sāzmān-e Farhangi-honari-ye Shahrdāri-ye Tehrān).

Talai discusses traditions in Esfahan, Shiraz and Tabriz that were fostered at the local courts of Qajar princes (in Shahrnazdar 2004a:86). Talai suggests that the teaching repertoires in Esfahan during the Qajar period were more 'flexible' (*en'etāfpazir*) and less 'fixed' (*sābet*) than in Tehran (ibid.:89), but this is difficult to substantiate. Research on both historical and contemporary practice has focused almost exclusively on Tehran and much work remains to be done on traditions elsewhere.

Published Versions of Mirza Abdollah's Radif

Notwithstanding the existence of alternative repertoires, the term '*radif*' generally implies some relationship to the body of pieces transmitted by Mirza Abdollah and his followers, on which the mainstream of Iranian classical music today is based. It is therefore this *radif* that forms the main point of comparison with performances in Chapter 4. What survives of Mirza Abdollah's original are the names of *gusheh*s as played by his pupils (Hedayat 1928, Forsat al-Dowleh Shirazi 1966 [originally published 1903]) and the tradition as recorded, notated and transmitted orally. Prior to the mid-1980s, a small number of published versions were available, most of which are listed by Nettl (1987:6–9) and During (1984a:127–9). The first publication of Iranian music using staff notation, Vaziri's *Dastur-e Tār* (1913, Berlin), was not a *radif* as such but a teaching manual which included material from the *radif* of Mirza Abdollah plus technical exercises, short compositions by Vaziri, and arrangements of pieces by composers such as Schubert, Beethoven and Rossini, and was clearly influenced by Vaziri's studies in Europe. His later publications (1933 and 1936, both published in Tehran) were also instruction manuals (two for *tār*, one for violin), as was the first publication of a *radif*, that of Abol Hassan Saba (1902–1957) in the form of tutors for *santur* (c.1965), violin (c.1967), and *setār* (c.1970) (all originally published in the 1950s).

Notations and sound recordings of *radif*s have been produced for different purposes, primarily for teaching, preservation and scholarship. Thus, whilst Saba's *radif* was intended for teaching, that of Mussa Ma'rufi (Barkeshli and Ma'rufi 1963) was the result of a government initiative to publish a 'definitive' *radif*. Many musicians at the time felt the need for a publication which would preserve Iran's musical heritage; and the resultant lavish volume was regarded for many decades as the most complete notated version of the *radif*. Although less 'instrument-specific' than the books of Saba, this *radif* is nevertheless best suited to *tār* (or *setār*), and relevant tunings are given for each *dastgāh*. The history of this publication is interesting for what it reveals of the tension between the idea of the one 'authentic' *radif*, and the many individual versions of it.

The Ministry of Fine Arts wished to publish a *radif* which might be judged as representative of the tradition, possibly regarding standardization as a symbol of modernity and progress.[15] The preface describes how a committee of prominent figures was assembled in order to agree the contents: Ali Akbar Shahnazi (Hossein Qoli's son), Abol Hassan Saba, Nur Ali Borumand, Ahmad Ebadi (Mirza Abdollah's son), Musa Ma'rufi and Rokneddin Mokhtari. Needless to say, consensus was not reached and Ma'rufi was eventually asked to provide the version for publication (interestingly, these details are included only in the Persian preface and omitted from the French translation). No further information on the sources of this *radif* is given, but Ma'rufi himself in a critical open letter published in 1964 describes it as the fruit of 30 years work and expresses disappointment that its sources are not acknowledged. He goes on to explain that the basis of this *radif* is that of Darvish Khan, Ma'rufi's first teacher of *tār* (and pupil of Mirza Abdollah and Hossein Qoli). It was transcribed by Ma'rufi and subsequently refined over many years as he encountered the version of Mirza Abdollah's and Hossein Qoli's *radif* as transcribed by Vaziri, and Hedayat's transcription from the playing of Mehdi Montazem al-Hokama.[16] This *radif* can thus be regarded as a true synthesis of several versions, but all derived from the same line of musicians.[17] Unlike the *radif* of Saba, which includes just a few central *gusheh*s in each *dastgāh*, intended to make it more accessible to pupils, Ma'rufi sought to be as

---

[15]   For similar processes in South Asian music, in particular the role of the 'Experts Committee' of the Music Academy of Madras between 1930 and 1952, see Allen (2007). Davis also discusses the standardized 'official' version of the Tunisian *ma'luf* repertoire, which was promoted as 'The Tunisian Musical Heritage' and which largely ignored local variants (1997).

[16]   None of this information is given by Zonis (in her 1964 review), Nettl or During when discussing this *radif*.

[17]   A recording of this *radif* played by Soleyman Ruhafza on *tār*, and introduced by Ma'rufi, was also made (c.1959–60. See Chapter 4, footnote 27; also Nettl 1987:78).

comprehensive as possible (the publication has 471 individually named sections), to the point of including materials which might not normally be regarded as being part of the *radif* (Nettl 1987:7). Another grievance expressed by Ma'rufi was the prohibitive price and limited print run of the 1963 publication; this was to be a 'sumptuous state-sponsored publication clearly intended to serve as monument to tradition and as a Pahlavi proclamation to the world of the enduring legacy and high artistic status of Persian classical music' (Wright 2009:27), an elite and ostentatious document rather than an affordable book to be used for teaching. Since the 1980s, this *radif* has been republished several times (less lavishly) and is now widely available.

Another published *radif*, that of vocal master Mahmud Karimi (whose main teacher was Abdollah Davami) as taught by him at the University of Tehran and at the Markaz-e Hefz-o Eshāeh-ye Musiqi-ye Irāni (Centre for the Preservation and Propagation of Iranian Music, henceforth Markaz), was recorded for the Iranian government in the mid-1970s and includes both sound recordings and transcriptions by Mohammad Taghi Massoudieh (Massoudieh 1978). Like Ma'rufi, Karimi endeavours to be comprehensive (with 145 numbered items); and Massoudieh's detailed transcriptions perhaps make it more useful for scholarly study than for teaching. Another source for part of Davami's *radif* is a transcription of *dastgāh Shur* by Lotfi, part of an introductory text (1976, published in French) and which differs in a number of ways from Karimi's version.[18]

Among the early *radif*s available as sound recordings, one of the most important was that taught by Nur Ali Borumand (1906–1978) at both the University of Tehran and the Markaz in the 1960s and '70s. This version was recorded by National Iranian Radio and Television in 1972 with Borumand on *tār*, and although it has fewer *gushehs* (249) than that of Ma'rufi, is claimed by many to be more authentic (During 1984a:128, 1991a:62–3). Borumand's significance lies partly in the fact that he studied with several masters who were in direct receipt of Mirza Abdollah's repertoire (see During 1991a.62, Nettl 1987:142–3). Further, his main teachers, Esmail Khan Qahramani and Haji Aqa Mohammad, were among the most highly regarded of Mirza Abdollah's pupils; Qahramani reputedly knew his master's *radif* better than anyone. The *radif* which Borumand studied intensively with Qahramani over a period of about 12 years (During 1991a:63) is thus widely considered to be closest to Mirza Abdollah's original, particularly since the transmission through Qahramani and Borumand was not affected by Darvish Khan's attempts to 'popularize' the tradition.[19] Whilst Borumand's recording appears not to have been published during his lifetime – neither Nettl (1987:8–9) nor During (1984a:128, 1991a:62–3) are specific on this point – cassette recordings were in informal circulation.[20] This *radif* was finally published in 1991, first on cassette and later CD, together with transcriptions by Jean During (1991a). Borumand's influence as a teacher is discussed below.

Another recording which should be mentioned is a set of long-playing discs published in 1976, under the supervision of Kambeez Roshanravan, by the Institute for the Intellectual Development of Children and Young Adults (Kānoon-e Parvaresh-e Fekri-ye Koodakān va Nowjavānān). Intended for the general education of the public (rather than the direct teaching context), this recording, rather unusually for the time, includes liner notes on the musical system (in Persian and English). Included in the category of *radif* by Nettl, who describes it as a 'composite *radif*' (1987:9, but not mentioned by During), this publication differs in certain ways from other recorded *radif*s. First, it features several musicians (including some of Borumand's pupils), thereby

---

[18]   As mentioned in Chapter 2, a distinction is made between *radif-e sāzi* (instrumental *radif*) *and radif-e āvāzi* (vocal *radif*): these differ in certain respects, whilst sharing essential elements. Nettl discusses the rhythmic differences between instrumental and vocal *radif*s (1987:104). However, whilst students of plucked and struck stringed instruments with a decaying sound quality (*tār, setār, santur*) generally study *radif-e sāzi*, those learning instruments with a sustained sound such as *kamāncheh* (bowed spike-fiddle) and *nei* often learn *radif-e āvāzi*. Thus, a strict instrumental-vocal divide isn't entirely applicable; moreover, *tār, setār* and *santur* players often learn the vocal *radif* in the course of training.

[19]   Kiani claims that Borumand was the *only* musician in receipt of Mirza Abdollah's *radif* as transmitted by Qahramani (2004:149). Although the list of Borumand's teachers given by Nettl (1987:142–3) includes both Darvish Khan and Musa Ma'rufi, as his first teacher of *tār*, Darvish Khan's influence was fairly minimal; similarly, the period of study with Ma'rufi was early on and relatively short.

[20]   Caron and Safvate mention a recording of Borumand's *radif* (1966:117), but no details are given. It is unclear whether this recording was generally available at the time, particularly since no other sources mention it. In the mid-1960s, Borumand allowed certain non-Iranian scholars, including Tsuge, Nettl and Blum (see Nettl 1987:9, 78), to record parts of his *radif*, and transcriptions of this material are included in their publications (for instance, Tsuge 1974:402–45. Some of Tsuge's transcriptions are also in Zonis 1973:50, 70).

introducing listeners to the sounds of different instruments. Rather than *gushehs* being presented in sequence from beginning to end, the first few *gushehs* of each *dastgāh* are played individually and then sequentially; the next few *gushehs* are then presented individually and in succession in the same way; once all of the *gushehs* have been played, there is a complete rendition of the *dastgāh*, but in shortened form with only the central *gushehs*. To the extent that this recording represents an intentionally abbreviated 'compilation' from the *radif*s of different masters (including both Ma'rufi and Borumand's) rather than one particular master, it is rather atypical; on the other hand, since any *radif* is effectively a consolidation of material from different masters, it is perhaps less unusual than might at first appear. Despite certain limitations, it is nevertheless of interest and is included in the analyses of Chapter 4.

Both Nettl (1987:6–9) and During (1984a:127–9) list several other sources for the *radif*, including lists of *gusheh* names, transcriptions and sound recordings, for instance those by Forutan and Hormozi, played on *setār* (1972) and described by During as 'free *radif*s, that is to say less strict' (1984a:128), and that of Hossein Qoli recorded by his son, Ali Akbar Shahnazi (*tār*).[21] During has suggested that there may still be versions of the *radif* in private collections (1984a:129), and only when such links in the chain between Farahani and the present day are discovered will it be possible to piece together a more complete history of the *radif*.

Since the late 1980s, there has been a marked increase in *radif*-related publications, including recordings, notations and instruction manuals, but also for the first time publications with accompanying (sometimes analytical) commentary. In 1987, santurist Majid Kiani published the *radif* of Mirza Abdollah (a version very close to his main teacher, Borumand) as a set of five cassettes. Another set, published in 1992 by Hossein Alizadeh (another of Borumand's students), is of particular interest for its inclusion of analytical discussion. Another analytical version of Mirza Abdollah's *radif*, in notated form, was published by Dariush Talai in 1997 (in Iran), followed by an expanded version in 2000 published in the United States. As the *radif* has gained in significance, so the number of published versions has increased. One organization in particular has played a key role in this: the Mahoor Institute of Culture and Art, which also produces the scholarly journal *Mahoor Music Quarterly*. Since its establishment in 1987, Mahoor has issued recordings and print publications of various kinds, focused primarily on Iranian classical music and regional traditions. Their catalogue now includes a wide range of contemporary and historical recordings (including previously unavailable recordings from the early twentieth century), and many different versions of the *radif*, which are marketed in Iran and abroad. Whilst Mahoor is not the only publisher in this area, their extensive range of *radif*-related material gives some indication of the central position that the repertoire now occupies in the music culture. It is interesting that at the very time when the idea of a single authoritative version of the *radif* has been promoted (see below), there has been a corresponding rise in the number and variety of published versions of the repertoire.[22]

Discourses of Stability

Alongside the increasingly accepted idea of the one 'authentic' *radif* has emerged that of the *radif* as unchanging (and unchangeable; 'an unalterable model', During 1991b:203), as in the following statement by prominent singer Parisa (former student of Karimi):

> I have witnessed the honest rigor of Karimi's work. Under no circumstances would he allow the shifting of a single note in a *gushe*. With his idiosyncratic scientific precision, he took painstaking care to transmit the entire

---

[21]   According to Nazeri, Hossein Qoli chose not to follow his father and brother but instead developed his own *radif*, which despite its shorter length Nazeri considers to be more artistic ('*honarmandtar*'), more complex ('*pichidehtar*'), deeper ('*amiqtar*') and more useful for a performer ('*bishtar be dard-e navāzandeh mikhoreh*') (23.4.10). Talai (in Shahrnazdar 2004a:93) concurs with this, adding that he is particularly fond of this *radif*, a view I have encountered among other musicians with whom I have discussed Hossein Qoli's *radif*, which has been somewhat marginalized by that of Mirza Abdollah. Nowadays, this *radif* is more widely available, not least through print and recorded versions published by Mahoor (http://www.mahoor.com/default.aspx, accessed 16.10.13).

[22]   See http://www.mahoor.com/default.aspx (accessed 16.10.13).

unadulterated text of the *radif* to his students. A *gushe* taught by him, say, twenty years earlier, would not be altered one iota, when tackled in his class, twenty years later. (in During 1991b:221)[23]

This view presents a strong discourse of stability, with a symbolic investment in the unchanging *radif*, despite clear evidence of change since Qajar times. As Nettl observes, 'The idea that it [the *radif*] does not change reflects the abiding importance of certain cultural values, and the documentable fact that the *radif* is actually a recent restructuring of older materials which has changed a good deal since 1900 is typically ignored' (1983:208). One of the most important figures promoting such discourses was Nur Ali Borumand, whose claim in the 1960s and '70s to be teaching Mirza Abdollah's *radif* with minimal change from its 'original' was problematic.[24] Beyond such discourses, it is clear that the *radif* is by no means singular nor stable. In addition to the various extant versions, the disjuncture between verbal discourse and musical practice is evidenced in the fact that, for instance, there are some important differences between the version of *dastgāh Shur* as rendered by Karimi's main teacher, Davami (transcribed and published in Lotfi 1976), and that published as Karimi's own *radif* (transcribed in Massoudieh 1978). During similarly discusses ways in which the *radif* of *Segāh* has changed since the late nineteenth century (1984a:133–4).

As noted earlier and by several musicians and scholars, there is evidence that teaching *radif*s originally developed from playing repertoires:

It seems that in the past musicians have enriched the *radif* by enlarging it with more or less personal compositions or arrangements of airs drawn from diverse origins ... Nothing can prevent a musician, if he thinks it appropriate, to add to it another passage and try to teach that passage. (During 1991b:203)

The *radif* is like a grammar of language ... a linguistic grammar is always formulated after the language itself develops; and the *radif* and technique have also developed in the course of history as a result of the creativity of artists. (Alizadeh in Sarkoohi 1989:32)

According to this view, pieces originally developed in performance became incorporated into the taught repertoire over time. Nazeri also suggested that the *radif* emerged from improvisatory practice (23.4.10), and Payvar claimed that Saba's *radif* was based on listening to Habib Somai's playing which he 'formed into a *radif*' ('*be soorat-e radif darāvord*', 8.11.90). There are thus two perspectives, interestingly reflected in key words above: one regarding changes to the *radif* as 'adulterations', the other viewing them as 'enriching'. Whilst it seems to have been acceptable for earlier generations to develop, and sometimes publish, their own teaching repertoires, the discourses of authenticity which emerged in the 1960s (discussed below) encouraged teachers to use extant models. Talking in 1992, Meshkatian explained that teachers usually choose to teach a particular *radif* depending on their knowledge and training, rather than develop their own (20.7.92). However, he qualified this from his own experience, explaining that whilst he teaches the *radif* of Mirza Abdollah (he studied mainly with Borumand), he includes certain *gusheh*s that he considers worth learning from other *radif*s (such as Hossein Qoli's). This suggests a continuation of the practice by which masters develop teaching repertoires using several sources (precisely what Ma'rufi and Saba did in their published *radif*s). Similarly, Mohammad Reza Shajarian has written about the process of collecting and comparing different *radif*s in developing his own teaching repertoire (Ghaneifard 2003:155). Notwithstanding such practices –

---

[23] Note that whilst Parisa speaks of the 'entire unadulterated text of the *radif*', During claimed (based on interviews with Karimi) that the *radif* taught by Karimi was just part of his complete repertoire.

[24] The title of this version, *radif-e Mirza Abdollah be ravāyat-e Nur Ali Borumand* ('the *radif* of Mirza Abdollah as told/related by Nur Ali Borumand'), implies minimal change from the original ('*rāvi*', from which '*ravāyat*' is derived, means narrator or oral poet). However, in During's 1991 publication, '*be ravāyat-e Nur Ali Borumand*' is translated into French as '*Version de Nur 'Ali Borumand*', suggesting a more personal interpretation. In fact, discourses of stability notwithstanding, Borumand is reputed to have told pupils that he learnt the *radif* from Qahramani, but subsequently 'corrected and improved' it. Some sources have even speculated that Borumand deleted recordings by Qahramani to conceal the extent of changes made.

and despite evidence of diverse teaching repertoires prior to Farahani's codification, regional variations, and the existence of numerous versions of the *radif* today – the *idea* of the *radif* as unchanging has great potency.

Understanding the *Radif* as a Basis for Creative Performance

Radif *as 'Model'*; Radif *as 'Framework'*

Although in some respects a straightforward concept, the complexities of the term '*radif*' are revealed in the many definitions in the literature and among musicians. On the one hand, the *radif* is a body of repertoire transmitted from master to pupil:

> ... the fundamental canon of material upon which performances and improvisations are based. (Nettl 1972:12)

> The principal [*asli*] meaning of *radif* is the most documented [*modavvantarin*], most defined [*moayyantarin*], most established [*tasbit-shodeh-tarin*] melodies which have passed down to us from previous generations. (Meshkatian, 20.7.92)

At the same time, there is the idea of the *radif* as a structure which embodies the rules of musical composition and through which such rules are learnt:

> ... the arrangement of *gusheh*s inside the twelve or fourteen modal systems *as well as the ways of playing these gushehs* ... (123) uniquely a rhythmically free modal model ... [which] may be elaborated not for itself, but in order to teach a method of playing or improvising (126) ... The model is not only the basis, but also the example of free play in the style of such and such a master or school. (During 1984a:123, my emphases)

The *radif* thus serves both as a model repertoire and as a collection of procedures for its re-creation: as illustration and prototype. The idea that musical structures embody the rules for their own renewal is also found outside the Iranian tradition; in the words of Nattiez, 'music generates music' (1983:472), and Rice responds, 'I prefer [the] ... claim that people generate music at the same time that it acknowledges the formative power of previously constructed musical forms' (1987:474).[25] In a sense, all music functions 'both as models and as examples of performance' (Nettl with Foltin 1972:21). As several writers have noted (for example, Nettl with Foltin 1972:19, Nettl 2009:197), there are no essential structural differences between the learnt *radif* and performances based on it, yet a clear distinction is made between the theory of the *radif* and the practice of performance. Nettl compares the *radif* to 'studies' in Euro-American art music, 'building blocks' (1983:326) rather than performable music. And indeed, the *radif* is not generally performed as such (although there are musicians, *radif-navāz*, who play the *radif* more or less note-for-note, this is rather unusual and not highly valued). To be a good teacher requires a formidable memory to learn and transmit the music's intricate details. The mark of a good performer, however, is the ability to exercise creativity on the basis of the learnt repertoire.

But how exactly does the *radif* operate as a model or framework? And how do musicians conceptualize and talk about this? Among those who have theorized the nature of models or frameworks for creative performance, Lortat-Jacob (1987b:47) suggests four types: '*modèle-composition*', a relatively fixed piece (such as a pre-composed composition or a recording of an improvisation); '*modèle-formule/modèle forme*', a less-defined model such as a modal or metric structure; '*modèle composite*', where improvisation is based on the combination of several models; and '*modèle donné ou à découvrir*', one which is presented in

---

[25] Regarding the generative properties of music, evolutionary biologist Richard Dawkins suggests that 'there are other kinds of things [besides DNA] which deserve the title of a replicator'. He uses the term 'meme' (1976) to refer to 'the brain equivalent of a gene ... Like the DNA that makes up our genes, memes can multiply, mutate and evolve, but unlike DNA they breed not in nature, but in culture, through human communication' (Wyver 1990:19–20). One of Dawkins' examples is the transmission of a song from person to person, in the process of which the song may evolve and change, and also be subject to natural selection (1976:194). For a detailed application of Dawkins' ideas to music, see Jan (2007).

performance, perhaps as the most basic of several parts in a piece, or else a model which can only be extracted analytically by comparing different versions of a piece (1987b:46–9). Lortat-Jacob's conflation of 'model' and 'framework' into '*modèle*' perhaps reflects slightly different terminological mappings in French (he also uses '*cadre*' in discussing the – particularly temporal – framework of a piece). One issue is terminology; another is the applicability of these categories to different traditions: as we will see, the *radif* doesn't fit any of these categories absolutely.

Whilst the terms 'model' and 'framework' are often used interchangeably in the literature, I would suggest a subtle and important distinction which may be helpful in the Iranian context. 'Model' would seem to imply an extant, exemplary version(s) of a piece which is learnt and subsequently becomes the basis for performance; 'framework', on the other hand, suggests a skeletal structure which is not in itself a 'piece', but elements of which are embedded within a piece: that is, core features essential to the piece's identity, but always learnt with some elaboration. Individual *gusheh*s can be thought of as the *model* for performance, but there is also a *framework* within each *gusheh* comprising its essential elements. In this sense, 'framework' corresponds most closely to Lortat-Jacob's fourth category, the 'model to be found' (1987b:48). However, unlike the explicitly recognized 'model' function of the *radif*, the more elusive framework is not generally acknowledged or discussed by musicians, but can be identified through analysis. Thus, musicians:

> … arrive at mastery of a particular *gushe* through generalizing possible configurations and combinations on the basis of the various teaching versions and performances of it … the underlying process of segmentation may receive verbal expression to the extent that phrases occupying particular areas are labeled (e.g. as *shoru'*, *khateme* or *tahrir*). Nevertheless, such terms are residues, markers of the already interiorized rather than classificatory aids to acquisition. (Wright 2009:41)

Nettl has written about the nature of models[26] for creative performance and the wide range of specificity, or 'density':

> In comparing various types of models, we find that those of jazz are relatively dense, those of Persian music, of medium density, and those of an Arabic *taqsim* or an Indian *alap*, relatively lacking in density. Figured bass, and Baroque music in which a soloist improvises ornamentation, are perhaps the densest models of all. (1974c:13)

He also discusses 'audibility', whether 'the model comprise[s] the material that is actually heard by the student or performer' (ibid.:15), and which is related (but not necessarily correlated) to density:

> In some systems it [the model] is actual music that may also be performed without improvisation, in some it is basic sound material that the musician learns but does not execute in a true performance, and in still others it is largely theoretical subject matter, consisting of verbal instructions and exercises. (ibid.:16)[27]

There is clearly considerable variation in the extent to which musicians discuss, and are even aware of, such models and Nettl has commented on the elusive nature of a central 'core' or framework in Iranian classical music:

> In contrast to jazz (in which a specific series of chords or a popular tune, either of which can be performed in isolation, is the basis of the improvisation), there is difficulty in isolating models upon which improvisation

---

[26]   Nettl's use of the term also covers the semantic field of 'framework' as discussed above. In later writings, he circumvents the terminological issues by using the broader and less problematic 'points of departure' (POD), see footnote 1.

[27]   Nettl cites Karnatic music as an example of this, where 'if we say that the PoD is "the raga", then we also ask in what manifestation a raga is internalized. It is these exercises, with their raga-specific melodic segments and the variations in emphasis provided by the juxtaposition to contrasting talas, that provide the initial individualization of a raga, followed by memorized alapanas from the teacher's store of knowledge. Eventually, when these simple exercises and didactic pieces have been mastered, the student learns Varnams, short metric pieces in which the main characteristics and requirements of a raga are synthesized' (2009:189).

is based. That models exist we must take for granted. But they seem … hardly to be accessible in audible form. (with Foltin 1972:12–13)

This may seem a curious observation for a tradition where a fairly well-defined body of material is held to be the basis for performance. Yet, as the analyses of Chapter 4 will show, performances include much material that is not part of the *radif* (although usually related to it in some way), and vice versa: the *radif* includes much material which is not heard in performance. To summarize: on one level of understanding, the *radif is* the explicit model for creative performance; but within it lies an implicit, more abstract skeletal framework, a core of essential material which can be found by comparing different versions and extracting common material, a method used by Farhat to identify what he calls the 'basic melodic formula' of a *gusheh* (1990:29). Moreover, since students are encouraged to learn several *radifs*, it seems likely that similar processes are at work as they 'internalize' the central features of a *gusheh*.

Radif *within a Broader 'Performance Model'*

Notwithstanding its central role, discussion with musicians and observations in the literature make clear that the *radif* is only a part of the information which musicians draw upon in performance. Having suggested that the *framework* for performance lies *within* each *gusheh*, it is equally possible to understand the *model* from which musicians work as being broader than the *radif*, in that their understanding of a *gusheh* is formed not only from the memorized repertoire, but from the many versions assimilated through years of listening and playing. As During observes: 'whatever is the nature of the model, most traditional improvisations extend the more or less conscious synthesis that the musician brings about from all the improvisations that he has heard' (1987b:34–5). At the time of performance, these interact with a musician's knowledge of the *radif*; and of course each performance situation presents its own dynamics. Discussing the latter with reference to *qawwali*, the music of Sufi gatherings in Pakistan and North India, Qureshi (1987) distinguishes between 'occasion': the norms of a particular situation (the *qawwali* assembly, for example), and 'event': a specific instance (a *qawwali* assembly at a particular time and place). In the case of Iran, aspects of occasion might include performance setting (recording session, formal concert, informal gathering), whilst aspects of event might include audience identity and mood, the performers' state of mind, the time of day, and the relationships between musicians. The effect of context, particularly on the subtle and intimate communication between musician(s) and audience, and often correlated with size and formality of performance venue, was discussed briefly in Chapter 2. Elsewhere I have suggested that a musician's prior knowledge and accumulated musical experiences (including those outside the classical tradition), both aural and motor, comprise a 'performance model' (Nooshin 1996:97), unique for each individual and operating in a complex relationship with their experience of each performance event and with the broader music culture. Not only do many of these change over time, they also interact with one another: for instance, changes in the musical culture directly affect the performance situation, but also impact indirectly through changes in musicians' informal listening, audience expectations and so on. Similarly, a musician may try out new ideas which, if successful, become incorporated into their performance model, even becoming idiosyncratic over time. Moreover, the way in which a performance proceeds depends on its course up to that point, and is influenced by aspects of occasion and event. In this way, each event has the potential to feed back into the continually-changing performance model, thereby affecting future performances.[28]

To the suggestion that listening and other experiences contribute to a performance model as described, Meshkatian responded:

---

[28]   See Berliner (1994, for example, pages 495–6) for similar observations regarding jazz. It seems that musicians in many traditions work from such a performance model, an individual and continually developing knowledge-base built up over many years. There are clear parallels between the idea of a performance model presented here and that of schema discussed in Chapter 4.

You wouldn't call this *radif*, but it plays an important role. Any musician who has listened to and learnt all the good moulds/models [*olgoo*] of Iranian music differs greatly from one who, however creative, has not listened to these. (20.7.92)

Amir Eslami and Hooshyar Khayam (current and former lecturers at the University of Art) take a broader view of what a performance model might include:

AE: The *radif* is a sound source [*manba'-e sowti*], like any sound source. Folk music can be your source, Mozart can be your source, Indian folk music can also be your source, or Hungarian folk music. If you want to improvise or compose, you need a sound source on the basis of which to express yourself [*bar asāsesh harf bezani*]. The two sources which are closest to our culture are Iranian folk music and the *radif*.

HK: Each of us has a collection of sonar objects: the *radif* is our sonar object; the performance practice of Hassan Kassai can also be our sonar object; the performance practice of Kurdish music is our sonar object; the music of Harrison Birtwistle .... (26.11.10)

During my research, in only two instances did I come across musicians referring to what might be thought of as a performance model as described here: Amir Eslami and Daruish Talai used the terms *manba'-e zehni* ('cognitive source') and *olgoo-ye zehni* ('cognitive model') respectively; the latter, Talai explains, comprises the '*gusheh*s and your relationship with them' (in Shahrnazdar 2004a:91; later in the same interview, however, he uses this term to refer simply to the *radif*). For Eslami, the model can be much broader, as indicated above.

The performance of Iranian classical music depends on many factors, from the all-pervasive general (music) culture to the specifics of each performance situation. Linked to all of these and at the heart of performance, I suggest, is the dynamic performance model, and the relatively stable underpinning repertoire of the *radif*. As During (1987b:38) observes, since audiences cannot access a performer's (internal) cognitive model, renditions are assessed against an 'ideal model', formed by hearing many versions of a piece.[29] Each performance experience consolidates and 'brings in its turn, its contribution in terms of building on and imperceptibly transforming the ideal model' (During 1987a:21). Thus, 'tradition' can be understood as a collective, ever-changing and cumulative process, to which each interpretation contributes. The specific 'tradition' of the *radif* appears to function both as an 'ideal' version of the repertoire, as a 'performance model' from which musicians work, and as a canonic repertoire transmitted from generation to generation.

Radif *as Model: Musicians' Discourses*

How, then, do musicians describe the ways in which the *radif* functions as a model or framework for performance? Much of the non-Persian language literature on Iranian classical music uses European terms with no mention of local terminology. As noted, whilst certain aspects of the music are readily discussed and have associated terminologies, others are rarely verbalized. In conversation, musicians willingly talked about the role of the *radif*, but mostly using non-musical terms. Meshkatian used the term *olgoo* to refer not just to the *radif*, but everything which forms part of the performance model as described above (20.7.92). *Olgoo* corresponds most closely to the English 'mould', 'model' or 'exemplar'. More general in meaning is *chāhārchoob*, used by several musicians including Payvar (8.12.90), Nazeri (23.4.10), and also by During (8.12.90), and which translates as 'framework' or 'structure'. Whilst *olgoo* was used to describe both the broad musical tradition and the specific repertoire of the *radif*, *chāhārchoob* most often referred just to the latter. Berenjian used *zirbanā* ('foundation', 10.11.89), which in a non-musical context usually refers to the foundations of a building; similar words used by others included *pāyeh* ('foundation', 'basis', Payvar, 8.11.90) and *asl* ('principle', Payvar, 8.11.90, Berenjian, 7.12.89). Another term, *qāleb*, was also used, as in the following from Safvate, 'the *radif* is truly a mine of forms and molds [*qāleb*] for music' (in During 1991b:215; quoted in Chapter 2). Eslami and Khayam described the *radif* as a *manba'* ('source') or 'sonar object'

---

[29]   As noted in Chapter 2, few lay listeners have detailed knowledge of the classical repertoire, but instead tend to focus on the sung poetry. During's comments therefore apply to audiences of musicians and informed listeners.

(in English, 26.11.10); and Alizadeh uses the term *johar* ('essence') to indicate musicians' broad musical knowledge, also likening the *radif* to an alphabet or set of tools:

> Anyone who wants to create must be linked to the roots [of the music]. They should know the true essence [*johar*] of Iranian music and its *radif*s, as an alphabet, as tools. But after this period, the artist faces the question of what to do with these tools ... Art should have its roots in the past and a view towards the future. (in Sarkoohi 1989:35, 36)

Some musicians were particularly eloquent when describing the role of the *radif*, often using striking metaphors to make their points. Cited in Chapter 2, the following from Nazeri is worth quoting again; here, the *radif* is both 'basis', 'foundation', 'mould' and 'light':

> In reality, the *radif*s came about so that a musician could place their foot on a firm basis [*bastar*] from which to fly. Like an architect who wants to construct a building needs a firm foundation [*pāyeh*] ... it's a mould [*qāleb*] for learning and for moving in the right direction; like a light that guides you ... so you can be free to express things. Someone who isn't standing on a firm foundation but on loose or shaky ground, they can't fly. They can't travel in a proper and exact way, or with precise vision. (23.4.10)

Terms such as those given above were used to describe the general role of the *radif* and broader musical influences; however, the more abstract skeletal 'framework' (the embedded core of common material) of each *gusheh* is rarely discussed. Whilst the absence of discussion (itself perhaps a result of and in turn perpetuating the dearth of terminology) might suggest that this level of conceptualization is not significant, the existence of teaching *radif*s at varying levels of difficulty (with essential elements maintained, see below) strongly indicates that such conceptualization is indeed at work, even if not verbally articulated.

The *radif* is central to creative practice in Iranian classical music: it is both a model for performance and contains within it an abstract 'framework' comprising the essential elements of each *gusheh*. At the same time, the *radif* can be understood as part of a broader performance model. Since the latter is individual for each musician (and largely subliminal), the relationship between a specific performance and the model on which it is based is somewhat elusive. A central focus of this study is therefore to understand how musicians use their cognitive and spatio-motor knowledge to generate performances which are both unique and which also lie within the bounds of acceptable variation.

Teaching and Learning Processes in Iranian Classical Music

Teaching and learning processes can reveal a great deal about the relationship between the *radif* and creative performance, and how musicians progress from one to the other. Such processes are fairly well documented in the literature: Caron and Safvate (1966) and During (1984a) each devote a chapter, and the monograph by Nettl with Foltin (1972) a whole section to this topic while other publications mention it briefly (Lotfi 1976, Sadeghi 1971, Nettl 1983, 1987, Nooshin 1996:103–31). The following discussion is based on the literature and talking to musicians, as well as observation (and historical recordings) of teaching sessions. Processes of musical transmission have inevitably been affected by the rapid social, political and cultural changes described in Chapter 2; those which are particularly relevant here include the institutionalization of music education and the accompanying rise in musicians' social status, the introduction of notation, and the arrival of sound recording. These will each be considered below.

Teaching Contexts

Prior to the twentieth century, Iranian classical music was generally taught in the privacy of a master's home. This was consistent with an Islamic society in which attitudes to music are highly ambivalent; much music-making, including teaching, was a private affair, and learning to sing or play an instrument entailed becoming accepted into the *maktab* ('school') of a master. In 1868, Frenchman Alfred Jean Baptiste Lemaire (1842–1909) arrived in Iran, having been appointed by Nasereddin Shah to take charge of military music activities. Lemaire instituted a series of classes at the Dārolfonun school in Tehran, including instruction in both theory and instrumental practice. This was the first form of institutionalized music education in Iran. In 1918, the first music school, Madreseh-ye Musik, was opened by the Ministry of Education (Vezārat-e Maāref). Ali Naqi Vaziri (1887–1979) became the principal in 1928, and the name was changed to Madreseh-ye Musiqi-ye Dowlati (Government Music School). An army colonel who had received musical training in France and Germany, Vaziri is generally regarded as the great modernizer of Iranian music (see Zonis 1973:187). At his school, pupils of secondary school age studied the usual curriculum of subjects in addition to learning Iranian music and Western music theory: '"solfège" and notation, *tār*, violin and piano were taught there' (During 1984a:29). In 1938, the school became the Honarestān-e Āli-ye Musiqi.

Initially, both Iranian and Western music were taught at the Honarestān, but in the 1940s these strands were separated into different institutions. The founding in 1945 of the Anjoman-e Doostdārān-e Musiqi-ye Melli (Society for National Music) by Ruhollah Khaleqi (1906–1965) was an important step towards the eventual establishment of the Honarestān-e Melli-ye Musiqi (National Music Conservatory) in 1949, which specialized in Iranian classical music (together with Western theory and notation) and which remained the main teaching institution for Iranian music until the 1960s (after 1949, the Honarestān-e Āli-ye Musiqi focused exclusively on Western music). Khaleqi became the first principal, and many of those who taught there in the 1950s and '60s were former pupils of Vaziri, including Khaleqi himself (*setār*), Ali Akbar Shahnazi (1898–1985, *tār*), Mehdi Mefta (1910–1996, violin), Abol Hassan Saba (violin, *setār* and *santur*), Hossein Ali Mallah (1921–1992, violin), Musa Ma'rufi (1889–1965, *tār*) and his son Javad Ma'rufi (1912–1993, piano). By the 1960s, the Honarestān had expanded, and many of the teachers also recorded regularly for radio. However, it still only catered for secondary school pupils, after which students continued their studies privately.[30]

It was not until the mid-1960s that higher musical studies became available, initially within the Fine Arts Faculty at the University of Tehran, followed in 1969 by the formal establishment of the Music Department. Now it was possible to study at degree level, specializing in either Western or Iranian music. Those wishing to train as a classical musician in the 1970s would typically start learning an instrument or voice at an early age, either privately or at the Honarestān-e Melli; many subsequently entered university where they would study with a series of masters teaching *radif* and, for instrumentalists, the art of accompanying a singer (*javāb āvāz*) in addition to subjects such as harmony, counterpoint and music history. In the early 1970s, masters such as Nur Ali Borumand (*tār*), Ali Akbar Shahnazi, Mahmud Karimi (1927–1984, voice), Asghar Bahari (*kamāncheh*) and Dariouche Safvate (*setār*) taught at the university, followed in the late 1970s by some of their pupils, including Mohammad Reza Shajarian (b.1940, voice), Mohammad Reza Lotfi (1947–2014, *tār*) and Hossein Alizadeh (*tār* and *setār*).

In 1970, the Markaz-e Hefz-o Eshāeh-ye Musiqi-ye Irāni was opened under the auspices of the National Iranian Radio and Television organization with the support of its director, Reza Ghotbi.[31] The aim was to gather together musicians not involved with the radio (and therefore not generally known to the public) to create a centre of research and teaching in order to preserve the tradition of Iranian classical music. Safvate was the founder and director until 1980, and in the early years masters such as Borumand, Said Hormozi (1897–1976, *tār*), Yusef Forutan (1891–1978, *tār*), Bahari, Abdollah Davami (1891–1980, voice), and Karimi taught there. Younger musicians were invited to study, carry out research, and later to teach there, including Lotfi, Alizadeh, Meshkatian (1955–2009, *santur*), Kiani (b.1941, *santur*), Talai (b.1953, *tār* and *setār*), Jalal Zolfonoun (b.1937, *tār* and *setār*) and Parisa (b.1950, female voice), many of whom were talented students at the university (Zolfonoun was a lecturer). Students at the Markaz were also given funding to allow them to focus on their studies (Talai in Shahrnazdar 2004a:19). As well as teaching activities, the centre housed an archive, rehearsal and recording facilities, and an instrument-making section. Simms describes the establishment of the Markaz as 'a serious government intervention and commitment to the tradition of Persian music while continuing its policies of modernization' (Simms and Koushkani 2012a:133), and it served as

---

[30] Behroozi (1988:529–59) gives a detailed history of the main music education institutions in Tehran, and much of the information above is based on this; see also Darvishi (1995:29–49), Zonis (1973:186–93) and During (1984a:29–30).

[31] Sources give different dates for the establishment of the Markaz, but the most likely is the autumn of 1349 (1970).

a meeting place for those interested in preserving the traditional music, as well as giving young musicians access to some of the most knowledgeable older musicians, many of whom would not normally have agreed to teach at a public institution. With the focus on tradition, those teaching at the Markaz generally eschewed the use of notation.[32]

After the 1979 Revolution, the situation changed somewhat as musicians came under pressure in the new Islamic state, particularly during the Iran-Iraq war (1980–88) when public music-making was severely curtailed. However, with the Revolution also came a 'return to roots' interest in traditional music (mentioned briefly in Chapter 2), and a dramatic rise in demand by aspiring amateur musicians.[33] Payvar reported a significant increase in students learning *santur* with him after 1979 (8.11.90), and 10 years after the Revolution Alizadeh also noted the growing interest in Iranian music, particularly among young people (in Sarkoohi 1989:33). Nazeri recalled the heady days of the early 1980s:

> Even religious families started listening to the radio and television; cassettes came, tape recorders came. Many families sent their sons and daughters to music lessons. For example, there was a cassette called *Gol-e Sad Barg* published in 1363 [1984; a recording by Nazeri]. When it was published, believe me there was a revolution in *setār*, such a story [*yek dāstāni shod*], in the space of 8 or 9 months, I'm not saying 1 million people, but something around this number came to participate in classes, girls and boys. (21.8.99)[34]

The Music Department at Tehran University was closed shortly after the Revolution, but re-opened in 1990, and since then several other music departments have been established. At the time of writing, four institutions in Tehran offer music degrees (Tehran University, Dāneshgāh-e Azād, Dāneshgāh-e Sooreh and Dāneshgāh-e Honar, the last located in the city of Karaj, 12 miles west of Tehran); further afield, music can be studied at university only in Shiraz and the northern city of Rasht. After a period of closure, the Markaz was re-opened as Markaz-e Hefz o Pajoohesh-e Musiqi-ye Irāni (Centre for the Preservation of and Research on Iranian Music; Kiani 2004:155), and since 2000 Majid Kiani has served as director. Over the last 20 years or so there has been a proliferation of private music schools, both in Tehran and the provinces, and lessons are also offered in the cultural centres (*farhangsarā*) which were established across Tehran in the late 1990s. However, whilst private tuition and lessons in techniques such as those of Carl Orff are well established, music education in its broader sense is not part of the school curriculum and is unlikely to be for some time due to social and religious sensitivities.

Although music education has tended to be centralized in Tehran, there are teaching institutions in other cities. As far back as 1927, Saba was asked to head a newly-established branch of the Madreseh-ye Musik in Rasht, and this later changed name in line with its sister school in Tehran. More recently, in the early 1980s, During reported that a number of private music schools were operating in the provinces (1984a:30). Since then, the number has mushroomed; visiting one such school in Esfahan in 2008, I was told that there were approximately 40 across the city. Beyond private lessons, however, it is difficult to gain a formal advanced musical training outside the capital.

An interesting feature of the training system, discussed below, is that students generally learn with more than one teacher (but not usually at the same time) in order to enrich their knowledge of the repertoire. Elsewhere I have presented a teaching genealogy for the Tehran tradition from Farahani and his sons to the early 1990s, showing the closely-knit complex of musical transmission (Nooshin 1996:126; see also

---

[32]   See Talai (in Shahrnazdar 2004a:18–20), Kiani (2004), Miller (1999:37–56) and Simms and Koushkani (2012a:127, 133) for further information on the history and activities of the Markaz.

[33]   For discussion of the impact of the 1979 Iranian Revolution on music and musicians in the early 1980s see During (1984b), Nooshin (2005a:235–45) and Simms and Koushkani (2012b). It should be noted that despite important developments since 1979, the most significant aspects considered here are largely rooted in changes which began much earlier, in the mid-nineteenth century, and have continued to the present day.

[34]   Simms also notes the importance of this album, 'often described as the biggest selling cassette of Persian music and "Sufi music" in history', and briefly mentions other innovative aspects of Nazeri's work in the 1980s (Simms and Koushkani 2012b:25).

Nettl 1987:185).[35] A distinction is often made among older musicians between students of Mirza Abdollah and those of Hossein Qoli; in fact, both were taught by Qolam Hossein, and moreover Mirza Abdollah was Hossein Qoli's first teacher. Several prominent figures of the first half of the twentieth century, including Darvish Khan and his pupil Abol Hassan Saba, inherited from both 'strands', and, moreover, both of these musicians had many pupils through whom they transmitted their own syntheses of the *radif*s of Mirza Abdollah and Hossein Qoli. According to During, since Darvish Khan was obliged to teach as a living, he found ways of arranging and simplifying the material to keep his pupils interested (1984a:127). The gulf between amateur and professional is clear here, the implication being that an amateur would not have been compelled to make such changes. As will be discussed, the recent history of Iranian classical music has been marked by a tension between what might be called the 'purist' approach and those who followed the 'modernizing' ideas of Vaziri. By the early 1970s, there were two main currents, also reflected in the different approaches of the Honarestān-e Melli on the one hand, and the University of Tehran and the Markaz on the other. Many of those teaching at the Honarestān were associated with the radio, and were regarded as somewhat acculturated by 'authenticist' musicians (see During 1984a:25 and Kiani 2004:152).

As noted, Nur Ali Borumand played a particularly important role in teaching the *radif* of Mirza Abdollah at the University of Tehran and the Markaz from the mid-1960s to the early 1970s, and after that privately. Although little known among the general public, he was highly regarded as a teacher because of his detailed knowledge of the repertoire. Borumand was raised in an aristocratic household frequented by musicians, and received his first lessons on *tār* from Darvish Khan at the age of seven. When he was 16, he travelled to Germany to study and whilst there took piano lessons. Borumand continued his musical studies during his time in medical school, but after losing his sight returned to Iran and devoted himself to Iranian music (Nettl 1987:142–5). However, it was not until much later that he started teaching *radif*. Many prominent musicians born after c.1940, including Shajarian, Lotfi, Alizadeh, Meshkatian and Jamshid Andalibi, studied with Borumand at some point. Borumand is highly respected among this generation and his influence can be discerned both in their performances and teaching methods; moreover, Borumand has also influenced the work of Nettl and During, both of whom studied with him and who have interpreted his ideas in rather different ways.[36] I will return to Borumand below.

Since the early twentieth century, then, formal institutions have operated alongside more informal environments. Many masters continued to teach at home, whilst also becoming attached to one or more state or private institutions. It is difficult to determine exactly how this affected teaching processes. From a situation in the early twentieth century when this music was heard and taught within quite restricted circles, increased availability and social acceptance of music education in the public domain, partly attributable to the respectability afforded by institutionalization (and westernization), led to improved social status for musicians and eventually music as a graduate profession. As noted, many contemporary performers are music graduates, something which has afforded them a broader outlook and awareness of different kinds of music, a significant shift compared with even 50 years ago.

Teaching Methods

So much for the contexts of teaching; I now move on to discuss teaching methods. Whilst some of those described by Caron and Safvate (1966), Nettl with Foltin (1972) and During (1984a) are no longer used, it is useful to compare them with current practice and consider what has changed and why. Before the twentieth century, Iranian classical music was taught entirely by rote: the *radif* was learnt *gusheh* by *gusheh* and in the early stages pupils were required to imitate their master and memorize his *radif* precisely, almost in the manner of a pre-composed text.

According to Borumand (Nettl with Foltin 1972:19), individual teaching was more usual than group teaching during his youth. Shahnazi, master of *tār* at the Honarestān-e Melli, reportedly used an interesting

---

[35]   This contrasts with the clear lines of transmission evident in Hindustani music, as shown by Kippen for three *gharānā*s of *tablā* playing (1988b:68, 70, 72).

[36]   See also Nettl (1974b, 2005:179–81) and Sarami (1990) for further discussion of Borumand's life and works.

method by which a student would have an individual lesson, during which they would learn a phrase. They would then practise the phrase, either alone or with the help of a fellow student or one of Shahnazi's assistants, whilst Shahnazi saw another student.[37] They might notate it or even record themselves playing; after about 20 minutes, the student would return to Shahnazi, who would hear them and correct any mistakes. At the following lesson, the phrase would be reviewed briefly before proceeding to the next (During 1984a:31). During also describes a common technique, used by Borumand, whereby a master teaches a phrase to a small group who respond communally; the master corrects the students as necessary, after which they each play individually.[38] Karimi also used this method, but required students to sing in turn at the start rather than together. In the case of Borumand, the fact that groups comprised students playing different instruments underscores the role of the teacher as a transmitter of musical repertoire, rather than an instrumental specialist. Moreover, whilst Borumand and Karimi both corrected pupils who played or sang material incorrectly, neither appeared to comment a great deal on the *manner* of students' renditions, nor on aspects of technique. Meshkatian also discussed this method (20.7.92), and in April 2010 the author observed *ostād* Mohammad Reza Lotfi using it in his Āvā-ye Sheydā Music School in Tehran with a group of about 20 fairly advanced students, young men and women mainly in their 20s, playing various struck and plucked stringed instruments. Given that both Meshkatian and Lotfi studied with Borumand, it is clear that they chose to continue employing practices through which they themselves learnt. During suggests that whilst such methods work well with small groups, the main disadvantage is that reduced individual contact makes it difficult for a pupil absorb their masters' style (ibid.:32). A significant advantage of group teaching, however, are the opportunities to experience different variants of the same phrase as played by fellow pupils: through hearing which are corrected by the teacher and which allowed, students internalize the rules and boundaries of the permissible.[39] Khatschi describes a slightly different method of group teaching:

> One method is for the teacher to give each of a group of pupils a particular bit of music to memorize (by playing it without the use of written music), and then to require them to teach these sections to each other. (1962:33, in Nettl with Foltin 1972:19)

Significantly, the methods described all combine elements of group and individual teaching and learning: the individual classes of Shahnazi incorporated group work, whilst the various group methods also include some 'one-to-one' teaching. It seems that both are important: the former to learn the rules of variation, the latter to absorb aspects of style. And since musicians generally study with more than one teacher, they also come to an understanding of both the subtle differences between versions of the *radif* and the shared features (During 1984a:126, Nettl with Foltin 1972:19).

The *radif* is often said to be taught at three levels of difficulty: *radif-e moqaddamāti* (or *radif-e ebtedāi*, 'elementary *radif*'), *radif-e motevasset* ('intermediate *radif*'), and *radif-e āli* ('higher *radif*') (Meshkatian, 20.7.92). This final stage corresponds with that generally found in published *radif*s such as those of Borumand and Ma'rufi. For the elementary *radif*, Meshkatian explained that teachers may simplify material, often teaching only the central *gusheh*s, or use a simpler published *radif* such as that of Saba. During also describes how *radif*s were previously simplified for beginners 'in a very interesting way, whilst

---

[37]   Teaching assistants were apparently quite common in earlier practices. As Nettl reports, 'Descriptions of teaching traditions (During 1991, 244–46; Khatschi 1962, 3–35) indicate an approach in which a master teaches certain select students whose task is to pass on material to a larger group. Whilst these intermediaries (Safvat uses the term *khalife*) appear to be on the one hand superior students, they are, on the other (During 1991, 245), described as musicians who are uncreative and can thus be relied on to pass material along unchanged' (2009:194–5).

[38]   Lessons given by Borumand at the University of Tehran (15.10.1968) and by Karimi at the Honarestān-e Melli (2.1.1969), recorded by Bruno Nettl. I am very grateful to Professor Nettl for generously making these recordings available to me.

[39]   Blacking used a similar technique in order to elicit the rules of variation in Venda music: 'On some occasions I made deliberate mistakes, and was therefore especially interested if I was not corrected: this would mean that I had sung an alternative melody which, though not that which my teacher knew, was perfectly acceptable according to the canons of Venda music' (1967:33).

maintaining the essential inflections and plectrum strokes' (1984a:30). Similarly, Nettl reports Borumand's view that 'the proper way to learn the radif was in three stages – simple, intermediate, and complete; the simple version would contain everything of essence, and the others would be elaborations of the simple version' (2009:194). The fact that a *gusheh* can be simplified yet still retain an essential core of material (the 'essence') suggests that musicians do indeed conceptualize an underlying 'framework' even if not explicitly discussed. The existence of *radif*s at different levels of difficulty adds a further dimension to the relationship between the 'one' *radif* and multiplicity of *radif*s discussed earlier. Caron and Safvate also describe a three-stage process, but differing somewhat from that above, the final stage being the discipline of accompanying a singer (1966:191–3).

Learning to Improvise

An interesting aspect of the Iranian classical system is that masters rarely discuss details of variation, interpretation or improvisation which eventually become central to their pupils' performances: they are ostensibly concerned solely with transmitting a body of repertoire. Not only is there little technical vocabulary with which aspects of improvisation might be discussed; there is also a sense in which this is incompatible with the spirit of the music. There is even doubt as to whether improvisation can be taught. Meshkatian suggested that improvisation is not a 'transferable' skill ('*enteqāli nist*', 20.7.92) and, as described in Chapter 2, Payvar maintained that the ability to improvise is a god-given ('*khodādādi*') gift (8.11.90). Notwithstanding recent changes discussed below, one might reasonably ask how students learn to improvise, given the dearth of verbal explanation. It is clear from the earlier discussion that many teaching methods allow students to experience and play different permutations of the same material. Not only is it standard practice to memorize more than one *radif*, a master will often teach different versions of the same *gusheh*. Indeed, many *dastgāhs* include more than one *darāmad* (opening) section and Nettl suggests that these are intended to demonstrate 'options, of teaching improvisation, as it were, by showing that the same materials can be presented in different arrangements' (1987:97). Thus, 'a teacher can transmit the concept of individual variation or improvisation while retaining also the idea of adherence to stylistic orthodoxy' (Nettl with Foltin 1972:20). This 'demonstrating options' can also take the form of more subtle changes which a teacher may introduce into their playing. Clearly, experiencing variation is important for learning to improvise, and it is therefore significant that the teaching methods of Iranian classical music provides many such opportunities. Similar techniques are found elsewhere, as described for example by Rasmussen for the training of Quranic reciters in Indonesia where her teacher, Maria Ulfah:

> ... develops her students' expertise by offering them several versions of the variation or, alternatively, by repeating, with astonishing precision, long, intricately embroidered phrases that they are then expected to repeat perfectly in collective memesis. Once her students can do the same on their own – but without precisely imitating her example – the intervallic shapes, phrasing, and ornamentation of *Zanjaran* will be added to their musical bag of tricks ... By practicing musical ideas until they become 'natural', students have some hope of letting divine inspiration take over at the moment of performance ... (2009:77)

Zadeh also reports on similar teaching strategies for the North Indian vocal style of *thumrī*:

> In my lessons, she [the teacher] would sometimes demonstrate numerous ways of varying and ornamenting the compositions she taught me, singing different versions, one after another. This would normally continue for a few minutes, in an extended show of inventiveness and creativity. Sharma would then instruct me to listen to my recordings of my lessons, choose some five or six versions of the composition from the many that she had sung and memorize them, so as to be able to use them in my own performance. (2012:39)

As noted, there are no essential structural differences between the set repertoire of the *radif* and the performances based on it, and this partly explains how information is transmitted to pupils with relatively little discussion: in memorizing the *radif*, pupils learn fundamental principles and rules of variation embedded within the repertoire, comprising a basic 'tool kit' (Rasmussen's 'bag of tricks') for creative performance.

For instance, both *radif* and performances make 'use of repetition, sequence, development of a motif, and division into sections each based on a short motif' (Nettl 1972:176). Simms also notes that 'Like so much else in this tradition, the process of learning how to do this [improvise melismatic *tahrir* phrases] is implicitly contained in the study of the radif through inductively assimilating materials, idioms, and stylistic parameters that are subsequently creatively rearranged and varied' (Simms and Koushkani 2012a:247) and Talai concurs: 'The *radif* contains within it all that one needs to know in order to improvise' (personal communication, May 1986). In other words, musicians seem to learn the 'rules' of musical re-recreation in much the same way that children learn spoken language, through extended exposure and without conscious attention to grammatical rules; and the role of the *ostād* is not to teach improvisation as such, but to transmit material through which (together with other musical experiences) students eventually learn to improvise. In the words of Borumand, 'We do not teach improvisation. You learn the radif, and it teaches you to improvise' (in Nettl 2009:185). The discourses thus accord the *radif* a curious agency in relation to its own regeneration and embodiment of important aspects of the music: 'The *radif* with its own special order [*nazm*] guides the pupil towards techniques which are related to the culture of Iranian music' (Alizadeh in Shahrnazdar 2004b:33). It is the *radif* which is the active agent. Extending this, Khayam uses an organic analogy, suggesting that the music 'grows' (*rosht*) from previous musical expressions, reminiscent of the earlier discussion regarding music's generative properties.

It is generally accepted that only after many years of study is a pupil ready to start improvising. Nettl and Foltin describe a gradual move towards improvised performance in which, 'the student has the opportunity of departing very gradually from the teaching version, at first perhaps doing little beyond adding ornaments, repetitions, and brief extensions, later striking out more on his own' (1972:20). If students do indeed learn to improvise largely through memorizing the *radif*, this would explain why they were previously discouraged from improvising before they were fully immersed in the tradition. Moreover, since anyone who studies the music long enough will eventually acquire the knowledge necessary to improvise, verbal explanation is also redundant:

> Djamchid Chemirani talked very little in the class. At times, he would remind us about some necessary points, but, generally, he tried to make it possible for the student to grasp things directly by himself, through his own mind and feelings. (Mirabdolbaghi, in During 1991b:212)

In other words, once the *radif* has been played for many years it becomes cognitively and physically embedded such that it inevitably informs all performance, a view corroborated by other musicians. Meshkatian suggested that the educational value of the *radif* lies as much in the processes of learning as in the material itself (20.7.92) and Talai describes reaching a point 'known as internalization':[40]

> At this level of achievement, the performer thoroughly appreciates the principles of the radif, and although he might forget the details, the concepts nevertheless remain embedded in his mind ... Based upon what is remembered of the *radif*, he is now able to rearrange and reproduce the phrases in a new way. This happens without thinking or even being aware of what is happening. (2000:1)

An emphasis on contemplation is an important part of the discourse; Nettl relates how Borumand required him to play the *radif*:

> ... frequently, to look at it from all sides, listen to it, examine it, contemplate it. Perhaps contemplation acts as a stimulus for students to learn to understand the way the structure of the *radif* teaches the techniques and concepts of improvisation. (Nettl 1983:328)

Whilst the majority of writings on Iranian classical music focus on the tradition in Tehran, during his research Nettl had the opportunity to compare performances by Tehran-based musicians with those of self-taught

---

[40]   Talai doesn't give the Persian term for this 'internalization'. Further, like many musicians and commentators, he describes the process primarily in cognitive terms, rather than as an embodied experience.

musicians from the northeastern province of Khorasan. Despite the difficulty of learning the *radif* solely from published notations and recordings, Nettl and Foltin found that the performances of these musicians were:

> ... usually shorter and less impressive than those of more formally schooled musicians ... [but] one cannot maintain that they differ, as a group, from the others in the techniques of improvisation and the details of performance practice. (1972:20)

This is of interest in view of the idea that the repertoire embodies the rules for its own renewal. For the Khorasani musicians, the published materials functioned in a similar way to the memorized repertoire of 'schooled' musicians. Of course, students learn much more than just musical material from teachers, including appropriate gestures and body movements and often a certain philosophy and attitude to life, an approach to teaching sometimes described as *akhlāqi* ('moral').[41] During claims that performances by musicians who have learnt from recordings and scores are 'deprived of gesture' (1984a:34), although clearly physical aspects can also be learnt through observing other performers. Ultimately, it is usually necessary to study with a master in order to be accepted into the tradition, training pedigree often being important in a musician's standing.[42]

To summarize this section: on the one hand, there is a canonic repertoire within which re-creative potential is embedded; on the other, teaching methods which enable students to understand that potential: a formalized system of imitation and memorization which facilitates experiencing different versions of the repertoire and different permutations of phrases; and all with a minimum of verbal rationalization.

Notation and Sound Recording in the Teaching Context

Alongside the establishment of educational institutions, and with it professionalization and the associated rise in musicians' social status, it is arguably the introduction of notation and sound recording that have impacted most profoundly on the teaching and learning of Iranian music since the early twentieth century. Before this, the music was transmitted orally, *sineh be sineh* ('chest to chest'). 'Western' staff notation has been known in Iran since at least the mid-nineteenth century with the arrival of European musicians such as Lemaire, but was not generally used in the classical tradition before 1913, the date of Vaziri's first publication. Although most classical musicians today (except the very oldest) can read music, notation is less prevalent than might be expected given the generally high standing of musical literacy in Iran. There is a paradox here: while notation has been denigrated by some as inappropriate to the tradition, within the broader culture, notation – through association with Western music – is generally considered to be *elmi* ('scientific') and thereby accorded a certain prestige. Kiani describes how in the early 1970s, older masters who weren't musically literate were excluded from teaching at the recently established Music Department at Tehran University (even though they were teaching at the Markaz), which sought to prove its modernizing credentials.[43] Until the late 1970s, published notations were relatively few, mainly *radif*s and teaching manuals (some including material from the *radif*, for example, Vaziri 1913, 1933, 1936, Payvar 1961); since the late 1980s, however, there has been a significant increase, including various *radif*s, teaching manuals, collections of compositions for Iranian instruments and so on.[44] In addition, students often make notations during or after class to help them practise. The *radif* is difficult to memorize, with many minute details and repetitions to be learnt precisely, and although

---

[41]   In an observed lesson (April 2010), Lotfi regularly interspersed his teaching with philosophical reminiscences, poetry, anecdotes and general commentary on life. Similarly, Nettl suggests that 'the radif teaches the musician on three levels: techniques, general principles of music, and general principles of social life' (2009:195).

[42]   This contrasts with the case of Afghanistan, where amateur musicians 'were proud to be self-taught, perhaps precisely because training in music was associated with being a hereditary [and hence professional] musician' (Baily 1988:118).

[43]   Neuman reports on similar attitudes in India, citing the work of Indian musicologist V.N. Bhatkhande, writing in 1916: 'Our old Sanskrit Granthas ... having thus become inapplicable to the current practice, we naturally have come to be thrown on the mercy of our illiterate, ignorant, and narrow-minded professionals' (2012:427).

[44]   These almost exclusively use five-line staff notation, although new notations have been developed for certain percussion instruments such as *tombak* (goblet drum) and *daf* (frame drum).

some claim that the discipline of memorizing without notation is valuable, many pupils and even teachers now use both notation and sound recording.

The introduction of notation into teaching has not been uncontested, partly because of the perceived incompatibility between the speed of learning that it facilitates and the years of study considered necessary to attain the required immersion.[45] Moreover, some in the late 1960s believed that notation 'violated fundamental values, variability and personal interpretation, that are the basis of the repertory' (Nettl 1987:119), and although teaching manuals are used in the classroom, the *radif* itself is rarely taught from notation. Acknowledging musical literacy to be a useful skill for all musicians, Meshkatian explained that he always taught the *radif* by rote,[46] and During expresses a widely held view that 'the *radif* can only be transmitted directly "from chest to chest" (*sine be sine*) in which imitation plays an essential role' (1984a:31), perhaps because notation tends to privilege visual over aural and tactile memories. In discussing his teacher's methods, *tombak* player Zia Mirabdolbaghi recalls:

> One day a student, before leaving the classroom and unaware of being watched by the teacher, began to jot down something on a pad of paper. Djamchid Chemirani walked over to him quickly, asked him to hand over the pad, and added with a smile: 'It's better to forget than to write down!' This, of course, made the students' task more difficult, but it produced much finer results. They simply had to exercise their memories! (in During 1991b:212)

Nettl presents a contrasting view:

> ... some older individuals – were of the opinion that notation was extremely useful, that its introduction was one of the best things that had happened to Persian music in many centuries, and that indeed the survival of Persian music depended on it. (1987:119)

Similarly, Payvar believed that notation makes teaching and learning more efficient and rejected the idea that it adversely affects pupils' memorizing skills. However, whilst he allowed pupils to use notation for practising, in class they were expected to work from memory (8.11.90). The increasing use of published *radif*s and notations in teaching may partly explain changing attitudes, from the acceptance of many related versions to the idea of the one definitive *radif*.[47] However, whilst notation has found a place in teaching, albeit controversial at times, it is largely redundant in performance given the level of performer freedom, and rarely used. Even pre-composed (non-improvised, usually ensemble) pieces such as *pishdarāmad*, *tasnif* and *reng*, tend to be played from memory.

Alongside notation, the cumulative effect of an expanding mass media (especially radio), recording technology, and the emergence of public concerts from the early twentieth century, facilitated access to a great variety and quantity of music. Sound recording, and particularly from the 1960s the relatively cheap medium of magnetic tape, enabled students to experience many different performances,[48] to use recording as a memory aid and eventually to record themselves playing. According to Parisa, Karimi gave students recorded sections of the *radif* to help them practise between lessons (1985:80). I also observed that in the lessons of female

---

[45]   It is worth observing that notation renders students less dependent on teachers' willingness to share their knowledge, something which gave the latter immense power in the past. Weidman similarly notes that Karnatic music in the late nineteenth century was marked by intense secrecy and competition between teachers, from which notation had the potential to 'effect a liberation' (2006:212).

[46]   However, he added that once students have learnt two or three *dastgāh*s by rote, they will have gained the necessary knowledge to learn other *dastgāh*s correctly from notation. Currently, students at the University of Tehran learn two or three *dastgāh*s over the four years of their degree; at the University of Art students are expected to study all 12 *dastgāh*s (Amir Eslami, 26.11.10).

[47]   The introduction of notation has similarly impacted on concepts of variability in other traditions. El-Shawan (1987:156), for example, considers the effects of notation use on improvisation in Egypt.

[48]   Wright describes how singer Touraj Kiaras supplemented formal lessons with informal exposure, 'largely through listening to gramophone records, a solitary experience of a medium paradoxically both permissive and authoritarian' (2009:1). For further discussion of the role of notation and sound recording in the teaching and learning of Iranian classical music, see During (1984a:32–4).

singer Mahsa Vahdat (April 2010), the first thing that students did on arrival was to turn on their recording devices and place them on the table around which members of the class were gathered. Certainly, it seems common today for pupils to record lessons, with the knowledge and often encouragement of teachers. Like notation, sound recording also has the potential to impact on concepts of variability: to repeatedly hear the same rendition of a piece would have been inconceivable before the early twentieth century. Moreover, the potential range of students' musical experiences has expanded vastly, with implications for creative practice, as discussed in Chapter 2.

Recent Developments in Teaching

Despite the profound changes which have impacted on Iranian classical music over the past century, the methods of teaching and learning appear not to have changed substantially. Notwithstanding the drive towards modernization and increased rationalization in some areas, the repertoire is still taught – by and large – with a minimum of explanation, with rote imitation and memorization remaining central. Indeed, among the differences between the teaching methods described above, certain patterns emerge, suggesting that oral-aural, non-verbalized teaching, involving repeated exposure to musical variation, is ideally suited to the transmission of a music where internalized structures and processes eventually become the foundation for creative performance. This in turn points to an integral relationship between a musical tradition and the methods by which it is transmitted.

Since the 1980s, however, some teachers have started to include more explanation, including discussing techniques of improvisation with pupils. Hossein Alizadeh, well known for his work as an improviser and spokesperson and advocate for music education in Iran, was one of the first to do so, using analytical methods to explain structural details and to show how material can be extended in performance.[49] In 1992, he produced a set of cassettes comprising his rendition of the *radif* of Mirza Abdollah (essentially in the form taught and recorded by Borumand), and which includes at the end of each *dastgāh* analytical discussion comparing opening and cadential (*forud*) phrases, as well as other motifs and patterns shared by the various *gusheh*s of each *dastgāh*. For example, the *radif* of *Segāh* is followed by a section in which Alizadeh plays the similar openings of *gusheh*s *zābol*, *muyeh* and *bastenegār*, explicitly demonstrating a relationship which would traditionally have been inferred through listening and playing.[50] These recordings are of great interest, suggesting a nascent analytical awareness in teaching practices. To the extent that Alizadeh's method is to play short fragments in order to highlight points of comparison, it represents a continuation of traditional methods; moreover, there is no attempt to offer students detailed analysis. Where it departs fairly radically from tradition is that relationships between *gusheh*s, particularly shared motifs and patterns, are explicitly presented. There is also a section in which *gusheh*s in different *dastgāh*s are presented comparatively (some in abbreviated form), although with minimal verbal explanation.

Talking almost 15 years after the publication of these cassettes, Alizadeh explained his views on music education and training:

> Look, there was a time when the method of oral training had reached a point of simply repeating. I mean, the
> *ostād* repeated something a thousand times, and that with a scowl as if to say 'don't ask me any questions!',
> the pupil was obliged to repeat![51] In this situation, much time was lost and there was no time for the pupil

---

[49]   Alizadeh has been actively involved in various types of music training, including within higher education and as a composer of music for children, as well as adapting the methods of Carl Orff for use in Iran (Sarkoohi 1989:37; see also Alizadeh 1998).

[50]   Interestingly, the recording of a lesson by Borumand (see footnote 38) includes some limited (and much less detailed) discussion of this kind. Thus, in *dastgāh Māhur*, he explains the main differences between *gusheh*s *rāk* and *arāq* to his pupils. He also plays some of the phrases at a slower speed, allowing pupils to follow more easily. There is, however, no discussion of improvisation. The fact that Borumand was one of Alizadeh's main teachers may have influenced the latter's more 'rationalized' approach to teaching.

[51]   There are strong resonances here with teaching practices in Hindustani music, for example the description by Shujaat Khan of lessons with his father Vilayat Khan (cited in Neuman 2012:435). Having been told to go and practise

to develop their individual creativity; only in exceptional circumstances did this come about. Oral training will only be effective when we have reached a proper understanding of the material. The development of the improviser's and *radif* player's memory is one of the important aspects of teaching Iranian music. As much as the player must develop a good technical facility ['*panjeh-ye narm*', 'supple hand'], they also need an agile mind ['*zehn-e chāboki*']. Memorizing the *radif* and the *gushehs* is important for practising this. There is a special discipline in learning the *radif*, but without doubt when teaching is accompanied by analysis and discussion, the pupil's mind accepts it better. If your only aim is to fill your mind with the *radif*, you will forget it very quickly (31) … criticism and analysis play a very important role … it is in this way that teaching can shape creativity. (in Shahrnazdar 2004b:31)

Whilst the work of Alizadeh cannot be taken as typical of teaching practices today, such ideas are certainly 'in the air'.[52] Even back in 1990, Payvar responded to a question about the teaching of improvisation with greater openness than might be expected from a musician of his generation, 'No, improvisation is not taught. It should be, but we are not yet organized enough to do this. Maybe one day there will be such classes' (8.11.90). Meshkatian reported that students often ask teachers to improvise so that they can record and analyse the music later. He partly attributed this interest in understanding creative processes to a new generation of broadly educated musicians who are no longer content to simply listen and imitate (20.7.92). Another development is the publication of notated analytical commentaries, such as the version of Mirza Abdollah's *radif* by Talai (2000), perhaps the clearest structural presentation of the *radif* to date, with motivic and phrase repetitions clearly marked and set above one another. Each *gusheh* includes a brief line-by-line commentary, although not all of the terms are explained.[53] This publication seems to anticipate being used in the teaching context:

> We have presented the *radif* in a pedagogic way as viewed by a native player, in whom the *radif* is already a state of mind. This forms a new method that can transmit the principle elements of the *radif*. The separate, yet related musical concepts of these elements (such as rhythm, figures, phrases, development and modification of each unit, repetitions, and embellishments), are all analyzed and visualized here. In the analytical annotations section, we deal with the form of *gushehs*, characteristics of their component parts or phrases, and their occurrence in different *gushehs*. (2000:2)

There is, however, no indication as to whether Talai uses this 'new method' in his own teaching.

Observing a teaching session at Mohammad Reza Lotfi's music school in Tehran in April 2010, I was struck both by the extent of his verbalization, and by his aesthetic approach to teaching. In class, Lotfi talked about the relationships between *gushehs*, the role of various scale degrees, and aspects of phrasing and musical shaping, as well as distinguishing between what he called *sākhtāri* ('structural') and *qayr-e sākhtāri* ('non-structural') *gushehs*.[54] Nazeri exhorted students to play the *radif* with artistic expression ('*bā bayān-e*

---

some music, Shujaat asks what the *rāg* is and his father responds: "'Again you are asking me?! Thinking? Thinking! I told you not to think! None of your business. Just play!"'. Neuman comments, 'I believe that the ustad's initial demand – don't ask, just practice – is less a call for a surrender to power and more a means to establish musical intimacy and creativity in a manner possible only by forcing repetition outside, as far as is possible, the frameworks of classificatory knowledge … The process of categorization has a necessary place, but only after the student is *taiyaar*, or ready' (2012:453–6). Neuman suggests that this teaching method is a means of 'protecting the mind' (2012:446) while more important forms of bodily knowledge are developed and 'the body-instruments (the throat, fingers, and ears) are trained to gain an intimacy with the aesthetic spaces of *rāg* … to "move on their own" and "see" æsthetic spaces that the mind can only later apprehend' (2012:436, 438). See discussion below.

[52]   For instance, see Jamali (2004) for an MA thesis proposing a new framework for teaching and learning melodic and rhythmic improvisation. Jamali teaches at the University of Rasht in northern Iran.

[53]   For example, Talai uses the terms 'signifier' and 'developing signifier'. The former is defined somewhat loosely in the glossary (provided by Manoochehr Sadeghi): 'The *gusheh* is recognized by its principle part called the signifier' (2000:616), and there is no indication of an equivalent Persian term. Further, the terms are not applied consistently: in *Segāh*, the first mention of a 'signifier' is in relation to *naghmeh* (ibid.:259), the third *gusheh* of the *dastgāh*, even though the preceding *darāmad* (notated on page 310) also has recognizable 'principle parts'.

[54]   See Chapter 4 for further discussion.

honari') – 'if you play the *radif* both correctly and with feeling and with beauty, it's worth hearing [*agar radif ham dorost bezani, ham ehsāsmand, ham zibā, qābel-e shenidan ast*]' – even drawing comparisons with poetic recitation. This invoking of the aesthetic differs somewhat from reported earlier practices in which the teacher's main task was to impart the repertoire with minimal interpretive information. By contrast, Lotfi's teaching was saturated with the aesthetic. He advised pupils not to make the mistake of regarding the *radif* as something that is only educational ('*āmoozeshi*'), encouraging them to play it with a good sound. Throughout the lesson, he paid intricate attention to detail, deconstructing the music phrase by phrase. The class was a two and a half hour session during which Lotfi played passages alone and then invited the group to shadow him; at other times, he would ask individuals to play a *gusheh* memorized since the last lesson, and would regularly stop them and comment on both playing style and sound quality.[55] Other pupils thus benefitted from hearing these interventions; moreover, whilst Lotfi did most of the talking, he occasionally asked students to comment on and critique each other's playing. Notwithstanding the interesting, potentially democratizing, trends suggested by this approach, as one of the foremost masters of his generation the lines of authority were very clear. Lotfi commanded immense respect and almost sacred deference from his students and others;[56] the classroom was set up with his chair on a raised platform at one end, almost in the manner of a throne, with pupils seated on cushions on the ground. Due to the size of the room, Lotfi used a microphone to amplify his voice and instrument (in the case of the lesson observed, *setār*).

The fact that Alizadeh and Lotfi have lived and studied abroad may well have influenced their teaching practices, but their methods are consistent with the changing identity and outlook of musicians and with other changes within the musical tradition and beyond. Nonetheless, some still maintain that traditional methods are the only satisfactory way of teaching this music. Talking in 2011, Amir Eslami and Hooshyar Khayam described a range of current practices, including both individual and group teaching; some teachers using notation, others continuing with oral-aural methods; some discussing aspects of musical structure and improvisation, others imparting the *radif* with minimum explanation. In the absence of extant models, Eslami has developed his own method (not dissimilar from that of Alizadeh) which includes analysing *gusheh*s with students, something which he claims few currently do:

> The pupil doesn't understand what they are playing. The teacher doesn't talk about the structure [*sākhtār*] or explain what is happening. When I teach, it's more analysis [*tajzieh-o-tahlil*] and explanation [*towzih*]. Alizadeh started to do this and there are a few musicians who recognize this problem and when you talk to them they say 'this is how I teach my pupils; I always explain to them, analyse, get them to talk about the music'. I make the pupil understand that, for example, this is the structure of *zābol*. In order to be able to improvise, they must understand the structure of a *gusheh*. (26.11.10)

Eslami recalls that as part of a Festival of Improvisation held in Tehran in 2000, a number of established musicians were asked about their views on improvisation:

> We asked them 'how do you teach improvisation?' And they all said 'improvisation cannot be taught. Improvisation means that you memorize the *radif* and you have enough creative ability yourself to become an improviser'. That's all. But today's generation is not prepared to memorize 233 *gusheh*s to become an improviser; it isn't important to them. The success of improvisers such as Alizadeh is that they haven't just played the *gusheh*s; they have really thought about what is happening in this *gusheh*. They have understood the *gusheh* and they ask themselves 'what do I need to do to express myself within the structure of this *gusheh* and still say something new?' In my view, this should be brought into teaching in order for improvisation to find meaning. Teachers didn't used to do this; they would just say 'play, play, play' until you reach a point where you

---

[55]   In her vocal teaching, Vahdat similarly focuses pupils' attention on sound quality and nuances of the musical line, with painstaking attention to detail, as well as on the poetry (lessons observed April 2010).

[56]   As an indication of this, following the lesson observed, several aspiring pupils were waiting outside the teaching room for an 'audience'. Some had travelled very long distances just to enquire about lessons and to talk to Lotfi personally. One young man, from the southern city of Bushehr (more than 1,000 kilometres from Tehran) had nowhere to stay in the capital and was returning home the same day.

can improvise. But today's generation says 'no, why should we put in so much time. Tell me what the structure of this *gusheh* is and what I have to do: is this phrase descending? Rising? Where's the central pitch?' (ibid.)

In the context of these recent changes, Dard Neuman's work on Hindustani music offers an interesting perspective, arguing that the withholding – or at least the deferral – of explicit theoretical knowledge allows for a greater focus on embodied aspects of the music. As in Iran, repetition plays a central role in training and Neuman describes three levels of 'practice-mastery' to which repetition leads, the highest of which:

> … marks the point where fingers or throat gain agency, where the executing body parts develop a life of their own, no longer moving automatically according to prescription, composition, or habit, but now exploring musical places (jagah) on their own … where the body-instruments appear as somehow autonomous and separate from one's self. (2012:438, 442)

Neuman argues that such embodied agency, where 'properly trained fingers actually compel the mind to imagine' (ibid.:442) and where the body becomes an active agent in finding 'spaces' for the variation and development of learned materials, is only possible through traditional methods (ibid.:440). According to this view, creativity, at least initially, comes not 'from a directing mind but rather from independent moving body-instruments … It is the hands and throat that must be trained to guide the mind, not vice versa' (ibid.:445). In contrast to an approach which seeks theoretical grounding and efficiency (note Alizadeh's comment that 'much time was lost' in traditional teaching), and according to which excessive repetition appears redundant, Neuman argues that a too-early engagement with theoretical knowledge and notation undermines the processes of embodiment, thus prohibiting the development of creativity. Similar observations have been made for Karnatic music, where the constant repetition of phrases by pupils provides an important means by which musical knowledge becomes embodied (Weidman 2006:275), effecting a process of what Pressing terms 'overlearning' (1998:53). I return to the role of motor memory in Chapter 4.

Whilst it is difficult to predict future trends, it seems quite possible that teaching practices will move further in the direction described here. Notwithstanding that, as in South Asia, traditional methods are in many ways ideally suited to the music, they are increasingly called into question by musicians who are keen to explore and extend the music and who are less interested in preserving the tradition for its own sake than in using it to express the contemporary moment. Lying at the heart of the music system, processes of teaching and learning are unlikely to remain untouched by broader changes.

Problematizing the *Radif*

Radif *as Discipline;* Radif *as Canonic Authority*

> I too believe that the authenticity [*esālat*][57] of traditional music should be preserved, and taught, and made available to the people, but I do not believe that the only authentic [*asil*] art is that which repeats the past …
> I do not claim to be authentic or traditional [*sonnati*]. I follow a path which in my opinion has roots in the past and a view to the future. I do not wish to write songs and play the *tār* as they did a hundred years ago. I have no desire to do that. (Alizadeh in Sarkoohi 1989:36)

> … the perception of a core repertoire – however defined – as something sacrosanct is an essentially reactionary concept, and one that is not without its problems, for in the very process of creating a defensive shield around a corpus felt to be under threat it chokes back the normal flow of internal innovation and development. In other circumstances this could have led to the preservation of a frozen repertoire of pre-composed material,

---

[57]   *Asil* (adj.: 'rooted', 'authentic', 'noble', 'pure'; can also refer to someone of noble birth), and *esālat* (noun: 'rootedness', 'authenticity', 'nobility', 'purity') derive from *asl* ('principle', 'foundation', 'root', 'basis') and cover various shades of meaning. In this context, the closest English equivalent is 'authentic'. As discussed in Chapter 2, Iranian classical music is usually referred to as *musiqi-ye sonnati* or *musiqi-ye asil*, in which the latter indexes the music's noble/courtly associations.

unwrapped on special occasions to be shown off as a prized cultural possession, even if to all intents and purposes a dead museum exhibit, but the particular characteristics of Persian classical performances, in which there is an insistence upon creativity as an essential element, fortunately meant that consistency could never be absolute. (Wright 2009:12)

So far, the *radif* has been presented as an enabling repertoire, one which facilitates creativity. However, there is also a sense in which the structures of, and discourses around, the *radif* have served to contain, even constrain, creative practice. In the final section of this chapter I examine the relationships of authority invested in the *radif*, and how they serve to 'discipline'[58] Iranian music, a topic which has received little attention in the literature. As several authors have noted, the *radif* is 'by and large ... now regarded as a closed corpus, and the concepts of tradition and authenticity in their various ways close off experimentation in modal and rhythmic structure' (Wright 2009:28).[59] Comparing this with Ottoman music, Olley observes, 'While the *radif* provides a model for improvisation, it also strictly defines the content and limits of improvisation, so that it may equally be viewed, from outside the tradition, as a barrier to creativity, as opposed to the "real" spontaneity of the *taksim* (e.g. Feldman, 1993:12–13)' (2010:15). Beyond the specifics of the repertoire itself, there is the *idea* of the *radif* as an authorial canon: to be part of the tradition requires respect for its authority; to work outside the *radif* automatically places one outside the tradition. There are interesting parallels with processes of canon-formation, and the privileging of one body of repertoire over others, elsewhere.[60] Samson's observations for Europe certainly resonate with the case of Iran:

> ... it allowed the significant to push into obscurity the only marginally less significant ... and this authoritarian quality became increasingly pronounced in the early 20th century ... It is this ideological quality, the 'constructedness' of the canon, that has especially interested critics in recent years. (2001:7)

Samson suggests that it is in the nature of a canon to act 'as an instrument of exclusion, one which legitimates and reinforces the identities and values of those who exercise cultural power' (2001:7). Similarly, one can argue that the *radif* embodies the traces of its own position in the musical hierarchy. One way in which it does this is through the inscription of difference. As a system of knowledge, the *radif* depends on a series of binary positionings according to which the normative is urban (vs rural), male (vs female), high-art (vs popular), (originally/authentically) court music (vs public), Persian-centric (vs regional ethnicities; also Iranian vs 'foreign'), spiritual (vs corporeal)[61] and so on. This subsuming of Others, whether in terms of class, gender, ethnicity and so on, in what is often presented as a complete, all-embracing repertoire, even expressing notions

---

[58]   From Bergeron and Bohlman (1992).

[59]   See also During (1991b:204), Talai (2000:2), Wright (2009:122) and Lucas (2010:12, 14, 36). According to Wright, the 'classical music is tied reverentially to the past' (2009:122), and Lucas observes, 'Whether one plays the radif or improvises upon a given dastgah one can see a bedrock of unity that is premised on the *radif*'s completeness and status as a cultural heritage. Musical unity and stability are maintained through keeping the radif closed ... Whether it was a system that was perfected in the past or has lost some of its perfection because some melodies were lost, it remains the way it is because it is from the past ... If someone was going to add to the radif it should have occurred in the past' (2010:36–7).

[60]   For example, see Bohlman (1988, Chapter 7, on folk music canons) and Goehr (1992); also, with reference to repertoires related historically to the Iranian tradition, Harris (2008) and Fossum (2010:34–7, 2012). In the latter, 'the most important component of the canon of Turkmen instrumental music are the idiosyncratic versions of traditional pieces that masters develop in performance', particularly those preserved in recordings (2012). In the case of Iran, one might also consider the exclusions apparent in the marginalization of certain musicians and playing styles. For instance, some performers that I talked to noted that Ali Akbar Shahnazi (son of Hossein Qoli) was effectively sidelined by the better connected and more politically-savvy Borumand. A far superior performer, Shahnazi also composed and he adopted a flexible attitude to the *radif* as well as encouraging creativity in his pupils (Kalhor 16.6.12). Another musician mentioned by Kalhor whose very individual and creative style of *tār* playing has been largely forgotten is Morteza Ney-Davud (c.1900–1990).

[61]   Wright observes that writings about this music 'never speak of anything as basic as pleasure ... The body is likewise restrained, its physical responses held in check ... for all its lightness the final *reng* is a dance that is no longer danced' (2009:121–2). Alongside the spiritual/corporeal divide is another that contrasts the spiritual with more cerebral approaches to performance, the former conveyed through the notion of *hāl*.

of nationhood, is made possible partly through the *radif*'s closed nature: there is no space for new voices. Whilst Iran's geographic and other diversity (*gushehs* such as *masihi* reference Christianity, for instance) is indexed through the names of *gushehs* and *dastgāhs*, these are contained within, and domesticated on the terms of, the dominant culture. As Lucas observes, 'Gushes named for people and places in Iran's imagined past contribute to the construction of the nation's continuity with a suitable past while also homogenizing and "Persianifying" this past' (2010:35). And what about the voices of women musicians so evident in Safavid iconography and later?[62]

As will be discussed in Chapter 5, some younger musicians have started to question the hegemony of the *radif* and its 'blocking of aesthetic alternatives' (Born 2005:24).[63] Nazeri observes, 'There are a few people trying to bring about a new colour [*rang-e digari*] and create a new direction [*masir-e digari*]', but – invoking broader issues of cultural change and political control – he suggests that:

> When this happens, it often gets crushed [*sarkoob*]. From Safavid times until now, any progressive movement which started in our country was stopped by those in power, or by foreigners. Why? Because they were afraid. We must always be traditional. If we have progressive thoughts [*andisheh-ye pooyā*], they wouldn't be able to control us. (21.8.99)

There are resonances here both with Agawu's assertion of ethnomusicologists' investment in reifying difference through keeping the musics that they study 'traditional' and with what Rosaldo calls 'imperialist nostalgia' (1989), 'the condition in which people of the West long for what has been lost through their own projects of colonization ... the colonial and postcolonial fascination with the "authentic native"' (Bigenho 2002:5, 19).[64] Ostensibly operating outside power, there is in fact a struggle at the heart of Iranian classical music centred on the relationship between tradition and modernity, in which the *radif* has become something of a symbolic battleground. In the discussion below, I explore some of the competing discourses around the *radif*, most of which depend on ideologically-freighted binaries: tradition vs modernity; authentic/pure vs inauthentic/impure; national vs foreign, and so on. As a system of knowledge, it is important to understand how the *radif* 'constitutes a kind of power ... [and how] those who produce the discourses also have the power to make it true' (Hall 1992:295), and the processes by which it has been transformed from a simple musical repertoire and starting point for creative performance into a conceptual entity and iconic emblem evoking notions of purity, authenticity, tradition and identity.

Radif *as a Contested Domain: Discourses of Authenticity*

Most commentators agree that it was during the 1960s that the *radif* came to prominent public attention for the first time, in part through initiatives such as the lavish government publication (Barkeshli and Ma'rufi 1963) which gave an official stamp of approval, and the activities of the Markaz. Talai recalls that in his early years of study:

---

[62]   For another comparative perspective, see Weidman on 'the exclusions that the consolidation of classical music had brought about' in the context of Karnatic music (2006:22). Whilst constitutional change and processes of modernity led to a greater involvement of women in Iranian public life, it was only after 1979, and (somewhat ironically) under an Islamic regime, that women began to play a truly active role in the classical tradition, primarily as instrumentalists (partly due to restrictions on female singing in public). By 2012, there were more women studying at university (including music students) than men, a situation which would have been unimaginable before 1979.

[63]   Born uses this phrase with reference to the electronic music centre IRCAM in Paris, but it also seems pertinent to the Iranian context.

[64]   Singleton also writes about the preoccupation with 'tradition ... a powerful ruling weapon on which colonialism depends, on which the post-colonial world feeds, but which is ultimately a fabrication, and which blocks the formation and emergence of new narratives' (1997:95). See also Alizadeh's comments in Chapter 2 on the ways in which 'tradition' (*sonnat*) is often understood locally as an indicator of backwardness. One can see this clearly in an article published in 1971, '*Musiqi-ye Asil va Musiqi-ye Sonnati*' (*Majaleh-ye Musiqi*, issue 134), in which writer and musician Hossein Ali Mallah (former student of Vaziri) suggests that more traditionalist musicians are not only out of step with a modernizing society, but potentially play a negative and regressive role (cited in Fayaz 1998:109).

... learning the *radif* was gradually being forgotten; when we were young and worked on the *radif*, only a very few people accorded it any importance and it was treated unkindly [*bā bimehri*]. In my opinion, one of the most important things that the Markaz did was to revive [*ehyā, zendeh-kardan*] the *radif*, so that people started paying attention to it and teaching it. (in Shahrnazdar 2004a:90)

Kiani similarly notes:

Broadly speaking, before the establishment of the Music Department at Tehran University, traditional *dastgāh* music was not known within society. I mean, we had a few unknown [*gomnām*] old masters who knew the *radif*s and Mr Borumand himself was the only person who had learnt Mirza Abdollah's *radif* from Esmail Ghahramani. (2004:149)

Through the work of musicians at the Markaz in particular, the *radif* became increasingly central to public discourse on music, mentioned on recordings and programme notes, and with a growing number of published *radif*s – notated and recorded – particularly from the late 1980s. This was also reflected in musicological writings. For example, Nettl (largely based on time spent in Iran in the late 1960s) suggests that the *radif* symbolizes the essence of Iranian culture (1987:160–61), and Modir similarly points to the *radif*'s symbolic importance (1986b:72–5). And the trend has continued. Talking in 2004, Talai suggested that even in the preceding 10 to 15 years the *radif* had become more valued ('*arzeshyāftan*'; in Shahrnazdar 2004a:90).[65] Today, the market is saturated with *radif*-related publications and among the general public the *radif* is generally considered to embody the tradition of Iranian classical music. The crowning glory of this trajectory was that in 2009 the *radif* was added to UNESCO's Representative List of the Intangible Cultural Heritage of Humanity.[66]

Despite its growing centrality, or perhaps because of it, the *radif* has increasingly become the focus of debate, much of it ostensibly concerning the relationship between *radif* and performance, specifically the extent to which the *radif* should serve as a springboard for creativity or rather be studied as an end in itself (paralleling the views reported earlier according to which changes were regarded as 'adulterations' or, alternatively, 'enriching').[67] However, the debate is about much more than a musical repertoire and its interpretation: it is fundamentally about the relationship between past, present and future, between tradition (often conflated with nationhood) and modernity (often equated with identity loss), and between (preserving) the local in an increasingly global environment.[68] Such issues are clearly not exclusive to Iran but affect

---

[65]   He partly attributes this to the fact that 'In the past three decades, both Iranian and western musicologists have been initiated into Persian music by scholars – such as Alinaqi Vaziri, Ruhollah Khaleqi, Nurali Borumand, and Dariush Safvat – who believed that the *radif* was the only worthwhile Persian music. As a result, musicologists doing research in Persian art music today have often placed too much emphasis on the *radif* as a modal system' (Talai 2000:8).

[66]   http://www.unesco.org/culture/ich/index.php?lg=en&pg=00011&RL=00279 (accessed 8.12.13).

[67]   There are interesting parallels with debates over 'authentic' performance in Western art music. As Kivy observes, 'there seem to be two obvious ways in which to understand the concept of historically authentic performance practice: as a means or as an end in itself. As a means, performing practice can be construed either as our pathway to the realizing of the composer's performing intentions or as our pathway to the realizing of contemporary sound. In the former case, its authority lies in the authority of intention; in the latter in the authority of sound' (1995:233). For further parallels between the case of Iran and discourses within the 'Historically Informed Performance' movement in Europe and North America, see Nooshin (2013).

[68]   Whether one concurs with Bigenho's view of modernity (after Mary Louise Pratt) as an 'ideological story that the West tells about itself, to itself and to others. The story – one of progress, enlightenment, and rationality – is presented as universal and naturalized as inevitable' (2002:141), it can certainly be argued that we should be thinking in terms of 'modernities' in the plural rather than singular. Bigenho refers to 'peripheral modernities', adding that 'the nation-state as an organizational form produces contrasting, even contradictory, forms of modernity' (ibid.:167). Further, as others have noted, 'the very categories of "modern" and "traditional" are productions of modernity', highlighting one of the 'paradoxes of modernity, the ways in which the "traditional" takes on a profile precisely in relation to the "modern"' (ibid.:165). Indeed, as noted in Chapter 1, and following the work of Timothy J. Mitchell, the tradition/modernity binary should be understood as emerging from the dialectic between the West and its colonial Others: 'Modernity in this sense is not a creation of the West but of an interaction between the West and the non-West' (2000:24).

many musicians in situations where 'traditional' music has found itself out of step with modern lifestyles, new performance contexts and so on. Ethnomusicologists and others have reported on divergent discourses and actions, from the strongly preservationist, including so-called 'safeguarding strategies' which may also potentially ossify traditions,[69] through to the argument that traditions can only survive by changing. The same debates are found in Iran where they have in recent years spilled onto the pages of journals, magazines and newspapers, as musicians have taken the opportunity to set out their positions. For example, as discussed below, in 2004 *Mahoor Music Quarterly* published a series of exchanges between Majid Kiani and Hossein Alizadeh, prominent musical figures whose views often represent far ends of what can broadly (and somewhat crudely) be characterized as a spectrum between 'tradition as preservation' and 'tradition as creation'; between following the letter of tradition and what one considers to be its spirit.

An important strand of the debate concerns competing discourses around terms such as *sonnat* ('tradition') and *esālat* ('purity', 'nobility', 'rootedness'), which first gained currency in the 1960s as part of what Fayaz terms the 'authenticity movement'. This was partly a response to the rapid pace of westernization at this time, but also a reaction against Vaziri's earlier modernizing reforms and the perceived acculturation of the 'radio musicians'.[70] The Markaz eventually became the spiritual home of this movement, which was led by Dariouche Safvate (founder and first director of the Markaz) and Borumand. The discourses started to become more moralistic and authoritarian at this time, and *esālat* became (and continues to be) one of the most value-laden concepts in Iranian music with musicians increasingly judged on their supposed connection to and respect of 'the past', understood primarily as the pre-Pahlavi Qajar past. Most music publications since the 1970s (except for a few tutor books) tend to be marked by a nostalgia for the Qajar period and are particularly concerned with 'knowing the ancestors' ('*tabārshenāsi*', Fayaz 1998:104) invoking the past to validate the present, notwithstanding that this was in large measure based on an imagined re-creation of Qajar music. Furthermore, many in the 1960s believed that such authentication required music to retain its national and cultural identity in ways that were expressed through metaphors of racial 'purity' (see Nooshin 2013). Thus, the discourses promoted by musicians such as Borumand and Safvate depended on a binary division between music considered 'authentic', 'pure' and 'traditional' and its implied Others. Furthermore, such discourses were underpinned by some of the existing dualisms mentioned above as well as the linking of notions of 'artistic authenticity' and 'historical authenticity', or at least a certain interpretation of the historically authentic (Fayaz 1998:105), which were quite new to Iranian music.[71] Once again, we return to the question of how difference is imagined in relation to creative practice. And it was the *radif* that became the main vehicle through which such binary positionings were normalized, as this iconic repertoire of the Qajar courts acquired a new quasi-ideological centrality, symbolizing fidelity to tradition, playing a central role in the processes by which authenticity was 'produced'[72] and serving as a 'buttress[ed] against defilement by unauthentic versions' (Bohlman 1988:10, referring to the Anglo-American folk canon of the Child ballads). This position gained authority through institutional support, and eventually through the writings of musicologists, both in Iran and outside.

In response to this conflating of artistic and historical authenticity, others have sought to reclaim the meanings of *sonnat* and *esālat* by emphasizing the importance of creativity and change (*tahavvol*), not in binary opposition to, but as part of the ongoing process of tradition-making. Both Alizadeh and Shajarian have expressed strong views on this issue:

---

[69]   Amongst writings which address such issues, see Howard (2006).

[70]   For further discussion of Vaziri's work and reactions against it see Darvishi (1995:207–68), Talai (2000:7–8), Wright (2009:11–13) and Simms and Koushkani (2012a:121–2).

[71]   See Nooshin (2013) for further discussion of this movement, its key figures, ideologies, motivations and discourses, as well as the role of non-Iranian ethnomusicologists in 'keeping the music traditional'. Talai also discusses discourses of purity in the 1960s and the role of musicologists from outside Iran (in Shahrnazdar 2004a:18–19). Note that the term 'authentic' is henceforth presented without inverted commas, but should of course be understood as contested and socially-constructed.

[72]   See Clifford (1988:228).

All those things which have taken shape under the name of *musiqi-ye sonnati* did not exist right from the beginning, but were gradually created in the course of history in response to social and cultural needs. How can one accept that only those in the past had the right to create and to express an opinion, but that people in the present and the future cannot be creative? ... A poet is not judged by the number of poems of Hafez or Mowlavi that he knows by heart. In the work of an artist, one's acquired knowledge and relationship with the past are important, but only to the extent of being a support for creativity and innovation. (Alizadeh in Sarkoohi 1989:36)

These *radif*s didn't fall from the sky! They were made by people. If we don't add to them, one day they will be forgotten. So they must be added to. (Shajarian in Ghaneifard 2003:155)[73]

Similarly, Nazeri commented on critiques of his work as not being authentic:

It has nothing to do with being inauthentic [*qayr-e asil*]. When an artist has reached a certain point and is in control [*tasalot*], whatever he does is correct [i.e. within the tradition]. At the time, many people complained about my work; but if you put it under the magnifying glass, you see that all the fabric [*bāft*] of *musiqi-ye sonnati* was clear but the mould was broken up [*qāleb be ham khordeh bood*]. (23.4.10)

When you've worked with the *radif*s they are in your being [*vojood*].[74] So musicians who are a little more progressive and in control, instead of like school children coming and repeating the *radif* or the work of others from the Qajar period, they create something which is traditional but which is also new: without breaking any of the bases [*qāedehā*], without imitating foreign forms [*form-e khāreji*], and without spoiling any kind of authenticity [*har gooneh esālat*]. (21.8.99)

Whilst tradition is a good thing, he warned:

Some musicians have the state of mind [*zehniyat*] and awareness not to fall into the ditch of tradition [*chāh-e sonnat*, lit: 'well of tradition']. You see, tradition is a good thing, but when there is a prejudicial ditch in front of it, when you go looking for it [*sorāqesh*], it can be a dangerous thing. And this is why some musicians are dogmatic [*moteasseb*]. They are only prepared to accept those things which have come from the past and been dictated to them: you should play like this and not any other way. I never wanted to repeat the works of Qajar times. Whatever we performed was something of which its kind [*nowesh*] hadn't been heard before, but which also was not inauthentic ['outside of authenticity', *khārej az esālat*]. (21.8.99)

Much of the debate concerning the relationship between tradition and change has coalesced around the *radif*. Talai discusses the range of performance practice in a somewhat neutral manner, describing the *radif* as 'a means and a framework for transmitting music' ('*yek āmel va qāleb-e enteqāl-dahandeh-ye musiqi*'; in Shahrnazdar 2004a:90), observing that 'now, the balance [*mizān*] between how much you use this frame or how much you distance yourself from it depends on different playing styles [*shiveh-ye navākhtan*]'. Whilst some performers, 'play what they have learnt from their teacher. Others change it a little [*ān rā kami taqir midahand*] and another group are those who at the time of performance, change what they have learnt a great deal' (ibid.:91). He then proceeds to question the resulting binary: 'we need to find better terms for improvising [*bedāheh-navāzi*] and playing the *radif* [*radif-navāzi*]' (ibid.:96), suggesting that the scope of

---

73   Whilst Talai claims that 'The process of *radif* formation is ongoing; in the twentieth century, several new *gushehs* have been added to the repertory' (2000:6) – and he gives examples of *gusheh*s added by older masters such as Saba, Davami and Karimi – the processes described here have, since the mid-twentieth century, worked against the addition of new *gushehs*.

74   Lotfi used similar physical imagery during teaching: 'When you listen to the *nei* of Kassai, for instance, you understand his relationship with the *radif*; he is using the *radif* but with creativity [*khalāqiat*] and putting the essence of his soul [*jān māyeh*] into the music. It's as though he has swallowed the *radif* and it has become part of him; anything he plays will be authentic [*asil*]. Anything he plays will be national [*melli*], not Arab or Turkish or Western or anything else' (lesson observed April 2010).

'*radif*' could be extended to refer to all classical music performance, not just the teaching repertoire and performances close to it: 'we need to clarify what we mean by *radif*, whether we really want to separate *radif* from the performance of *dastgāh* music and only name the fixed repertoire *radif*, or open out our view and call [all] *dastgāh* music *radif* in both forms [*shekl*, i.e. taught form and performance]' (ibid.:91). According to Talai, 'There are many people who like to listen to the *radif* like a work [*āsār*], like Mr Borumand's performance [*ejrā*] of the *radif* (in ibid.:93).

Talai's proposal might be read as an attempt to bridge the gap between what have become quite polarized views. Everyone agrees on the centrality of the *radif* ('the *radif* is everything', see below); however, there is less agreement on what to do with it once it is memorized. For musicians like Alizadeh, Nazeri and Kayhan Kalhor, the *radif* is the beginning of the journey, not the end. The intensity of the language shows that these questions *matter* to musicians, and they are therefore worth quoting at length. Alizadeh claims that traditionalists have pushed people, especially the young, away from classical music; Nazeri calls for a more artistic approach (*barkhord-e honarmandāneh*) to the *radif*.[75]

> Some musicians, from the day that they go to work to the day they go to the grave, repeat the same lessons that they learnt in class; they say there should be nothing other than this. I don't know what kind of thinking this is. It's obvious that you must learn the *radif*s in their different versions [*ravāyat*]. It's an alphabet; this is the class. But a musician must be educated to think, so they are ready to fly [*sar-e koo-ye parvāz*]. Some musicians never do this. It is not in his culture to fly; his culture is not to search [*jost-o-joo*] or research [*tahqiq*]; not to discover [*kashf*]. But art [*honar*] without discovery has no meaning. I believe that an artist must always discover a new course [/direction, *masir*]. If we are simply meant to repeat what they did in Qajar times, so what meaning does art have? How can we answer to history? (21.8.99)

> Traditionalists [*sonnatgarā*] say that you have to play *radif* every day. And that's all. You can't improvise, that's forbidden. And we have people who do this and every time they perform they play *radif*. And if they want to play in their homes they play *radif* again. The *radif* is everything, but you don't have to play it all the time. It's like a book from first grade. When you go to school, you learn the alphabet so you can read and write. It's like studying literature, you don't write the same book that you studied. This is something to start from, because in the old days there weren't tutor books or methods. So they had to teach orally by making small pieces for students to memorize, a small easy formula. But the traditionalist attitude is 'this is like Koran', and they think you have to play it over and over again. (Kayhan Kalhor, 4.8.99)

> There are musicians who have closed the door to other kinds of music, and want to preserve the music in a pristine state ['untouched'; *dastnakhordeh*]. You can live with the *radif*, learn it, play it every day, worship with it, but give others the right to live with other tools. This is how music can have many dimensions. Its place in teaching and preserving values is clear; but it also has a place in innovation [*noāvari*] and creativity. (Alizadeh in Shahrnazdar 2004b:34)

The comparison with the Koran is revealing; for some, the *radif* has indeed attained the status of a sacred text. Alizadeh concedes that the tradition needs both improvisers and those who focus on memorizing and preserving the *radif*; and these are not necessarily the same people. However, he argues that the latter should not prevent their pupils from improvising or listening to other kinds of music (in Shahrnazdar 2004b:34).

At the other end of the spectrum are musicians such as Safvate and Majid Kiani, closely associated with the Markaz. Publications by and interviews with these individuals are replete with references to the 'true', authentic tradition – meaning closely based on the *radif*, but also invoking notions of spirituality embodied in the term *hāl* – and their performances also follow the *radif* closely.[76] Kiani uses the expression *shirin-navāzi* ('sweet playing', 2004:152), in a derogatory sense as in 'crowd pleasing', to describe performances which,

---

[75]   There are parallels here with Lotfi's aesthetic approach to teaching. Similarly, discussing the role of the *radif*, Shajarian comments: 'The aim is to reach beauty [*Hadaf residan be zibāi ast*]' (Eftekhari 1999:142).

[76]   See During (1994:189–209) for discussion of authenticity, particularly relating to aspects of spirituality, and the concept of *hāl* (161–88).

in his view, stray too far from the *radif*. The discourses of these 'self-appointed guardians of authenticity' (from Agawu 2003:195) have been promoted outside Iran by writers such as During and Clifton Miller.[77] Describing the role of the Markaz in the 1970s, Talai argues that it: 'defended music and informed people about real [*vāqei*] and pure/noble [*asil*] music. It trained a generation of musicians who had aims [*hadafdār va hadafmand*], who believed in what they were doing' (in Shahrnazdar 2004a:20). Interestingly, many of the musicians who studied at the Markaz, including Alizadeh and Lotfi, went on to become some of the most important innovators in Iranian classical music from the mid-1970s, often placing them in a contradictory position to those who continued the preservative work of the Markaz (see Nooshin 2013).

Beyond the discourses of musicians, one of the few scholars to have examined the links between terms such as *sonnat* and *esālat* and notions of musical authority is sociologist Mohammad Reza Fayaz, who engages critically with some of the rhetoric which has characterized this debate and which can be seen across a range of areas in music education, production, theory and criticism. Asking why the concept has evoked such anxiety, Fayaz suggests that the 1960s 'return to purity' (*bazgasht be esālat*, Talai in Shahrnazdar 2004a:18) was not just – or maybe even – about the music, but a means of validating a particular ideological position (see Nooshin 2013). This anxiety over the 'authentic' is also evident in other areas of cultural production, notably post-1979 Iranian cinema with many films set in rural locations and featuring child actors. Such films often evoke a romanticized image of an idyllic past when life was simpler and more connected with nature, and with children representing a lost innocence, in much the same way that the 'authentic' music movement sought a pure, untouched tradition embodying an Iranian 'essence', thus also perpetuating the myth of musical and racial purity. Fayaz notes similar discourses in the post-1979 preoccupation with rural folk traditions, presented as a 'healthy' music and extensively collected and documented over the past several decades (1999:107).

Whilst the specific case of Iran reflects local concerns about the relationship between tradition and modernity, the resonances with debates over questions of 'authenticity' elsewhere are striking. Music philosopher Peter Kivy begins one of the most thorough explorations of 'authenticities' in Western art music performance, as follows:

> The highest praise one can bestow nowadays on a musical performance, in many influential circles, is to say that it was 'authentic'. So powerful has the medicine of authenticity become, indeed, that those who find a musical performance to their liking, but unable to pass for authentic according to whatever tests are currently endorsed by those whose imprimatur carries weight in these matters, must reach out for some new or distant sense of the term in order to like what they like without losing their respectability. 'Authentic', then, has become or is close to becoming a synonym for 'good', while seeming to confer upon a performance some magical property that it did not have before. It is the musical version of the doctrine of the real presence. (1995:1)

There's no need to labour the parallels with Iran; nor the religious overtones. Kivy identifies various positions used to argue for so-called 'historically authentic performance' (ibid.:108), these being 'authenticity as intention' (ibid.:9), 'authenticity as sound' (ibid.:47), 'authenticity as practice' (ibid.:80) and what he calls 'the other authenticity' or 'personal authenticity' (ibid.:108).[78] He proceeds to ask 'why [to] be authentic ... why should the performer realize the composer's performing intentions?' (ibid.:145), something that has become so naturalized that to ask the question is tantamount to asking 'Why Should I Be Moral?' (quoting F.H. Bradley's essay in moral theory), since 'being authentic', like 'being moral' is often regarded as 'an end to be desired for her own sake, and not as a means to something beyond' (F.H. Bradley, quoted in Kivy 1995:146). Kivy discusses the tension between 'historical authenticity' and aesthetics, and how the former has:

---

[77]   Both During (1991b:251–6) and Miller (1999) offer a vitriolic admonishing of musicians who have 'sold out' to the tradition in order to reach wider audiences.

[78]   Compare this to the work of Bigenho in which the 'contested grounds of authenticity in Bolivian music performances' are examined in relation to 'the space between cultural experiences that are *felt*, *represented* and *exchanged* as authentic' (2002:16). Bigenho distinguishes between 'experiential authenticity, cultural-historical authenticity, and unique authenticity' (16); the second lies 'within the realm of the always slightly imperfect representation, as it purports a continuity with an imagined point of origin, situated in a historical or mythical past' (18).

... begun to overpower what might be called 'reasons of the ear' to the extent that it no longer seems intellectually respectable, in musical circles, to adduce reasons of the ear *against* the claims of historical authenticity. In other words, now reasons of the ear, although they have not ceased to be relevant, have become relevant in only one direction. If you like the way authenticity sounds, that may be a reason in its favour; but if you don't, or if you like something else better, that is, from the critical point of view, no reason at all. (ibid.:xi)

Similarly, to move away from the *radif* for 'reasons of the ear' (as will be discussed in Chapter 5) immediately places one in the realm of the 'inauthentic'.

Authenticity Personified

If the *radif* has become a symbol of musical authenticity, then Nur Ali Borumand is arguably its personification. Borumand played an important role in promoting discourses of authenticity in the 1960s and '70s, and his teaching positions at both the University of Tehran and the Markaz made him immensely influential. What is particularly interesting, however, is how contemporary musicians 'claim' Borumand as a means of validating their own positions. An example of this can be seen in an exchange between Majid Kiani and Hossein Alizadeh in issues 22 and 23 (both 2004) of *Mahoor Music Quarterly*. The first includes an interview with Kiani on the history of the Markaz during which he discusses the views of Borumand and other teachers such as Hormozi and Forutan on a range of issues including musical practices of the 1950s and '60s and the purported poor quality of music broadcast on the radio at the time (2004:152). Kiani describes how, in the early days and under Borumand's influence everything at the Markaz was research-oriented, from discovering the exact tuning of Hossein Qoli's *tār* to the precise rendering of each phrase of the *radif*. The focus was on research rather than performance: 'we didn't perform to record; we played and sometimes recorded in order to critique our work' (2004:153). Gradually, some musicians started to innovate (*noāvari*) and refine their playing techniques, leading to a shift from research to 'production' (*towlid*) in the form of commercial cassettes and, as Kiani relates, from a focus on 'serious music' (*musiqi-ye jeddi*) to *musiqi-ye āmehpasand* (literally 'popular music', suggesting music to please a large number of people). According to Kiani, Borumand regarded this as a diversion from the centre's original aims, and one of the main reasons that he left (2004:150).[79]

In a response to this interview, published in the following issue, the stated purpose of which was to clarify certain historical facts, Alizadeh contests Kiani's narrative. Replying to his criticism of musicians such as Vaziri who composed for large ensembles, Alizadeh claims that whilst Foroutan (presented by Kiani as interested only in the 'pure' tradition) did not have the opportunity for his music to be performed by a large group, there is evidence that he imagined his pieces in this way. Similarly, according to Alizadeh, Hormozi wanted his music to be played by a large orchestra and even wrote pieces for groups of *tār*s. As for Kiani's criticism of the radio, Alizadeh reports that Davami, far from avoiding the radio (as Kiani claims), used to teach with it turned on. And so on.

Such debates among musicians are not unusual. What is interesting here is that Kiani and Alizadeh both appeal to Borumand as the ultimate arbiter: the former holding him to be a 'defender' of authenticity; the latter presenting an image of someone open to new ideas and supportive of young musicians. Alizadeh describes his own compositional work in the mid-1970s when, together with fellow students, he was exploring 'how to undertake [instrumental] group[80] work whilst maintaining beauty [*zibāi*], principles [*osool*] and artistic values [*arzesh-e honari*] in the framework of Iranian music' (2004:216). Without the encouragement of masters such as Borumand, Alizadeh says, the students at that time would not have had the courage to try new things. He takes Kiani to task for seeking 'after the death of this master to make his views accord with ours' (ibid.); in other words using Borumand as a means of voicing his personal views. That both musicians claim Borumand's approval of their interpretation of tradition is interesting: Borumand has become an embodiment

---

[79]   Kiani uses this interview to refute some of the charges levelled at him as being dogmatic ('*moteasseb*'), difficult ('*sakhtgir*') and reactionary ('*gozashtehgerā*'): 'I don't want to be dogmatic, I just want to preserve our old music' (2004:154), emphatically stating that the only way to do this, and to avoid a museum culture, is to encourage young people to perform (156).

[80]   Often without a singer, which was quite unusual at this time.

of, on the one hand, 'historical authenticity' (Kiani) and on the other 'personal/artistic authenticity' (Alizadeh), simultaneously invoked to validate opposing positions.

Radif *as Symbol of Nationhood*

Closely related to the idea of the *radif* as an index of authenticity is its symbolizing of nationhood. As noted, the *radif* distinguishes Iranian music from neighbouring traditions with which it historically shares a great deal. One might draw parallels with the adoption of Shi'ism as Iran's state religion in the sixteenth century as part of a nationalist movement which sought to differentiate Iran from its Ottoman and Arab Muslim neighbours. Generally speaking, Iranian musicians' discourses are saturated with expressions of identity and belonging, no doubt related to the processes of modernization and westernization discussed, but also to a certain 'siege' mentality rooted in the perception that Iranian music has been under threat for centuries, whether from Islamic orthodoxy or through the westernizing policies of the Pahlavi period.[81] The renaissance of Iranian classical music after 1979 was in large part a result, and an indicator, of a renewed confidence in local culture. However, the relationship between past and present, and between local and 'other', is complex:

> It's from preserving the past that culture can continue, become modern and develop ... we have lost, and are losing, our roots very quickly. In order to develop and move forward, we need roots; and our musical roots are in our old music which must be preserved. Unfortunately, in replacing our culture with a foreign [*bigāneh*] one, we are losing our own roots. (Alizadeh in Shahrnazdar 2004b:26)

The debate around the *radif* and the relationship between tradition and change, then, is underpinned by issues of identity (and loss of): personal, musical, national; what Hooshyar Khayam describes as the tension between the desire for modernity and 'fear of losing' ('*az dast dādan*', 26.11.10) one's traditions. Much of the preoccupation with purity and authenticity described earlier is about preserving national identity in the face of external forces such as westernization and, more recently, globalizing processes. The extent to which aesthetic values are expressed in terms of national belonging is revealing: music criticism regularly invokes this trope such that aesthetic judgments are based on how 'Iranian' a piece sounds. One of the main criticisms levelled at Iranian rock music, for instance, is that it doesn't sound (obviously) Iranian, and therefore isn't 'really' Iranian but a form of Western cultural 'invasion' (*tahājom*). That the same is not usually said of music composed in 'Western classical' style by Iranian composers (orchestral music, for instance) says a great deal about the relations of cultural power and the status which 'music as art' has in Iran (see Nooshin 1996:107, 121, 155, 157; 2015). The naturalized and largely unquestioned connection between Iranian music and ideas of national identity feeds into a discursive othering of music deemed to be diluting or polluting, which in turn impacts on the *radif* which, as well as serving as an icon of musical authority, purity and authenticity, additionally takes on the burden of nationhood. At the same time, there is a broad awareness among musicians of the need to engage with a wider 'global' culture. In response to a question about culture loss (*kamrang shodan*; culture 'losing its colour'), Alizadeh stressed the need to define 'our' (*khodi*) culture and its relationship with global culture (*farhang-e jahāni*), expressed in terms of the interpolation of – and the impossibility of separating – self and other: 'it's here that the boundaries between our art [*honar-e khodi*] and that of others [*qayr-e khodi*] is not clear cut' (in Shahrnazdar 2004b:37), thus problematizing the binary between the local and the global.

Of course, there is a certain irony in the post-1960s positioning of the *radif* as symbol of 'nationhood as tradition', against the implied Others of modernity and westernization. As has been observed, the *radif* developed as a direct result of the processes associated with the arrival of modernity in Iran. Perhaps the most incisive analysis of the interconnected history of the *radif* and early twentieth-century nationhood is by Ann Lucas, who points to the development of the *radif* at the exact same time that the idea of a modern nation-state

---

[81]   It should be noted, however, that modernizers such as Vaziri also followed strongly nationalist agendas. See Chehabi (1999) for discussion of the role of music and music education in early twentieth-century processes of nation-building. During also discusses the close connection between music and 'language, nation and territory' in Iran (1994:101–37).

was forming around the turn of the twentieth century (2010),[82] when developments in communications and travel enabled 'nationwide groups like merchants, artisans, the new intellectuals and even the leading ulama [religious leaders] to identify and communicate with each other on a national basis' (Keddie 1981:36–7). Lucas argues that the *radif* can only be understood as emerging within the conditions of modernity, which 'contributed strongly both to the establishment of a national community and to musicians' discourses within that community' (2010:25).[83] At the same time, the notion of historical continuity remained important: the new nation-state 'needed a historic musical existence and collective music repertoire to legitimate its claims to united, perennial cultural existence' (Lucas 2014). Certainly it can be argued that the *radif* represented the first 'national' repertoire, one that could be imagined:

> ... as being shared by Qajar subjects in different parts of Qajar territory where notions of the nation of Iran were being propagated (3) ... the concept of *radif* depends on the unity of the Iranian nation and the modern cultural demand for music to reflect the unity of nation: ideas that had no relevancy for premodern music in the region, but conversely held great relevancy in the development of an Iranian nation during the Qajar Constitutional Period of 1906–11. (ibid.)

Lucas also suggests that as court musicians started to travel abroad, they were regarded as 'carrying the tradition of an entire nation ... All of this affirmed the unity of an Iranian cultural existence, even as it affirmed the right of *radif* musicians to claim their musical practices for all of Iran' (ibid.). She also points to the ways in which the *radif* is presented as a form of national heritage, indicated in part by 'the names of *dastgah*s and gushes ... [which] clearly speak to an Iranian national consciousness. They are named for people, places, poetic forms and other "Iranianisms"' (Lucas 2010:13, 37).[84] Notwithstanding the discourses that were to follow in the 1960s, in which the *radif* was transformed into an icon of tradition and the very antithesis of modernity, one can understand the nature of the *radif*, as a thoroughly 'modern construct[s] of cultural authenticity' (ibid.:35). Lucas links the attempt to promote 'an imagined continuity between modern music developments and past epochs' (ibid.:27) with broader processes of nation-building at the time, which also sought to connect Iran's present to a long and glorious past: 'The pursuit of the authentic radif not even a hundred years after it emerged was ultimately the pursuit of the nationalist myth ... while it embodies a sense of cultural heritage, this heritage is a modern phenomenon that uses history to legitimize modern and novel developments' (ibid.:33, 39).

In the early twentieth century, then, the music of the court became transformed into the music of the nation,[85] in contrast to regional 'folk' musics. And this connection between *radif* and nation has continued through the best part of a century. In Chapter 5, I consider the ways in which some musicians are challenging this by contesting essentialized notions of nationhood and cultural difference and forefronting new kinds of identities emerging in a globalizing world.

---

[82] Much of Lucas's discussion is predicated on the idea of Iranian nationhood as a modern phenomenon, something which has been widely debated in the literature. Whilst the word 'Iran' is several thousand years old, it is unclear how far back the idea of national belonging in its modern sense can be traced. See Kashani-Sabet (1999).

[83] There are interesting parallels with Afghanistan and the role of radio in 'creating the Afghan nation' from a fragmented tribal society (Baily 1994).

[84] There are similarities with processes of canon-formation and nation-building elsewhere, as noted by Samson (2001:7). Amongst other writings, perhaps the most detailed explication of such processes is Harris (2008), with reference to the Uyghur Twelve Maqam of western China.

[85] This is one reason why the label 'Persian classical music', found outside Iran, is problematic; the use of 'Iranian' marks this as music of the nation in a way which 'Persian' does not. Since the 1990s, a new term, *musiqi-ye melli* ('national music'), has emerged to refer to Iranian music composed for orchestra.

*   *   *

This chapter has explored various aspects of the *radif*, including its history, the ways in which it serves as a starting point for performance, and the processes by which it is transmitted. Despite sweeping changes to the musical culture and Iranian society in general since the early twentieth century, the latter appear not to have changed substantially, pointing to an intimate relationship between the music and methods by which it is taught and learnt. The second half of the chapter explored the symbolic significance of the *radif*, its embodiment of notions of authority, purity, authenticity and nationhood, and the contestations around it, claimed both by those purporting to follow the authentic tradition and by those seeking to extend it creatively. Clearly, the *radif* plays a fundamental role as the starting point for much of the creativity in Iranian classical music, and it is this creativity which forms the focus of the final two chapters.

PART III
Beyond Discourse:
The Practice of Creativity

Chapter 4
Creative Performance in Iranian Classical Music

Introduction: The Scholarly Context

At the heart of this book lies a desire to understand how Iranian classical musicians think and talk about creative practice, the creative process itself, and the relationship between the two. In particular, as already discussed in Chapter 1, I seek to interrogate the notion of 'improvisation', and the implicit or explicit binaries which the term sets up with its Others: composition and 'non-improvised' performance. From the start of this research it seemed to me that the discourse of improvisation, whilst usefully highlighting the creative licence of the performer, tells us relatively little about creative process, instead arguably providing a veil of mystique which potentially obfuscates the highly structured and compositional nature of the music. Clearly the discourse of improvisation only works in relation to the central linchpin of the *radif*. And yet, as soon as one probes beneath the surface, the ostensibly neat relationship between learnt *radif* and creative performance turns out to be far more complex than the accepted orthodoxy might suggest. Having considered the discourses through which musicians and scholars have framed ideas about creativity, in this chapter I turn to the music 'itself' and examine more traditional forms of performance practice, drawing on examples from an unpublished extended study of *dastgah Segāh*, with some reference to *dastgāh Māhur*.[1] Following this, Chapter 5 considers changes within the classical music since the Revolution of 1979, focusing on two musicians who are developing new forms of improvisational practice that move away from traditional allegiance to the *radif* and challenge dominant discourses concerning the relationship between improvisation and composition.

Before embarking on the analysis, I briefly survey the scholarly context and consider issues of methodology and approach. The original study on which this chapter is based follows a tradition of musicological scholarship dating back to the early 1960s in which much of the relevant literature before 1979 was in English, French or German (by Iranians and others) and published outside Iran. As well as those focused specifically on improvisational practice,[2] a number of publications concerned primarily with the *radif* also include consideration of performance practice.[3] In addition, several introductory books on Iranian classical music discuss improvisation, albeit in fairly general terms.[4] As noted in earlier chapters, there has been an increase in musicological scholarship in Iran in recent years and this has resulted in a few journal articles and dissertations in Persian exploring aspects of performance practice.[5] Whilst writings on this music almost invariably mention improvisation, few early publications discuss in detail how musical material is generated in performance. There are exceptions, including the study by Wilkens comparing performances by two *santur* players (1967), Massoudieh's study of *dastgāh Shur* (1968), several publications by Nettl (1972, 1974a, 1987, with Foltin 1972), and more recent work by Azadehfar (2006), Wright (2009) and Simms

---

[1]   The complete findings are presented in Nooshin 1996 (see also 1998, 2003) where 29 performances and four *radif*s of *Segāh* are compared in order to identify shared material and examine how musicians generate new material in performance. The choice of *dastgāh* and selection of examples was partly determined by availability of recordings and access to musicians, as well as covering a range in terms of performance dates, age of musicians, instrument/voice and so on. The study explored various aspects of the music, from large-scale sectional organization through to detailed motivic structure.

[2]   For example, Gerson-Kiwi (1963), Wilkens (1967), Massoudieh (1968), Sadeghi (1971), Jones (1971), Nettl with Foltin (1972), Nettl (1972, 1974a), During (1987c), Azadehfar (2006), Wright (2009).

[3]   See Khatschi (1962, 1967), Farhat (1965, 1990), Tsuge (1974), Nettl (1987), Kuckertz (1992).

[4]   See Caron and Safvate (1966), Zonis (1973), During (1984a).

[5]   A special issue of *Mahoor Music Quarterly* (volume 10, no. 37, Autumn 2007) was devoted to the topic of improvisation; however, most of the items are translations of articles previously published outside Iran in English or French rather than original research by scholars in Iran. Several are translations of entries from the 2001 *New Grove Dictionary of Music and Musicians* (ed. Sadie).

(Simms and Koushkani 2012a, 2012b). Whilst Sadeghi discusses improvisational techniques in some detail (1971:75, 135), offering insights from the perspective of a performing musician, most of his examples are in fact taken from the *radif*. Farhat (1990) presents transcriptions of improvisations of the central *gushehs* of each *dastgāh*, focusing on their essential characteristics rather than on creative process.[6] These studies evince a variety of approaches, but most share a broadly comparative methodology in which different versions of the same section of repertoire are juxtaposed. Many have written about sectional organization, particularly the ordering of *gushehs*, as well as the internal details of individual *gushehs*, including modal characteristics and techniques of elaboration (for example, Sadeghi 1971:95–120, Zonis 1973:104–25, Nooshin 1996:169–284) and motivic patterns (Gerson-Kiwi 1963:38, 42–3, Sadeghi 1971:80–85, Nettl with Foltin 1972, Nettl 1972, 1984a, 1987, Nooshin 1996:389–466, Simms and Koushkani 2012a:247–56). Whilst the idea of phrases as 'combinations of motifs and figures which may be repeated, sequenced or modified' (Sadeghi 1971:86) is a recurrent one, few have discussed how musicians actually apply these in performance.[7] Nettl has perhaps gone furthest in this respect, describing how techniques listed individually by others operate in relation to one another; at the same time, his focus remains primarily on the *radif*.[8] A more recent analysis by Azadehfar describes a particular performance of *dastgāh Shur* by Farhang Sharif (*tār*) and Mohammad Esmaili (*tombak*) at the 1998 Fajr Festival in Tehran's Vahdat Hall (2006:285–304). Whilst his main interest lies in rhythmic aspects, Azadehfar also considers other dimensions including a rare discussion of audience reception. Similarly, Wright offers a lengthy analysis of a single performance of *dastgāh Homāyun* by UK-based vocalist Touraj Kiaras, with whom he also consulted closely during the analytical process (2009:39–116). Wright provides a *gusheh* by *gusheh* commentary, examining aspects of structure as well as the relationship between *radif* and performance. The two volumes by Rob Simms and Amir Koushkani (2012a, 2012b) provide a comprehensive survey of the life and work of master vocalist Mohammad Reza Shajarian, and incorporate extended commentary in Shajarian's own words. They also include transcriptions and analyses of some of his key works, with a focus on the development of performance style and issues of interpretation. There is a particularly interesting comparison of two performances of the same piece – *Dastan* – both recorded in 1987, which highlights aspects of variability and stability between the two (2012b:82–9).

What is implicit in much of the literature, and which comes out particularly clearly in the work of Nettl, is that Iranian classical music is based on 'a group of general principles of musical structure' (Nettl 1987:64) which are found both in *radif* and in performance. Thus, as noted, Sadeghi devotes considerable time to discussing improvisation, but his illustrations are taken not from performances, as one might expect, but from published *radifs* (1971:75–135) since, as he explains: 'The examples chosen from printed books were in an improvisatory stage before they were notated' (ibid.:136).[9] Similarly, in the case of at least one of the *radifs* that Zonis takes her examples from, 'this author judges it to be extremely close to live performances' (1973:115).[10] Nettl and Foltin are more explicit about the relationship between the 'improvisational' and 'pre-composed':

> … composed pieces have, in their structure, many of the characteristics that are also found in the improvisations: repetition, variation, variation of a motif, extension, sequence, reliance on tetrachords. Thus, the traditional division between 'composed' and 'improvised' materials in Persian music may have limited value. (1972:12)

---

[6]   This book is based directly on Farhat's 1965 doctoral thesis.

[7]   During, for instance, lists and briefly describes techniques of elaboration in various publications, but rarely provides illustrative examples or discussion of specific performances (1984a:139, 1991b).

[8]   Much of Nettl's work appeared as a series of publications in the 1970s; some were later reprinted in the 1987 volume *The Radif of Persian Music*. The latter is primarily a study of the *radif*, but includes some discussion of improvisation, particularly with reference to *dastgāh Chāhārgāh* (based on material originally published in Nettl with Foltin 1972). The chapter on *Māhur* also considers improvisational choices, but focuses on the selection and ordering of *gushehs* rather than internal details of each *gusheh*.

[9]   Sadeghi includes a brief analysis of two performances (the second by himself) focusing largely on sectional organization, but with some discussion of motifs and elaboration techniques earlier in his text (1971:130–35).

[10]   This is the *radif* compiled by Musa Ma'rufi (Barkeshli and Ma'rufi 1963; see Chapter 3).

Given that the *radif* forms the basis for creative performance, it is perhaps not surprising that both are based on similar principles. However, there are some interesting anomalies which will be considered below. As discussed in Chapter 2, since the learning processes allow pupils to hear many permutations of the repertoire, they are thereby able to internalize both the 'stable' elements which remain unvaried from one version to another, and the kinds of variational techniques listed above which become the basis for composition in performance.

The Analyst's Dilemma

Certain aspects of the music system are readily articulated by musicians, most notably mode, for which there exists a developed and historically-rooted theoretical framework and associated terminologies, and which remains the most theorized area of Iranian classical music. However, when it comes to other aspects, particularly those relating to creative practice, there is much less verbalization. From the first English-language introduction to Iranian classical music by an author from outside the tradition, to a more recent study by an Iranian scholar, things seem to have changed little:

> Most of the theory of practice comes to an Iranian intuitively … the student simply absorbs the compositional procedures without being aware of them as such. For this reason, a musician is often unable to explain precisely what he is doing during his improvisation. Likewise, Persian music theorists, considering this aspect of music to be an intuitive procedure, do not discuss it in their writings. Therefore … the foreign musicologist has little indigenous methodology or terminology on which to base a study of improvisation. (Zonis 1973:98–9, 125, quoted in Chapter 2)

> Improvisation is in fact such a natural and almost self-evident procedure for the Persian theorist that he does not feel the need to explain it. Hence there is a lack of methodology to analyse improvised music in Persian theory. (Azadehfar 2006:118)

Of course, Iranian classical music in not alone in this respect. Discussing his work on oral-formulaic composition by Serbo-Croatian epic singers, Albert Lord notes:

> About the question of asking the singers themselves to explain how they compose – this is a rather difficult thing to do, in the sense that, although supposedly they should be able to tell you, as a matter of fact, they don't know. And their ideas of how they do it are ideas that have been suggested to them from outside rather than inside. Sometimes you can get valuable information from a singer by indirect questioning. Avdo Mededovic, who was our best singer, would not talk about it directly. (in Stolz and Shannon 1976:289–90)

For a study which seeks to understand the relationship between verbal discourse and creative practice, this poses some methodological challenges. Herndon and McLeod's observations seem pertinent here:

> While rules are known by an individual, he may not be able to state them explicitly or clearly; nor will an individual necessarily be able to replicate the totality of rules stated by any other individual … it remains a task for the researcher to formulate the tacit rules which members of a group are using in order to create their music. (1979:62)

Much of my work on Iranian classical music has sought to access such implicit knowledge ('tacit rules'); however, doing so though purely ethnographic methodologies requires making certain assumptions about the relationship between cognitive process and verbal articulation. John Baily has written about verbalization and the relationship with what might be called 'music theory'. He asks, 'What is the significance of verbalized music theory? Why do some societies have such theories and not others? What is their relationship to differing types of music, and are there some kinds of music which cannot be readily learned or performed unless one acquires this formal knowledge?' (1992:147–8). Similarly, one might reasonably ask whether such 'music theory' need necessarily be in the verbal domain. Whilst the teaching of the *radif* has generally involved little in the way of theoretical explanation (until recently at least), might the *radif* itself constitute a form of non-verbalized music theory? Wright is worth quoting at length on this in a paragraph which directly precedes his analysis of Kiaras's performance:

> … explicitly formulated analytical procedures do not form part of the learning process for Iranian musicians. But this is not to suggest that abstraction is absent: the very fact that musicians have to arrive at mastery of a particular *gushe* through generalizing possible configurations and combinations on the basis of the various teaching versions and performances of it to which they have been exposed is an indication to the contrary. Indeed the underlying processes of segmentation may receive verbal expression to the extent that phrases occupying particular areas are labelled (e.g. as *shoru'*, *khateme* or *tahrir*). Nevertheless, such terms are residues, markers of the already interiorized rather than classificatory aids to acquisition, and for Touraj Kiaras knowledge is preferably articulated through actions and judgements, so that we are again confronted with the problem of the extent to which the western analytical approach usefully reveals the unstated and not consciously realized or merely articulates in a laboriously explicit way matters that for the performer and informed listener are taken for granted or, if verbalized, are deftly and succinctly expressed by metaphor. (2009:41)

The relative absence of local verbalized theory in relation to creative process has been a perennial topic of discussion among scholars, who have tended to adopt 'Western' techniques: (usually) transcribing and subjecting the music to structural analysis, often adopting a comparative approach, but rarely in direct discussion with musicians (although a number of such scholars are themselves practitioners) and largely divorced from contextual considerations. This applies to the vast majority of studies conducted by non-Iranian scholars and Iranians working outside Iran, as well as local researchers.[11] Whilst the applicability of what are still widely regarded as Western analytical techniques to musical traditions globally has long been debated, this area of Iranian music research has been marked by a certain unease, particularly among non-Iranian scholars, who have sought to justify their methodologies. Of these writings, perhaps the most thoughtful is the Epilogue to Wright's book in which he assesses his analytical project in relation to the initial statement of intent (2009:117–22).

One of the most polemical attacks on what she calls 'the Western hegemonic tradition of musicology' (2003/4:86), and heavily informed by nationalist and postcolonial discourses, is by former University of Tehran music lecturer Azin Movahed, according to whom Iranian musicology after 1979 sought to:

> … establish its own norms of scholarship and scientific enquiry (86) … Realizing the necessity to examine their own music on grounds free from the influence of western views, Iranian musicians are now challenging the intensive imposition of western musical thought upon their music and prolifically writing and helping the development of indigenous musicology and scholarship …. (2003/4:88)

Whilst there can be little doubt that 'western musical thought' has had a profound impact on musical practice in Iran since the early twentieth century, as discussed already with regard to the adoption of dualistic discourses of creative practice, whether this was imposed from outside or adopted from within is a moot point. Moreover, this is arguably a separate issue from the impact of *musicological* thought on Iranian music scholarship, which remains to be adequately assessed. Reviewing the literature produced in Iran between 1979 and 2001, Movahed sets up a divide between scholars in Iran and 'western ethnomusicologists and Iranian musicologists trained in the west' (ibid.:107), suggesting that the latter are:

> Unable to unfold the magnitude of layers necessary in the study of Persian music. Many indigenous musicians share a common concern that western methodologies are incompatible with eastern philosophical interpretations and ignore the sophisticated expressive dimensions entwined in Persian music. (ibid.:107–8)

---

[11]   Intriguingly, although several authors mentioned here worked closely with practising musicians (Ella Zonis with Ruhollah Khaleqi, Bruno Nettl with Nur Ali Borumand, Jean During with Dariush Talai and Dariouche Safvate, Manuchehr Sadeghi himself a performing musician) their writings include little discussion of cognitive aspects of performance.

Thus dismissing in one fell swoop a whole body of literature, including much valuable work by scholars such as Mohammad Taghi Massoudieh who studied outside Iran. Exactly what an 'anti-imperialist' musicology based on 'alternative concepts that deviate[d] from the western methodologies of research widespread in the study of Persian music' (ibid.:85) might constitute is unclear. A perusal of recent musicological literature in Iran shows that scholars continue to use similar methodologies to those outside, whilst also developing their own approaches.[12] Moreover, despite Movahed's claim only to consider the work of those trained in Iran, one of the authors discussed, Dariush Talai, spent many years in France where he gained advanced degrees in music.[13] Whilst I would concur entirely with the need for Iranian musicology to develop its own distinctive identity, something which is starting to happen, that this can only come about through the wholesale rejection of Western methods seems at best naive, at worst isolationist and even damaging to local scholarship.

It may be instructive at this point to contrast Movahed's position with that of Agawu who, in the context of Africanist musicology, argues for a multiplicity of perspectives:

> How not to analyse African music? There is obviously no way not to analyse African music. Any and all ways are acceptable. An analysis that lacks value does not yet exist which is not to deny that, depending on the reasons for a particular adjudication, some approaches may prove more or less useful. We must therefore reject all ethnomusicological cautions about analysis because their aim is not to empower African scholars and musicians but to reinforce certain metropolitan privileges. (2003:180)

Clearly, the debate is about more than scholarly method: for Movahed, the development of local 'ethnomethodologies' represents a stand against the hegemony of the West. Power relations are also at stake for Agawu, but exercised through assumed essential differences between African and European modes of knowledge:

> The idea that, beyond certain superficial modes of expression, European and African knowledge exist in separate radically different spheres originated in European thought, not in African thinking. It was (and continues to be) produced in European discourse and sold to Africans, a number of whom have bought it, just as they have internalized the colonizer's image of themselves. (2003:180–81)

From this universalizing perspective, Movahed's essentializing of scholarly difference might, ironically, be regarded as symptomatic of a colonial mindset. Doubtless such debates will continue; and, my own discussion with musicologists in Iran suggests that Movahed's views are not shared by all, or even the majority. Nevertheless, these issues are raised here in order to highlight the contested nature of musical analysis. And, away from the polemics, if analysis can only ever be conducted in a culturally-relative mode, one risks losing potential insights from culturally-transcendent parallels which are not immediately evident within a single tradition.

One strategy adopted by those exploring the conceptual thinking underlying creative performance has been to involve musicians in the analytical process, with some even named as co-authors. Examples include Sorrell and Narayan (1980), Kippen (1985), Widdess (1994) and Sanyal and Widdess (2004) for Indian music, and Nettl and Riddle (1973, with input from Lebanese musician Ali Jihad Racy) for Arabic music. Whilst this approach can lend important insights, one should also recognize the additional interpretive filter and the need to negotiate between the views of musicians and the (always subjective) evidence of musical analysis. In his work with Nettl and Riddle, 'Racy himself, after seeing some of the analytical data, indicated surprise at the degree to which his performances followed certain patterns' (1973:13). Reflecting on his collaborative project with Touraj Kiaras, Wright acknowledges that such relationships between analyst and performer can be fruitful but asks whether, as is often assumed, they 'necessarily lead[s] to deeper insights and analytical refinements

---

[12] Azadehfar, for instance, describes his approach as being 'a combination of Western musicological and analytical study with Iranian musicology' (2006:8), but without elaborating on what the latter comprises. Zolfonoun is keen to stress that his analytical methods are 'compatible with international principles [*montabeq bar osool-e beynolmelali*]' (2001:24).

[13] Movahed herself completed a DMA performance doctorate at the University of Illinois (1993).

deemed valid and useful by both parties' (2009:117). Indeed, in contrast to a methodology which folds in the musicians' perspective, he suggests that 'it could make sense to discuss various parameters of a particular repertoire in a manner possibly alien to those who produced it, especially if this aided comprehension and appreciation amongst a non-native audience' (ibid.:118). The idea that an 'outsider' may offer insights not apparent from within a tradition is supported by Herndon, who argues for a multiplicity of voices:

> As to the question of who can, or who should, speak for a musical style, music culture, performer, or occasion, that, too, is negotiable territory. If possible, multiple voices, from many points of view … would weave a clearer picture of the music of a people. Such voices would include all ranges of practitioners, participants, non-participants, total strangers, and deep initiates … (We) should remember that no voice, by itself, is sovereign, absolute, and definitive. (1993:78)

In the case of the current study, the circumstances under which most of the initial research was undertaken in the late 1980s meant that contact with musicians was necessarily limited. Where possible, as in Chapters 2 and 3, their views have been foregrounded. In this chapter, however, I attempt to understand creative processes largely through my own analytical interpretation. Besides the (enforced) constraints under which I was working, it became increasingly evident that the verbal domain can offer limited insights when it comes to creative processes. I should be absolutely clear: my aim is not to replicate musicians' cognitive processes, but to present an inevitably interpretive understanding based on the available information. I accept that my methods are 'Western' in that they surely reflect my training, and to that extent they may well also be 'imperialist', but I would hope that many years of studying this music has nuanced my approach. In any case, the methodologies employed in each of the two analytical chapters (4 and 5) differ significantly, partly because of access to musicians but also because of the greater openness (indeed eagerness) of younger musicians to talk about how particular pieces came into being. These musicians tend to be music graduates and are therefore better able to grasp the nature of my musicological undertaking. Had it been possible to work more closely with the (generally older) musicians whose music is discussed in the current chapter, the conclusions might have been different; whether they would have been more 'valid' is another matter, as the experience of Wright bears out. Like Herndon, I also believe that, 'no one voice, by itself, is sovereign'; each scholar and musician brings their own perspectives and experiences, with the potential to contribute in some small way to our understanding of the music. Throughout this work, I have sought to negotiate the sometimes conflicting views of musicians and the evidence of musical analysis to reach an (always provisional, always partial) understanding of the rich diversity of ideas about creativity and their manifestation in practice.

One final point: as noted in earlier chapters, the 'voice' that has arguably been most neglected in studies of Iranian classical music is that of the listener. Whilst music analysts are increasingly attentive to the views of musicians, questions of reception have received relatively little consideration. Wright notes this lacuna (2009:122, 126), observing:

> On the presumption that the analyst *qua* expert listener can identify precisely those structures and processes that make the composition in question effective for ordinary listeners, even if they remain blissfully unaware of them, their reactions have remained largely unexplored. (ibid.:21)

Whilst the focus of the current volume is on creative processes from the perspective of production, it is important to signal the need for future research into reception and the meanings which Iranian classical music has for its audiences.

Under the Skin of the Music …

Preliminaries

In this chapter I address two main questions. First, given the centrality of the *radif* to discourses of creativity, what exactly is the relationship between learnt repertoire and creative performance and how do musicians move from one to the other? In general, as discussed below, this relationship is much clearer in some *gusheh*s than others. This leads to the second question: how is material generated in the performance of *gusheh*s where the connection with the *radif* is less clear?

A detailed introduction to the structures of Iranian classical music lies outside the scope of this study, and is readily available elsewhere. However, a brief summary is necessary to contextualize the analysis below. The *radif* of Iranian classical music comprises the 12 *dastgāh* ('system', five of which are considered subsidiary and sometimes referred to as *āvāz*), a collection of modally-related pieces known as *gusheh* ('corner').[14] The number of *gusheh*s varies from *dastgāh* to *dastgāh*, and between different *radif*s. Whilst musicians select which to include in a *dastgāh* performance, there are certain central *gusheh*s which are rarely omitted. The most important is the opening section, known as *darāmad*, which establishes the home mode of the *dastgāh*.[15] Following this, a series of *gusheh*s is presented, each with its own name and modal, melodic and, sometimes, rhythmic characteristics, each usually exploring progressively higher tonal areas and modifying the home mode by changing pitches or the relationships between them. The pitch climax of the *dastgāh*, the *owj*, comes towards the end and is followed by a descent to the final cadential *forud* section, which returns the music to the home mode and provides a satisfactory conclusion through characteristic patterns. In the course of the *dastgāh*, there may also be brief returns (also called *forud*) in short sections at the end of *gusheh*s. Generally speaking, then, the overall trajectory of a *dastgāh* tends to be arch-like (but with the highest point towards the end) with a series of waves of rising pitch and accompanying tension, eventually released in the final extended descent.

The modal character of each *gusheh* is determined by the functions of specific pitches, and as noted, this is one aspect of the music system marked by theorization and accompanying terminology: *shāhed* ('witness') refers to the modal pitch centre; *āqāz* ('start') indicates the initial pitch of pieces in a particular mode; and *ist* ('stop') is the pitch on which phrases usually end. Some writers use 'finalis' for the final pitch of a *gusheh*.[16] *Moteqayyer* ('changeable') is the name for variable pitches. Some *gusheh*s are found in more than one *dastgāh*, and this may involve a sharing of melodic material, overall shape or just the name. A performance usually remains in one *dastgāh*, although musicians sometimes move between *dastgāh*s using shared *gusheh*s as bridges, a technique known as *morakkab-navāzi*.

---

[14]   Whilst musicians are in broad agreement regarding the number of *dastgāh*s, there is some variation between different versions of the *radif*. Borumand's version of Mirza Abdollah's *radif* includes *Bayāt-e Kord* as a (short) *dastgāh* (which is not found in the other *radif*s under study), bringing to 13 the number of *dastgāh*s in this *radif* (see During 1984a:114, 1991a).

[15]   Most writers refer to the *darāmad* as a *gusheh* (see, among many examples, Caron and Safvate 1966:109, Zonis 1973:48, During 1984a:141 and Nettl 1987:26). However, Farhat defines *gusheh* as: 'The generic term for individual pieces, other than the *darāmad*, which make up the repertoire of a *dastgāh*' (1990:22). Similarly, Sadeghi lists '*darāmad*' separately from '*gushe*' (1971:51–2), although he later includes *darāmad* in a list of principal *gusheh*s of each *dastgāh* (ibid.:57–8). This apparent anomaly would seem to derive from the fact that in Persian one does not refer to '*gusheh-ye darāmad*', but simply to the *darāmad* of a particular *dastgāh* as in '*darāmad-e Segāh*', '*darāmad-e Chāhārgāh*' and so on. Regardless of whether the label '*gusheh*' is used, as a constituent section of the *dastgāh*, the *darāmad* is, strictly speaking, a *gusheh*. Therefore, terminological complexities notwithstanding, in this study the *darāmad* is treated as a *gusheh*.

[16]   *Shāhed*, *āqāz* and *ist* are of Persian/Arabic origin; finalis is Western in derivation. Farhat uses the latter in preference to 'tonic' with its 'direct associations with the harmonic system of western music' (1990:24). Moreover, the word 'tonic' might imply a certain modal prominence already indicated by *shāhed*. Zonis mentions 'finalis' by way of explaining the Persian word *ist*, which she equates with the finalis of Gregorian chant (1973:47). In contrast, During makes no mention of Persian terminology, simply substituting the French *note-témoin*, *note d'arrêt* and *note de conclusion* for *shāhed*, *ist* and finalis (as used by Farhat) respectively (1984a:108). In this, he appears to follow Caron and Safvate, who give both French and Persian terms, and who also distinguish between the *ist* (which can function as the final pitch of a *gusheh* as well of medial phrases) and *ist-e movaqqat* ('temporary' *ist*, only heard in the latter position) (1966:42–7). They translate *note de conclusion* from the Persian *forud-e kāmel*. In the tables of modal scales preceding Massoudieh's transcription of the vocal *radif* (1989[1978]:22–3), he uses the terms *sedā-ye shoru* ('starting sound'; and also the French *note de départ*) and *sedā-ye khātemeh* ('ending sound'; Fr. *note finale*) to indicate *āqāz* and finalis respectively. Whilst there is an important difference between a pitch which ends medial phrases and that which ends a complete *gusheh*, neither Farhat nor Massoudieh state whether the terms *finalis/sedā-ye khātemeh* are used by musicians or have arisen through analytical needs. The term used by Caron and Safvate – *forud-e kāmel* – is used by musicians, but not commonly found in the literature.

The core of Iranian classical music is in an unmetered style known as *āvāz* ('song', 'voice', not to be confused with the subsidiary *dastgāhs*). However, as noted in earlier chapters there are a number of metered (usually pre-composed) genres which developed in the early twentieth century and which can be played independently or as part of a *dastgāh* performance. These include *pishdarāmad* (opening instrumental ensemble piece), *tasnif* (song accompanied by ensemble, usually heard at the beginning or end of a performance), *chāhārmezrāb* (fast, rhythmic instrumental piece, often heard as an interlude during a performance) and *reng* (instrumental dance piece, often in ⅜ time and usually played at the end of a performance). In addition, several *gushehs* are based on poetic metres, such as *masnavi*, *hodi va pahlavi* and *rajaz* in *Segāh*. It should also be noted that the unmetered *āvāz* style has close links with poetry and much of the music is set to lyrics by Medieval mystic poets.[17]

Dastgāh Segāh

Since most of the analytical discussion which follows focuses on *Segāh*, I will introduce this *dastgāh* before proceeding to the analysis itself. Written references to *Segāh* date back to at least the late thirteenth century (Wright 1994:481), but how close the musical material was to the present day is uncertain. *Segāh* is also related to similarly-named modal systems in other parts of the Middle East, North India and Central Asia.[18] In Persian, *Segāh* means 'third place', referring to the finger position on the neck of the lute (the instrument on which much of the music theory of the region was historically based). *Segāh* bears a close relationship to *dastgāh Chāhārgāh* ('fourth place') sharing many *gushehs* in name and overall shape, but with a different modal configuration. The central *gushehs* of *Segāh* are as follows: *darāmad*, *zābol*, *muyeh*, *mokhālef* and *maqlub*, each based around successively higher pitches, with *maqlub* forming the climax, after which the music descends to the tonal area of the opening. In addition, there are a number of other (shorter) *gushehs* in the *radif*s of *Segāh*, heard with varying regularity in performance, as discussed below.[19] I will briefly describe the central *gushehs* and give some illustrative examples. As in other *dastgāh*s, the mode of *Segāh* is established in the *darāmad*; in effect, the mode of the *darāmad is* the mode of *Segāh*. The pitch of overriding significance is e-*koron* (approximate half-flat), which acts as *shāhed*, *āqāz* and *ist*, as well as finalis; indeed, a distinguishing feature of *Segāh* is the coincidence of these modal functions on one central pitch. The main tetrachord lies between e-*koron* and a-*koron* although other pitches are also used. Another characteristic feature of *Segāh* is the neutral third interval between the e-*koron shāhed* and the third below (c), a motif used extensively in the *darāmad* (particularly at the end), in the cadential *forud* patterns at the end of *gushehs*, and in the extended *forud* at the conclusion of *Segāh*.[20] Illustrative examples of the *darāmad* of *Segāh* (one *radif* and one performance) are presented in Figures 4.1 and 4.2.

Figure 4.1   *darāmad* of *Segāh*, Nur Ali Borumand (*tār*), *radif* 1 (accompanying CD, track 1)

[17]   Tsuge (1974) is a comprehensive study of rhythm and metre in Iranian music. See also During (1984a:142–7), Nettl (1987:32–4, 70–72), Miller (1999), Azadehfar (2006).

[18]   Powers (1989) provides an overview of the various manifestations of this modal system in the Middle East and parts of Central Asia. See also Ogger's (1987) detailed study comparing *Segāh* in the Persian and Iraqi traditions.

[19]   For further information on general characteristics of *Segāh*, see Zonis (1973:88–90), During (1984a:118–19) and Farhat (1990:51–5).

[20]   E-*koron* lies between e♭ and e♮. Although there is traditionally no concept of standard pitch, and performances and published notations are therefore centred around a variety of pitches, greater standardization in the course of the twentieth century led to the common use of two tunings – *rāst kuk* ('right tuning') and *chap kuk* ('left tuning'), usually a perfect 4th apart – in performing a particular *dastgāh* (see Caron and Safvate 1966:185–9, Sadeghi 1971:22–32, Zonis 1973:66–96). The choice of tuning often depends on the vocal range of the singer (if there is one). Most performances of *Segāh* use either e-*koron* or a-*koron* (or a nearby pitch) as the *shāhed* of the *darāmad*. For comparative purposes, the examples from *Segāh* in this chapter are notated with e-*koron* as the *shāhed* (of the *darāmad*). The actual sounding pitch of the *shāhed* is indicated in square brackets at the start of each example.

The *darāmad* of *Segāh* is usually followed by *gusheh zābol* (named after a town in southeastern Iran), which is characterized by a distinctive opening motif: an oscillation between e-*koron* and f, before moving up to an emphasis of, and resting on, g. The pitches and main tetrachord of *zābol* are the same as the *darāmad*, but the centre of melodic activity moves up to g (the *shāhed*). See Figures 4.3 and 4.4 for examples of *gusheh zābol*.

Zābol is generally followed by *muyeh* (lit.: 'crying', 'lamenting'); again, the pitches of the *darāmad* are maintained, but the main area of activity is now between g and b♭. *Mokhālef* ('contrary') usually follows *muyeh* and is the most important *gusheh* after the *darāmad*. *Mokhālef* is based around the sixth degree of the scale of *Segāh*, but with changed pitches (a-*koron*, b-*koron* and e♭), constituting the first significant modification of the home mode. Like *zābol*, *mokhālef* has a distinctive opening: an emphasis of c, usually followed by a movement down to g and up to c again, as seen in the examples of *mokhālef* in Figures 4.5 and 4.6.

The climax (*owj*) of *Segāh* is *gusheh maqlub*, which uses the same pitches as *mokhālef*; however, whilst the main tetrachord of *mokhālef* lies between g and c, *maqlub* emphasizes the area between c and e♭, the highest focal pitch in *Segāh*.[21] Note that this flattening of pitches in the upper octave – the e-*koron* of earlier *gusheh*s becomes e♭ in the higher ranges of *mokhālef* and *maqlub* – is also found in other *dastgāh*s. Bearing in mind that much of this music was originally based on the voice, it is possible that vocalists found e♭ (in the case of *Segāh*) less strenuous in the higher register than the slightly sharper e-*koron*, leading over time to a gradual flattening of the upper octave e-*koron*. See Figures 4.7 and 4.8 for examples of *maqlub*. Following *maqlub*, the music descends (usually through a series of shorter *gusheh*s) to the home mode and an extended *forud* section. Farhat discusses the importance of this final *forud* in re-establishing the modal area of the *darāmad* after the (generally) extended section in the higher-pitched *mokhālef* mode (1990:55).

The order of central *gusheh*s presented here, whilst consistent with that usually found in the *radif*s of *Segāh*, is subject to some variation in performance, as discussed below. Similarly, the pitch functions described may be varied, with performers occasionally using an alternative (most usually adjacent) pitch, particularly for the *āqāz* and *ist*. The finalis, however, rarely changes, because of its role in maintaining modal identity. Similarly, the *shāhed* is not variable, since its relationship to other pitches is the most important factor in defining the mode.

Discussion of the *gusheh*s of *Segāh* in the literature is generally cursory and focused almost exclusively on mode. Zonis (1973:88–90), During (1984a:118–19) and Farhat (1990:51–5) describe the characteristics of the main *gusheh*s, with musical examples provided by Zonis and Farhat. Farhat also gives a 'basic melodic formula' (1990:52) for the central *gusheh*s, drawn not from one performance but abstracted from several. These authors make little distinction between aspects of mode which may be characteristic of a *gusheh*, and those which are essential. Nor is there any consideration of how *gusheh*s are interpreted in performance.

It is important at this point to clarify use of the term 'mode', the complexities of which are discussed at length by Powers (1980c, 1989) with particular reference to the Middle East. In the present study, 'mode' is taken to mean a set of pitches in a hierarchical relationship (Powers' 'tonal category'). In one sense, *gusheh* is the main modal unit of Iranian music, each *dastgāh* comprising a series of *gusheh*s in different (but related) modes, connected by the home (*darāmad*) mode. However, whilst 'mode' and '*gusheh*' are often presented as essentially synonymous in the literature, there is an important difference between them, since two *gusheh*s may share the same mode (in the sense of 'tonal category') but be distinguished through particular melodies and rhythms, as is often the case with shorter *gusheh*s. In *Segāh*, *naqmeh-ye maqlub*, *masnavi* and *hazeen*[22]

---

[21] *Maqlub* is usually notated with an e♭ (or equivalent, depending on the pitch of the *shāhed* of *Segāh*). However, in the *radif*s of Karimi (*radif* 2; Massoudieh 1989[1978]:149) and Ma'rufi (*radif* 4; Barkeshli and Ma'rufi 1963) it is notated using e-*koron* (the latter has e-*koron* at the start of *maqlub*, changing to e♭ part-way through). There are various indicators that these may be misprints. In the recordings accompanying *radif* 2, Karimi sings an e♭ in the upper octave, and in the published notation of this *radif* the return to e-*koron* towards the end of *maqlub* (in the lower octave) is marked in a manner that would be unnecessary had there been an earlier e-*koron*. Moreover, all of the renditions of *maqlub* in the analysed performances use e♭ in the upper octave.

[22] Farhat describes *masnavi* and *hazeen* as 'vagrant' *gusheh*s or '*tekkes*', relatively short and less important *gusheh*s which can be found in any *dastgāh* and which maintain their melodic shape whilst being assimilated to the mode of that *dastgāh*. He gives examples of *masnavi* in *Shur*, *Bayāt-e Esfahān* and *Afshāri*, and of *hazeen* in *Navā*, *Shur* and *Chāhārgāh* (1990:111–12, 184–6, 188–90). Figure 4.9 lists the occurrence of *masnavi* and *hazeen* in all 12 *dastgāh*s in *radif*s 2 and 4.

Figure 4.2   *darāmad* of *Segāh*, Pashang Kamkar (*santur*) and Jamshid Andalibi (*nei*), performance 15 (accompanying CD, track 2)

Note: All musical transcriptions are by the author. See Appendix B for a key to the symbols used. Sound recordings of Figures 4.1 to 4.8 are on the accompanying CD.

Figure 4.3   *gusheh zābol*, Mahmud Karimi (voice), *radif* 2 (accompanying CD, track 3)

Figure 4.4   *gusheh zābol*, Farhang Sharif (*tār*), performance 13 (accompanying CD, track 4)

Figure 4.5   *gusheh mokhālef*, Nur Ali Borumand (*tār*), *radif* 1 (accompanying CD, track 5)

use the mode/tonal category of *mokhālef*, but are characterized by specific melodies and, in the first two, rhythms, and thus identifiable as separate *gushehs*. They are in the mode of *mokhālef* but are separate entities from *gusheh mokhālef*. Thus, '*mokhālef*' indicates both the specific *gusheh* with its own melodic and modal characteristics, and the broad modal area within which other *gushehs* are heard. This subtle distinction creates a level of analytical complexity rarely discussed by musicians. Another example: *hodi va pahlavi* and *rajaz* share the *darāmad* mode (tonal category), but are independent *gushehs* with distinct melodic and rhythmic features. Similarly, *bastenegār*, a short *gusheh* largely defined by its distinctive rhythm, can be heard in any *dastgāh* or (theoretically, at least) *gusheh*. In *Segāh*, it is usually heard in the mode of *zābol* and occasionally in *mokhālef*. *Shekasteh muyeh*, a *gusheh* which sometimes appears briefly towards the end of *Segāh* as a bridge between the modal area of *mokhālef* and the return to the *darāmad* mode (but which may also be heard before *gusheh mokhālef*), is in the mode of *muyeh*. *Hesār* and *hozān* were the only shorter *gushehs* in the analysed versions of *Segāh* not to be based in the mode of a primary *gusheh*, and for these two, therefore, 'mode' and '*gusheh*' coincide. Whilst there are exceptions, generally speaking it is prominent *gushehs* such as *darāmad* and *mokhālef* which include other, shorter, ones within their modal ambit.

As noted, material in the mode of *Segāh* is heard at the beginning of the *dastgāh*, in order to establish its identity, and at the end to provide closure and reinforce the sense of return. The distinction between 'mode' and '*gusheh*' is important here. The opening is known as *darāmad*, whilst the ending is called *forud*; the latter shares the mode/tonal category of *darāmad* and some of its other characteristics but is clearly recognized as a separate section. The short *foruds* in the *darāmad* mode heard at the end of *gushehs* in the course of the *dastgāh* are generally considered part of the *gusheh* which they conclude.

The distinction between *gusheh* and mode is rarely discussed in the literature, but is often implied in the terminology used. Of those who do discuss this (briefly), Farhat suggests that the Persian *maqām* ('position') is equivalent to 'mode' (1990:23), and certainly prior to the development of the *dastgāh* system, this would have been the main local term signifying mode or melody-type (as still used in related traditions in the region). Indeed, until recently, some older musicians still used '*maqām*' to refer to individual *dastgāhs* (see Khaleqi 1983a). Another term for 'mode' is '*māyeh*' (Pers: 'source', 'basic material'; Farhat 1990:23,

Figure 4.6   *gusheh mokhālef*, Lotfollah Majd (*tār*), performance 10 (accompanying CD, track 6)

During 1991b:60–63).[23] In lessons, Firooz Berenjian expressed the distinction between mode and *gusheh* indirectly by explaining that a particular *gusheh* was '*dar favāsel-e mokhālef*' ('in the intervals of *mokhālef*') or '*dar nowthā-ye mokhālef*' ('in the notes/pitches of *mokhālef*'). Similarly, in the commentary following Alizadeh's recording of the *radif* of Mirza Abdollah (1992), he describes certain *gushehs* as being '*dar*

---

[23]   Khaleqi also uses the word *māyeh* (1982:63–74), although his definition of and distinction between *gām* (scale), *māyeh* and *maqām* is rather unclear. This is partly due to the way in which he attempts to explain Persian modal theory in terms essentially derived from Western music, itself indicative of the period when this book was originally published (1938). Farhat (1990:23) also claims that the English 'mode' is used by some musicians. Although the latter is not something I have encountered, this may have been the case in the early to mid-1960s when the material published in 1990 was originally written.

Figure 4.7　　　*gusheh maqlub*, Mahmud Karimi (voice), *radif* 2 (accompanying CD, track 7)[24]

Figure 4.8　　　*gusheh maqlub*, Parviz Meshkatian (*santur*), performance 16 (accompanying CD, track 8)

mahdoodeh-ye darāmad' ('in the limits/region of *darāmad*'). Although this aspect of mode is not generally discussed, then, vocabulary does exist to describe the way in which one *gusheh* operates within the modal domain of another.

From Radif *to Performance*

The primary starting point for the analysis which follows is the simple fact that *Segāh* is created anew at each performance. However, this must take place within certain boundaries if the identity of the *dastgāh* and its constituent *gusheh*s is to be maintained. In exploring the relationship between *radif* and performance, one could focus on many aspects of the music. Here, I begin by examining the large-scale organization of *Segāh* and how musicians shape performances in terms of constituent *gusheh*s and modal sections.[25] The second half of the chapter will consider the internal details of each *gusheh*, seeking to understand how musicians use the learnt repertoire to create new material in performance.

The performances of *Segāh* analysed as part of the larger study from which the examples below are drawn include a range of musicians in terms of age, educational background and training lineages, performing in different contexts, and spanning a period from the 1950s to the late 1980s. Some are live recordings of concerts, others are commercial recordings or recorded radio broadcasts (from Iran and abroad). All of the main instruments of the classical tradition are represented and the sample includes renditions by the same musician on different occasions, and by teachers and pupils or fellow pupils, all of which was useful for comparative purposes. Further details of the performances are given in Appendix A. The *radif*s analysed were: the *radif* of Mirza Abdollah as transmitted by Nur Ali Borumand (*tār*) (*radif* 1, often referred to as the *radif* of Borumand); the vocal *radif* of Abdollah Davami, recorded and taught by Mahmud Karimi (*radif* 2, published as Massoudieh 1978);

---

[24]　Note that due to the layout of the notation, it has not been possible to align the words exactly under the corresponding pitches in Figure 4.7.

[25]　Using a similar approach to Nettl's discussion of constituent *gusheh*s and their ordering in *dastgāh*s *Chāhārgāh*, *Shur* and *Māhur* (with Foltin 1972, 1987). Simms and Koushkani also present an analysis of the distribution of *dastgāh*s and *gusheh*s in 42 recordings by Shajarian (2012a:225–38). In my original study (Nooshin 1996), each performance and *radif* was analysed in several ways, according to: (a) broad modal sections; (b) the order and length of individual *gusheh*s; and (c) the metric character, length and *forud* notes of the subdivisions of each *gusheh*. The resulting data was presented in a series of tables (1996:553–81; see also Appendix A in this volume) and discussed in detail (184–227).

the *radif* published by the Institute for the Intellectual Development of Children and Young Adults (*radif* 3, various musicians and instruments); and the *radif* compiled by Musa Ma'rufi (*radif* 4, unpublished recording).[26] In addition, the violin *radif* of Abol Hassan Saba in two versions (c.1967, Volumes 1 and 2, *radif*s 5 and 6), although available only in notated form and therefore not as useful as the recorded *radif*s, was also referred to. Two further recordings were consulted, but not used directly in the analysis: the first played on *santur* by Majid Kiani (1987) and the second on *tār* by Hossein Alizadeh (1992). Both are former students of Borumand, and the recordings are almost identical to *radif* 1 but are finer renditions. The listing and descriptions of *gusheh*s of *Segāh* given by Farhat (1990:51–5) were also a useful supplement.[27]

Whilst the transition from one *gusheh* to the next is not made explicit in performance (for instance, by means of an announcement as often found in recorded *radif*s in line with their pedagogical function) but simply understood by informed listeners, in performances 18, 25 and 26 *gusheh*s are identified before and/ or during the rendition, since these were intended to illustrate the tradition for a non-Iranian audience. For performance 2, the *gusheh*s were listed on the concert programme notes; similarly for performances 9 and 17, *gusheh*s were named on the cassette and album covers respectively. These listings, however, are fairly general and none provide information on the internal sectioning of *gusheh*s (there were also some discrepancies between the *gusheh*s listed in programme notes and those actually performed). Nettl has written about the difficulties of analysing performances for their constituent *gusheh*s (with Foltin 1972:17–18), tentatively suggesting two kinds of *dastgāh*, the first of which (including *Segāh*) can be relatively easily divided into constituent *gusheh*s, whilst the second is less easily analysed in this way (*dastgāh Shur*, for instance; Nettl 1987:105). The situation is made more complex by the technique known as *eshāreh* ('hint', 'allusion') in which a *gusheh* is briefly alluded to within another; thus, *zābol* may include a brief allusion to *gusheh muyeh* ('*eshāreh be muyeh*'). Moreover, as discussed in Chapter 3, whilst some musicians remain close to the *radif*, presenting clear-cut sections based on the main *gusheh*s, others use materials from the *radif* more freely, in which case *gusheh* identification can be difficult.

Whilst the relationship between *radif* and performance is central to the current discussion, as noted in Chapter 3 identifying a specific model or models on which a particular performance is based is problematic, not least because musicians typically learn more than one version and because in performance they may draw on musical experiences that go beyond the *radif*. Although difficult to ascertain the extent to which published *radif*s (notated and recorded) differ from the orally-transmitted *radif*s of individual masters, most

---

[26]   The background to this recording is rather interesting and worth relating in full here. Played on *tār* by Soleyman Ruhafza (1907–1980) in apparently informal surroundings, the recording is introduced by Ma'rufi, and clearly intended to preserve his *radif* for future generations. The rendition is based directly on that published by the Iranian government and discussed in Chapter 3 (Barkeshli and Ma'rufi 1963). It was deposited at the University of Tehran, and a copy of the recording of *Segāh* was made available to me courtesy of Professor Bruno Nettl. Whilst the date is unknown, according to Tsuge (1974:98), Ruhafza recorded this *radif* under Ma'rufi's supervision between 1959 and 1960 (Tsuge transcribes part of this *radif* in his study). It is likely that this is the same recording as that deposited at the university and therefore *predates* the print version. In 2009 (well after the original work presented here was undertaken), Ruhafza's recording was published by the Mahoor Institute of Culture and Art whose website explains: 'The radif compiled by Musa Ma'rufi is based on the radif of Mirza Abdollah and the radif of Aqa Hoseyn-Qoli. It has also been adapted to the radif of Mehdi-Qoli Hedayat. But since there has never been a consensus among the Persian music masters on the gushe's of radif, around four decades ago, many of the celebrated masters of Persian music including Nur-Ali Borumand, Ali-Akbar Shahnazi, Abolhasan Saba, Ahmad Ebadi, Rokneddin Mokhtari, and Musa Ma'rufi gathered together at the invitation of Institute of Fine Arts to edit and finalize every single gushe of radif. These controversial sessions lasted for a whole and a half year but in vain due to the divergence of views among those masters. Finally, they agreed that everyone does compile, transcribe, and publish their own version separately, and afterwards the council conducts analysis on them. Through such a procedure, the radif of Musa Ma'rufi was selected to be published. Musa Ma'rufi was masterful at playing tar. He was one of the prominent students of Darvish Khan. Ma'rufi in compiling his radif which was published in 1963 has artistically taken into account the radif of Mirza Abdollah and the radif of Aqa Hoseyn-Qoli, and the works of Ali-Naqi Vaziri as well. The deceased Soleyman Ruhafza, on the recommendation of Ma'rufi, has performed the due radif by tar' (www.mahoor.com/cd/Pedagogical-Works/ Radif-of-Seven-Dastgahs-of-Iranian-Classical-Music-647.aspx, accessed 15.12.12).

[27]   Although *radif*s 1, 2 and 4 were available in printed form, in the case of the first two I chose to make my own transcriptions for the purposes of analysis, whilst also referring to the published sources for points of comparison. For *radif* 4, analysis of the progression and relative lengths of sections was based on the sound recording (again, with reference to the published notation).

of the musicians with whom I talked invoked the former to illustrate their points. Moreover, the literature presents published *radif*s as representative of, if not identical to, the oral tradition of teaching. Given that such publications are in wide circulation, and generally regarded as reliable sources, I have taken these to be representative of the taught repertoire.

Sectional Organization

Starting with the analysed *radif*s of *Segāh* (those available as sound recordings), the diagram below (extracted from the listing for each *radif* in Appendix A) shows that all four were constructed around a core progression of modal areas, each centred on one of the main *gushehs* (*darāmad* (D), *zābol* (Z), *muyeh* (Mu), *mokhālef* (Mo)) and tracing a gradual rise in pitch until the climax on *maqlub* (Maq) and return to the *darāmad* mode for the final *forud*:

D	Mu	**Z**	**Mu**			**Mo**	**Maq**	Mo	Mu [*shur*][28]	**D** (*radif* 1)
D		**Z**	**Mu**	Hes		**Mo**	**Maq**			**D** (*radif* 2)
D		**Z**	**Mu**			**Mo**	**Maq**	Hoz[29]	Mo	**D** (*radif* 3)[30]
D		**Z**	**Mu**	Hes Hoz	**Mo**		**Maq**	Mo	Hoz Mu	**D** (*radif* 4)

In general, the analysed performances also shared the same core modal progression, but with one important difference: the omission of *maqlub*:

D		**Z**	**Mu**		**Mo**			**D**

This core, derived from comparing 26 performances, was presented in the form above in only one rendition (performance 22, Hossein Malek).[31] In the other 25, the core was varied in different ways. In some, the music returned to a modal area (or gave a 'preview' before the main modal section); for example, whilst *muyeh* was usually positioned between *zābol* and *mokhālef*, in a number of performances it was also heard later in the descent following *mokhālef*; in some cases, *muyeh* was substituted in this position by *shekasteh muyeh* (SMu, a short *gusheh* in the mode of *muyeh* but with its own distinctive melody. 7, group; 17, group). Elsewhere, *muyeh* was omitted from its more usual position before *mokhālef*, but included in the later descent, again often in the form of *shekasteh muyeh* (10, Majd; 25, Borumand). Another variation to the basic core was the inclusion of less prominent *gushehs* such as *maqlub*, *hesār* (Hes) and *hozān* (Hoz), usually after *mokhālef*. In general, the most frequent variational strategy was a combination of re-statement (or pre-statement) of modal sections and the inclusion of extra *gushehs* (1, group; 3, Saba; 8, Bahari; 15, group; 8, Payvar; 20, group; 27, Shajarian and Payvar; 29, group). Other musicians both re-stated central modes, added extra *gushehs*, and omitted *muyeh* from its earlier position, including it (and/or *shekasteh muyeh*) after *mokhālef* (5, Zeidollah Tului; 6, Reza Shafeian; 9, Shafeian; 16, Meshkatian; 23, During). In several of these performances, *hesār* (and in performance 8, *zābol*) became an alternative to *muyeh* in the later position.

---

[28]   The unusual group of *gushehs* in the mode of Shur towards the end of *radif* 1 is discussed below.

[29]   *Hozān* (Hoz) is not mentioned by Farhat, and in the *radifs* under study only appeared in *radifs* 3 and 4. According to Sepanta (1959:9), *hozān* is an old *gusheh*, rarely heard even in the 1950s. However, part of the phrase which comprises this short *gusheh* was heard towards the end of *hazeen* in *radif* 1 (but not separately named) and in several performances, where it seemed to function as a *forud* pattern. The same pattern was also found in a similar position in several other *gushehs* (both in *radifs* and performances), as discussed below.

[30]   The order of *gushehs* in *radif* 3 is rather unusual, since they are introduced individually and subsequently combined in small groupings to demonstrate sub-sections of the *dastgāh*. This *radif* was not intended for the direct teaching context, but as a general educational tool. The modal trajectory presented here is an abstraction from the progression of sections in this *radif*.

[31]   Performance number and name of musician(s) are given in parentheses. For further details of the performances, see Appendix A.

In only two performances (13, Sharif; 12, Malek) was the order of any of the main modal sections changed: in performance 13, *muyeh* was played before *zābol*:

D   Mu ⟵——————⟶ Z   Mo   Hes   D   SMu   D

And performance 12 (the only performance not to begin and end in the *darāmad* mode) began with *zābol* rather than *darāmad*:

Z ⟵————⟶ D   Z   Mu   Mo

Whilst Malek did tend to emphasize *zābol* more than other performers, this ordering of sections is nonetheless surprising given that it contrasts directly with another performance in which he presents the modal core in its most basic form (22).[32] Finally, just two performances omitted one of the central modal sections: all 26 included *darāmad* and *mokhālef*, but *zābol* and *muyeh* were omitted from performances 14 (group) and 24 (Safvate) respectively.

Notwithstanding the limited sample size, the analysed performances and *radif*s shared much in their modal organization, and a number of patterns were evident. In performance, a core progression of four modal sections (and the final return to the *darāmad* mode) was varied using repetition and omission of sections, as well as the addition of *gusheh*s outside the central core. Whilst only two performances were identical in their modal organization (10 and 25), there were other commonalities: all 26 included the four main modal sections (other than the omission of *zābol* and *muyeh* in performances 14 and 24); all began and ended in the *darāmad* mode (except for performance 12); and in all but three, *zābol* followed *darāmad* as the second modal section. *Muyeh* was the only central mode whose position regularly changed, usually heard either directly before, or in the descent after, *mokhālef*. Furthermore, in many of the performances (but less apparent in the *radif*s), the progression in the first part of *Segāh* (between *darāmad* and *mokhālef*) was less complex than in the second (from *mokhālef* onwards), which is where most of the shorter and modally-independent *gusheh*s were heard.

And there are other patterns. Consider the following (performance 3) in which *mokhālef* is 'sandwiched' between two sections in the mode of *muyeh*:

　　　　…　　**Mu   Mo   SMu**　　…

This was subject to variation: for instance, *radif* 1 had the same pattern but with *maqlub* additionally inserted 'within' *mokhālef*:

　　　　…　　**Mu   Mo   Maq   Mo   Mu**　　…

In performances 8, 20 and 29, *hesār* was substituted for *muyeh* in the post-*mokhālef* descent:

　　　　…　　**Mu   Mo   Hes**　　…

And performance 27 combined the above two variations:

　　　　…　　**Mu   Mo   Maq   Mo   Hes**　　…

In other words, just as the overall modal organization of *Segāh* comprises a continually varied core of *gusheh*s, so individual parts of the core are varied in their internal sectioning.

---

[32]   Taken from a Bärenreiter Musicaphon disc (published early 1960s), performance 12 was rather unusual. The music fades out during *mokhālef*, and seems to be cut before the end of the performance, perhaps because of time limits. The recording was made by Alain Daniélou and edited under his direction.

In Nooshin 1996 (p.192), I present a flowchart summarizing the progression of modal sections in the analysed versions of *Segāh*, and the various 'pathways' by which musicians move through the *dastgāh*. In that teachers explicitly name *gusheh*s, which are usually learnt in the order that they appear in the *radif*, sectional organization is fairly well-articulated. Thus, the close correspondence between *radif*s and performances in this respect is unsurprising. However, certain interesting anomalies (considered below), and the fact that sectional organization seems to represent a range of variation around an analytically abstractable core, suggests that in learning different versions of the *radif*, students come to understand the 'core' (for each *dastgāh*) and its variational potential, subsequently applying this in performance.[33]

Structuring Principles, Controlled Variation

The discussion above has identified certain patterns in the sectional organization of *Segāh*: most fundamentally, the performances all included *darāmad* and *mokhālef*, with *zābol* and *muyeh* omitted from only one performance each; the analysed *radif*s were built around the same core, and in essentially the same order, but with the addition of *maqlub*.[34] Generally speaking, performances were more diverse than *radif*s in their sectional organization, but adhered to similar principles: there was a certain unity among the performances, but not as tight a core as in the *radif*s. At the same time, no two analysed versions of *Segāh*, even by the same musician, were identical in their sectional organization. To summarize: in performance the central core was varied through the re-statement, movement or (occasionally) omission of main *gusheh*s and/or the inclusion of shorter *gusheh*s: all began in the *darāmad* mode and ended in the same mode (with the exception of one *radif* and one performance), and shared an overall shape characterized by a gradual rise in pitch and associated tension, reaching a pitch climax towards the end, followed by a descent to the home mode. The central *gusheh*s thus seem to occupy particular positions in the architectural structuring of *Segāh*; indeed it might be suggested that they attain significance through their positioning at critical points. Since this arch shape is also heard in other *dastgāh*s, it is possible that it accords with certain aesthetic criteria:[35] *gusheh*s may be added, omitted or re-arranged as long as the overall trajectory of rising tension and eventual release is maintained. For example, whilst *maqlub* formed the *owj* of *Segāh* in all of the *radif*s, it was omitted from 18 of the performances, where instead *mokhālef* assumed the climactic role otherwise fulfilled by *maqlub*. Similarly, certain sequences of *gusheh*s were simply not (or rarely) heard: *muyeh* rarely preceded *zābol* (only in *radif* 1 and performance 13); *maqlub* never preceded *mokhālef*; *shekasteh muyeh* was generally played in the descent at the end of the *mokhālef* modal section; in the few renditions where it appeared before *mokhālef*, *shekasteh muyeh* was heard again after *mokhālef* (in *radif* 2, the only *radif* to include *shekasteh muyeh*, there was a return to it in the form of an *eshāreh* in the descent at the end of *maqlub*); and the following progression – *darāmad* moving directly to *mokhālef*, followed by *zābol* – was not found in any of the analysed versions of *Segāh*. Clearly, certain kinds of modal progression lie outside the acceptable, largely unspoken, limits of variation.

When one considers the positioning in performance of the two longest and most structurally complex *gusheh*s – *darāmad* and *mokhālef* – an interesting pattern emerges. Many of the analysed performances seemed divisible into two main halves: the first starting with *darāmad* and the second with *mokhālef* (the only significant shift from the home mode of *Segāh*), with both followed by a series of shorter *gusheh*s.[36]

---

[33] Limits of space preclude discussion of such aspects of sectional organization as the use of measured and unmeasured material, the relative lengths of *gusheh*s and modal sections, and the internal organization of *gusheh*s. For further discussion see Nooshin (1996:194–210).

[34] In Simms and Koushkani's analysis of the inclusion of *gusheh*s in four performances of *Segāh* by Shajarian, all included *darāmad*, *zābol*, *muyeh* and *mokhālef*, just two included *maqlub* and only one included *hesār* (2012a:231).

[35] See Nettl (1987) for discussion of this with reference to *dastgāh*s *Chāhārgāh*, *Māhur* and *Shur*.

[36] The second half of *Segāh* (beginning with *mokhālef*) started between 46 and 78 per cent of the way through performances (and between 50 and 60 per cent of the way through in just under half of the performances analysed). A similar situation was found in *radif*s 2 and 4, although *mokhālef* started later (62 and 55 per cent of the way through respectively) due to the prominence of *hesār* between *muyeh* and *mokhālef*; and in *radif* 1 *mokhālef* started earlier (40 per cent of the way through) as a result of the series of extra *gusheh*s associated with *rohāb* at the end of this *radif* (the unusual organization of *radif* 3, noted earlier, makes it difficult to specify a figure).

In the case of *darāmad*, these shorter *gushehs* were generally modally independent (though still closely related), whilst those following *mokhālef* tended to share the same mode. Nettl has written about the relative lengths of *gushehs* and their positioning within *dastgāh Chāhārgāh* (1987:53–4), and suggests three types of performance: in the first, *gushehs* are of approximately equal length; in the second, the *darāmad* is the longest, followed by progressively shorter *gushehs*; and in the third, the performance is divisible into two main sections each led by a major *gusheh*, usually followed by shorter renditions of others. Whilst the examples of *Segāh* analysed here do not correspond exactly with any of these typologies, they seem closest to the third, but with the shorter *gushehs* accorded more importance than in Nettl's sample.

As well as the inclusion, ordering and internal organization of broad modal sections and individual *gushehs* of *Segāh*, I have elsewhere considered their relative lengths (Nooshin 1996:204–10; see timings in Appendix A of this volume). The *darāmad* was on average the longest modal section in performance, followed by *mokhālef*, *zābol* and *muyeh*, in that order. *Gusheh* length thus correlates with internal sectional complexity. However, in the analysed *radifs*, the order of *zābol* and *muyeh* (in terms of relative length) was reversed; and whilst *darāmad* was (on average) still the longest, it constituted a smaller percentage of the overall *dastgāh* in comparison with performances. Instead, *gushehs* outside the central core, some of which were not included in the performances, comprised a greater percentage of the *dastgāh*. In terms of specific performances, only one (performance 14) followed the overall average for modal section length: *darāmad* being the longest, followed by *mokhālef*, *zābol* and *muyeh*. In six performances, the order was *darāmad*, *mokhālef*, followed by *muyeh* and then *zābol*, closer to the relative lengths of sections found in the *radifs*. Five of these were by older musicians, suggesting that this may represent an earlier practice in which *muyeh* was more prominent than *zābol*.

To summarize the discussion so far: there seem to be a number of principles at work in the ordering of modal sections in *Segāh*, including the overall shape and trajectory of the *dastgāh* and its organization around two main modal sections, *darāmad* and *mokhālef*. Such principles are not explicitly discussed during teaching, and it seems likely that through experiencing different versions, they are abstracted and become part of a musician's internalized knowledge. In the absence of local terminology indicating the ways in which a musical idea or structure may be varied around certain (usually implicit) principles, I use the term 'controlled variation'. This controlled variation was evident in the inclusion and ordering of *gushehs* and broad modal sections, in the overall shape of the *dastgāh*, and also in relation to modal pitch functions.

The Relative Importance of *Gushehs*

It is clear from talking to musicians and from the literature that the *radif* embodies notions of musical hierarchy: every *gusheh* has its place. Nettl has suggested that in this respect it is reflective of Iranian society with its prevalence of elaborate hierarchies (1980, 1983:139, 207, 1987:153–6). A number of authors have discussed the relative importance of *gushehs*. Farhat distinguishes between the main *gushehs* of a *dastgāh*, and what he calls *tekke*: short pieces which are heard in several *dastgāhs* (1990:22, 109–12; Zonis makes the same distinction, 1973:100–101). Sadeghi also suggests a tiered structure, but identifies three levels (1971:56–7). The first, '*shah gusheh*' ('king *gusheh*', a term previously used by Caron and Safvate [1966:112]), are generally the longest and most subject to variation. They usually constitute a major departure from the home mode and might also be a longer section in which other *gushehs* are heard. Sadeghi's next category, 'secondary *gushehs*' (equivalent Persian terminology is not given), are of medium length and subject to less variation than *shāh gushehs*, serving to 'fill the gaps between the principal sections of the *dastgah*' (1971:57). Finally, what Sadeghi calls 'additional fixed *gushehs*' (similar to Farhat's *tekkes*) are shorter and less important, and often have a regular metric and/or rhythmic structure, sometimes derived from a specific poetic form. Using similar terminology, During distinguishes two main types: '*shah gushes*' and '*gushes de moyenne importance*', each of which comprises two further subdivisions (1984a:141–2). In contrast to these tiered categories, Nettl suggests a continuum, listing 12 types from most to least important, using criteria such as the specificity of a *gusheh* to one or more *dastgāhs*, its internal complexity, and metric character (1987:24–9).

Whilst none of these authors state whether such categories are used by musicians, distinctions *are* in fact made between *gushehs* of greater and lesser importance, but pupils are expected to reach an understanding

Figure 4.9   Occurrence of *gushehs hazeen, hesār* and *masnavi* in all 12 *dastgāhs* in *radif*s 2 and 4

	hazeen		hesār		masnavi	
	radif 2	*radif* 4	*radif* 2	*radif* 4	*radif* 2	*radif* 4
Māhur	x	x	x	x	x	x
Shur		x			x	x
Bayāt-e Tork					x	x
Afshāri	x		x		x	x
Abu Atā						x
Dashti					x	
Homāyun						x
Esfāhān		x				x
Navā		x				
Rāst Panjgāh	x					
Segāh		x	x	x	x	
Chāhārgāh		x	x	x	x	

of this through prolonged exposure to the music in its varied permutations. The importance of a *gusheh* seems to depend on a number of factors including: regularity of appearance, length, complexity of internal organization, variability, metric character and specificity to a particular *dastgāh*. For instance, certain *gushehs* are essential for a satisfactory rendition and therefore always included (*darāmad* and *mokhālef* in *Segāh*); other important but less essential *gushehs* are heard in most performances (*zābol* and *muyeh*); and others only in some (*maqlub* and *hesār*). And regularity of appearance correlates with other aspects: thus, *darāmad* and *mokhālef* were the only *gushehs* heard in all 26 analysed performances, and were also the longest and most internally complex. *Zābol* and *muyeh*, on the other hand, were shorter, less complex and included little in the way of associated *gushehs* or measured material. Significantly, where *muyeh* was more prominent – in the analysed *radif*s – this correlated with more complex internal organization (see Nooshin 1996:578–9).

Whilst some *gushehs* are specific to one *dastgāh*, others are found in more than one. However, whilst *gushehs* of the same name in different *dastgāhs* may share musical material (but usually in different modes), the connection between them is not always so clear. Further, a number of *gushehs* such as *kereshmeh*, *bastenegār* and *zanguleh* can be heard in any *dastgāh*, and are usually short, with a relatively fixed rhythmic structure (indeed, often defined through this) and least subject to variation (Sadeghi's 'additional fixed *gushehs*' and Farhat's '*tekkes*'). In general, the most important *gushehs* are specific to a particular *dastgāh*, whilst less important *gushehs* may move freely between them.[37] In the analysed *radif*s, *darāmad* and *mokhālef* are specific to *Segāh*,[38] but other *gushehs* are found elsewhere. The sharing of *gushehs*, however, varies from one *radif* to another: in *radif* 4 (and in Farhat's listing) *zābol* is also in *Homāyun* and *Rāst Panjgāh*; and *muyeh* appears in *Shur* in the listing of Khaleqi as given in Khatschi (1962:77–80), but in none of the analysed *radif*s of *Shur*. And the series of *gushehs* associated with *rohāb* at the end of *radif* 1 (but in none of the other analysed *radif*s) are also found in several other *dastgāhs*. The three *gushehs* in the versions of *Segāh* analysed here most

---

[37]   However, the special relationship between *Segāh* and *Chāhārgāh* should be noted. Although differing in modal structure and cadential formulae, these *dastgāhs* share the same central *gushehs*, both in name, broad melodic outline and specific motifs. In this case, the sharing does not indicate a less central role for these *gushehs*.

[38]   Since *darāmad* simply means 'opening', the use of the same term for the opening *gusheh* does not constitute a sharing between *dastgāhs*; the musical material in each case is quite distinct and specific to the particular *dastgāh*.

commonly found in other *dastgāh*s were *hazeen*, *hesār* and *masnavi*. Figure 4.9 lists their occurrence in all 12 *dastgāh*s in *radif*s 2 and 4:

However, patterns of *gusheh* distribution are complex. A *gusheh* found in *Segāh* in *radif* 1 may not be found in any other *dastgāh* in that *radif*, but may occur in another *dastgāh* in a different *radif*. Limits of space preclude detailed discussion of this, but the important point is that generally speaking the more central a *gusheh* is to a particular *dastgāh* the less likely it is to be heard in another.

Finally, it is worth noting that not only is there a hierarchy between the various *gusheh*s of a *dastgāh*, but also between *dastgāh*s. And the criteria seem similar: length, organizational complexity and distinctive material. Thus, *Shur*, the longest *dastgāh*, is generally considered the most important. *Navā* and *Rāst Panjgāh*, on the other hand, share many *gusheh*s with other *dastgāh*s, and are regarded as more derivative and less important. Whilst the relationship between *dastgāh*s is not the focus of the present study, it is nevertheless interesting to note similar principles operating at different structural levels: in this case, the criteria governing the relative importance of *gusheh*s appear to be similar for different *dastgāh*s.[39]

The Case of *Hesār* and Other Anomalies

It is clear from the above discussion that the analysed *radif*s and performances of *Segāh* share much in their modal and sectional organization, generally including the same central *gusheh*s and maintaining a similar overall trajectory. This supports the idea that through exposure to different *radif*s and listening experiences, musicians internalize aspects of the music which are later applied in performance. It also aligns with the dominant discourses which place the *radif* at the centre of creative practice. And yet there were some intriguing differences between the *radif*s and performances which somewhat contradict such discourses and which I will consider here. Perhaps most significant is that despite the relatively wide range of *gusheh*s in *radif*s 1–4 (see Appendix A), these appeared rather sparsely in performance; the latter mainly comprised the central *gusheh*s with brief forays and allusions to others.[40] Moreover, certain *gusheh*s which played a central role in the *radif*s were less important in performance. For instance, *muyeh* was the only central *gusheh* to be significantly longer (on average) in the *radif*s than in performance, and this also correlated with its more complex internal organization in the former. Only in performances by older musicians did *muyeh* assume prominence, pointing to a possible diminishing role for this *gusheh*. Similarly, whilst *maqlub* was present in all four analysed *radif*s (and particularly prominent in *radif* 2), it was only heard in eight performances; in the others, *mokhālef* served the same climactic function. *Hesār* was prominent in both *radif*s 2 and 4, being the longest *gusheh* after the second *darāmad* in the former, and comprising several sections in the latter (but notably absent from *radif* 1); in both, it was positioned between *muyeh* and *mokhālef*. Yet *hesār* was included in only 11 performances, 10 of these very briefly and in a *different* position: in the final descent from *mokhālef* to the *darāmad* mode. Only in performance 23 (During) was *hesār* heard in the same position as in *radif*s 2 and 4: before *mokhālef* (seemingly taking the place of *muyeh* which was omitted before *mokhālef* in this performance).[41]

It is unclear why *gusheh*s such as *maqlub* and *hesār*, which seem to play a fairly central role in the *radif*s, should be heard rather infrequently in performance, and often with changed roles and/or positioning. This would seem to contradict the idea that students infer the importance and positioning of a *gusheh* from the *radif*. I'd like to explore a number of possible explanations, focusing on the case of *hesār*. First, as suggested for *muyeh*, this may simply be indicative of the changing tradition: *hesār* has retained its central position in some *radif*s but become short and largely optional in the performance tradition. The fact that

---

[39]   For further discussion of the relative importance of *dastgāh*s see Nettl (1987:34–9).

[40]   Nettl makes a similar point in his brief analysis of *Segāh* (1987:61–2). However, the relatively small sample (seven short performances) and the absence of detailed analysis of other *dastgāh*s makes it difficult to know whether this is specific to *Segāh* (although Nettl does makes similar observations with regard to *dastgāh Shur* (ibid.:74)).

[41]   In Nettl's analysis of *Segāh* (1987:61–2), *hesār* is also absent from all but one of the analysed performances. Similarly, in his extensive analyses of *Chāhārgāh*, Nettl notes an interesting difference between the 'lengthy exposition' of *hesār* in the *radif*s and the relatively brief appearance of this *gusheh* in the analysed performances' (ibid.:51).

those performances which included *hesār* tended to be by older musicians lends weight to this. It may also be significant that *hesār* appeared in those *radif*s originally published as notations (*radif*s 2 and 4, although in the former these were transcriptions of the accompanying sound recording; *hesār* is also in Farhat's listing), and not those originally available just as sound recordings (*radif*s 1 and 3). Other factors may be relevant. *Radif* 1, considered by many to follow the older tradition, does not include *hesār* (although it is in Borumand's *radif* of *Chāhārgāh*), and indeed During's suggestion that *Segāh* was originally a short *dastgāh* without 'the modulation to *hesār* and *mokhālef*' (1984a:133–4), might explain its omission from this version. Borumand's importance as a teacher, and the fact that approximately one third of the analysed performances were by him or his students (although they would also have learnt other *radif*s), may partly explain the relative absence of *hesār*. However, one of the performances to include *hesār* (11) was by Borumand himself, accompanying Golpayegani (voice; a student of Borumand), despite *hesār* being omitted from his own *radif*. *Hesār* was also in performance 1, a rendition by Shajarian and Lotfi (both former pupils of Borumand), but does not appear in their other performances. No-one else who included *hesār* in performance was directly associated with Borumand.

In separate discussions, Payvar and During claimed that *gusheh*s can move freely between *dastgāh*s in performance, particularly between *Segāh* and *Chāhārgāh*, and both therefore regarded as insignificant the fact that *hesār* is omitted from Borumand's *radif* of *Segāh*. Payvar suggested that the length of *hesār* in *radif* 4 is attributable to the completeness of this publication, collected as it was from many different sources (8.11.90, see footnote 26). However, this does not adequately account for the absence of *hesār* from so many of the analysed performances and, where it *is* present, its consistent brevity and positioning after *mokhālef*. Payvar also suggested that the change from a-*koron* to a♮ makes *hesār* difficult to play on the *santur*.[42] Whilst this may indeed be a factor, still 4 of the 11 appearances of *hesār* were played on *santur* (by 2 of the 5 santurists in the sample), suggesting that the issue of tuning is not of overriding significance.

Hesār is the only *gusheh* to substantially alter the home mode of *Segāh*, effectively transposing it up a (perfect) fifth, and stressing the interval between b-*koron* and a♮. It might therefore be speculated that the omission of *hesār* from more recent renditions may indicate a move away from modally diverse performances, perhaps as the result of a changing aesthetic and bringing the Iranian classical tradition closer to that of the Arabic *taqsim* and possibly to earlier Iranian practices (see Chapter 3, and Farhat 1990:19–20). In line with this, there is also evidence that the skill of moving between modally distant sections of repertoire, known as *morakkab-navāzi* (or *morakkab-khāni* for singers), is gradually being lost; it is seldom heard today, despite being regularly mentioned in the literature of the 1960s and '70s. However, this does not explain the prominent position which *hesār* appears to enjoy in *Chāhārgāh*, where its relationship to the home mode of the *dastgāh* is no different from that of *hesār* in *Segāh*.

The case of *hesār* becomes even more interesting when one considers three *gusheh*s – *masnavi*, *shekasteh muyeh* and *hodi va pahlavi* (and also *rajaz*[43]) – in which the reverse was found: these appeared in approximately half of the analysed performances, but were absent from the instrumental *radif*s. However, all three were in the vocal *radif* (2) and *masnavi* is also in the vocal *radif* of *Chāhārgāh*; *hodi va pahlavi* forms part of both vocal and instrumental *radif*s of *Chāhārgāh*. The inclusion of these *gusheh*s in so many of the analysed performances might be an example of the temporary movement of *gusheh*s between *dastgāh*s suggested by Payvar and During. Alternatively, it might indicate a more permanent change, with a 'migration' of *gusheh*s from *Chāhārgāh*. Since many instrumentalists also study the vocal *radif*, one can see how such *gusheh*s might find their way into instrumental practice. It is also possible that instrumentalists who included them were following current trends in the performance tradition. Nevertheless, given that these three *gusheh*s were only

---

[42]   Whereas most Iranian instruments have the complete range of pitches available without retuning, *hesār* can only be played on *santur* if the a-*koron* in the upper octave has been retuned to a♮, and the *gusheh* is then played in that octave (as in performance 27, for instance). Alternatively, the a♮ can be omitted, as in performances 6, 9 and 29, in which *hesār* was characterized by a stressing of b-*koron*, particularly from the upper c. Of the 11 analysed performances which included *hesār*, only those on *santur* omitted the a♮, this being an important pitch in the other versions. Performances of *hesār* on *santur* also tended to be shorter than on other instruments.

[43]   Usually associated with *Chāhārgāh*, *rajaz* was heard in two of the analysed performances, in both cases following *hodi va pahlavi* in the final *forud* section.

found in the vocal *radif*, it does seem rather curious that the majority of performances in which they were heard were instrumental rather than vocal.[44]

Another apparent anomaly is the group of *gushehs* in the mode of *Shur* towards the end of *radif* 1: *rohāb*, *masihi*, *shāh khatāi* and *takht-e tāqdis*. These were not in any of the other analysed *radifs* of *Segāh* (but are in other *dastgāhs*), nor in any of the analysed performances. Given the importance of Borumand's *radif*, this is somewhat puzzling. Indeed, these *gushehs* provide a rather odd ending to *Segāh*, and although claimed both by Payvar and During to represent earlier practices (see also During 1984a:134), are not found in any of the earlier published *radifs* of *Segāh*. Payvar suggested that they may originally have been played at the end of *Segāh* and gradually found their way into other *dastgāhs*, such as *Navā* where, he claimed, they sound better (8.11.90). If so, perhaps Borumand was invoking an older tradition by including these *gushehs*, which by the mid-twentieth century had been dropped from other *radifs* and from the performance tradition of *Segāh*.

As discussed, whilst the *radif* occupies a central position in Iranian classical music, its role in performance varies: some musicians remain close to the learnt repertoire (in the current sample, performances 4 and 22 are close to the *radif* in their sectional organization) whilst others draw freely from other sources, including the performance tradition. Moreover, musicians vary in their proximity to the *radif* in different performances (see performances 12 and 22 by the same musician for two extremes) and even within the same performance different aspects of the music may align more or less closely with the *radif*. Performance 4 followed the *radif* closely in its complement of *gushehs*, but included rapid changes of metric character (not characteristic of the *radif*, but of the particular performer, Ahmad Ebadi) with only a few extended sections in unmeasured *āvāz* style (the longest, just over one minute, being relatively short for a performance of this music). Similarly, performance 23 (During) was the only one in which *hesār* was heard in the same position as in the *radifs* and was also the only performance to include *gusheh hozān*. On the other hand, this rendition included *hodi va pahlavi*, not found in the instrumental *radifs*, and also *rajaz* (one of only two analysed performances to do so), not found in any of the *radifs* of *Segāh*. Performance 7 (Lotfi and Shajarian) was closest to the instrumental *radifs* in its many subdivisions of *muyeh*, but also included *shekasteh muyeh*, only heard in the vocal *radif*. Performances 1 and 6 included all of the *gushehs* found in the vocal *radif* but omitted from the instrumental *radifs*, and in addition both presented *hesār* as a rather marginal *gusheh* after *mokhālef*; at the same time, performance 1 was one of only eight to include *maqlub*, which was central to the *radifs*. Finally, whilst the focus here is on general patterns of *gusheh* organization rather than discussion of individual renditions, it is worth noting the relative lack of correlation between versions by musicians related as teacher and pupil, or pupils of the same teacher. It is likely that the practice of studying with more than one master works against clear-cut lineages, encouraging 'cross-fertilization' between different versions of the repertoire.

What, then, does this discussion of sectional organization tell us about the relationship between *radif* and performance? And in what sense can this aspect of the music be considered 'improvisational'? First, it is evident that there is a core progression of *gushehs* and modal sections essential to the identity of *Segāh* for which the *radif* provides a framework and by which performances are structured. There is certainly scope for – indeed an expectation of – variation, but this is always within certain boundaries, which have arguably emerged in relation to implicit aesthetic criteria. To this extent, the sectional organization of *Segāh* perhaps lies closer to the 'variation' end of Nettl's continuum (1974c), rather than the improvisational, with the *radif* serving as a fairly clear framework around which variation takes place. At the same time, there were some notable and somewhat surprising differences between *radif* and performance, suggesting a more complex relationship. The fact that performances consistently diverged from the *radif* on certain points seems to indicate a performance tradition operating alongside, and perhaps somewhat independent from, the *radif*. As During observes:

> I would say there is a mainstream of – we shouldn't call it *radif* – but of musical structure, motifs and *gushehs*. Everybody more or less follows this mainstream. And within this main current there is a small line which is more or less didactic, which is the *radif*. Musicians learn the *radif*, they learn the sequences, the modulations, the

---

[44] In his analysis of *Chāhārgāh*, Nettl found that the group of *gushehs* *hodi*, *pahlavi* and *rajaz* 'seems to be extremely rare in performances, but in the *radifs*, it has somehow held its own' (1987:45), essentially the reverse situation to that found in this analysis of *Segāh*.

models and so on; [but] after they have taken their examination in *radif* [in the case of university students], they follow the mainstream, and when they perform *Segāh* they perform it according to the main trends. (8.12.90)

The analyses certainly lend support to the idea that in addition to formal *radif*-based learning, students acquire a great deal of knowledge from informal musical experiences.

Variational Potential in the *Gusheh*s of *Segāh*

So much for the broad sectional organization of *Segāh*. What about the relationship between *radif* and performance in terms of the musical material of each *gusheh*? To what extent are specific phrases, motifs and so on transferred into performance? In the second half of this chapter I turn to the ways in which musicians draw on material learnt from the *radif* to re-create the repertoire at each performance, ultimately asking to what extent the concept of improvisational practice might be useful for understanding such processes. As part of the larger study from which this material is drawn, a number of different versions of the same *gusheh*, in *radif* and performance, were compared in order to examine how the identity of each *gusheh* is established and maintained, despite continual variation. Is it possible, for instance, to identify core characteristics for *mokhālef* (in much the same way as I have sought to do for *Segāh* as a whole), effectively what I describe in Chapter 3 as the abstract 'framework' of the *gusheh*: essential elements which can be extracted by comparing different versions but which are not found in skeletal form within the tradition and not explicitly discussed by teachers? And what are the limits of variation beyond which *mokhālef* loses its identity? One of the points to emerge from this study (Nooshin 1996:228–84) and which I have also discussed elsewhere (Nooshin 1998:80–91), is that *gusheh*s vary significantly both in their density of obligatory material and, by correlation, in the extent to which they can be varied. This is of central relevance to the discussion that follows and I will therefore briefly outline the main findings here.

Several different versions (from both *radif*s and performances) of five *gusheh*s – *darāmad* (four versions), *mokhālef* (four versions), *maqlub* (six versions), *hazeen* (six versions) and *hodi va pahlavi* (four versions), chosen because they illustrate well the range of *gusheh* variation in *Segāh* – were selected, transcribed and compared.[45] In the case of *maqlub*, *hazeen* and *hodi va pahlavi*, it was possible to identify specific melodic/motivic material found both in *radif* and performance, but this was more difficult for *darāmad* and *mokhālef* where there was little in the way of a pre-defined structure or material specific to that section of repertoire. Instead, the identity of these *gusheh*s depends almost entirely on aspects of mode, most notably for the *darāmad*: the range and main area of melodic activity, and e-*koron* as *shāhed* and finalis. Less consistently central, but nevertheless important, were the *āqāz* (starting) pitches, *ist* (medial phrase endings) and some short motivic patterns to be discussed, including the neutral third interval (motif (viii)) between the e-*koron* *shāhed* and the lower c which strongly characterizes *Segāh* (see Figures 4.1 [end of phrase] and 4.2). Beyond this, the only obvious common material between the (four) analysed versions of the *darāmad* was the phrase in Figure 4.10, heard in both performances but notably absent from the *radif*s.

Turning to *mokhālef*, mode was also important in defining the *gusheh*, particularly the specific pitches used, the main area of melodic activity, and the *shāhed* (c). In comparison with the *darāmad*, the analysed versions shared more in their musical material, including a clearly defined opening section and a core of motifs and phrases which appear to be characteristic of *mokhālef* (see Figures 4.5 and 4.6). However, in terms of the *radif*-performance relationship, there was little shared material between the analysed performances and *radif* 1, there being much more commonality with *radif* 2, including several motifs and a melismatic *tahrir* passage heard in the third and final section (see Figure 4.11).[46]

---

[45]   Various aspects of the music were considered, including modal character, overall *gusheh* structure, and the use of motivic and other characteristic material (with a particular focus on elements of pitch and melody). Due to limits of space, I present only the main conclusions here. As well as these five complete *gusheh*s, I also compared the openings of *zābol*, *muyeh* and *mokhālef* in a number of different versions. For further discussion see Nooshin (1996:228–84).

[46]   *Tahrir* is a melismatic vocal technique (also imitated by instrumentalists) involving the embellishment of a single note or series of repeated pitches (usually with upward movement to the adjacent pitch), or an extended vocal melisma,

Figure 4.10   Performance 15, Jamshid Andalibi (*nei*) (see Figure 4.2); and Performance 20, Ahmad Ebadi, *setār* (Nooshin 1996:586–9 includes a full transcription of *darāmad* in this performance)

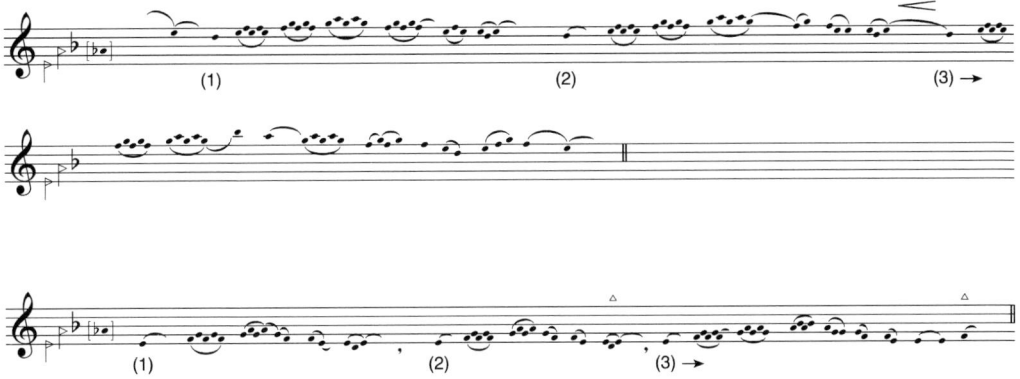

Figure 4.11   *mokhālef*: staves 1 and 2 from Performance 10, Lotfollah Majd (*tār*) (see Figure 4.6); stave 3 from *radif* 2

Moving to the more pre-defined *gusheh*s, mode continued to be important but specific thematic material also played a defining role. *Maqlub*, for instance, has a clear sectional structure, and a distinctive opening melody which differentiates it from *gusheh mokhālef*, in the context of which it is usually heard (see Figures 4.7 and 4.8). Similarly, the identity of *hazeen* (in the mode of *mokhālef*) depends not only on modal characteristics,

---

most often at climactic points towards the ends of phrases. See Caron and Safvate (1966:159–64), Tsuge (1974:171–4), Lotfi (1976:18–20), Ayako (1980) and Alizadeh (1992).

but also on its opening phrase and overall trajectory through which the music descends from c (*shāhed* of *mokhālef*) to e-*koron* (g/a-*koron* in performances 9 and 15), the *shāhed* of the *darāmad*. The positioning of *hazeen* at the end, and its focus on the lower part of the mode, of *mokhālef*, is also an important aspect of this *gusheh*. Finally, *hodi va pahlavi* is based in the *darāmad* mode (but often includes brief 'excursions' to other *gushehs*), and comprises a recognizable melody with a distinctive rhythm (based on a poetic metre of the same name). Among the analysed *radif*s, only the vocal *radif* included this *gusheh*, reflecting its close association with poetry; at the same time, amongst the six analysed performances to include *hodi va pahlavi* (1, 2, 4, 6, 15, 23), only performance 1 was a vocal rendition.

Comparison of these five *gushehs* also pointed to a correlation between length and prominence of a *gusheh* and its variability. Thus, the *gusheh* that was most varied (*darāmad*) was also the longest and most frequently heard (together with *mokhālef*). As *gushehs* progressively decreased in relative length and prominence, so did their degree of variation. Based on this, it is possible to suggest a continuum with the main *gushehs* of *Segāh* positioned according to length, prominence and what might be termed 'variational potential':

darāmad	+
mokhālef; *zābol*; *muyeh*	
maqlub	
hazeen; *shekasteh muyeh*	
naqmeh-ye maqlub; *masnavi*; *hodi va pahlavi*	–

Whilst it is only possible to assign *gushehs* approximate positions, this continuum reflects the range of variation found: those from *maqlub* downwards are generally denser in obligatory material, both rhythmic and melodic, have a relatively stable and pre-defined metric structure, and are varied less in performance. Note, however, that an unmetered *gusheh* does not necessarily entail more variability. For instance, neither *hazeen* nor *maqlub* are regularly metred, but both have fairly fixed melodies in which the rhythm is quite stable and varied relatively little. One of the difficulties in assigning exact positions on this continuum is that *gusheh* identity is established and maintained in different ways: *darāmad*, *mokhālef*, and also *shekasteh muyeh*, are identified primarily through modal characteristics, opening and closing motifs, and relative positioning within *Segāh*, and less through specific melodies, rhythms/metres or overall structure. On the other hand, *gushehs* such as *naqmeh-ye maqlub*, *masnavi* and *hodi va pahlavi* are defined both by mode, but also – and particularly – through specific melodic and rhythmic/metric material (the first in a regular duple metre; the latter two based on poetic metres).

Also of interest is the fact that less pre-defined *gushehs* were more varied in length. The analysed versions of *darāmad*, for instance, ranged from 17 seconds in *radif* 1 to just over six minutes in performance 20; and whereas the *radif* examples were comparatively short, both comprising a single unmetered section, the performances were more complex: performance 15 had two halves with the musicians alternating, before coming together to conclude the *gusheh* (Figure 4.2); and Ebadi's performance (20) included a metered section (*chāhārmezrāb*) separating the two halves of the *darāmad*. The analysed versions of *mokhālef* were less varied in length: from 75 seconds in *radif* 2 to just over three minutes in performance 10. Once again, the *radif* examples were shorter (but with a smaller differential) and were entirely unmetered. The examples from *maqlub* had a much smaller range in terms of length, from 16 seconds in performance 1 to 40 seconds in *radif* 2; significantly, however, and in contrast to *darāmad* and *mokhālef*, the *radif* examples were *longer*, perhaps reflecting the greater importance of *maqlub* in *radif*s relative to performance, as discussed earlier. Similarly, *hazeen* (like *maqlub* a relatively short *gusheh* with a fairly well-defined structure) varied from 18 seconds in performance 9 to 41 seconds in *radif* 3 (a similar range to *maqlub*). As with *maqlub*, the longest examples were in the *radif*s rather than performances.

The primary reason for presenting this summary of findings from the earlier comparative analysis is to make two main points relevant to the discussion which follows. First, the fact that the *gushehs* of *Segāh* differ considerably in the extent to which they are varied in performance – what I have called variational potential and what Nettl terms 'improvisatoriness' (2009:194) – suggests that different kinds of creative process may be at work, the understanding of which is not necessarily well served by the all-encompassing term 'improvisation'. Whilst longer, more prominent *gusheh*s offer greater licence, many of the shorter *gusheh*s have clearly defined melodic, rhythmic and structural elements and their performance might therefore be more appropriately termed 'variation' (Nooshin 1998:80–91). Indeed, a *gusheh* such as *hodi va pahlavi* is so clearly defined that renditions might be better described as 'interpretation', as of a pre-composed piece. The metaphor used by Herndon to describe such a range of variational potential seems apposite here: 'I think of this as a series of rubber bands of differing sizes, ranges … they expand or contract (at differing rates, sometimes) and … each rubber band has a point to which it can be stretched … There are ranges of performance in individuals, groups, genres, styles, forms, contexts, cultures, and so on' (ed. Herndon and Brunyate 1976:198). In the same way, individual *gusheh*s can be 'stretched' to varying extents before they lose their identity. Whilst this range of variation is briefly mentioned in the literature in connection with the relative importance of *gusheh*s, few have explored it in detail (Nettl and Foltin 1972:32–3 do discuss it for *Chāhārgāh*). When I asked Parviz Meshkatian why some *gusheh*s are more varied than others, using *hodi va pahlavi* as an example, he initially offered a response couched in theoretical terms, '*hodi va pahlavi* is a melody, whilst *darāmad* is a mode'; however, he quickly moved into the characteristic Iranian metaphoric mode of expression: 'for example, if we think of *darāmad* as a garden, then *hodi va pahlavi* is a tree in that garden' (20.7.92). Berenjian also replied to the same question in aesthetic terms: 'because *hodi va pahlavi* is very beautiful [*zibā*] and complete [*kāmel*], you can't really bring yourself to change it [*ādam delesh nemiyād ān rā avaz bokoneh*]' (18.9.90). Many years later, and having found relatively little reference to this issue in the literature or among musicians, I was struck by Lotfi's use of terms implying a distinction between more and less pre-defined *gusheh*s. In a class that I observed, he described some *gusheh*s as *sākhtāri* (lit.: 'structural') and others as *qayr-e sākhtāri* ('non-structural');

> *Tarz* is a particular melody-model [*melodi-ye model-e khāssi*] which is always the same [*hamisheh hamoon ast*] and on which you can't compose [*rooyesh ham nemisheh āhangsāzi kard*]. Some *gusheh*s end in themselves [*be khodeshān khātemeh paydā mikonand*], and if you try to compose on it, it will no longer be *tarz*. Some *gusheh*s are *sākhtāri*, like the *darāmad*. *Tarz* is non-structural [*qayr-e sākhtāri*]. (20.4.10)

Asked by a student how one knows which *gusheh*s are structural, Lotfi responded, 'From the *radif* of course. Our yardstick [*melāk*] is the *radif*. It is our book from which the grammar is described' (20.4.10). Thus, whilst a continuum may be useful in understanding the range of variation, both the analyses and the statements above suggest a distinction between two types of *gusheh* (in *Segāh* at least, but judging by Lotfi's comments in other *dastgāh*s also) in terms of the development of musical material in performance: in longer *gusheh*s (*darāmad* and *mokhālef*) certain techniques are used to develop and extend material, whereas in less central *gusheh*s (*maqlub*, *hazeen*, *hodi va pahlavi*), such techniques are embedded within the *gusheh* itself. This is discussed further below.

The second, and related, point brings us back to the relationship between *radif* and performance. We have already considered some of the anomalies in terms of sectional and modal organization. In the case of the examples just discussed, whilst the relationship between learnt repertoire and creative performance is fairly clear in shorter *gusheh*s such as *maqlub* and *hazeen*, in the case of *gusheh*s such as *darāmad* and *mokhālef* it is more complex. These tend, on average, to be (often much) longer in performance than in *radif*, not surprisingly since musicians (are expected to) expand upon the material of the *radif*. However, the analyses showed that not only is there much material in performance that is not found in the *radif*s (as one might expect), but the reverse is also true. Beyond the central defining elements, there is generally a sparse 'transfer' of material – specific phrases, melodies, rhythms – from *radif* into performance. One might therefore conclude that whilst the *radif* is important in teaching the defining elements of a *gusheh* and its variational potential, in the case of more central *gusheh*s it does not function as a precise framework, instead offering a means by which musicians learn general aspects of style and techniques for developing material. This also supports the idea, mentioned above, that the *radif* operates alongside the broader performance tradition from which musicians draw and which is itself enriched with each new interpretation of *Segāh*.

I will briefly mention some examples from the comparative analysis to illustrate the complexity of the *radif*-performance relationship and to give a sense of the issues. In some *gusheh*s, the analysed *radif*s were very similar to one another, almost forming a separate core, related to but independent of the analysed performances (this was the case, for instance, in the internal sectioning of *hazeen*, see Nooshin 1996:251–7). Conversely, the analysis of *darāmad* identified material shared between performances but included in neither of the analysed *radif*s (see Figure 4.10). Since the analysed versions included performances by Borumand whose *radif* was also under study, it was particularly interesting to note differences between his performances and *radif*. For example, whilst *mokhālef* began in the lower octave in two analysed performances by Borumand (25, 26), this was not a feature of his own *radif* (although it was heard in *radif* 4, and also in the final *reng* of Borumand's *radif*). Even within the same *radif*, there were anomalies: *hodi va pahlavi* in *radif* 2 included a section in *maqlub* which followed the structure of this *gusheh*, but which was closer to other renditions of *maqlub* than that in *radif* 2 itself (ibid.:244–50). There were also instances where performers included material derived from the *radif*, but from a different *gusheh*. Thus, performance 17 (voice, Abdol Vahab Shahidi) features a rising motivic sequence towards the opening of *muyeh* which was not in any of the other openings of this *gusheh*, but *was* in all of the analysed *radif*s in *mokhālef* (and in several performances, but not performance 17; ibid.:238–50), suggesting that this pattern was perhaps learnt as part of *mokhālef* and subsequently 'transferred' to *muyeh* in performance. A final observation: in some *gusheh*s, there seemed to be a particularly close relationship between the vocal *radif* (*radif* 2) and the analysed performances. For example, whilst in the instrumental *radif*s (1 and 3) *muyeh* began with a characteristic motif from the opening of *zābol* (starting on e-*koron*), by contrast, *radif* 2, together with all the analysed performances, began directly with material specific to *muyeh* (starting on g/bᵇ). Similarly, the analyses of *mokhālef* and *maqlub* highlighted closer parallels in the use of material between the performances (instrumental and vocal) and *radif* 2, than with the instrumental *radif*s. Correlations between *radif* 2 and the analysed performances were also noted earlier in relation to the inclusion in (particularly instrumental) performances of a number of *gusheh*s only found in the vocal *radif*. The apparently close relationship between the vocal *radif* and the analysed performances is significant: although musicians generally learn several *radif*s (including, for instrumentalists, the vocal *radif*), given Borumand's importance as a teacher and his direct connection with many of the musicians in the analysed sample, one might expect there to be closer correlations between the performances and *radif* 1.

Another point to emerge from the analyses which it has not been possible to discuss in detail is that similar principles of organization are found at different levels. For instance, just as the overall organization of *Segāh* is subject to controlled variation, so too are individual *gusheh*s, which are heard in a large number of variants but always within certain limits; and the same applies to individual sections within *gusheh*s. Similarly, *Segāh* is varied less at the beginning and end of the complete *dastgāh*, and this is also the case for individual *gusheh*s. And just as the overall contour of *Segāh* is arch-shaped, so, generally speaking, are individual *gusheh*s, as well as phrases within *gusheh*s. Finally, analysis of *hodi va pahlavi* (Nooshin 1996:257–63) showed the modal trajectory of the complete *dastgāh* distilled within one *gusheh*. It seems likely that such principles are an important unifying factor in the music.

Each *gusheh* of *Segāh* exists in a (potentially infinite) number of variants, but this variation is controlled within certain limits. Whilst rarely discussed by musicians (beyond significant elements of mode), such limits are essential to identifying sections of repertoire and re-creating them in performance, and are thus an important part of the subliminal knowledge of both musicians and informed listeners. For a study which seeks to understand the relationship between learnt repertoire and creative practice, perhaps the most important point to emerge from this discussion is not only that there is a continuum of *gusheh*s in terms of variational potential, but that there are essentially two types of *gusheh*: in one, the *radif* functions as a fairly clear framework for performance; in the other the relationship is more complex. For the latter, one might reasonably ask where the musical material generated in performance comes from, a question which forms the focus of the final part of this chapter.

Understanding the Creative Process

It should by now be clear that whilst there are parallels between the *radif* and performances based on it, the relationship between the two is far from straightforward. In particular, the musical evidence (and some musician discourses) suggests two kinds of *gusheh*. In the remainder of this chapter, I explore this idea further through selected examples which show how techniques for developing musical ideas are embedded within the *radif*. Early studies of Iranian classical music tended to characterize performance as a patchwork or mosaic in which memorized motifs and phrases are juxtaposed.[47] I argue that whilst memorized material is important, for *gusheh*s such as *darāmad* and *mokhālef* performance is more akin to what Treitler describes (in the context of Medieval chant) as 'an interwoven texture of *materials and procedures* ... internalized non-verbally by singers who practice them daily and have been doing so since childhood' (1991:77, my emphases). My contention is that in the process of learning the *radif* and through other experiences, students internalize both specific material (motifs or melodies, for instance) and, crucially, compositional principles or techniques for developing that material.[48] These become assimilated into a musician's knowledge base and later 'abstracted' for use in performance as described below. Whilst I have written about this elsewhere (Nooshin 1996, 1998, 2003), the aim here is to draw together and explore further some of these ideas, including potential parallels with other areas of human creativity. Essentially, I am seeking to understand what 'surface structure' compositional techniques might reveal of underlying 'deep structure' processes. The analysis is based on the same versions of *Segāh* discussed above, with some reference also to examples from *dastgāh Māhur*.

With the exception of those mentioned at the start of this chapter, the literature includes few detailed studies of performance practice in Iranian classical music. However, several authors list the kinds of techniques used in performance. Zonis mentions and gives examples of: repetition, comprising literal repetition, *zir-bam* (the shifting of octaves characteristic of *santur* and violin performances), sequence, and varied repetition (rhythmic and/or melodic modifications); ornamentation, including (tremolo), trills, *tekiyeh*[49] and arpeggios (in somewhat 'westernized' performances); and centonization, 'the joining together of familiar motives to produce longer melodies, particularly at the ends of phrases' (1973:105–14; see also Simms and Koushkani 2012a:247–56). Nettl similarly lists repetition and melodic sequence, but also includes extension, augmentation and contraction, as well as the combination of techniques, such as 'repetition, followed by upward transposition that is followed by a second transposed version given in extended form' (1987:40). Both Sadeghi (1971:95–119) and During (1987c:139) essentially list these same techniques but without illustrative examples. Beyond these listings and brief examples, however, few explore the creative process by examining the use of such techniques in specific performances.

Amongst the various techniques or procedures through which material is generated, the most fundamental is repetition; however, repetition is rarely exact and most typically involves the variation of ideas somewhat analogous to the intricate detail of Iranian visual arts to which the music is so often compared.[50] Just as the perpetual variation of a small number of motifs produces highly complex yet unified patterns in the visual arts, so here a few basic procedures and motifs result in potentially infinite musical variations.[51] Repetition is also important for its germinal role with respect to other procedures:

> One of the essential principles of free play ... is repetition. The ear likes to hear the same motif or modal structure, but on the other hand, repetition engenders lassitude. The great art consists, therefore, of respecting an apparent symmetry whilst developing the motifs or the modal or rhythmic structures. Thus, the potential

---

[47]   See Gerson-Kiwi (1963), Sadeghi (1971:75–135), Nettl with Foltin (1972) and Zonis (1973:104–25). Racy comments on 'the unfortunate and persistent stereotype of "Islamic music" [goes] – a continuous and persistent mosaic-like repetition of motifs and filigrees' (2009:320).

[48]   Both Zadeh and Berkowitz make a similar distinction, the former between 'stock expressions' and 'strategies' (2012:21), the latter between 'musical "objects" that must be committed to memory so that they can be produced spontaneously when improvising ... [and] musical "processes" that must be learned and rehearsed so that they can be used to develop formulas in improvised performance'; amongst the latter Berkowitz lists 'transposition, variation and recombination' (2010:40).

[49]   'Leaning', where a note is briefly alluded to in the manner of an upper auxiliary note, particularly characteristic of singers. See Sadeghi (1971:111–13) and Zonis (1973:109, although she does not use the Persian name).

[50]   See, for example, Zonis (1973:108–9). Wright offers a careful critique of such loosely drawn parallels (2009:120).

[51]   Again, drawing parallels with North India, Zadeh makes similar observations regarding the 'desire to explore the potential inherent in a limited amount of (musical and/or textual) material' (2012:37).

of a motif is sometimes explored in a systematic, almost logical way: it is transposed, developed, abridged, lengthened, etc. (During 1984a:195)[52]

Comparing the Iranian and Turkish traditions from an historical perspective, Olley notes the greater 'complexity and diversity of creative procedures for motivic development' in the former in contrast to:

> ... what we might call 'structural development' in the Turkish tradition ... [and which] may be due to the absence of a significant theoretical or compositional tradition [in Iran] from the Safavid era until the late nineteenth and early twentieth century ... This led to a focus on non-rhythmic improvisation, which, in the absence of a theoretical or compositional tradition which might have led to a structural conception of the modal system, engendered a musical style in which unlimited variation of a limited number of musical ideas predominated. (2010:29)

In my earlier work (Nooshin 1996, 1998, 2003), I identify a number of compositional or developmental 'procedures' in *Segāh*, focusing on various types of extension, but also considering techniques of varied repetition, contraction, sequencing and so on, some of which are discussed below. The analyses corroborate the observations above, suggesting a small number of elemental procedures and their variants which lend the music a highly unified character. The rest of this chapter extends the earlier analyses, whilst also examining possible insights to be gained from exploring the music through the lens of different approaches to creativity, both from within and – viewing musical creativity as one manifestation of the general human urge to create – beyond music studies.

Oral Formulae and Generative Phrase Structures

In 1960 Albert Lord published *The Singer of Tales*, a landmark in the field of oral literature, based on his own work and that of his teacher, Milman Parry. Drawing on evidence from Serbo-Croatian epic singers' use of 'oral formulae', Lord presented novel ideas about the authorship and mode of composition and transmission in the Homeric epics. According to Lord, the oral poet has a stock of learnt formulae which, on the one hand, allow rapid 'composition in performance'; on the other, 'rather than induce similar performances, the "formulaic style" because it avoids the necessity of exact memorisation gives the performer the opportunity to make each performance unique' (Finnegan 1977:65):

> The Poet had at his disposal this series of traditional patterns built up over the years (so there was something in the theory of multiple authorship), but he was not passively dominated by them: he *used* them to create his own poems as he performed them. (ibid.:60)

Further, Lord suggested that a high density of formulae evidences (originally) oral composition and transmission, his conclusion regarding the *Iliad* and the *Odyssey*.

There are obvious parallels with music where formulae (whether motifs, patterns, phrases and so on) play an important role in composition, whether in performance or in notation. Whilst Lord regards formulaic patterns as particularly characteristic (indeed, indicative) of oral transmission, Finnegan presents examples of formulaic patterns in musical and poetic texts in both written and memorized oral traditions (ibid.:69–70) and considers the complex relationship between these often interdependent modes of composition and transmission. Other scholars have explored the use of formulae in (notated) Euro-American art music.[53]

---

[52]   In the glossary to Talai 2000, Sadeghi offers the following definition: 'repetition: A favourite technique, among many to modify and expand the improvisation. Could be achieved by expansion, "*zir* and *bam*" (high and low), variation, and sequential techniques, with rhythmic, melodic, and ornamental modifications' (2000:615). Similarly, 'developing: Development and expansion of a previous phrase, usually shorter, simpler, and possibly from a different tonal level' (ibid.:612).

[53]   See, for example, Reti (1961), Walker (1962), Schoenberg (1967), Gjerdingen (2007) and Berkowitz (2010). Reti discusses the ways in which motivic relations and transformations form the thematic basis for much Western art music. Gjerdingen reports on the widespread use in the eighteenth century by *galant* style composers of certain 'exercises and

Notwithstanding this view of formulae as facilitators of creativity, they have also been considered in a less positive light as indicating a lack of creativity, particularly when used as 'fillers' while musicians work out the next step. In his study of jazz improvisation, so anxious is Smith to counter this charge that he rather overstates the case, claiming that 'the ability to compose rapidly rests not on the memorization of stock formulas, but on the ability to create new phrases by analogy, using the patterns established by the basic formulas' (1991:38).[54]

Formulae play an important role in Iranian classical music, which is replete with certain 'stock' ideas. This can be heard at the most detailed level, for example in the form of motivic patterns (which may be specific to a section of repertoire, or characteristic of particular instruments/voice or musicians), through to the various developmental procedures found in the context of formulaic phrase structures, to be discussed below. Many of the same formulae are found both in *radif* and performance; indeed, I would suggest, following Lord, that creative performance would not be possible without them. Wright observes with reference to Middle Eastern music in general that:

> … what is created in the course of performance may involve, say, varying a melodic *Gestalt*, usually in fairly predictable ways, but is especially likely to involve cut-and-paste processes resulting in new arrangements of known formulae, particularly in instrumental performance, where mastery of technique provides ready-made physical moves that can be strung together. (2009:37)

However, it should be stressed that the use of formulae is by no means a simple matter of selecting from an accumulated stock of ideas. For one thing, other than motivic patterns one rarely finds formulae in unvaried form: there is a constant process of variation. Coming back to Smith's point, the analyses suggest that the performance of Iranian classical music depends on both the memorization and restatement of existing formulae, *and* the creation of new formulae 'using the patterns established by the basic formulas' (1991:38). Second, as will be discussed below, the creation of phrases goes beyond the simple substitution of one formula for another, involving a complex network of choices in which formulae evince a high degree of compositional flexibility.

This discussion of formulae relates closely to the question of decision-making in performance. Whilst the choice of *dastgāh* and the selection and ordering of *gusheh*s is usually determined in advance (particularly in group renditions), detailed decisions as to how motifs and phrases are to be varied, extended and joined together are, generally speaking, not.[55] The immediacy of the performance situation suggests that such decisions are based on accumulated aural and spatio-motor patterns and formulae, no doubt using conscious decision-making processes, but with some degree of subliminality. As well as being partly determined by the spoken and unspoken musical 'rules' relating to a specific *dastgāh* or *gusheh*, decisions can be shaped by factors such as performance context, audience receptiveness, fellow performers and the unfolding of a particular performance (see Chapter 2). Sloboda's observations seem pertinent here:

> Excellence in improvisation results from having 'at one's fingertips' a large repertoire of procedures or options for accomplishing some end result within a limited time. In this respect it resembles fluent public speaking, or rapid mental calculation … In such performances, one can often not know the best step to take *unless one*

---

rules' (he refers to such formulae as 'schemata') set out in notebooks (*zibaldoni*) which 'provided an important repository of stock musical business from which a young composer could later draw' (2007:10).

[54] For further discussion of formulae in oral traditions see Stolz and Shannon (1976), Ong (1982), Foley (1988) and Rubin (1995). With specific reference to music, Kippen (1988b) and Zadeh (2012) both examine formulaic patterns in North Indian music, in *tablā* playing and *thumrī* vocal music respectively. Zadeh describes these as the 'building blocks of *thumrī*' (2012:6) and gives many examples of formulaic patterns on a spectrum between 'the exact repetition of chunks of musical material' (or 'stock expressions') and 'abstract, generational musical strategies'. What she terms 'variable outlines' and 'musical gestures' lie 'somewhere in the middle' (2012:20). Treitler (1974) compares the role of formulae in the Homeric epic tradition and Gregorian chant, asking what these might reveal of earlier oral transmission processes in the latter. Smith (1991) discusses formulae in jazz, as does Berliner (1994, in particular pp.227–30), who also references other writings on the subject (ibid.:799–800, note 4).

[55] As Nettl observes, 'Principally, the radif teaches the musician that moving from memorized radif to performance involves options, but options of particular sorts' (2009:195). Zonis discusses decision-making processes (1973:99ff.), noting also that the choice of *dastgāh* used to depend on the time of day (1973:99–100).

has determined the result of the previous step ... it is clearly not enough for an improviser to know how his or her performance *must* be structured ... the improviser must have rapid access to a large and well-organized body of knowledge ... Even the expert improviser will have a distinctive 'style' that reflects the way his or her improvisatory repertoire is chosen from the infinitely large set of possible options .... (1982:484, my emphases)

One might also fruitfully draw comparisons with non-musical domains such as chess, notwithstanding that for musicians aural and spatio-motor memories may be more important than the visual:

How does the master (chess player) know which moves to consider? It appears that through years of study and play masters develop a greatly detailed visual memory of chess positions. They use this knowledge to analyse the position before them and it determines which moves are worth considering. This knowledge is again used to determine how these possible moves must be modified to respond to the specific situation at hand, which seldom matches precisely any situation the master has studied before. (Weisberg 1986:12–13)

In the same way, Iranian musicians draw on a body of accumulated knowledge, including formulaic patterns which are varied according 'to the specific situation at hand'.

Perhaps the least varied formulaic patterns are the motifs from which phrases are constructed, a distinctive feature of Iranian classical music as noted above and by several writers.[56] In her early study, Gerson-Kiwi observes:

... one cannot but compare it with the huge surfaces of ancient carpets covered with hundreds of small compartments all of them filled with ornamental motives which are of a uniform style yet never repeated. Obviously, the creative impetus is similar in both arts .... (1963:22–3)

Similarly, Nettl notes that 'Persian classical music is composed of short bits of sound – we call them motifs, gestures, particles, which are manipulated, altered, repeated, developed, expanded, reduced' (1987:105). These 'short bits of sound' are the basic building blocks and seem to act in the manner of oral formulae as described by Lord, facilitating composition in performance. Whilst some motifs are characteristic of particular sections of repertoire, in general there is a great deal of unity in the motivic 'language' of the music.[57] Certain archetypal patterns are found throughout the repertoire: 'the same units appear in all modal environments, and thus represent a primary melodic structural level of the *radif*, though not one explicitly recognized in traditional music theory. They are abstract, androgynous melodic shapes devoid of any modal implications' (Simms and Koushkani 2012a:247).[58]

---

[56]   In the 1980 edition of *The New Grove Dictionary of Music and Musicians*, Drabkin defines motif as 'A short musical idea, be it melodic, harmonic, rhythmic, or all three. A motif may be of any size, though it is most commonly regarded as the shortest subdivision of a theme or phrase that still maintains its identity as an idea' (648). And Scholes offers the following: 'The briefest intelligible and self-existent melodic or rhythmic unit. It may be of two notes or more. Almost any piece of music will be found, on close examination, to be developed out of some figure or figures, repeated – at different pitches, and perhaps with different intervals, yet recognizably the same' (1970:661). Schoenberg devotes a whole chapter of *Fundamentals of Musical Composition* (1967) to 'The Motive', and begins as follows: 'Even the writing of simple phrases involves the invention and use of motives, though perhaps unconsciously. Consciously used, the motive should produce unity, relationship, coherence, logic, comprehensibility and fluency' (1967:8). Here, I use the term to indicate a short melodic pattern, usually of between two and five notes, from which longer melodies are constructed.

[57]   Whilst musicians rarely discuss such aspects of the music, in conversation Meshkatian used the expression *motif gardooni* ('spinning out'/'turning' a motif) to describe the development of a musical idea (20.7.92); I have not encountered this phrase elsewhere.

[58]   Simms further observes, 'As with Sadeghi's identifications (1970:84–5) and my own (1992:150), the repertoire of centonic units frequently recurring in the 1996 sample of Shajarian's avaz, especially within his tahrirs but in other parts of his phrase construction as well, is surprisingly small' (Simms and Koushkani 2012a:247). Simms discusses Shajarian's use of motifs or 'centonic units', particularly in melismatic *tahrir* sections, comparing these with the vocal *radif* of Karimi, and followed by a motivic analysis of a section from Shajarian's 1984 album *Bidād* (2012a:247–56). Nooshin (1996:229–84, 289–467) includes a detailed analysis of the motivic structuring and underlying rules governing melodic movement in *gusheh zābol*, including comparison of motifs in performances on santur and *tār*, and the possible impact of instrument

Another kind of formula is what I term 'generative phrase structures', gestalt phrase-models which are subject to variation, and which form the analytical focus of this section. Iranian classical music is shaped and paced in distinct phrases, something no doubt related to the central role of poetry. Indeed, musicians often use linguistic terms such as *jomleh* ('sentence') to describe aspects of phrasing, both instrumental and vocal. If the use of different motifs is one way in which phrases are varied, then at the next structural level it is these formulaic phrase-models that facilitate the generation of new material. Since, even in group renditions, it is unusual for more than one instrument to play simultaneously in the main *āvāz* section – instrumentalists generally take turns to explore the musical material, either answering each other or responding to the voice and playing between lines of poetry – the analysis below presents individual solo phrases extracted from complete *gusheh*s. I begin with examples from the *darāmad* of Segāh: compare Figure 4.12 with the almost identical phrases seen earlier in Figure 4.10 (from performances 15 and 20).

Figure 4.12   Performance 9, Reza Shafeian (*santur*), *darāmad*

Note the tripartite structure of the phrase: the statement of an initial idea (1) (with an arch-shaped contour), its repetition (2), after which the phrase is extended on the third statement (3), leading to a pitch climax and eventual resolution; in all three cases, this is followed by a short pause before the next phrase begins. Elsewhere I have used the term 'extended repetition' to refer to this kind of phrase structuring. Here, I am less concerned with the specific way in which the phrase is extended (to be considered later), and more in the fact that the structure accommodates different kinds of material, including motifs and development techniques, and is found in different *gusheh*s of Segāh. For instance, the phrases in Figures 4.13 and 4.14 are from *mokhālef*, the first from a performance by Safvate (24, *setār*), the second from another performance by Shafeian (6). In both, the initial section (1) is based on the same 5-note motif seen above, but here the phrase extension is prolonged through a *second* extension: in performance 24, using a pattern which is effectively a contraction of (1) (what I call procedure B^2);[59] in performance 6, the pattern is derived from the last few notes of (1) (B^4).

Many examples of this basic phrase structure were identified in the analysed versions of Segāh: in different *gusheh*s, using different motifs, and with phrases extended differently (including extension on the second rather than the third statement of (1)), as in the phrases in Figures 4.15 to 4.20. In Figure 4.15, Shafeian uses the same phrase structure, but with a 3-note motif as the basis for (1); in 4.16, Meshkatian uses a different motivic pattern altogether and the phrase has a second extension based on the whole of (1) (B^1); and so on. What these examples (and others presented in Nooshin 1996:319–30) suggest is that musicians learn, on the one hand formulaic phrase structures, and on the other ways of varying these structures, such that no two versions of a single phrase are the same. Further, it seems that these two elements (basic phrase structure and variational strategies) are not learnt separately but as a 'unit', either from the *radif* or from the performance tradition. In other words, the formulaic structure doesn't constitute a finished phrase in itself, but embodies the

---

morphology on motivic patterning. The following observation by Zadeh (for *thumrī*) is also applicable to Iranian music, particularly regarding the characteristic motifs often used to mark the opening and/or closing sections of *gusheh*s: 'The repeated use of particular musical units in a particular position within phrases creates a sense of musical syntax; it allows formulas to serves as familiar landmarks for listeners, delineating the structure even of unfamiliar musical phrases. This also affords the opportunity for musicians to manipulate listeners' expectations, for example by extending a phrase after a conventional closing figure or by interrupting closing figures so as to create a greater sense of resolution when they are finally performed in full' (2012:42).

[59]   My categorization of compositional procedures will be described below.

Figure 4.13   Performance 24, Safvate (*setār*), *mokhālef*

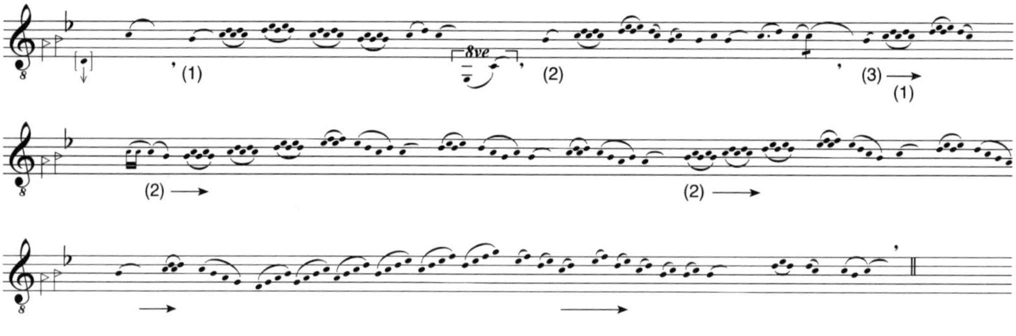

Figure 4.14   Performance 6, Shafeian (*santur*), *mokhālef*

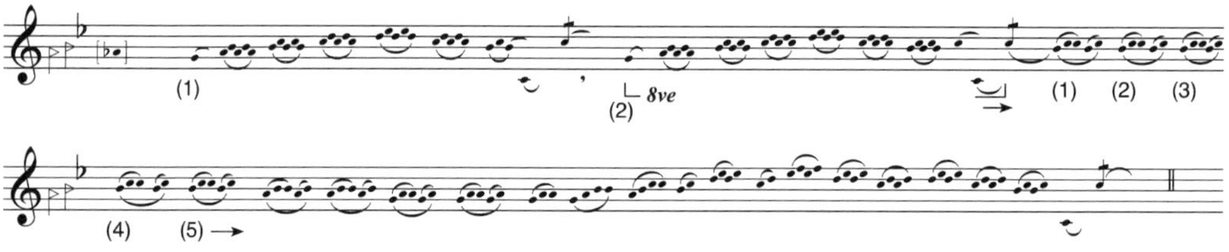

Figure 4.15   Performance 9, Shafeian (*santur*), *darāmad*

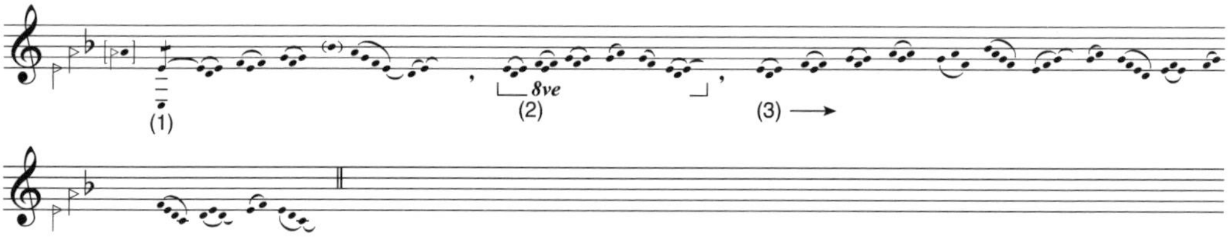

Figure 4.16   Performance 16, Meshkatian (*santur*), *mokhālef*

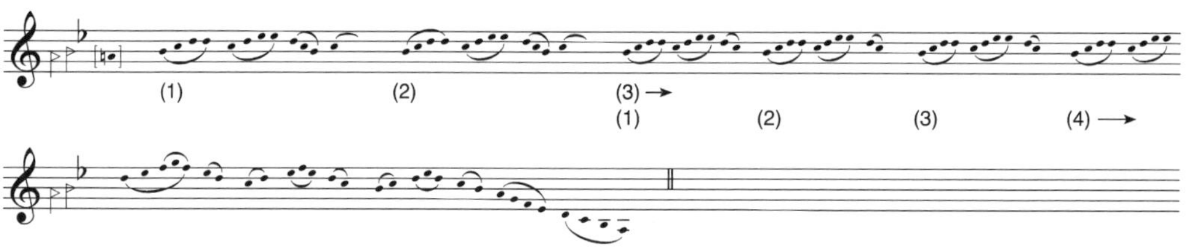

Figure 4.17   Performance 13, Sharif (*tār*), *mokhālef*

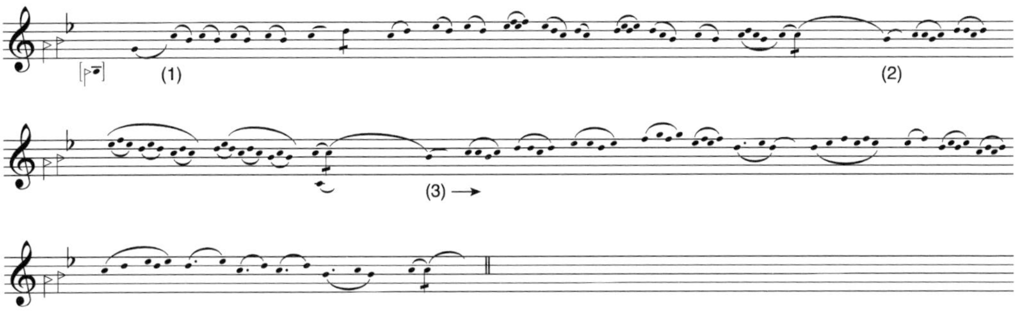

Figure 4.18   Performance 14, Shahnaz (*tār*), *darāmad*

Figure 4.19   Performance 24, Safvate (*setār*), *darāmad*

Figure 4.20   Performance 7, Shajarian (voice), *darāmad*

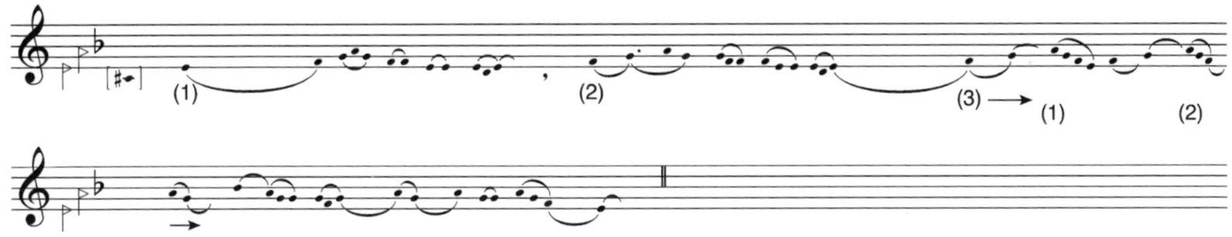

open-ended *potential* for the generation of new phrases, drawing on other formulaic patterns (mostly motifs and compositional procedures).[60]

The phrase structure described above was found in performances by different musicians and in different *gusheh*s of *Segāh*, but seemed particularly characteristic of *darāmad* and *mokhālef* and of *santur*ist Reza Shafeian. Despite its fairly regular appearance in performance, however, it was not found in any of the analysed *radif*s.

---

[60]   Similarly, Zadeh notes that (in *ṭhumrī*) 'multiple different types of formulas might overlap and be nested within each other when they are realized in performance' (2012:30).

As suggested for Figure 4.10, this may indicate that it primarily circulates within the performance tradition; or that it is in the *radif* of another *dastgāh* and has 'migrated' into performances of *Segāh*. In fact, one of the analysed *radif*s of *Segāh* includes a phrase which bears some similarity to those above, but differs in that it plays a specific cadential role in the *forud* sections of *gusheh*s (the same phrase is also heard in this position in performance 16) (see Figures 4.21 and 4.22).

Figure 4.21   *Radif* 1, Borumand (*tār*), *kereshmeh bā muyeh*

Figure 4.22   Performance 16, Meshkatian (*santur*), *darāmad*

A final example of this phrase structure was found in a different *dastgāh*, *Māhur*, and can be compared to Figure 4.16 (Meshkatian, *mokhālef*) with which it shares an identical first section (1) using the same motif, but subsequently extended differently: in Figure 4.16 there is a second extension based on the whole of (1), whereas in Figure 4.23 there is a single phrase extension. Nonetheless, the fact that such similar phrases are found in different *dastgāh*s, performed by different musicians, and with no exemplars in the analysed *radif*s, once again points to the importance of the performance tradition (particularly since Meshkatian and Alizadeh worked closely together) and to the role of these generative structures in providing a framework for creating new material.[61]

Figure 4.23   Performance 30, Alizadeh (*tār*), *Māhur*, *darāmad*

Returning to *Segāh*, a second generative phrase structure identified during analysis also embodied a tripartite structure but with a contour which was effectively the inverse of those above. Most of the phrases used one of two 4-note motifs (or variants thereof), the first of which is motif (i) in Figures 4.24 to 4.27. They share the same structure, the use of motif (i), and a similar first section (1), which, however, is extended differently in each case. Focusing on the two examples by Shafeian, although both use procedure B[3] in which the phrase is extended using the first part of (1), in Figure 4.26, the extension uses the first 12 notes of (1), whereas in Figure 4.27 it uses the first four, thereby generating two different phrases from essentially the same

---

[61]   An example of a phrase based on the same material (but in a different mode) is given by Sadeghi as part of the *tahrir* at the end of *gusheh sayakhi* in *āvāz-e Abu-Atā* in the *radif* of Saba (Sadeghi 1971:88; the phrase extension is different from Figures 4.16 and 4.23).

Figure 4.24   Performance 11, Borumand (*tār*), *zābol*

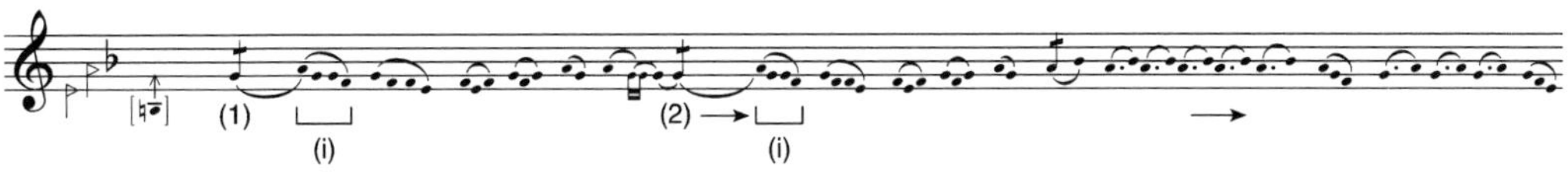

Figure 4.25   Performance 1, Lotfi (*tār*), *mokhālef*

Figure 4.26   Performance 6, Shafeian (*santur*), *zābol*

Figure 4.27   Performance 6, Shafeian (*santur*), *mokhālef*

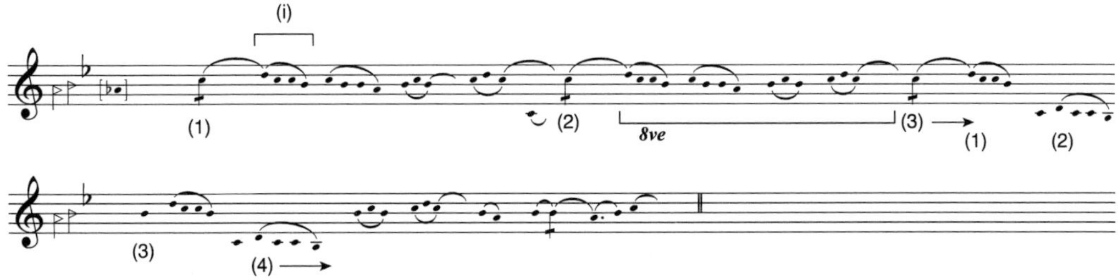

'raw materials'. Another example from performance 6 uses the same phrase structure but with a variant of motif (i) (see Figure 4.28).

Figure 4.28   Performance 6, Shafeian (*santur*), *zābol*

Here, (1) is stated twice, followed by a shorter section based on its opening. This is then played in sequence and repeated, before ascending to a climax on b♭, followed by a descent and eventual rest on g (the central pitch of *zābol*).

There were a number of phrases with the same essential structure, but using a different (closely related) 4-note motif, (ii) (or variants) (see Figures 4.29–4.32).

Figure 4.29   Performance 11, Golpayegani (voice), *mokhālef*

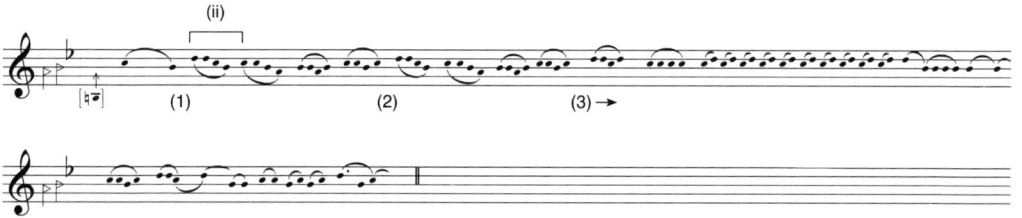

Figure 4.30   Performance 1, Lotfi (*tār*), *zābol*

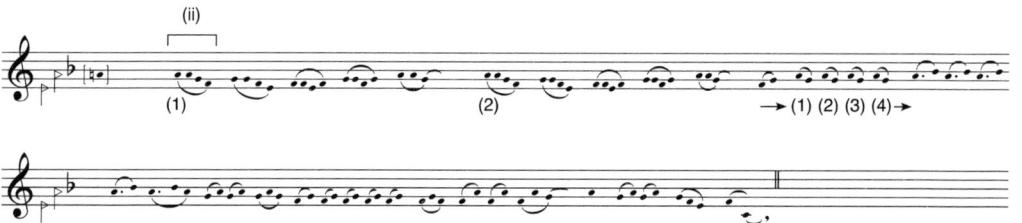

Comparing Figures 4.30 and 4.31, both use the same developmental procedure (B⁴, with the second extension of the phrase based on the last section of (1)); however, in the first, motif (ii) is the basis of the extension, whilst in the second, motif (ii) (varied) is not heard in full until the phrase extension itself, where it forms the main material for the second extension of the phrase (see Figure 4.33).

Whilst some examples of this generative phrase structure used motivic patterns other than (i) or (ii), these were particularly prevalent. As with the earlier examples, there were no instances of this second generative phrase structure in the analysed *radif*s.

Figure 4.31   Performance 22, Malek (*santur*), *zābol*

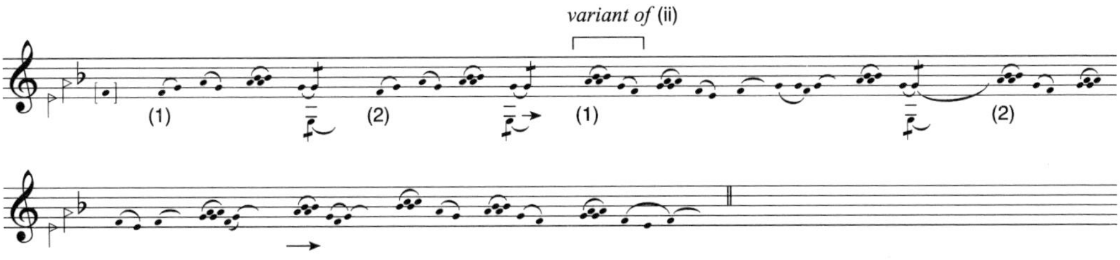

Figure 4.32   Performance 17, Shahnaz (*tār*), *darāmad*

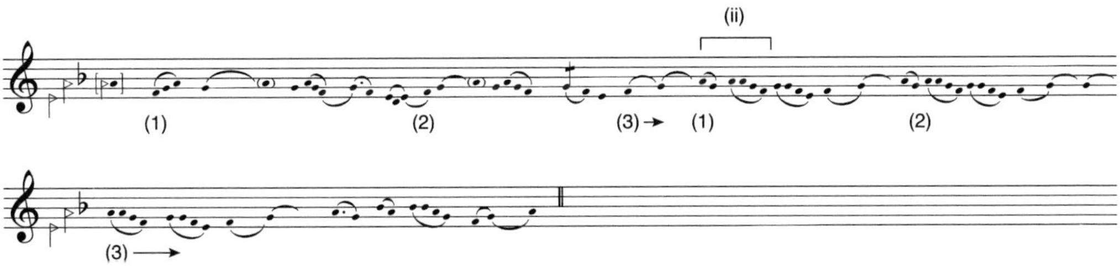

Figure 4.33   Procedure B⁴ in Figures 4.30 and 4.31

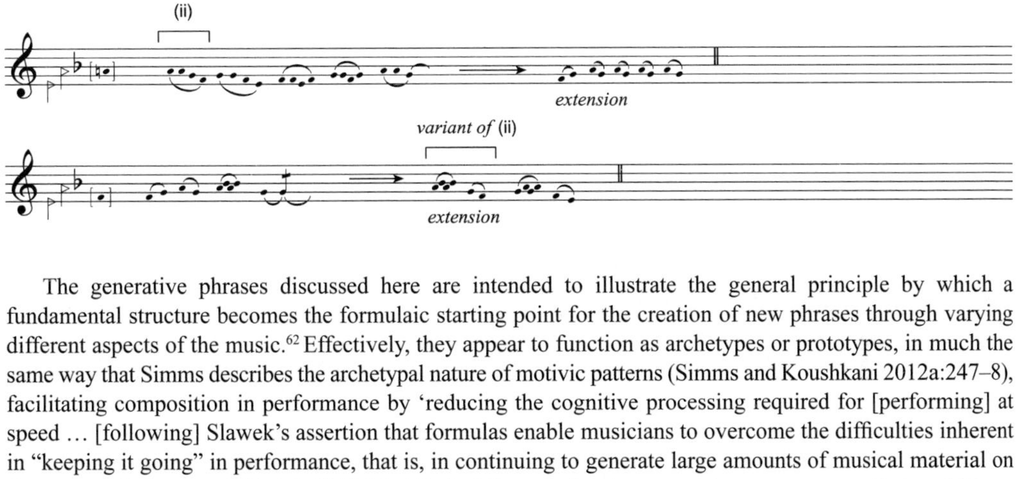

The generative phrases discussed here are intended to illustrate the general principle by which a fundamental structure becomes the formulaic starting point for the creation of new phrases through varying different aspects of the music.[62] Effectively, they appear to function as archetypes or prototypes, in much the same way that Simms describes the archetypal nature of motivic patterns (Simms and Koushkani 2012a:247–8), facilitating composition in performance by 'reducing the cognitive processing required for [performing] at speed … [following] Slawek's assertion that formulas enable musicians to overcome the difficulties inherent in "keeping it going" in performance, that is, in continuing to generate large amounts of musical material on the spur of the moment' (Zadeh 2012:15–16). And they are but two examples among many that could have been discussed. These phrase structures play an important role in less pre-defined *gushehs*, and indeed the above examples are all from such *gushehs* (*darāmad*, *zābol* and *mokhālef* in *Segāh*).

Formulaic patterns clearly play an important role in facilitating the creation of new phrases within certain parameters. In the case of motivic formulae there is a fairly clear process of transfer from *radif* to performance. However, for the generative phrase structures discussed, given that there were no examples in the analysed *radif*s, something more complex seems to be happening. Since the *radif* naturally represents an older (now

---

[62]   There seem to be possible parallels between the concept of generative phrase structures discussed here and Zadeh's 'variable melodic outline … realized differently on each occurrence' (2012:30, 28) in the context of *ṭhumrī* performance.

canonic) tradition, it is worth noting that most of the examples above are by musicians of the generation born after c.1940, suggesting that such phrase structures may have developed within the performance tradition and remain in circulation there.[63] In the next section, I continue to examine the relationship between *radif* and performance, but turn to specific compositional procedures.

Compositional Procedures: Extended Repetition

In this section, I consider how new musical material is created in the framework of generative phrase structures. As with the preceding discussion, much can be learnt through analysis of individual phrases; and indeed I will refer to some of the earlier examples to illustrate my points. Many of these share a characteristic feature: the statement of a motif or short melody at (or towards) the beginning of a phrase and its subsequent extension, usually with increased intensity and rise to a pitch climax followed by a descent to the phrase ending. This aspect of the music has been noted by Nettl (but surprisingly few others):

> … the characteristically wave-like intensity curve of the music, with its short stretches of intensification and its large number of minor climaxes, a feature that sharply distinguishes the Persian non-metric improvisation from the more grandly organized Indian *alap* …. (with Foltin 1972:33)

This can be seen clearly in Figure 4.10. Heard in performances 15 and 20, and in several other performances of the *darāmad* (indeed, the only specific 'melody' shared by more than one version) but in none of the analysed *radif*s, this phrase essentially embodies the structure described: a short idea is presented, repeated (after a brief pause) and – on the third statement – extended to a pitch climax before descending to the phrase end. In itself, this tells us little about creative processes; however, when considered in the context of the many ways in which this basic *principle* is varied, both in *Segāh* and elsewhere, it becomes more interesting. For instance, as noted, Figure 4.23 (from the *darāmad* of *Māhur*, performed on *tār* by Alizadeh) uses essentially the same idea but applied to a different opening pattern. The basic principle remains the same. Another example is from a performance by Shajarian (see Figure 4.34).

Figure 4.34   Performance 27, Shajarian (voice), *zābol*

In my earlier work, and in the absence of local terminology, I called this principle 'extended repetition' and identified several variants (Nooshin 1996:290–315). I should stress that the categories below emerged solely from the analysis and are not intended to reflect local conceptualization or discussion, of which there is virtually none. In seeking to identify regularities in the ways in which musical material is developed, I was struck by two things: first, how such principles seem to be learnt in one context and re-applied elsewhere, suggesting a process of (possibly subliminal) 'abstraction'; second, it became increasingly evident just how compositional and structured this music is, raising questions once again about the relationship between the prevalent discourse of spontaneous improvisation and the analytic evidence. I return to both points below. For detailed discussion of different kinds of extended repetition (and other compositional procedure such as phrase contraction, sequential patterns and so on) the reader is referred to my earlier work (particularly Nooshin 1996, Chapter 6). Here, I expound upon a number of ideas related to abstraction and the compositional

---

[63]   1940 (date of birth) serves as a somewhat loose dividing point between musicians in receipt of a more traditional training and the younger generation who tend to be (mostly music) graduates.

nature of performance. As in the previous section, the illustrative examples are mainly phrases extracted from complete performances and *radifs*.[64]

The most basic form of extended repetition (labelled A^1 for analytic purposes) is shown in Figures 4.10, 4.12, 4.23 and 4.34. Some of the earlier examples also use A^1 in varied form: in Figures 4.15, 4.17 and 4.19, (2) is slightly varied in relation to (1) ($A^{1(i)}$); and in Figure 4.24, the phrase extension occurs on (2) rather than (3) ($A^{1(ii)}$). Further variation can be seen in Figure 4.18 where the extension is based on a contraction of (1) ($A^{2(i)}$; superscript $^{(i)}$ indicates that (2) is varied in relation to (1)), and in Figure 4.29 the extension on (3) is formed from the opening of (1) (A^3). What these various examples – from different performances and performers, and different *gushehs* – show is how essentially the *same* developmental technique can be applied to *different* material. Moreover, the reverse is also seen: the same initial idea developed differently. For instance, compare Figures 4.10 and 4.12 with Figure 4.35.

Figure 4.35   Performance 17, Shahnaz (*tār*), *darāmad*

A particularly striking example is in Figures 4.16 and 4.23, compared above (the first from *Segāh*, the second from *Māhur*) in which the same initial idea is developed differently. Whilst Figure 4.23 uses procedure A^1, in Figure 4.16 there is a more complex form of extended repetition which I have termed 'multiple extended repetition' (B^1) in which, rather than the third statement of (1) leading directly to the phrase climax, (1) is instead repeated several times (without a pause between each statement), and only then does the music proceed to climax. In its simplest form, multiple extended repetition can also be seen in Figure 4.25 above (B^1, as in Figure 4.16), and in Figures 4.36 and 4.37.

Figure 4.36   Performance 17, Payvar (*santur*), *mokhālef*

Figure 4.37   Performance 5, Tului (*tār*), *mokhālef*

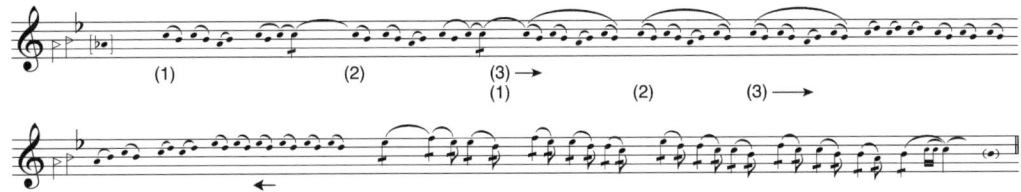

---

[64]   For discussion of such procedures in the context of a complete *gusheh*, see Nooshin (1996:360–67, 1998:102–10, 2003:277–9).

Figures 4.13, 4.20 and 4.32 are all variations of B^1 in which the second extension is formed from a *contraction* of (1) ($B^{2(i)}$). In Figures 4.26 and 4.27 the second extension is formed from the *first part* of (1) (B^3), and another example of B^3, from *dastgāh Māhur*, is shown in Figure 4.38.

Figure 4.38   Performance 33, Talai (*tār*), *Māhur*, gusheh *dād*

Several of the earlier examples use multiple extended repetition B^4 in which the second extension is based on the *ending* of (1): see Figures 4.14, 4.30 and 4.31. Finally, in B^5, the second extension is derived from material in the *middle* of (1) (Figure 4.22). There is further potential for varying B^3, B^4 and B^5 through using more or less of the beginning, middle or end of (1) in the second extension (see Figures 4.26 and 4.27).

Most of the above examples of extended (including multiple extended) repetition are from the analysed performances of *Segāh*, and from the central *gusheh*s, in which – as discussed – relatively little beyond aspects of mode and certain characteristic motifs and melodic ideas are transferred from *radif* into performance. None of the phrases presented were found in the analysed *radif*s, nor in performance versions of more pre-defined *gusheh*s. However, extended repetition *is* found in the *radif*, both in the central *gusheh*s where it is heard in the context of different material from that in performance; and, crucially, in less central *gusheh*s, where it often forms part of the defining core, transferred more or less intact into performance. An example of the former can be seen in the phrases in Figures 4.39 and 4.40 from *mokhālef* in *radif* 1, both built around multiple extended repetition (Figure 4.5 presents the complete *gusheh*).

Figure 4.39   *Radif* 1, Borumand (*tār*), *mokhālef* (B^1)

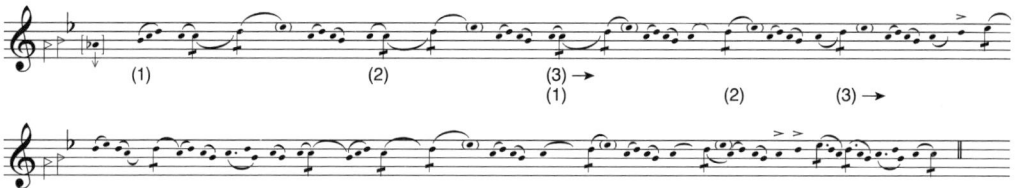

Figure 4.40   *Radif* 1, Borumand (*tār*), *mokhālef* ($B^{3(i)} \rightarrow B^{4(ii)}$)

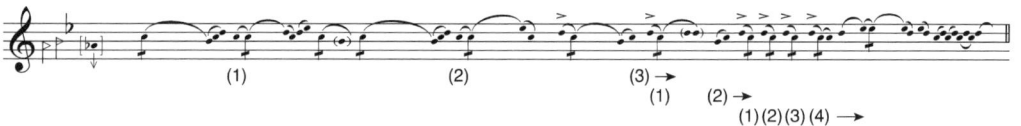

It thus seems likely that through memorizing these phrases within the *radif*, pupils also learn the structure of multiple extended repetition. Further, such phrases provide examples of alternative ways of extending material: in Figure 4.39, the extension is formed from the whole of the short opening section (see Figure 4.41); whereas in Figure 4.40, only the first four notes of the opening comprise the extension (see Figure 4.42), followed by a further extension using the last two notes of the first extension (see Figure 4.43).

Figure 4.41   Opening of phrase in Figure 4.39

Figure 4.42   First extension in Figure 4.40

Figure 4.43   Second extension in Figure 4.40

A similar phrase is found in *radif* 3: here (1) begins in the same way, but instead of extended repetition, the opening is repeated and played in slightly varied form a tone lower (starting on a-*koron* rather than b-*koron*) somewhat in the manner of a sequence, before ending the phrase (see Figure 4.44).

Figure 4.44   *Radif* 3, Tehrani (*santur*), *mokhālef*

Elsewhere in the *radif*, extended repetition forms part of the central core of some *gusheh*s. Perhaps the clearest example in *Segāh* is a single, distinctive phrase in *maqlub*, rarely omitted in performance (although it appears not to be *essential*, since it isn't in *radif* 2; see Figure 4.7, also Nooshin 1996:244–50) (see Figures 4.45 and 4.46). In Figure 4.45, (1) is stated twice and then extended using the 3-note motif (iii); this is repeated three times, after which the music rises to a climax on g and a sequential descent to a medial pause on the *ist* pitch, c. Figure 4.46 shares the same opening, which is repeated and extended on the third statement, with the melody leaping from c to f, followed by a longer sequential descent and rest on c. What is particularly interesting is that we have essentially the same phrase in two versions of the *radif*, and in each case the same opening material is extended differently. These, and earlier, examples suggest that such 'demonstrating options' is one way in which pupils learn to create new phrases. I return to this idea below.

I would like to pause briefly and consider how this particular phrase in *maqlub* is varied in performance whilst also maintaining its essence, including the embedding of extended repetition. The examples in Figures 4.47 and 4.48 share with *radif* 1: the opening movement from b♭ up to f and the descent to c; the compositional procedure (multiple extended repetition) and in Figure 4.48 the use of motif (iii) for the second extension (in Figure 4.47, Zarif uses a 2-note motif); the climactic upper g; and the following descending sequential passage to end on c.

Figure 4.45   *Radif* 1, Borumand (*tār*), *maqlub* (B⁴⁽ⁱⁱ⁾)

Figure 4.46   *Radif* 3, Tehrani (*santur*), *maqlub* (A²)

Figure 4.47   Performance 28, Zarif (*tār*), *maqlub* (B⁴⁽ⁱⁱ⁾)

Figure 4.48   Performance 21, Ebadi (*setār*), *maqlub* (B⁴⁽ⁱⁱ⁾)

The similarities with the same phrase in *radif* 1 are interesting, given that both are by older musicians and suggesting that they are perhaps following earlier practices as represented by Borumand's *radif*. Comparing these with Figures 4.49 and 4.50 from a performance by Meshkatian (b.1955), it is clear that whilst these phrases are close to *radif* 1 in some respects (Borumand was Meshkatian's main teacher), there are important differences, notably the absence of movement from b♭ up to f and down to c (this idea is instead varied at the start of Figure 4.49), as well as the use of *zir-bam* (the shifting of octaves characteristic of *santur* performances). For the phrase extension, Figure 4.49 uses a 4-note descending motif (iv), compared with the 3-note motif (iii) in *radif* 1. In Figure 4.50, there are two consecutive extensions: the first using motif (iv) descending from f to c and the second its first three pitches (f, e♭, d). Both end with a brief sequential descent using short motifs, in the manner of Figures 4.45, 4.47 and 4.48.

Figure 4.51 (like Figure 4.50, part of an *eshāreh* (allusion) to *maqlub* in a *chāhārmezrāb* in the *mokhālef* mode and closer to 4.49 and 4.50 in its material), differs from those above in using procedure B¹ (rather than B⁴), in which the second extension is formed from the whole of (1) rather than part of it. Like the earlier examples, the phrase ends with a sequential descent, but one which is gradual and uses the 4-note descending motif (iv) of (1).

Figure 4.49   Performance 16, Meshkatian (*santur*), *maqlub* (B[4(i)])[65]

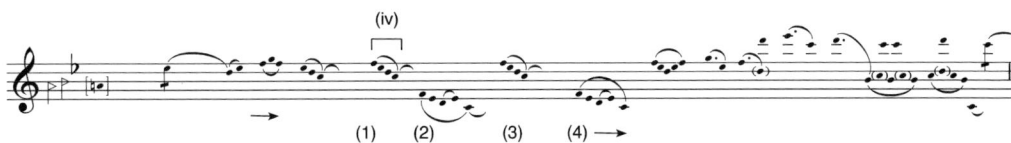

Figure 4.50   Performance 16, Meshkatian (*santur*), *eshāreh be maqlub* (*chāhārmezrāb-e mokhālef*) (B[4(i)] → B[3])

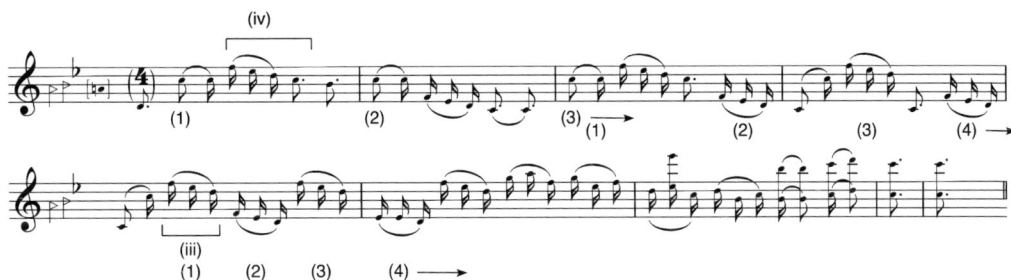

Figure 4.51   Performance 9, Shafeian (*santur*), *eshāreh be maqlub* (*chāhārmezrāb-e mokhālef*) (B[1])

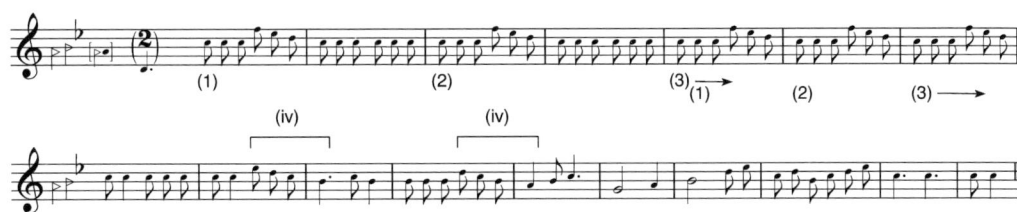

Figure 4.52   Performance 9, Shafeian (*santur*), *maqlub* (A[3(i)])

Figure 4.52 is from *gusheh maqlub* (rather than an *eshāreh* within *mokhālef*) in the same performance as Figure 4.51 and bears some similarities with Figure 4.46 (*radif* 3), particularly the use of extended repetition rather than multiple extended repetition (but with the extension based on the opening of the phrase) and in the subsequent gradual sequential descent to c via e♭ and d. In other words, whilst Figures 4.51 and 4.52 are from the same performance and same musician, the material seems to be derived from different *radif*s. The final two examples show how elements from different *radif*s can be assimilated within the same phrase: in both, the phrase openings and procedures are derived from *radif* 1, whilst the descending sequential passage of the second half is closer to *radif* 3. And although they share the same procedure (B[4]/B[4(i)]), the extension in

---

[65]   For the complete *gusheh* see Figure 4.8.

Figure 4.53   Performance 18, Payvar (*santur*), *maqlub* (B⁴)

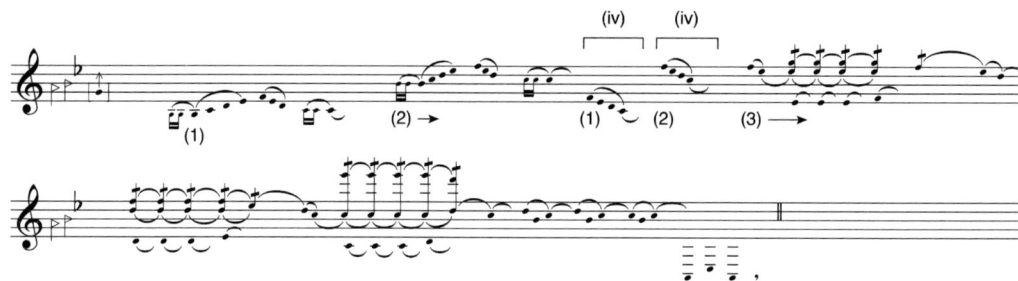

Figure 4.54   Performance 11, Golpayegani (voice), *maqlub* (B⁴⁽ⁱ⁾)

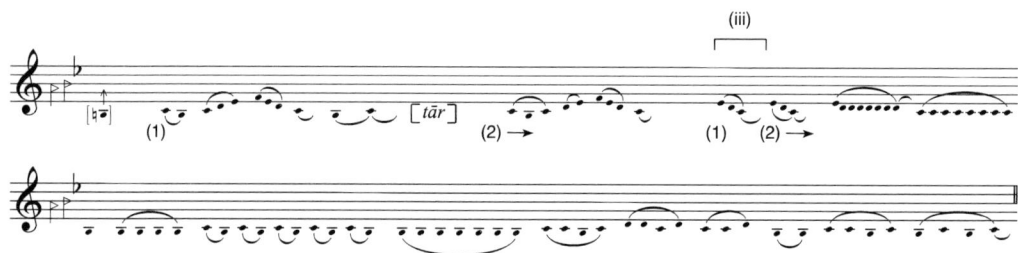

Figure 4.53 is based on the last four notes of (1) whilst in Figure 4.54 it is the last three (note also the use of *zir-bam* in Figure 4.53):

As observed, tracing direct lines of transmission between the *radif* of a master and the performances of their pupils is not straightforward. Besides the fact that musicians learn different *radif*s, the performance tradition from which they also learn includes musicians of different lineages. Whilst some of the phrases above derive material from one or other of the two *radif* examples (Figures 4.45 and 4.46), comparable phrases from the same performance and performer (Shafeian) seem to draw from different *radif*s. Similarly, Figures 4.53 and 4.54 use elements from both analysed *radif*s within a single phrase. There are of course other *radif*s not considered here (for example *radif* 2, see Figure 4.7), which may have provided the basis for some of the performances, but given the complexity of the learning system, it is impossible to account for all of the sources on which a performer may draw.

What do these examples tell us about the kinds of choices involved in the performance of this phrase in *maqlub*? The analyses suggest that musicians are faced with a number of decisions, for example whether to begin with the type of opening heard in both *radif*s (Figure 4.55), and varied in Figures 4.53 and 4.54 (Figure 4.56), or, instead with that found in Figures 4.50–4.52, involving a leap from c to f rather than a scalar ascent (see Figure 4.57). And then there are further choices including whether to repeat the opening idea, or proceed directly to the phrase extension; where the phrase extension should start; which part of the first section of the phrase the extension should use; and whether the final sequence should be a gradual descent from e♭/g to c/e♭ (as in Figures 4.46, 4.52–4.54) or a sequence constructed of short motifs (Figures 4.45, 4.47–4.51). As with the generative phrase structures, this range of variables enables musicians to re-create the phrase, at the same time maintaining its prototypical structure and identity.[66] As noted, given time constraints, it is unlikely that such decisions are all made consciously at the time of performance; instead, over many years, these various options become 'embedded' in a musician's aural and motor memory.

---

[66]   For further discussion of the ways in which similar material is extended differently, see the comparison of the opening of *muyeh* in six performances and three *radif*s of *Segāh* (Nooshin 1996:270–72).

A number of phrases with a structure similar to those above, but in *gusheh*s other than *maqlub*, were also identified. Figures 4.58–4.60 from *hazeen* use multiple extended repetition (B⁴) (based a 4th lower than the *maqlub* examples). Figure 4.61, from the *forud* at the end of performance 26 by Borumand, is similar to those above, including 4.58 (*radif* 1), suggesting that the phrase (embodying multiple extended repetition)

Figure 4.55   Opening of Figures 4.45 and 4.46

Figure 4.56   Opening of Figures 4.53 and 4.54

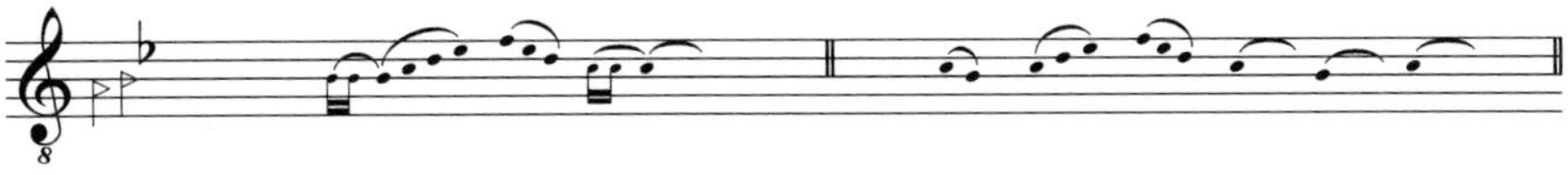

Figure 4.57   Opening of Figures 4.50–4.52

Figure 4.58   *Radif* 1, Borumand (*tār*), *hazeen* (B$^{4(ii)}$)

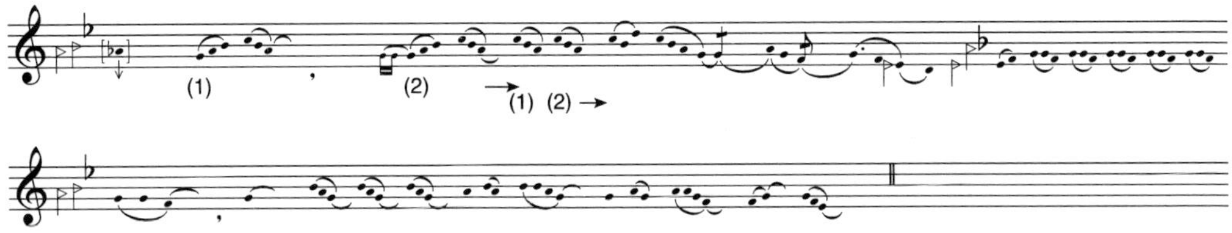

Figure 4.59   *Radif* 3, Tehrani (*santur*), *hazeen* (B⁴)

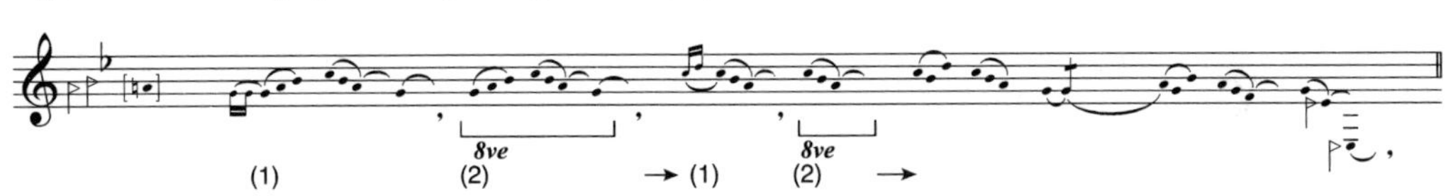

Figure 4.60   Performance 16, Meshkatian (*santur*), *hazeen* (B⁴)

is learnt as part of the *radif* in *hazeen* and subsequently used in different contexts/*gusheh*s in performance.[67] Note, however, that Figure 4.61 is closer to 4.59 and 4.60 than it is to the example above from Borumand's own *radif*.

Figure 4.61 Performance 26, Borumand (*tār*), *forud* of *Segāh* ($B^{4(i)}$)

Figures 4.45 to 4.60 show how extended repetition, and in particular B^4, is an integral part of *maqlub* (and *hazeen*) in a number of analysed *radif*s and performances. Indeed, I have suggested elsewhere that the similar positioning of this phrase in both may function as a tension-building device (Nooshin 1996:244–57). Moreover, the same phrase, embodying the same procedure, is found in *gusheh*s *hozān* and *pas hesār* in *radif* 4, and at the end of *mokhālef* in *radif* 5, as well as in the descent at the end of *maqlub* in *radif*s 2 and 6. I would propose that in learning this phrase in the *radif* – in different *gusheh*s and at different pitch levels – musicians internalize both the procedure of multiple extended repetition and the phrase shape, including the physical movements involved in playing it, which can subsequently be deployed in the context of other *gusheh*s in performance.

The embedding of compositional procedures within the pre-defined structure of certain *gusheh*s can also be seen in *dastgāh Māhur*. Take the examples in Figures 4.62–4.64 from *gusheh*s *feyli* and *khosravāni*. Figures 4.62 and 4.63 use procedure B^1 in which the whole of (1) becomes the basis for the second extension; Figure 4.64 is built around procedure B^3 in which the second extension is formed from the first part of (1). As in *maqlub*, this phrase forms part of the essential core of *khosravāni* and is subject to minimal variation in performance. Like *Segāh*, there is a hierarchy of *gusheh*s in *Māhur*, and *khosravāni* is one of the shortest and least varied. *Feyli*, on the other hand, is a fairly central *gusheh* and the phrases above are not transferred directly from *radif* into performance but extended differently, as shown below. Figure 4.65 is from the opening of *feyli* in a performance by Shajarian and shares with Figure 4.62 the distinctive opening scalar ascent and emphasis of g (a clear transfer directly from *radif* to performance).

Figure 4.62 *Radif* 1, Borumand (*tār*), *Māhur*, *feyli* (B^1)

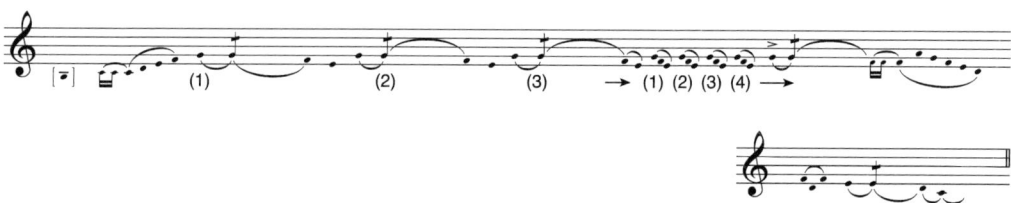

Figure 4.63 *Radif* 2, Karimi (voice), *Māhur*, *feyli* (B^1)

---

[67] Given the absence of *hazeen* in performance 26, this phrase seems to be a brief allusion to it in the final *forud* section following *mokhālef*.

Figure 4.64   *Radif* 1, Borumand (*tār*), *Māhur*, *khosravāni* (B³)

Figure 4.65   Performance 32, Shajarian (voice), *Māhur*, *feyli* (A¹⁽ⁱ⁾)

However, whilst in Figure 4.65, the phrase extension begins *after* the sustained g, in Figure 4.62 the sustained g is itself part of the idea from which the extension is built. The opening of *feyli* in a performance by Alizadeh (Figure 4.66) begins in the same way, but the initial motif is extended using the last three notes of the first section of the phrase (motif (v)), moving up to a climax on a (as in the other examples) by sequencing the same 3-note motivic pattern (vi) heard in Figure 4.65, and descending once more to rest on c.

Figure 4.66   Performance 31, Alizadeh (*tār*), *Māhur*, *feyli* (B⁴)

Note that all three examples of the opening of *feyli* (Figures 4.62, 4.65, 4.66) use repeated motifs in the area between e and g to build up tension, but each uses a slightly different motif (see Figure 4.67).

The discussion so far has focused on extended repetition as found within individual phrases. For examples in the context of a complete *gusheh*, see Figure 4.4 (*Segāh*, *zābol*, Farhang Sharif, *tār*) where the extended repetitions are indicated on the transcription. The opening of *zābol* is characterized by two phrases: the first moves from the starting pitch, e-*koron*, to emphasize g, the new *shāhed* (central pitch) after the preceding *darāmad*; the second (which in this performance starts in the upper octave) usually begins with a characteristic

Figure 4.67   Motifs used in the opening of *feyli* in Figures 4.62, 4.65 and 4.66

motif (f, g, a-*koron*, g) followed by an exploration of the area between f and a-*koron* (e-*koron* and b♭ are also heard peripherally).[68] In this performance, a 5-note motif (variation of motif (i)) becomes the basis for extended repetition $B^{3(ii)}$ in which the extension of (1) is based on the phrase opening; here there are two extensions, eventually leading to a climax on c and a descent to g at the beginning of the third stave. Following a pause, the same 5-note motif is stated three times before moving into a downward sequence and a return to the pitch centre of the opening (e-*koron*). Shifting back to the upper octave, we hear $B^{4(ii)}$ in which the extension is taken from the end of (1) (g, f, e-*koron*, motif (iii)), leading to a climax on a-*koron* and eventual rest on e-*koron*; the phrase ends with two motifs characteristic of *Segāh* ((vii) and (viii)). Motif (vii) in particular, with its neutral third interval between c and e-*koron* clearly marks the identity of the *dastgāh* at the end of *zābol*.

   Extended repetition in its various permutations is an example of a compositional procedure, a technique for extending and developing musical material. The aim of this section has been to present examples of this procedure and to show how similar principles can be applied to quite different musical material, and vice versa how the same material is developed differently. Also of interest are the differences between less central (more pre-defined) *gusheh*s such as *maqlub* and *hazeen* in *Segāh* and *khosravāni* in *Māhur*; and more central (less pre-defined) ones. Whilst in the latter, procedures and melodic material learnt from the *radif* appear to be abstracted and used in different contexts in performance, in the former procedures are often embedded within the *gusheh*, 'attached' to specific material and transferred directly into performance, suggesting that these ostensibly less significant *gusheh*s are in fact an important means by which musicians learn compositional principles. It is also worth noting that compared with the analysed performances, the *radif*s used a smaller range of types of extended repetition (A^2, A^3, B^1, $B^{2(i)}$, $B^{3(i)}$, B^4 and $B^{4(ii)}$ in *Segāh*, for instance). Whilst a larger sample might have yielded more, this suggests that certain procedures may not be learnt from the *radif* at all but developed on the basis of principles learnt through the *radif* and subsequently circulated in the performance tradition. The importance of the latter as a source of learning has already been noted with regard to generative phrase structures.

Interlude: Thoughts on Extended Repetition

In the course of analysis, which involved studying many examples of extended repetition, in *radif* and performance, I have become particularly interested in this compositional procedure, which essentially provides a means for building tension within a phrase: the first section establishes the basic material, the second generates tension through repetition, and this is intensified further in the extension up to phrase climax before eventual release in the final descent. In other words, embedded within the structure of extended repetition are the most fundamental developmental techniques of Iranian classical music – repetition, variation and extension – which arguably represent points along a continuum of ways of developing a phrase, moving away from the original. Perhaps it is this combination, the building of tension and the incorporation of fundamental compositional techniques, that makes extended repetition such a prominent feature of the music. Wright notes that the performance of Iranian classical music 'is organized so as to present a series of contrasts and oppositions, expansions and contractions, tensions and resolutions' (2009:124). And indeed extended repetition is a supreme example of a structure which facilitates 'gradual intensification followed by sudden release' (ibid.:126), arguably paralleling the build up and resolution of tension within complete *gusheh*s and *dastgāh*s; such resolution 'guarantees the narrative finality of return after venturing forth' (ibid.:125). Thus, what Wright describes as the 'potential psychological satisfaction to be gained from the completion of the smaller-scale narratives represented by the structure of each *gushe*' (ibid.:126) can also be

---

   68   For a detailed analysis of the opening of *zābol* in 10 performances and three *radif*s of *Segāh*, see Nooshin (1996:267–9).

said of individual phrases built around extended repetition. Further, there are interesting parallels to be drawn between extended repetition and certain forms of (often very emotive) oratory found in Iran, particularly that known as *rajazkhāni*, the heightening and eventual resolution of tension within individual musical phrases often mirroring the shape of recited phrases in such oratorical discourse.[69]

Clearly the generation and resolution of tension is not specific to Iran, and I have elsewhere drawn attention to, and briefly discussed, certain parallels between extended repetition and apparently similarly-structured phrases in other traditions, most notably Euro-American art and popular music (Nooshin 2003:279).[70] This is not something that I have explored extensively, but have noticed from time to time. The intention is not to propose some kind of universal musical structure, but it does raise for me the question of whether extended repetition satisfies certain principles of anticipation and release, and if so what the broader 'cross-musical' implications might be. Certainly, the fact that it is possible to identify similarities between the structures of Iranian music composed in performance and pieces composed elsewhere using notation is intriguing in the context of a study seeking to interrogate the improvisation/composition binary and to understand the relationship between the compositional and the improvisational.

Compositional Principles and Generative Processes: Abstraction and Parallels with Spoken Language

The preceding discussion suggests that there are certain principles (procedures, techniques) through which musical material is generated in performance. Some of these are derived directly from the *radif*; others seem to develop and circulate within the performance tradition. Whilst such principles might be thought of as formulaic strategies, as with generative phrase structures they are found in varied forms and may be used to create new procedures. Of particular interest is the fact that compositional techniques appear to be learnt within the *radif* or through informal listening, and subsequently *abstracted*, such that the principles embedded within them are re-applied to different material; and vice versa, that the same or similar material is developed differently. This suggests that at some (unverbalized) level, the constituent elements of a learnt phrase are not simply interchangeable, but extractable and available for use in different contexts in performance. In other words, compositional principles have an identity independent of a particular context, even if they are not explicitly named and discussed by musicians. As Wright observes:

> Up to a point, the *radif* material itself embodies its potential transformation in that it inculcates the processes by which it may be creatively varied and extended. It is worth adding in the present context that the operations of segmentation that this implies, even if not verbalized, are clearly analytical in nature, and are indeed rendered explicit in the notation of the *radif* by Tala'i [1997]. Although in this instance the purpose may have been partly visual economy, it nevertheless represents the outcome of analytical perceptions that identify motivic elements and thereby render them potentially detachable, to be recombined in different configurations. (2009:26)

The idea of abstraction also enables the analyst to generate hypothetical phrases by bringing together melodic ideas from the repertoire and abstracted principles. Consider the phrases in Figures 4.68 and 4.69. Both begin in the same way, but the extension in Figure 4.68 is formed from the *middle* of (1), whilst that in Figure 4.69 is based on the *end* of the first section of (1). As with the earlier examples from *maqlub*, the opening offers certain options: how many times to repeat (1); whether to repeat exactly or to vary; which part (or all) of (1) to use in the subsequent phrase extension; and what the nature of that extension should be.

---

[69]   During (1987c:138) explores this relationship further.

[70]   Since first formulating my ideas about extended repetition, I have come across a number of instances where scholars have identified similar constructs in other musics. For instance, Fossum observes in the context of Turkmen *dutar* music that, 'Like Nooshin's Persian musicians, Ahal School musicians seem to absorb "compositional principles" in the process of learning a pre-composed repertoire ... [and subsequently] apply these "principles" at appropriate moments in the inherited composition. In fact, on two occasions in Summer 2009, musicians I was interviewing pointed out ways that they had used a device akin to Nooshin's "extended repetition" to intentionally change a piece' (2010:180–81). Zadeh mentions a similar structure in North Indian *ṭhumrī* which she labels 'successive variation' (2012:38).

Figure 4.68   Performance 20, Ebadi (*setār*), *darāmad* (B^5)

Figure 4.69   Performance 20, Ebadi (*setār*), *darāmad* (B$^{4(i)(ii)}$)

Figure 4.70   (B$^{3(i)}$)

Figure 4.71   (A^3)

On this basis, it becomes possible to generate phrases using the same opening but applying different procedures (see Figures 4.70 and 4.71).

Following extended periods of discussion with musicians, listening to, analysing and playing individual *gushehs*, the researcher reaches a point where they have to some extent assimilated the underlying 'rules' of the music. An extension to the current analysis could be to generate different versions of *gushehs* for evaluation by musicians. This approach has been adopted by several scholars who have sought to identify generative principles within a body of music, often drawing on ideas from linguistics.[71] Clearly, gaining musician feedback on generated material may provide interesting insights into creative processes. Whilst the aim here is not to devise a generative grammar for Iranian classical music,[72] the possibility of abstracting underlying principles points to potential parallels with linguistic creativity. I therefore digress briefly at this point to consider some of the broader issues before suggesting ways in which such ideas may be useful in understanding creative processes in Iranian music. There is of course a vast literature on the subject of generative linguistics, but for the purposes of this discussion the central ideas as originally formulated by Noam Chomsky (1957, 1965) will be briefly outlined.[73] Generative linguists seek to explain the processes by

---

[71]   See Kippen (1985, 1988b) and Kippen and Bel (1992) for such a project using *bol* patterns of North Indian *tablā* music. Hughes (1988) also solicited feedback from Javanese musician Sri Hastanto on pieces generated through his devised grammar for the genre *gendhing lampah*, and used the feedback to refine the grammar further.

[72]   See Nooshin (1996:419–41) for an abstraction of some of the apparent rules governing motivic patterning in performances of *zābol*.

[73]   See Chomsky (1957, 1965, 1972, 1980, 1986), Lyons (1981) and Aitchison (1987, 1989) for the debate among linguists on these issues as well as Chomsky's later revisions of his earlier work. Going back to the discussion of oral formulae, several writers have explored the role of formulaic patterns in everyday speech, challenging some of Chomsky's original ideas. See Mackenzie (2000) and Wray (2002, 2008).

which native language speakers are able to continually create sentences from a finite vocabulary and grammar, sentences which are both (usually) grammatically correct and understood by other speakers, even though they may never have been previously uttered. Chomsky argued that language use requires an inherent and developed creative faculty of all human beings (in contrast to widely-held views at the time which regarded language acquisition as largely a matter of conditioned observation and imitation):

> Chomsky started out with the basic assumption that anybody who acquires a language is not just learning an accumulation of random utterances but a set of 'rules' or underlying principles for forming speech patterns …
> It is these 'rules' which enable a speaker to produce an indefinite number of novel utterances, rather than straight repetitions of old ones. (Aitchison 1989:92–3)

Thus, language speakers acquire both syntactic rules and vocabulary to which these can be applied to convey semantic meanings. For those outside linguistics seeking to understand the workings of the human mind, such ideas were immensely influential. Within music studies, from the late 1960s, scholars began to speculate that similar processes might be at work and that musical systems, like languages, are based on a set of internalized 'rules' (or 'grammar') and a 'vocabulary' (motifs, phrases, rhythmic patterns and so on) to which the rules are applied to generate new material. Whilst some even used terminology taken directly from generative linguistics – Blacking, for instance, suggested that the 'deep structure' of music comprises a musician's knowledge and the processes underlying the 'surface structure' of the sonic product (1967, 1970, 1973) – clearly parallels only hold to a point. For one thing, deep structure in language relates to *meaning* and syntactic rules are bound by semantics. Even were it possible to identify syntactic rules for music, the question of meaning remains highly problematic. Another important difference is that between reception and production, or what Chomsky terms 'competence' and 'performance' (see Blacking 1971b:21 and Cook 1990:73–4).[74] There is also the question of how musical 'grammars' may be bound by aesthetics, and this is where feedback from musicians is particularly valuable. In a landmark critique of the use of linguistic models in music scholarship, Feld (1974) questions the premise that music is sufficiently close to language to justify the application of such models, noting in particular that devised musical grammars often lack context sensitivity. However, he concedes that linguistic theory may be useful, particularly in explaining the rules which govern a music, the boundaries of variation, and understanding music as a form of human knowledge. Language clearly comprises a range extending from poetry and literature to everyday speech, and including both written and spoken, a point made by Powers in another important article in which he likens the improvisations of Indian musicians to extempore oratorical discourse rather than language in general and asks whether music should be regarded as a parallel to poetry, to ordinary conversation, or some other linguistic form (1980b:42–3). Powers argues that musics differ in the extent to which they lend themselves to the language comparison (their 'linguisticity'), suggesting that 'the more any musical practice is subject to constraints of ensemble performance, the less easily amenable it will be to quasi-linguistic analysis' (1980b:42). According to Powers, solo improvised traditions, particularly those of the Indian subcontinent and the Middle East, are most suited to such analysis. A contrasting view, albeit less concerned with applying linguistic models *per se* and more about understanding

---

[74]   Among others, Boilès (1967), Blacking (1971a, 1973 and 1984), Seeger (1969), Bee and Chenoweth (1971), Durbin (1971), Nattiez (1973), Becker and Becker (1979 and 1983), Lerdahl and Jackendorff (1981), Prociuk (1981), Pelinski (1984), Kippen (1985, 1988a and 1988b) and Hughes (1988) have applied ideas and models derived from or influenced by generative linguistics. See also Bright (1963), Aiello (1984) and Monelle (1992) for more general discussion of music-language parallels; Garfias (1990) offers an ethnomusicological perspective on such parallels with regard to music and language acquisition. Elsewhere (Nooshin 1996:52–63), I give an overview of some of these publications. The reader is also referred to Feld (1974) and Hughes (1991) for further discussion of the use of linguistic models within ethnomusicology. Outside ethnomusicology, a collaboration between a musician and linguist resulted in a generative grammar for (Western) tonal music (Lerdahl and Jackendorff 1983; see also Winograd 1968), and other projects have included a generative grammar for Swedish songs (Lindblom and Sundberg 1970) and a computational grammar for jazz (Johnson-Laird 1988, 1991). Extending this work into the area of reception, Lerdahl (1988) discusses the relationship between the 'grammar' which may underlie a particular piece and that by which listeners understand it. See also Berkowitz (2010) for more recent discussion of the parallels between speech and musical improvisation, particularly in relation to the cognitive processes involved in learning to improvise.

local aesthetics, is presented by Monson who considers the ways in which jazz musicians, in discussing *group* performances, 'use the metaphor of conversation to describe aspects of the improvisational process' (1996:73). She notes the 'pervasiveness of language images in African American music' (ibid.:85) generally, and among jazz musicians in particular 'linguisticity' is highly regarded from an aesthetic viewpoint: 'Good jazz improvisation is sociable and interactive just like a conversation; a good player communicates with the other players in the band. If this doesn't happen, it's not good jazz' (ibid.:84). Through detailed musical analysis, Monson examines 'the structural similarities between conversation and musical performance and the relationships among the aesthetics of social interaction, musical interaction, and cultural sensibility' (ibid.:8).[75]

There is clearly a long history of theorizing on music-language parallels within musicology, ethnomusicology and music psychology; the main reason for invoking these parallels in the context of this study is in relation to one specific process: abstraction. Abstraction is central to the ideas of generative linguistics and, as we have seen, also seems to be at work in the performance of Iranian classical music. I would suggest that the kind of musical abstraction identified in the earlier examples may be analogous to the ways in which (a) a lexicon of vocabulary and (b) syntactic rules and principles learnt by a language speaker in the context of a specific statement are subliminally separated from one another and re-used to create new statements that are both unique and grammatically correct. Thus, in the phrases analysed, 'compositional procedures' and 'musical material' might be compared to syntax and vocabulary: just as language users (subconsciously) learn grammatical rules from hearing and using existing sentences, and from being corrected, and re-apply these to generate new sentences, so it can be hypothesized that Iranian musicians subconsciously abstract basic principles from their accumulated musical knowledge and experiences and re-apply these in performance. In the same way that linguists have sought to explain the generative nature of language in terms of underlying (deep structure) rules which generate unique surface structure sentences, so the examples above suggest that musical statements which are both unique and part of the tradition are generated through common underlying principles. Whilst acknowledging important differences between linguistic and musical creativity, what the creative processes of Iranian classical music seem to share with spoken language is the experiencing and internalizing of extant 'statements', the abstraction of ideas from them, and the subsequent generation of new statements.[76] Notwithstanding the difficulty of defining a formal 'grammar' for this music, certain rules are clearly at work; otherwise, musicians would be unable to generate new material knowing that it lies within acceptable boundaries.

Limited though this analysis is to one musical tradition, the discussion above raises the possibility that some of the underlying creative processing in music and language may be similar, perhaps based on the same 'deep and restrictive principles that determine the nature of human language and [which] are rooted in the specific character of the human mind' (Chomsky 1972:102). Clearly such ideas are not new; one of the central theories of the comparative musicologists and others interested in the origins of music was an early form of human communication that 'shared elements of language and music' (Nettl 1956:136, 1983:166). What *is*

---

[75]   Many ethnomusicologists have pointed to the ways in which musicians draw parallels between music and speech; see, for instance, Berliner (1994) and Zadeh (2012:16). And of course scholars in other disciplines have used ideas from linguistics. The anthropologist Lévi-Strauss was particularly concerned with the relationship between language and society and 'whether the different aspects of social life (including even art and religion) cannot only be studied by the methods of, and with the help of concepts similar to those employed in linguistics, but also whether they do not constitute phenomena whose inmost nature is the same as that of language' (1972:62). Hawkes (1977:19–58) discusses the influence of structural linguistics on anthropology.

[76]   Several authors have noted similar processes of abstraction. Berliner describes how students of jazz 'begin acquiring an expansive collection of improvisational building blocks by extracting those shapes they perceive as discrete components from the larger solos they have already mastered and practicing them as independent figures' (1994:101). And, in the context of European art music of the eighteenth century, Zadeh reports on Gjerdingen's discussion of how formulaic patterns can be 'broken up, recombined, varied or made to overlap in individual compositions' (2012:19). Similarly, Roger Vetter relates his experiences leading *gamelan* ensembles in North America, during which it became necessary for him to undertake such abstraction for non-Indonesian learners and 'do such things as articulate underlying structure, present melodic and rhythmic vocabularies as building blocks of more complex musical utterances, and impart abstracted principles of musical syntax. I make explicit for my students many languagelike features of the music system of which native performers might not be consciously aware unless they have been exposed to the conceptualizations of someone who has studied their tradition' (2004:120).

new is recent research in both evolutionary musicology and neuroscientific studies of music which supports such theories regarding evolutionary and neurological connections, and the existence of a 'protolanguage', 'a communication system that had the characteristics that are now shared by music and language, but that split into two systems at some date in our evolutionary history' (Mithen 2006:26, see also 172–6, 191–204 and Brown 2000:271–300). Of particular interest is evidence from 'brain imaging studies ... that music and language are part of one large, vastly complicated, distributed neurological system for processing sound in the largest-brained primate' (Falk 2000:212).[77] Whilst detailed discussion of cognitive modelling lies outside the scope of this study, some of these recent findings seem to resonate with the ideas above and suggest possible connections between cognitive processing in musical and linguistic creativity.[78]

And perhaps these connections go beyond music and language: human beings are adept at acquiring types of knowledge – linguistic, mathematical, musical and so on – which depend on the accumulation of data, their comparison and abstraction, and the subsequent generation of new patterns or ideas. Dyson's discussion of abstraction in the context of understanding how jazz musicians learn to improvise reveals some interesting similarities with the points above:

> Fully skilled players are able to transfer previously learned information to any new standard and can even improvise well over tunes that are not well known to them, because their schema now allows greater flexibility and the highest levels of abstraction. At this level, players will not be consciously thinking about the melody, key centres or the harmonic progression whilst improvising on standards with which they are familiar. Like the advanced chess players, they are unconscious of all detail and process, and think aurally or respond to ideas in terms of direction, resolution and unfolding the musical ideas in the moment. The schema incorporates technical, theoretical, visual, aural, motor, kinaesthetic and imaginary elements moulded into the unique style and voice of the individual for the purpose of optimal musical exploration and expression. (2006:79)

Dyson draws on the concept of 'schema', used widely in the cognitive sciences – 'an abstract framework in the mind that both structures and is structured by experience' (ibid.:9) – in order to understand how musicians' accumulated aural, motor, conceptual, social and other knowledge becomes cognitively and physiologically embedded:

> Despite the sheer breadth of mind and body processes explained by the various schema theories, what they share is the need to understand how the human mind works in a dynamic sense in real life, and particularly how the individual learns and continues to learn and apply knowledge and skills to various different environments and situations ... The primary schema components required in jazz improvisation would appear to be aural and motor, with aural memory and auditory feedback triggering and driving the requisite motor schemata to produce the improvised musical line ... The process of learning to improvise at its simplest involves the development and interactivity of a number of schemata ... From the available information (the background musical knowledge will vary greatly from individual to individual), the player imagines a phrase and in executing it adds to their aural memory, stock of theoretical knowledge and embodied motor skill within the schema assemblage. Kinaesthetic and motor feedback on the flow and route of the movement plus auditory feedback and comparison of the intended

---

[77] Levman (1992) offers a useful summary of the main strands of the debate (up to that point) regarding the evolutionary relationship between music and language; see also Peretz (2006).

[78] There has been much neuroscientific interest in parallels between music and language processing. Of particular relevance to my argument here is the work of Aniruddh D. Patel, notably his landmark article 'Language, Music, Syntax and the Brain', which draws on 'neuroimaging data and cognitive theory to propose a specific point of convergence between syntactic processing in language and music' (2003). See also Patel (2008), Patel et al. (2008), and the work of Robert J. Zatorre on auditory processing. My thanks to Seth Ayyaz Bhunnoo for drawing my attention to this work. Also of interest is recent research into the neurobiology of improvisation, such as that conducted by Berkowitz and Ansari in which brain imaging data was collected whilst musicians were improvising (Berkowitz and Ansari 2008, 2010, and Berkowitz 2010, Chapter 7), and similar studies by Brown, Martinez and Parsons (2006). It could be argued that a truly comprehensive understanding of creative processes in music can only come about through a combination of analytic, ethnographic and psychological approaches; at the same time, such psychological testing usually involves removing subjects from 'normal' performance contexts, with implications for the validity of the findings.

idea and the actual notes played, will also be added to the schema and alter its structure and connections. This schema assemblage will then be used to organise (non-consciously) the next attempt at an improvised line, which will once again increase the store of multi-modal information available to the player. (ibid.:68–70)

Widdess also draws on schema theory in his work on North Indian classical music, and in particular the ways in which performing musicians use 'pitch schemas … the static, quasi-spatial, hierarchical relationships among a group of defined pitches (such as a scale)' and 'contour schemas … a temporal sequence of pitches underlying, and repeatedly embellished or varied in, a group of melodic phrases' (2011:194).[79] In the case of Iran, the 'schema assemblage' aligns with the 'performance model' (discussed in Chapter 3), comprising musicians' knowledge (aural, cognitive, motor) of the *radif* and the performance tradition, including information on the overall structuring of the *dastgāh*, the limits and rules of variation for each *gusheh*, compositional procedures, specific melodic material, generative phrase structures, motivic patterns and so on. All of these are in dynamic interface with their unique musical experiences, preferences and idiosyncrasies, as well as aspects of occasion and event such as other musicians, audience interaction and expectations, the social context of the performance situation and so on.

The central point to emerge from the above discussion of compositional procedures is that creative performance in Iranian classical music transcends the simple memorization of alternative versions of phrases and their selection and re-arrangement in the manner of a patchwork, as suggested in some previous literature.[80] Rather, the analyses show that in the case of the central *gushehs*, performance involves the application of procedures previously learnt, abstracted and subsequently applied in different contexts and with different musical material.[81] Moreover, these may be combined to generate new procedures which when applied to new material generate ideas which themselves become the basis for further development (see Nooshin 1996:319); in this way, the performance tradition comprises an ever changing kaleidoscope of expression.

Spatio-Motor Factors: 'the fingers give it to you'

An important aspect of performance relates to spatio-motor factors and the role of embodied knowledge in the generation of material, particularly the ways in which interaction between the human body and musical instrument may facilitate (or conversely prohibit) certain movement, and thus, sound patterns. John Baily has written extensively on this topic (1977, 1985, 1989, 1991, 1992, and Baily and Driver 1992) and its relationship to aspects of cognition, with particular reference to the *rubab* and *dutar* (plucked lutes) of Afghanistan (and also to blues guitar playing). He observes:

> The way the human body is organized to move is, in certain respects, a crucial element in the structure of music. A musical instrument is a type of transducer, converting patterns of body movement into patterns of sound … The morphology of an instrument imposes certain constraints on the way it is played, favouring movement patterns that are, for ergonomic reasons, easily organized on the spatial layout. Thus, the interaction

---

[79]   For discussion of the concept of schema in relation to music, see Snyder (2000) and Rubin (1995). More generally, Zadeh observes that 'Cognitive psychologists suggest that schemas operate widely in our everyday lives, acting as scripts to generate typical patterns of behavior in familiar situations' (2012:3).

[80]   Dyson similarly discuses 'the common reductionist approach to learning to improvise [in jazz, which] … focuses on learning scales, motifs, fragments and other patterns from harmonic sequences, which are gradually assembled in progressively longer sections to form a whole solo' (2006:218). There are also striking parallels with Hindustani music as reported by Neuman: 'Although Hindustani music involves the stitching (or weaving) of parts (pakar and chalan), the purpose is not only to aid memory but also to facilitate elaboration (vistar and barhāt). From the perspective of the musician, a bandish ought to be broken down into key phrases, but the bandish is not itself a mere assemblage of those phrases. Rather, the phrases and place (jagah) are areas for the student and musician to discover. The bandish is breakable into significant parts but it is not understood as a patched whole … The bandish is a woven whole that exists to be broken apart and built around' (2012:444).

[81]   As noted, the work of Zadeh suggests parallels with Hindustani vocal music, where the 'repeated use of abstract musical strategies [which] produce entirely different musical phrases' (2012).

between the human body, with its intrinsic modes of operation, and the morphology of the instrument *may* shape the structure of the music, channelling human creativity in predictable directions. (1992:149)

Baily (1977) shows how well adapted the structure of the *rubab* and different types of *dutar* are to the music played on each, and the difficulties which arise when music usually played on one instrument is transferred to another. He suggests that a two-way process over time has resulted in instrument morphology partly determining musical structure, as well as instruments being constructed 'to suit particular motor patterns in order to fulfil certain musical requirements' (1985:242). Creativity thus results in part from 'deliberately finding new ways to move on the instrument, which can then be assessed, and further creative acts, guided by the aesthetic evaluation of the resultant novel sonic patterns' (ibid.:257–8). According to Baily, motor patterns form part of the underlying musical 'grammar' which, once learnt, function generatively to create:

> … 'grammatically' correct novel sequences with a minimum of conscious planning by the player. This capacity is exploited in certain styles of music that deliberately cultivate improvisation, such as North Indian Classical music, but is probably operative in any instrumental musical skill. According to this model, musical creativity often involves using the 'motor grammar' to generate novel melodic sequences, some of which are then selected by the creating musician to form his new 'compositions'. (1977:329)

He cites the work of Blacking and Kubik on certain African traditions where the basis of music-making rests as much on patterns of body movement in relation to an instrument as on sonic patterns (1985:238–42).[82] For example, Blacking found:

> The most significant common factors of the *kalimba* [thumb piano] tunes are not their melodic structures, but the recurring patterns of 'fingering' which, combined with different patterns of polyrhythm between the two thumbs, produce a variety of melodies … [the] tunes … are variations on a theme, but the theme is physical and not purely musical. (1961:29)

Similarly, Dyson considers neurological evidence that body memory enables 'non-conscious elements [to] come into play which release consciousness for other activities whilst motor areas are organising information so that the brain can control movement in response to a wide range of environmental and kinaesthetic variables' (2006:26), evincing a complex interplay between the auditory, visual, tactile and kinaesthetic. In the words of jazz saxophonist Harold Ousley, 'Sometimes, the ideas come from my mind, and I have to find them quickly on my horn … other times, I find that I am playing from finger patterns; the fingers give it to you. As I play, my fingers are walking through the yellow pages, so to speak. They roam around and they come up with ideas that I like' (quoted in Berliner 1994:190).[83] In contrast to such discourses, recent research in the area of embodied music cognition on the relationship between music, movement and meaning, and between action and perception, has proposed a more integrated understanding of the mind-body relationship. From this perspective, the mind itself can be regarded as embodied (see Leman 2007, and Godøy and Leman 2012). Thus, Henley suggests that the physical 'automaticity' achieved within the 'body mind' over many years of playing is partly what allows the 'intellectual mind' the space to make creative decisions (2013). Others have used the idea of the 'biopsychosocial' ('BPS') body, first developed by psychiatrist George L. Engel in the 1970s, to theorize the complex interplay of physiological, psychological and social factors involved in creative performance (see Bhunnoo 2013).[84] Whilst much of the work in this area is in relation to music

---

[82]　Others who have discussed this aspect of music-making include Sudnow (1978) with reference to jazz piano playing, Stokes (1992:70–81) in discussing the Turkish *baglama* long-necked lute, Stock (1996) writing about Chinese *erhu* fiddle music, Dyson (2006) on learning processes in jazz, and Neuman (2012) on Hindustani music.

[83]　See similar observations by Neuman for Hindustani music (2012); Berkowitz refers to the 'brains in the fingers' (2010:37), quoting from a figured bass manual from the 1930s.

[84]　For further work in the area of embodied cognition in music, see Iyer (2002), Keller and Rieger (2009; the Editorial to a special issue of *Music Perception* on 'Musical Movement and Synchronization') and Moran (2013).

created in performance, spatio-motor factors may also play a role in notated composition. Grunfeld notes how Berlioz's proficiency as a guitarist shaped his compositional thinking:

> Everything that Berlioz composed is conditioned by the fact that he was not subject to the tyranny of piano habits. The way he spaces out his orchestral chords, the way his phrases are shaped and his rhythms change reveal a fresh, flexible mind that has been trained in the school of guitar rather than the boxed-in formulas of keyboard harmony. (1969:202, in Baily and Driver 1992:70)[85]

The only person to have explored spatio-motor factors in Iranian music is Baily himself (albeit briefly), who examines the relationship between instrument morphology and musical structure with respect to the two main long-necked lutes of Iran, the *tār* and *setār*, which he compares with those of Afghanistan (1977:318–19). Through learning the *radif* and other musical experiences, performers acquire a store of aural and physical patterns, the latter comprising habitual ways of moving on the instrument, which are also shaped by the kinds of phrase structures and motivic patterns discussed earlier and which become embedded over many years. Quotations from musicians already cited are relevant here, for example Berenjian's observation that 'As a result of playing different *radif*s, there are certain movements which are in the musician's hands [*dar panjeh-ash*]' (10.11.89, quoted in Chapter 2). The extent to which such movements are shaped by the structure of the long-necked lutes which have historically dominated this tradition is an interesting question and an avenue for future research. Several musicians with whom I talked suggested that the prevalence of sequential patterns is indeed related to this. Again, I quote from Berenjian:

> It's because of the long neck of the *tār* and *setār* [and moving up and down it]. Maybe if the *nei* had been more popular, it would have been different. You don't hear someone play this [sings an ascending sequence], or very rarely, on the *nei*. It usually has long held notes, according to the logic of the *nei* itself [*manteq-e khod-e nei*]. (30.7.90)

Elsewhere I have examined the ways in which the morphological properties of the *santur* and *tār* predispose musicians to certain kinds of movement, and therefore particular motivic patterns (Nooshin 1996:389–466). Beyond this, one can observe that the *santur* facilitates rapid movement between octaves in a way which is less feasible on other instruments, and the use of a large range and octave tremolos are therefore noticeable features of *santur* performances. Whether in relation to generative phrase structures, motifs or other formulaic patterns, the examples presented in this chapter provide ample evidence of the importance of embodied motor memory, and the cumulative effect of playing this music over many years in developing habitual ways of moving on the instrument.

Concluding Comments

This chapter has sought to examine some of the generative processes at work in the performance of *dastgāh Segāh* (with some reference to *Māhur*), specifically the complex journey from *radif* to performance, and to explore potential parallels with other areas of human creativity. The general consensus among musicians and scholars is that the *radif* underpins all creativity in Iranian classical music, to the extent that – since the repertoire is accorded an agency through which musicians learn everything they need to know in order to perform – discussion of creative processes has traditionally been deemed unnecessary. However, the analyses suggested that whilst *radif* and performance versions of individual *gusheh*s share important features, for instance in their ordering and relative importance, and hence length and degree of variation, when it comes to specific musical material the relationship is less straightforward, particularly in the more central *gusheh*s. Whilst similar material and compositional techniques are found in both, these are often in different contexts: the same material attached to different techniques, and vice versa. On this basis, it was proposed

---

[85]   Similarly, Slawek discusses the work of jazz guitarist Pat Martino, whose 'conceptual framework derives from his realization that the structure of the guitar leads to a conception of musical organization that is fundamentally different from the piano' (2009:213).

that material and techniques learnt together within the *radif* become abstracted from one another, for later use in performance. Not all *gusheh*s feature such abstraction, however: in less central *gusheh*s such as *maqlub* in *Segāh* or *khosravāni* in *Māhur*, material and techniques in the *radif* are maintained as a unit in performance, often as part of the *gusheh*'s essential core. Thus, the analyses suggested two kinds of *gusheh*, the performance of one involving abstraction, the other not. In the latter, performance might more appropriately be described as 'variation' or 'interpretation', thus problematizing the blanket use of the concept of 'improvisation'.

The idea of 'controlled variation' was used to describe how sections of repertoire are varied, but always within understood limits and in relation to an analytically abstractable, but rarely articulated, core of defining material. Controlled variation is evident both in the sectional organization of *Segāh* (such as in the choice and ordering of *gusheh*s), and in the range of variation within individual *gusheh*s. The same principle also seems to operate at a micro-structural level in relation to modal pitch functions, generative phrase structures, compositional procedures and so on.

It became clear from the analyses that musicians draw on the performance tradition as well as the canonic *radif*, and that each rendition of a *dastgāh* contributes to the re-creation of the performance tradition, changing it, enriching it, and providing ideas for other musicians. Thus, returning to the discussion of Chapter 1, the performance tradition can be understood as the cumulative contributions of many individuals over time, 'inherited from thousands of unknown talents and geniuses before' (Grainger, in Blacking 1987:45). In comparison, the *radif* remains relatively stable. In terms of creative procedures, whilst there is a basic unity in the techniques of composition, the main difference between the analysed *radif*s and performances seems to be the latter's wider latent potential: *radif* versions consistently form a tighter core of variants compared with performances.[86] Moreover, there is an interesting dynamic: on the one hand, it was suggested that procedures and patterns heard only in performance today may have originally derived from the *radif*; conversely, given the likelihood that the *radif* itself evolved from performance repertoires (as discussed in Chapter 3), one can see how procedures now embedded in the *radif* might at one time have been part of the performance tradition. The use of examples from the *radif* by Sadeghi (1971) and Zonis (1973) to illustrate 'improvisational' procedures was noted earlier.

In general, then, the *radif* can be understood less as a note-by-note framework (although it may function in this way in more pre-defined *gusheh*s or in renditions by performers who choose to remain close to the *radif*), and more as a source from which musicians learn both techniques of composition and specific melodic material, which can later be abstracted and used creatively. And, in learning several *radif*s pupils internalize different ways of developing the same material. The analysed versions of *Segāh* and *Māhur* included instances where the musical material of a phrase was derived directly from the same *gusheh* in the *radif*, whilst *the way in which the material was developed* was from a different *gusheh* or indeed another version of the *radif*. At the same time, as Wright suggests, 'even if only one version is internalized ample opportunity is provided to identify and isolate repeated (and therefore repeatable) segments, and to absorb the combinatorial grammar of the patterns in which they occur, thus proceeding via an intuitive form of analysis to master the norms of creative variation and recombination' (2009:38). All of this reinforces the idea that the music, like language, embodies the rules for its own renewal; further, it seems likely that the perpetuation of any musical tradition depends on such a set of embedded rules – the musical DNA – learnt consciously or subconsciously by both performers and listeners over many years.

Returning to the central questions of this chapter and the volume as a whole, and in particular how ideas about musical difference in relation to creative practice are imagined and articulated, the analyses here indicate that music created in performance within the Iranian classical tradition is highly structured and formulaic (these formulae are not used passively, however, but as a starting point for creativity), such that it is possible to identify specific compositional principles through which the music is developed. To this extent, the music can arguably be described as compositional. At the same time, local discourses continue to stress the improvisational, and there clearly are important aspects of the music which accord with this, including the relative lack of advance planning and the fact that musicians rarely talk about structuring or discuss the music in compositional terms. As argued in Chapter 1, then, it would perhaps be more helpful to an understanding of creative process to reconsider the somewhat rigid noun-based binary categories, and recognize the complex

---

[86] Simms notes a similar tendency in the motivic structuring of performances by Shajarian compared with the vocal *radif* of Karimi (Simms and Koushkani 2012a:251).

interpolation of the compositional and improvisational. In the final chapter, I examine some of the changes within the classical tradition over the past 40 years or so, focusing on the emergence of new ideas about creative practice.

Chapter 5
Postlude: 'Roots in the past and a view towards the future': Contemporary Developments in Iranian Classical Music Performance

Introduction

> It all goes from imitation to assimilation to innovation. You move from the imitation stage to the assimilation stage when you take little bits of things from different people and weld them into an identifiable style – creating your own style. Once you've created your own sound and you have a good sense of the history of music, then you think of where the music hasn't gone and where it can go – and that's innovation. (Walter Bishop Jr., quoted in Berliner 1994:120)

In his study of creative processes in jazz, Berliner describes creativity as the 'Act of Fusion and Transformation' (1994:138). Similarly, the Iranian classical musician spends a lifetime accumulating knowledge and experiences through which creative expression takes shape. For the past 150 years or so, this expression has been rooted in the *radif* such that for most musicians it is almost unthinkable to work outside the *radif*; to do so effectively means working outside the tradition. However, as discussed in earlier chapters, the relationship between the *radif* in its various forms and the practice of creative performance is complex. Moreover, there is a sense among some musicians that the *radif* can act as a constraint to creativity, in part through its closed nature, but also through the moralistic discourses of canonicity and authenticity which have become associated with it. Despite its centrality, then, the authorial power of the *radif* is being contested, particularly by younger musicians – broadly educated, cosmopolitan, and with access to a wide range of musics – who are less prepared than their predecessors to follow the tradition for its own sake, who are seeking a new kind of relationship with the *radif* and developing a musical voice which is both rooted in tradition and responsive to the contemporary moment. In this final chapter, I briefly survey recent developments, beginning with the work of key figures who, from the late 1970s introduced new ideas into the classical tradition and who paved the way for more recent changes. I then discuss the work of two musicians who are amongst those experimenting with new kinds of improvisational practice in Iran today.

Post-Revolutionary Renaissance

The historical narrative of Iranian classical music presented in Chapter 3 followed a trajectory from the music's pre-Qajar roots, through the many changes of the twentieth century. The second half focused on the period from the late 1950s to the late 1970s, one characterized by two predominant currents: proponents of musical 'purity' on the one hand, led by figures such as Safvate and Borumand and centred on the Markaz-e Hefz-o Eshāeh-ye Musiqi-ye Irāni and the University of Tehran; and, on the other, musicians associated with National Iranian Radio and Television, denigrated by the first group as somewhat acculturated. Borumand died in 1978, just before the Revolution of February 1979 wrought seismic changes in the political and cultural spheres. Elsewhere I have discussed the impact on musicians of the post-1979 period, and specifically government attempts to implement cultural policies consonant with Islamic tenets. What is of interest here is less the effect of specific official directives than the upsurge in national consciousness, an important driving force in the revolution itself and which had profound consequences for music. Despite overbearing restrictions on musicians in the 1980s, particularly during the eight-year war with Iraq, Iranian classical music experienced an extraordinary renaissance. Whether due to limitations on other kinds of music (such as popular music, which was banned in public between 1979 and 1998), or indeed a way of resisting limitations, or part of the mood of national enfranchisement following the overthrow of a ruler widely considered a puppet of the West, the 1980s witnessed an unprecedented public interest in traditional music, as I describe elsewhere (for example, Nooshin 2005a:241). This grass-roots awakening drew in many who had hitherto been largely excluded from the classical tradition, including many women and people from traditional and religious backgrounds who would previously have rarely listened to music or participated in music-making. The early 1980s marked an important watershed in the social acceptance of music in Iranian society, with the added irony that this should have happened under an Islamic government. Whilst concerts more or less stopped in the early 1980s, and there was little music on radio and television other than revolutionary anthems and military music, classical musicians were able to produce cassettes, which were eagerly anticipated and widely distributed, in some cases becoming an emotive focus for the new mood of national and political consciousness. Key figures such as Shajarian, Nazeri, Alizadeh and Lotfi became akin to national heroes. Most significantly, for the first time in many decades, classical musicians set poetry which resonated with the contemporary moment and music thus found a new social relevance which it had arguably not had since the 1906 Constitutional Revolution. For instance, when Shajarian, Lotfi and the Sheydā Ensemble performed the piece '*Sepideh*' ('Dawn')[1] at one of the first public concerts permitted after the Revolution (in December 1979), the song made such an impact that it soon became an unofficial national anthem, and has endured in popularity to the present day.[2]

The intention here is not to provide a detailed social history of Iranian classical music in the post-1979 period, but to convey a sense of the heady atmosphere of the early 1980s: at the same time that musicians were dealing with crippling official restrictions, there was a new mood of openness and possibility, a time to try new things, following on from changes which musicians such as Alizadeh and Lotfi had started in the mid- to late 1970s. Many of these were subtle, including the use of instruments such as the *daf* frame drum, which had fallen out of use in the classical music since the late nineteenth century; the setting of new kinds of poetry such as that of Mowlana (Rumi) and contemporary poets including Hooshang Ebtehaj (pen name Sayeh, lit: 'shadow'), Javad Azar, Aslan Aslanian and Mojtaba Kashani; and the use of additive metres such as $\frac{5}{8}$ and $\frac{7}{8}$, again something quite new to the classical music.[3] Some of these changes can be attributed to the disproportionate number of musicians of Kurdish heritage trained and working in the classical tradition (members of the Kamkar family, Shahram Nazeri, Jamshid Andalibi, Kayhan Kalhor, Saeed Farajpoori and others) who introduced regional elements.[4] Whilst the basic foundation of the music, and the centrality of the *radif*, remained unchanged (as evidenced by performances from this period discussed in Chapter 4), the cumulative effect was a new sonic aesthetic: Iranian classical music of the 1980s *sounds* different from the pre-1979 period; in the words of Kalhor, 'music started to breathe at this time' (interview, 16.6.12). It isn't easy to describe, but one might say that the music gained a new sense of direction and purpose.

Significantly, most of the musicians leading the changes were the heirs, not of the radio and television musicians of the pre-revolutionary period, but predominantly former students of Borumand and others at the Markaz and the university in the late 1960s and 1970s.[5] In other words, it was those most steeped in

---

[1]   Music by Lotfi; lyrics by Sayeh. '*Sepideh*' was published on *Chavosh no. 6* (cassette) in 1980 by the Chāvosh Cultural and Artistic Institute, Tehran, and later re-issued on CD: *Sepideh, Concert-e Goroohe Shaidaa* (no date; Avaaye Shaidaa Cultural and Artistic Institute, Tehran).

[2]   The most prominent groups during the 1980s were the Sheydā Ensemble and the Āref Ensemble, the first formed in 1974 by Shajarian and Meshkatian (and named after the prominent Constitutional Period poet, Mirza Abbas Khan Sheida, or Sheida-ye-Esfahani 1873–1949), and the second in 1977 by Meshkatian, Alizadeh and Lotfi. Referring specifically to the work of the Chāvosh Institute, a cultural and publishing centre established in 1978 and which grew out of the work of these ensembles, Sadighi and Mahdavi (2009) note that more orthodox musicians disapproved of the use of classical music as a vehicle for social, and sometimes political, comment at this time.

[3]   The only place where it was heard previously in the classical music was *gusheh chāhārpāreh*, which could be rendered in $\frac{7}{8}$ time.

[4]   See, for instance, the $\frac{5}{4}$ section in *zābol* in performance 15, played by Pashang Kamkar (*santur*) and Jamshid Andalibi (*nei*), both Kurdish musicians. Simms and Koushkani (2012b:24–5) also discuss the post-1979 folk influence on the classical music, particularly through classically-trained Kurdish musicians.

[5]   It should be noted that some of the musicians associated with the Markaz before 1979, such as Majid Kiani and Dariush Talai, continued their work much as they had before 1979 and remained detached from the changes described here.

the 'authentic' tradition promoted by Borumand who were destined to become the most radical innovators. Following on from the discussion in Chapter 3, one might surmise that it was the rigour of their training and their knowledge of the *radif* that, in a potent cocktail with the prevailing social currents, gave them both the courage and the tools with which to innovate.

The war with Iraq ended in August 1988 and Ayatollah Khomeini died in June 1989. The social and political changes which followed the end of the war and the death of the Revolution's spiritual leader led to greater liberalization. By the early 1990s, musical life had regained some stability, including the re-opening of the Music Department at Tehran University in 1990. The legacy of the previous decade, however, meant that many were no longer prepared to follow the inherited tradition unquestioningly (although some still did) but continued the trajectory of exploration. Among the many individuals and groups active at this time, it is only possible to mention a few, those I consider to have been the most influential. In selecting for discussion a small number of musicians whose pioneering work in the 1980s and '90s set the stage for a broader culture of innovation now coming to fruition, I acknowledge the many others who contributed to the development of Iranian classical music at this time. Nor has it been possible to discuss the music itself in detail but only to trace broad trends in creative practice.

One of the key innovators, and someone who has dominated Iran's musical landscape since the late 1970s, is Hossein Alizadeh (b.1951). Active as composer, performer (*tār, setār, tanbur*), educator, instrument designer (developing the *shurangiz* plucked lute, for instance), and a tireless campaigner and public spokesperson for music, I have referred to him extensively in earlier chapters and three of his performances are amongst those analysed in Chapter 4. Alizadeh studied at the University of Tehran before pursuing advanced studies in composition and musicology in Berlin. He was one of the founders of the Āref Ensemble in 1977, and also worked with the Sheydā Ensemble; he has performed with most of Iran's leading musicians and toured widely internationally. Alizadeh's lengthy discography includes compositions for orchestra, including many film scores, as well as solo and ensemble pieces.[6] Such is his influence and prolificness that it is hard to select individual works for mention here. However, as discussed in Chapter 2, one of his most important contributions has been the promotion of instrumental music and challenging the dominance of the voice. In 1989 he established the Hamāvāyān Ensemble, with the aim of performing 'new interpretations of classical Persian music',[7] particularly with regard to the use of the voice. In *Rāz-e No* (*A New Mystery*, 1998, Mahoor Institute of Culture and Art. M.CD-38), the three voices – two female, one male – are treated as though they are instruments in a manner unlike anything heard before in Iranian music. The album was published in the summer of 1998, following performances at Tehran's Vahdat Hall in March of the same year, and caused something of a stir with its interweaving of voices to form a sonic tapestry in which the individual parts alternately stand out from, and merge back into, the musical texture. The work simultaneously serves as a tongue-in-cheek response to official restrictions according to which solo female singing is prohibited in public (other than at female-only concerts) but 'choral' singing, where individual voices cannot be distinguished, is permitted. Alizadeh plays with this idea: there is no lead singer as is customary in Iranian classical music, but the group is also more than simply a 'chorus'. Another important album, *Endless Vision* (2004, Hermes Records), is a recording of a performance at Tehran's Niāvaran Palace in 2003, a collaboration between Alizadeh and Armenian master *duduk* player Djivan Gasparyan which brings together the Hamāvāyān Ensemble with a group of Armenian musicians. This is the first collaboration between such prominent Iranian and Armenian artists, serving also to acknowledge Iran's long-standing Armenian community. The album was nominated for a Grammy Award (in the traditional music category) in 2007. Still active today, Alizadeh has, over several decades, exercised an immense influence both on his peers and younger musicians; like that of many contemporary artists, his work is testimony to the long road that Iranian music has travelled from the comparatively closed milieux of earlier generations.

I would now like to consider the work of a group which has been at the forefront of innovative practice in Iranian classical music for over two decades: the Dastān Ensemble. Established in 1991 and led by Hamid

---

Talai, in fact, spent most of the 1980s outside Iran, studying and teaching in France and the United States.

[6]   A comprehensive list of his works can be found at www.hosseinalizadeh.net/Portfolio.aspx (accessed 22.8.12). See also Nooshin (2001).

[7]   http://en.wikipedia.org/wiki/Hamavayan_Ensemble (accessed 22.8.14).

Motebassem (*tār* and *setār*), the membership was fairly fluid in the early years, including at various points Morteza Ayan (*tombak*), Mohammad Ali Kiani-nejad (*nei*), Kayhan Kalhor (*kamāncheh*) and Ardeshir Kamkar (*kamāncheh*). Since 2000, the ensemble has comprised the following: Motebassem, Hossein Behroozi-nia (*bārbat*), Pejman Hadadi (percussion), Saeed Farajpouri (*kamāncheh*) and Behnam Samani (percussion; his brother, Reza Samani, occasionally joins the group as an additional percussionist). Dastān has to date released numerous albums, the first being *Booye Norooz* (1992) with compositions by Hamid Motebassem, and has performed widely in Iran and worldwide. At the time of writing, the musicians were based in Germany, the Netherlands, the United States, Canada and Iran. Dastān's music is characterized by a freshness of compositional palette, interesting timbral combinations, and a rhythmic-metric vitality which for many years distinguished them from other groups (until others started to follow). The musicians are all composers in their own right, and their works are regularly performed by the band; band members have also produced solo albums, or in collaboration with other musicians.[8] Dastān does not have one regular vocalist but maintains its identity as a group of instrumentalist-composers who invite vocalists to work with them for particular projects. Over the years, they have collaborated with many of the best known singers of Iranian music including Shahram Nazeri (*Through Eternity*, 1999, Sounds True; *Looliān*, 2005, Avay-e Novin), Sima Bina (*Hanaie: Flowers of the Desert*, 2002), Parisa (*Shoorideh*, 2003, Network 24.253; *Gol-e Behest*, 2004, Network), Iraj Bastami[9] (*Booye Norooz*, 1992) and Salar Aghili (*The Endless Ocean*, 2007, Network 495120; *In the Name of the Red Rose*, 2009). More recently, they have worked with Homayoun Shajarian, son of Mohammad Reza Shajarian.[10] One indication of Dastān's success is the extent of their influence among young musicians, particularly in their search for new modes of expression. Asked about the role of innovation in Iranian classical music, in an on-stage interview before a performance at London's Queen Elizabeth Hall in February 2011, Motebassem replied:

Someone who sets out on the path of art must be daring enough [*jesārat dāshteh bāshad*] to make changes [*taqyir va tahavvol*]; for innovation [*noāvari*] there must be courage in the work so that changes can be made. (5.2.11)

Another musician who invokes the discourse of courage is Kayhan Kalhor, a member of the Dastān Ensemble until 2000, when he left the group to pursue a solo career. Talking in 1999, he said:

I think musicians are becoming more courageous and feeling freer to express themselves. This is something that traditional music or traditional anything doesn't teach you. And I see this as an achievement of all these changes. And the position of the *radif* is definitely different now. (4.8.99)

Like Alizadeh and the members of Dastān, Kalhor is active as both composer and performer (*kamāncheh*, *setār*). Trained in Iran, his early activities included performing with the Sheydā Ensemble from the age of 17. He subsequently pursued higher education in Italy and Canada. Important early works include the album *Shab, Sokoot, Kavir* (*Night, Silence, Desert*, 1996, with Mohammad Reza Shajarian) and his first solo album (produced outside Iran), *Scattering Stars Like Dust* (1998, Traditional Crossroads 4288). Kalhor has been an inspiration to many young musicians and has almost single-handedly brought about a renewed interest in the *kamāncheh* (bowed spike-fiddle), which from the early years of the twentieth century became overshadowed, and often replaced, by the violin, as a result of which there was little technical development or exploration of its capacities. Kalhor has introduced many new techniques, including pizzicato, harmonics, double-stopping and strumming, and using the *kamāncheh* percussively. He also draws strongly on folk elements, including

---

[8]   Dastān's artistic leader, Hamid Motebassem (b.1958), started composing in the late 1980s. His first published work was the album *Bāmdād* (*Dawn*, 1990), performed by the Āref Ensemble, directed by Bijan Kamkar.

[9]   Iraj Bastami (1957–2003) was a classical vocalist who died in the Bam earthquake of December 2003.

[10]   Motebassem's most recent project, the Simorgh Project, is based on one of the stories from Iran's national epic poem, the *Shāhnāmeh* by Ferdowsi, and includes Homayoun Shajarian as vocalist (see http://www.simorq.org/Project.133.0.html, accessed 22.8.12).

from his Kurdish heritage and from the province of Lorestan in western Iran. This can all be heard clearly on *Scattering Stars like Dust*, the publication of which marked Kalhor's arrival on the 'global' world music stage:

> Within Iran I was already known for what I do on *kamāncheh*, new techniques, playing it differently. But outside Iran there wasn't anything like that of me on the market. I wanted to show young musicians that you can be traditional *and* you can sound different and modern within the tradition. You can develop your own techniques but use them in a traditional way. So with this album I was saying 'here I am, and here is the modern tradition'. (interview, 16.6.12)

The album is based entirely in *dastgāh Chāhārgāh* and follows the central *gusheh*s fairly closely (only omitting *hesār*). Kalhor's innovative approach and stunning virtuosity is evident from the start: the fast-paced and dramatic 7-time opening of track 1 uses percussive plucking quite unlike anything heard before on *kamāncheh*.[11] Kalhor described the influence of plucked instruments on his playing style, partly because the first *radif* that he studied was for *tār*, but also through listening to recordings of the early twentieth-century *kamāncheh* master Baqer Khan (Mirza Hossein Qoli's son-in-law), whose playing includes a great deal of staccato and detached notes:

> Traditionally many *kamāncheh* and violin players learnt the vocal *radif* and imitated singers, but I didn't do that, because when you do that on *kamāncheh*, there is no correct accentuation, and that was what was missing in *kamāncheh*. In my earlier music, I played more like plucked instruments because I was influenced by Baqer Khan and others. Over the last 20 years, I've been trying to develop a more balanced style which is not too plucked or *tār*-like. (16.6.12)

Not until 1'45" does the bowed *kamāncheh* enter, but even then the music continues rather unconventionally with metrically-free sustained notes layered over the tight patterns on the accompanying *tombak* goblet drum (played by another virtuoso, Pejman Hadadi), which maintains the rhythmic momentum. This opening track uses a variety of textures, has a strong dance-like character – a cross between a *reng* and a *pishdarāmad* – and includes folk elements as well. Like Alizadeh, Kalhor has worked towards developing instrumental music independent of the voice, including extended solo performances:

> I like what I can do with a singer but I don't want to be melded in it or to be the only thing that I do. I like to do that once in a while to satisfy my traditional side, but I think there are many things we can do with a single instrument that we haven't done yet. And that should be an example for our new musicians, because instrumental music has been traditionally left alone, not developed as it has been in North India, for example. And we should be doing that more. You see many performing ensembles today, but less often do you see a single player as a soloist. (16.6.12)

In this album, Kalhor draws a range of sounds from the instrument as if to compensate for the absence of variety which might be provided by a singer (and thus poetry) and other instruments.

Since the late 1990s Kalhor has performed and recorded with many musicians around the world, including four albums with Indian *sitar*ist Shujaat Hussein Khan, with whom he formed the group Ghazal (*Lost Songs of the Silk Road*, 1997, Shanachie; *As Night Falls on the Silk Road*, 1998, Shanachie; *Moon Rise over the Silk Road*, 2000, Shanachie; *Rain*, 2003, ECM); the Kronos Quartet (*Caravan*, 2000, Nonesuch); Iranian-Kurdish *tanbur* master Ali Akbar Moradi (*In the Mirror of the Sky*, 2004, World Village); Turkish musician Erdal Erzincan on *bağlama* (*Wind*, 2006, ECM); and the Brooklyn Rider String Quartet (*Silent City*, 2008, World Village). He met some of these musicians through the Silk Road Ensemble, which he has been a member of for a number of years and has composed several pieces for, including 'Blue as the Turquoise Night of

---

11   *Scattering Stars Like Dust* (1998, Traditional Crossroads 4288), track 1, 'I. Introduction'. Note the multiple extended repetition at 4'52".

Neyshabur' which was performed at the BBC Proms in London in August 2004.[12] Since 2000, Kalhor has also been part of the group Masters of Persian Music, led by Shajarian and also including Alizadeh. Looking at the wide range of Kalhor's collaborators, and at the profiles of the other musicians above, it should be clear that we are dealing with a very different kind of musician, even compared with the 1960s. These 'new' musicians are well-educated, cosmopolitan, eclectic in their musical tastes and liberal in their approach to tradition; several now reside outside Iran. All have undergone rigorous training in the classical repertoire but – as discussed in Chapter 3, where I have quoted from several of them – the *radif* is regarded as a starting point rather than an end in itself. Their work thus presents a challenge to some of the dominant discourses around notions of tradition.

One final musician from whom I have quoted extensively in Chapters 2 and 3 and who merits mention here is Shahram Nazeri. Active as singer and *setār* player from the 1970s onwards, Nazeri was, together with Shajarian, the leading vocalist of the classical music renaissance of the 1980s. He was one of the first to set the poetry of Mowlana (Rumi), now so popular among musicians. I have interviewed Nazeri twice (in 1999 and 2010) and on both occasions he described his work developing a new kind of vocal technique. This is apparent to some extent in the 1999 album *Through Eternity* (with the Dastān Ensemble) – an album which, incidentally, begins with unaccompanied solo voice, flouting the usual conventions of Iranian classical music – and even more so in *The Passion of Rumi* (2007, Quartertone Productions), a collaboration with his son, Hafez, who is the composer and also plays *setār* on the album.[13]

New Approaches to Improvisation: Case Study – *All of You* (2010)

The musicians above have been immensely influential in instilling the idea among young performers that one can be true to tradition whilst nurturing an individual voice; and – crucially – giving them courage to find that voice. But other factors have also played a part. Most importantly, the period of liberalization following the election of President Mohammad Khatami in 1997 led to a flourishing in the arts generally; and for music specifically there were some important changes, many of them centred around Tehran, but with the impact felt well beyond the capital. These included the establishment of cultural centres (*farhangsarā*) around Tehran, which provided venues both for music and other kinds of performance, and for classes; new record labels, most notably the Tehran-based Hermes (established 1999), a company which promotes contemporary and experimental new music; the opening of three new music departments in Tehran (Dāneshgāh-e Āzād, Dāneshgāh-e Sooreh and Dāneshgāh-e Honar);[14] new radio stations such as Rādio Payām and Rādio Javān ('Youth Radio'); and so on. These developments have been somewhat piecemeal and there was (and still is) little co-ordinated government policy in relation to music. Indeed, many musicians in the late 1990s continued to complain about the lack of government support, particularly for music education which remains excluded from the school curriculum. Also important at this time were moves to re-establish international diplomatic relations after almost two decades of relative isolation. With the concurrent arrival of the internet and the increasing impact of globalizing processes, a new generation of musicians (many of them music students or graduates and mostly from fairly affluent backgrounds) found themselves more connected with the outside world and able to access a much wider range of music and attendant ideas about creativity than earlier generations. In Chapter 2, I mentioned the discursive parallels frequently drawn between Iranian classical music and other ostensibly improvised traditions, and there has certainly been a growing interest in exploring new ideas around improvisation: as seen, for instance, in the Festival of Improvisation held in

---

[12]   www.silkroadproject.org (accessed 26.9.14).

[13]   See also Simms and Koushkani (2012b:25) for further discussion of Nazeri's work in the 1980s.

[14]   Since 1969, the University of Tehran had been the only institution offering a degree in music.

Tehran in 2000,[15] and recent new ensembles experimenting with improvisational practice,[16] some of which have released albums on the Hermes label.[17]

There is another dimension to this story: the growing interest in new forms of improvisational practice can perhaps be related to the emergence of what has been dubbed the 'civil society discourse' during Khatami's period of office (1997–2005) and marked by a steady shift from the prevalence of a single patriarchal voice (= *radif*?) to a more polyvocal public domain. Recent critiques of the *radif* and its authorial power might therefore be understood in relation to the growth of a civil society consciousness in Iran.[18]

In the final section of this book, I focus on a case study which exemplifies the work of those who are seeking to redefine their relationship with the *radif* and with tradition, and to find a new language for improvisation in Iranian music. What is particularly intriguing about the two musicians discussed here is that they have articulated a clear framework for their creative practice, and made it available in the public domain: at a seminar held in Tehran after the release of their 2010 album, at academic conferences outside Iran, and so on. Indeed, their eagerness to construct a particular narrative around the music is striking. The following discussion is based primarily on two interviews held in November 2010 and July 2011, a presentation by the musicians at the Performance Studies Network International Conference at the University of Cambridge in July 2011,[19] and other documents provided by the musicians. Since part of the intention is to foreground their voices, I include extended quotations from interviews and other sources.

In December 2010, Hermes released the album *All of You* (*Tamām-e To*; HER-059), a collaboration between *nei* player Amir Eslami (b.1971) and pianist Hooshyar Khayam (b.1978). Hermes was established in 1999 by Ramin Sadighi with a mission 'To create an environment that is joyful and inspirational for generating new musical ideas'. The label publishes a wide variety of music from film soundtracks to experimental electronica and in just over a decade has established a reputation locally and abroad for quality recordings of interesting new music. In the discussion below, I focus on three pieces from the album, exploring the creative processes at work, primarily through the musicians' own words and thoughts which I was able to access in a way which was simply not possible for the analyses of Chapter 4.

First, some background information. Amir Eslami is a performer of *nei* and a composer. He gained a BA and MA at the University of Tehran and currently teaches (mainly composition) at Tehran Art University where he was also formerly Dean of Administration in the Faculty of Music. Hooshyar Khayam is a pianist and composer who gained his BA at Tehran Art University, specializing in piano performance (but also studying *radif* for four years on *kamāncheh*). He pursued advanced studies abroad, gaining a DMA in composition at the University of Cincinnati, before returning to Iran. Until 2011, he also taught at the Art University. Active as a concert pianist and recording artist, Hooshyar had released four albums for solo piano or violin and piano prior to *All of You*.[20] Significantly, like many of the musicians mentioned earlier, Amir and Hooshyar are active as both composers and performers, and indeed have both won international awards for their compositions.[21] These musicians have known each other for many years; in fact, Hooshyar was previously a student of Amir's

---

[15]   Funded by the cultural organization of the Tehran municipality, Sāzmān-e Farhangi-honari-ye Shahrdāri-ye Tehrān. A number of subsequent youth and student music festivals organized by the Ministry of Culture and Islamic Guidance have included an improvisation section. My thanks to Fariborz Rostami for providing information on the 2000 festival.

[16]   See, for instance, an extract from the group Piccolo performing at Tehran's Farabi Hall in October 2002 on Mojtaba Mirtahmasb's 2003 film *Sedā-ye Dovvom* (*Back Vocal*; 35'27"–36'22").

[17]   For example, *Tonal Practice*, featuring the Tehran Experimental Orchestra (HER031, 2006) and *Tehransaranieh* by Martin Shamoonpour (HER057, 2010). www.hermesrecords.com/en/Catalogue (accessed 2.8.14).

[18]   For further discussion of the civil society discourse in relation to music, see Nooshin (2005b:486–7, 2009b:351).

[19]   See http://www.cmpcp.ac.uk/conferences.html (accessed 25.7.14).

[20]   For further information, see www.hooshyar-khayam.com/Biography.aspx (accessed 15.6.14).

[21]   For instance, Hooshyar won first prize in the 2011 Franz Schubert International Composition Competition (http://schubert.kug.ac.at/en/international-competition-franz-schubert-and-modern-music/international-competition-for-composition-2011/preistraeger.html, accessed 12.8.13); Amir won third prize in the 2010 Shakuhachi Chamber Music Composition Competition for his piece 'Seasons' (www.amireslami.com, accessed 14.5.14) and first prize in the 2009 Bologna International Composing Competition, for 'Parsi (Memorial of Ferdowsi)' (http://www.concorso2agosto.it/edizioni-passate/, accessed 12.3.13).

at Tehran Art University. Many years later, they found themselves colleagues at the same institution. In terms of performance, however, they were working in quite separate spheres: Hooshyar as a (Western) classically trained pianist; Amir as an Iranian classical musician. Indeed, somewhat astonishingly, this album represents the first collaboration between musicians from these different musical backgrounds, and part of the creative challenge has been to find a common language. Hooshyar described as 'magical' the way in which their creative relationship started (26.11.10), and Amir recalled:

> It was very interesting. Hooshyar had released an album called *Thousand Acacias*. On the first track he just plays the piano strings with his bare hands. I really like this track. And one day, when I came home from the university – and this was not a good time for me – I looked out the album. I put on the first track and suddenly felt like playing. The piece was in *dashti* mode and somehow resonated with how I was feeling. I reached for my *nei* box, took an instrument at random and started improvising. By some co-incidence the *nei* was tuned to the same mode.[22] I recorded a line over the piano. The two lines worked well together and I decided to improvise again over the piano part, and to record it. (26.11.10)[23]

In all, Amir recorded three improvisations over the existing piano piece; he then mixed these and emailed the track to Hooshyar:

> It was a bad day, a very blue day and we were experiencing harsh times, socially speaking. And then I received an mp3 file from Amir. And the subject of the email was '???', I remember that very clearly. And when I opened it there was no explanation. I listened to the file with my wife, and we were both so affected by the music that we started to cry. It was a fascinating experience, a very hurtful experience I have to say, because it opened up something inside us which had been there for a long time. So I phoned Amir. It was after midnight. And I said, 'listen, we have to start working together, there's no way round it'. And that is how our working together started. It was an instant decision. And it stayed exactly like this even when we would sit and talk about making a new piece, even if our discussions were long, when we went to the recording room the process would be instant, very very fast. (16.7.11)

This was the genesis of '*Zakhmeh*' (which appears as recorded by Amir as track 3 of the album): a classically-trained *nei* player improvising over a pre-recorded piano track.[24] Note the context of isolation: there are no other musicians physically present, and no audience. I return to the question of audiences below. Over the next three months, Amir and Hooshyar recorded a further 9 tracks and the completed album was released in December 2010. Hooshyar explained: 'The album was recorded in my home studio with really limited equipment, but good equipment ... there hasn't been the slightest modification of sound by means of auto-tuning, adding of reverb, and so on' (16.7.11).

The first piece that Amir and Hooshyar worked on (physically) together, '*Qesseh-ye Mā*' ('Our Story'), was recorded in two versions, which they spent several sessions listening to and discussing in order to develop further their ideas about the possibilities of a new approach to improvisation (Eslami and Khayam 2011). After this initial period, subsequent pieces were generally recorded in the course of a day, usually starting with discussion around some kind of visual or narrative stimulus. Indeed, the pieces all have descriptive titles (a departure for Hooshyar who for many years refrained from using titles[25]), which generally came after the music and involved much discussion. Hooshyar described their various working methods:

---

[22] Since the *nei* has fixed pitches, performers use different instruments to play in different modes.

[23] Note that in these interviews (26.11.10, 16.7.11) Hooshyar spoke mainly in English whilst Amir spoke in Persian (quotations from the latter are translated by myself).

[24] In the Shahr-e Ketāb seminar described below, Hooshyar explained: 'I felt that there was something I wanted to say [in the original piano piece] that I couldn't, but that my friend was able to.'

[25] For instance, the tracks on *Sea's Seven Days* (2010, Contemporary Music Records) are simply entitled 'Day One', 'Day Two' and so on; and similarly on *Thousand Acacias* (2010, Hermes), 'Sonnet I', 'Sonnet II' and so on.

These tracks are all improvisations, but some are worked out and others are just raw improvisation, entirely from scratch from beginning to end. We even played in a dark room so as to focus entirely on the music. But others are worked out. They are ideas that we sat and discussed what we wanted to do. Nevertheless, we think of these as improvisational because of the 'in the moment' [*dar lahzeh*] development of ideas. But we think of them as different from traditional improvisation. (16.7.11)

Amir explained that when he and Hooshyar started work on the album:

We sat and thought about what we could do. First, we could simply compose. I could say 'Hooshyar, you write a piece for *nei* and piano'; and I would write a piece for *nei* and piano, with a score. And then we thought maybe this way of composition [*āhangsāzi*] would not be fruitful for the kind of work that we wanted to do. We thought to do improvisation. But what kind? We didn't plan to play *radif*. All these thoughts and questions brought us to the direction of a kind of improvisation that would be close to our expertise in composition, where there would be some pre-defined [*az pish ta'rif shodeh*] elements which we had discussed beforehand, in contrast to improvisation in [traditional] Iranian music in which nothing is defined beforehand other than the *maqām*: they say 'we're going to play *dashti-e sol*' and they start playing. Everything happens in the moment. Either it creates something good or it doesn't, you can't be sure. But in our way of working, as well as agreeing on the tonality and the *maqām*, we talked about the form and about particular themes. For example, we had a meeting and I brought along an 8-bar theme which I wanted us to agree on a form for … but once the general discussion had taken place, we just hit the record button and start playing. In other words, it was improvisation where we had discussed aspects of form, material, harmony, and other details. So, the main difference between our work and traditional [*sonnati*] improvisation is that we had some idea beforehand about what we wanted to do.

HK: We have acquired a certain common concept of structure. This is what is between me and Amir. We understand the ideal structure for a certain piece. It just happens in the instant. It's a sound, a sonority. It's that shared understanding that means in the moment [*dar lahzeh*] when we are shaping the structure of the music in a darkened room, I would know exactly where you [addressing Amir] would finish and you would know exactly where I start. How does that happen? We didn't discuss it beforehand. Even the pieces that we worked on together, we didn't discuss what kind of cadential formula you would have …

AE: And another thing that happened was that, despite the cultural differences between piano and *nei*, in terms of structure, repertoire, training – the training that Hooshyar had, the training that I had – an interesting thing happened that went beyond boundaries [*farātar az marz*]. (16.7.11)

Amir went on to describe events of the previous day (15.7.11), following their presentation at the Performance Studies Network Conference, when they had invited members of the audience to offer an idea for them to improvise upon. As a result, Professor David Dolan (pianist and Head of the Centre for Creative Performance and Classical Improvisation at the Guildhall School of Music and Drama, London) ended up improvising with Amir: 'This was a very interesting experience for me, but it depends on a compositional approach: David Dolan is a composer, Hooshyar is a composer, and so am I.'

On several occasions, Amir and Hooshyar commented on their initial surprise, both at how 'these two instruments from two different cultures blended so well together and found a common language [*bā yekdigar hamzabān shodand*]', and at how similar their own ideas and outlook were, despite their different musical backgrounds: 'we were so close together in this work from the start that the creative side happened in an amazing way [*beh towr-e hayrat angizi*]. In many ways we complemented each other' (Khayam, 26.11.10). There is certainly a sense of heightened intensity, even drama, in the relationship between the musicians/instruments. As noted, most of the pieces have a narrative basis and 'tell a story' of some kind. Whilst the pairing of *nei* and piano is somewhat unusual, in some ways it evokes the traditional combination of voice and lute: the *nei* is often likened to the human voice in its timbral qualities and extended sound; and the piano, in those places where it is strummed, brings to mind the sound of Iranian long-necked lutes.

Through the process of working together and thinking about the potential for creative practice beyond the *radif*, Amir and Hooshyar have articulated certain principles around what they call '*shiveh-ye nowvin-e bedāheh-navāzi dar musiqi-ye Irani'*, translated by them into English as 'A New Approach to Improvisation in Persian Music' (the title of their 2011 Cambridge presentation). They have given several presentations setting out the key differences between this approach and 'traditional improvisation' (*bedāheh-navāzi-e sonnati*),[26] including: prior discussion and agreement on certain aspects of the music, unlike traditional improvisation where only the broad modal area is agreed beforehand; taking inspiration from the *radif* and its modes but not following them exactly; the use of harmony and polyphony; and the fact the pieces all have literary and/ or dramatic connotations. Another departure from traditional practice is the use of extended instrumental techniques, rarely heard in Iranian music: Hooshyar strumming and plucking the piano strings and striking the instrument body; Amir using the *nei* percussively and generating sounds through rapid covering and uncovering of finger holes and various breathing effects (described below for the piece '*Khiyāl*'), as well as simultaneously singing and playing the instrument (a technique found in certain rural traditions). Thus, the music is largely rooted in the sounds and performance ethos of the classical tradition but few would consider it to be part of that tradition because of the differences already noted, most importantly its divergence from the specific material of the *radif*.

One of the most interesting aspects of this new approach to improvisation and the discourses around it is the centrality of compositional thinking, which Amir and Hooshyar describe as '*negāh-e āhangsāzāneh*' ('a compositional view/approach', see Hermes publicity literature) or '*tafakkor-e āhangsāzi*' ('compositional thinking'). This is expressed in various ways and found repeatedly in their written and spoken narratives. Amir, for instance, described the music as 'improvisation that is supported by compositional thinking' (26.11.10) and Hooshyar continued:

> We shape it structurally, we think about it. This is where it comes close to composition. They *are* compositions, we work them out. I think what we are doing has both qualities. We both have the experience of pure improvisation, but the common concept is that of structure. (26.11.10)

This 'new improvisation' takes note of:

> ... the science of composition [*oloom-e āhangsāzi*] and the structure and musical material and its elements such as harmony, form, rhythm, melody and effective aspects of composition such as the development and expansion of themes [*tem-hā*] and motifs [*motif-hā*]. (Eslami and Khayam 2011)

On several occasions, Amir and Hooshyar suggested that, as well as being a proficient performer, anyone engaging in this new kind of improvisation should have experience in composition (implying notated composition) and 'be familiar with techniques of expansion and development' (Eslami and Khayam 2010).[27] Moreover, they regularly invoked another distinctive feature of their approach: an economy of material whereby certain themes are explored, sometimes exhaustively, in a compositional way, such that the music is built up from a 'nucleus' ('*hasteh*') rather than stringing together many different themes without exploring their full potential:

---

[26]   In interview and in presentations, Amir and Hooshyar identify three main types ('*shiveh-hā*') of 'traditional' improvisation, two of which were discussed in earlier chapters. First, there are performers who alter the *radif* minimally in performance, using some ornamentation and variation in strumming patterns, for example; Amir and Hooshyar name Majid Kiani as the main exponent of this type of improvisation. Second, there are those who memorize the *radif* thoroughly but subsequently 'improvise[ing]' in a way that is based on the *radif* but is not the *radif*. Amir and Hooshyar also identify a third group, 'mainly the younger generation who have not really memorized the *radif* well. They play it; but only pass it by and something happens in their minds and they try to improvise on the basis of that' (Eslami, 16.7.11).

[27]   This view of the interdependence of composition and improvisation is reminiscent of the case of Clara Schumann (1819–1896), one of the most acclaimed improvisers of her time, whose father, Friedrich Wieck (also her main teacher) believed that her studies in composition 'would be of great help to her in improvising ... Wieck encouraged this facet of her training also as a means of creating compositions that she could perform and publish, because it allowed her to display her individual technique and creativity, and because it was expected of a virtuoso' (Goertzen 1998:239). Goertzen also reports that Wieck taught 'technique and harmony through improvisation' (244).

> The progression of phrases in [traditional] improvised performance generally depends on creating a large number of sentences in the form of a mosaic and musicians don't emphasise the development or expansion of themes. (ibid.)

This somewhat contradicts the analysis of Chapter 4 which evidenced a strong element of compositional development (and indeed a refutation of the 'mosaic' paradigm) in the performances analysed, all of which predate this new approach to improvisation. What is clearly new, however, is the conscious conceptualization of the music *as compositional* and the verbal articulation of aspects of compositional structuring, some of which are agreed beforehand. This contrasts with more traditional practice in which musicians rarely talked about their music in this way. In the 2011 Cambridge presentation, for instance, Amir and Hooshyar used a level of analytical discourse, including motivic analysis, identifying themes and their development, and using terms such as *gostaresh* ('expansion') and *degargoon-shodan* ('transformation'), which is quite new to Iranian music.

According to Hooshyar, the fact that their pieces are relatively short compared with more traditional extended performances is indicative of the economy of material mentioned. He partly related this '*kamgooi*' (lit: 'saying less', but with the implication of 'saying more with less') to cultural influences from outside Iran, specifically the philosophies of the Far East which have attracted some interest in Iran in recent years: 'this *kamgooi* also comes from the fact that we have read Haiku; we know about Tao' (26.11.10).[28] Amir described a similar approach in his teaching:

> My improvisation in this album has been influenced by a module called 'Composition in Iranian Music' in which I aim to teach my students just one thing: how to say the most with the least material. I really stress this way of thinking and am very strict about it. I tell them: 'Iranian music is full of melody; you can string together 30 or 40 melodies and make a piece. But I want you to take just *one* melody and explore it, expand it. This comes from my training in composition. (26.11.10)

He explained that most of the tracks on *All of You* have one or at most two themes: 'we really focus on the expansion and development of the sound space' ['*bast o gostaresh-e fazā-ye sowti*']; for these musicians, this seems to be one of the key differences between traditional and new forms of improvisation. Another is what they describe as 'figure melodies':

> When musicians perform upon the music of the *radif*, they adopt the exact figure melodies from that repertoire. They refer constantly to them, and this is the beauty of the work, the aesthetic criteria. And you, as a listener, would always distinguish specific figure melodies. You would say 'this is a *naqmeh*', 'this is a *jāmedarān*', and so on. Then you would understand through this process how these masters would modify and interpret these figure melodies. In our work we do not use any pre-existing figure melodies. We just take the scheme of what those figure melodies are like, and we build our own, as a representation of a specific musical style, which is the music of *radif*. It's just a hint to that, a reminiscence, without any actual quotation. (Khayam, 16.7.11)

There are also differences in the timeframe of performance (which partly relates to the economy of material):

> The other main difference is that our improvisation is not limited to those figure melodies, letting the time pass and give as much time as the performer needs to get into the mood, and the singer to get into the mood, and then the audience. It is not like that. Here, we are dealing with closed structures. We think about the structural scheme of the work and the framing of time in one piece. This is why our pieces are much shorter than you generally find in traditional improvisation. (ibid.)

Much of Amir and Hooshyar's discourse centres on the relationship between 'composition' and 'improvisation', of which both are intensely aware and keen to discuss the complexities of:

---

[28] Amir has also composed for the Japanese *shakuhachi* end-blown flute; see footnote 21.

HK: You shouldn't divide them. I would say there are two different processes of composition: one is not limited by the time, you have an hour to think about two bars of music and yet at the very last minute of that hour you suddenly realize this is how you should do it. This is an improvisation. On the other hand, you are, for example, Keith Jarrett, improvising on some jazz tune; but what you are really doing is certain technical work which you could call composition, definitely; the way that you define the structure, the arc, for example, going up and coming down, all the concepts you have from before and then you shape the music. So in the end, there isn't much difference, that much of a borderline between these two.

LN: You talked earlier about pieces where you discussed and agreed certain things beforehand; and those where you played without any prior planning. Do you feel that there was a different kind of creative process going on?

HK: The process was different but I would say that the result isn't.

LN: You can't hear it?

HK: Exactly. You would hear the work and you wouldn't know if we have discussed it beforehand or just created at the instant. And I think it doesn't really matter. It's the final work that matters. Those works that we have performed from scratch, from beginning to end, sometimes we think they are much stronger structurally than many of our own previous compositions that we worked on separately. (16.7.11)

Hooshyar went on to explain that it was possible to 'shape and define structure and still call your work an improvisation and not a composition', adding 'in just the same way that I believe the written down compositions of quite a few Western composers are basically improvisations' (26.11.10), bringing us back to some of the issues discussed in Chapter 1.

Another aspect of the music which contrasts with traditional practice is in the collaborative nature of the improvisational experience, which is in some ways closer to certain practices outside Iran.[29] As described in earlier chapters, creative performance in the main *āvāz* sections of Iranian classical music is essentially solo: even in group renditions, musicians either take turns to improvise, or one leads and another follows, usually voice shadowed by an instrument, but also more recently one instrument shadowing another. In the case of this album, the level of interaction and integration goes well beyond that usually found in the classical music. This is something that Amir and Hooshyar don't seem to have articulated explicitly, other than talking about how the musical experience has brought them closer together as friends, an empathy also noted by Kiavash Sahebnassagh in the January 2011 Shahr-e Ketāb seminar discussed below:

> … the empathy [*hamdeli*] of these two musicians is very rare in these harsh times. In our profession, how many people make music together with such empathy? These things are happening, but on a small scale and I always regard them with respect because it teaches us that we *can* have companionship [*hamneshini*], we *can* have empathy, and this is much much more important than even this music or this album.

Elsewhere I have written about the emergence of a strong collaborative ethos within grassroots Iranian popular music since the late 1990s (Nooshin 2009b:251), and framed this within wider discussions about civil society as a space where diverse voices can be accommodated and heard on (more) equal terms. Similarly, the creative processes at work here arguably represent a form of collaboration which both reflects, and is perhaps prescient of, broader social changes beyond music.

---

[29]   Indeed, one point that came out of discussion following my presentation of this material at various seminars and conferences in the UK and the US was the extent to which Amir and Hooshyar may have been influenced by improvisational practice outside Iran, including what several audience members considered to be somewhat dated practices. Whilst further discussion lies beyond the scope of this chapter, I would note that both musicians have strong international connections, Hooshyar having studied in the US, and both have travelled widely, so it is not unlikely that their ideas have in part been shaped by experiences beyond the Iranian context.

In order to illustrate the above points, I will now discuss three of the pieces on the album, '*Zakhmeh*', '*Khiyāl*' and '*Golrizoon*', before offering some concluding thoughts.

'Zakhmeh'

As described earlier, '*Zakhmeh*' ('Strum', 4′26″) marked the start of Amir and Hooshyar's working relationship and appears on the album as track 3.[30] The piece is actually the first track ('Sonnet I') from Hooshyar's 2009 album *Hezār Aqāqi* (*Thousand Acacias*)[31] over which Amir recorded on *nei*. The sonic result is somewhat disturbing, perhaps reflecting in some way the political backdrop against which the music was created.[32] The piece starts with harsh, strident strumming on piano (on the notes d, e♭, f and g), the strings played with bare fingers, and the resulting rhythmic momentum remains a constant driving ostinato throughout. After a few seconds the solo *nei* enters, followed by more 'layers' of *nei* over the piano strumming and glissandi, resulting in a polyphonic texture with interweaving *nei* lines in different registers. At the start, most of the propulsion is provided by piano, but at 2′24″ the *nei* parts also become more regularly metered. The piano strumming continues throughout, with fragments of a strong 5-beat (3+2) pulse in places, the piece ending with a final loud strum. Talking about '*Zakhmeh*', Hooshyar explained:

> This piece shows two things: first, the specific use of the piano, which comes from the quest for cutting all ties which connect this instrument with the Western world. And the word 'strum' gives you absolutely no connection to the instrument's origins in the West. But you have entire connotations with the East. Not a single note is played with a hammer; everything is strummed with the bare hands. There's not even a plectrum. Nothing. Second, this track is important because it was the first track that made us work together, it just happened haphazardly, entirely by accident. (16.7.11)

Hooshyar then proceeded to relate how the piece came into being. Interestingly, he accords the music itself a certain agency: it was the music that brought them together and *made* them collaborate.

In relation to the compositional process, Hooshyar described the building up of layers, both in the original piano piece and those recorded over it by Amir:

> So, the piano has various layers, the *nei* has various layers and then all these layers come on top of one another. It's an entirely different sonic experience. At the time, Amir thought 'this is only an experience – let's see what happens'. But it was a very sincere experience. (16.7.11)

Hooshyar explained that the track as originally recorded by Amir was how the music appeared on the final album without any further modification. He also talked about the title:

> HK: '*Zakhmeh*' is a peculiar title; we don't have the exact equivalent in English. Because it has two meanings. *Zakhmeh* is a process of strumming; but it also means wound.
>
> LN: So it has a double meaning?
>
> HK: Yes. And you wound your instrument …
>
> LN: You haven't put that meaning here [in the English track titles], you just put 'Strum'?
>
> HK: We just called it 'Strum' because we didn't know how to express that in English. (16.7.11)

---

[30]   The first three minutes of '*Zakhmeh*' can be heard on the accompanying CD, track 9.

[31]   Hermes Records HER-050.

[32]   The events described earlier by Amir and Hooshyar took place in the aftermath of the disputed presidential elections of June 2009.

According to Amir and Hooshyar, the mode is mainly based on *Dashti* (but using an e♭ rather than e-*koron*),[33] with some reference to *Navā*. However, they make clear that this is not tied to notions of these modes as found in the *radif*:

> HK: It is a large modification of the modes. So much that it is difficult to make any connection, because when you say '*Dashti*', you have associations and ideas about how to proceed from one *gusheh* to the next. But in '*Golrizoon*', for instance, you have many different *maqāms* and notes at the same time. Maybe you have one *Dashti* on one degree and another *Dashti* on another. In a sense, it is a polymodal approach to the music. (16.7.11)

'*Khiyāl*'

According to Amir and Hooshyar (Eslami and Khayam 2011), '*Khiyāl*' ('Illusion', track 6, 3'35") was the first to be planned as a polyphonic ('*chand-sedāyi*') piece and is perhaps one of the least obviously structured tracks on the album.[34] It begins with manipulated breathing effects on *nei*, creating a sound rather like a rain stick, over single piano notes – hammered and plucked, as well as light glissandi. The blown *nei* enters at 0'51" with a sustained note leading to a somewhat fragmented dialogue with piano, including a variety of percussive and other effects on both instruments. For most of the piece, the piano part revolves around a motif comprised of a perfect 5th descent from middle c to the f below, moving up to a♭ and b♭, with soft chords in between. The music gently fades out at the end with the piano repeating the c to f motif over muted percussive sounds on *nei*. As with '*Zakhmeh*', there is an element of double meaning in the title, which Amir and Hooshyar translate into English as 'Illusion' but which also means 'imagination'. In discussion, Hooshyar also drew links with the Hindustani vocal genre of *khyal*, once again showing a knowledge of non-Iranian traditions which would have been unusual among musicians before the 1970s. He described in detail the process by which '*Khiyāl*' came into being:

> Now, '*Khiyāl*' is interesting because what we did was an entirely different process. I went to my room one night. Amir was not there but it was in the middle of our working together. And I started playing on places of the piano which you normally wouldn't. I played harmonics, pizzicato, hitting on the iron and on the back of the instrument, on the body. Well, I wouldn't say hitting because I was really caressing my instrument. And I was enjoying it. So, I gathered a large pile of sonic events and put them into my computer. And then I asked Amir to come over, and he went to the room alone and played whatever he wanted to. Of course, we had talked about the tonality, about what I was trying to get …

> LN: So, it was two completely separate events?

> HK: Yes. And then Amir went home and I started my personal improvisation on these. I took the sonic events and started to build the work. I put on the drone, and then I started to insert these events, upon each other, and modify them. So, the composition started to take shape. And then I called Amir and we worked on it together, and he played some more. And this is what '*Khiyāl*' is. Now, when you listen to it you absolutely wouldn't guess, you wouldn't realize how it's put together. I have to say that maybe it is the most imaginative work of ours, at least from my perspective. And the closest to our hearts. Because in '*Khiyāl*' I think there is an entire separation of mind from the rational way of thinking about the music. Everything is done by instinct and everything is perceived by instinct at the time that you hear it.

> LN: Although, interestingly, the way it was constructed seems to suggest that it's far from simply going into a darkened room and playing together; there are many stages in the construction.

> HK: Yes, this is what you would think. But the result is exactly the opposite. (16.7.11)

---

[33]   On this album, the piano uses equal tempered tuning rather than being retuned as in some Iranian piano music.

[34]   The first two minutes of '*Khiyāl*' can be heard on the accompanying CD, track 10.

At the January 2011 seminar (see below), Amir responded to a question about the opening of '*Khiyāl*' by describing how he breathed into the instrument whilst moving his fingers, and Hooshyar subsequently manipulated the sound file to achieve the desired effect. It was clear from the discussion that the first few seconds of the piece had been worked on intensively to get the sound just right. Asked whether he thought it helps the listener to understand the piece if they know how it is put together, Hooshyar responded, 'I think it is sometimes important for them *not* to know these things so they can establish their own relationship with the sound' (16.7.11). In view of such comments, it's interesting that the liner notes for *All of You* provide no information on the tracks (just titles) and no commentary on the compositional process, in contrast to the saturation of commentary in other contexts.

'*Golrizoon*'

The penultimate track on the album is '*Golrizoon*' ('Flower Scatter', 5′28″), a piece for solo *nei* which incorporates a variety of sounds generated through extended techniques, including percussive effects using the instrument body.[35] The piece starts with a solo melody line, soon joined by another, merging into and away from the initial pitch and giving a feeling of the music gradually expanding from a central core. The resulting sustained lines are layered using a phased effect, gradually building up to a motif: f♯, g, a, g, f♯, g (first heard at 0′50″), which is then varied. At 1′48″ we hear the first statement of a folk tune fragment, at which point the texture reduces to a single line briefly before building up in layers again. A strongly rhythmic middle section in $\frac{7}{8}$ (3 + 2 + 2) starts at 3′06″, the contact sounds of the fingers on the holes producing an effect rather like horses' hooves. The blown *nei* re-enters at 3′40″ with the return of many ideas from the opening section, but this time over the now-established $\frac{7}{8}$ foundation. This pattern stops at 5′08″ and the piece ends with multiple lines interweaving ideas from earlier in the piece.

Hooshyar described '*Golrizoon*' and its genesis as follows:

> HK: '*Golrizoon*' uses no piano and it's an improvisation we did together, but all on *nei*. The piece is made of 13 tracks layered on top of one another. It was a response to a debate that has been going for a long time on whether Iranian music can be polyphonic. Or is it naturally monophonic? And this was our response, one way of doing it. The piece uses different modes at the same time, on top of each other; and using different registers and metres and phrase structures. (16.7.11)

Amir talked about the title and its relationship with the music:

> '*Golrizoon*' has different meanings. One is in the *zurkhāneh* when the *morshed* [master] comes and they scatter flowers [petals] on his head.[36] In this piece, the several melodies that come one after the other are like the scattering and fountain of falling petals. There is a [pre-existent] melody, '*Marjangi*' or '*Mard-e Jangi*' [lit: the man of war], from the music of Lorestan [western Iran], and this is an invitation to war. It says 'Why are you sitting? Get up! It's the time for war'. And the melody is under the layers of music. And there is something of a conflict [*tazād*] between the melody and the layers that come over it and are somehow an invitation to calmness and peace. And *golrizoon* is a form of peace, of calm. Even in the old days between the fighting heroes [*pahlavān*], when they scattered flowers it was an invitation to peace. This conflict is in this music and maybe it's a conflict that is in the whole world: some are always in the process of fighting; others are always inviting to peace. And these are always points of opposition to each other. And in this music there is also this atmosphere of conflict. (16.7.11)

Hooshyar described his role in the piece:

> HK: I was sitting with the computer and composing these with each other.

---

[35]   The first four minutes of '*Golrizoon*' can be heard on the accompanying CD, track 11.

[36]   *Zurkhāneh* is a traditional gymnasium, usually an all-male space which also has a strong spiritual dimension; music is central to the *zurkhāneh*.

AE: Hooshyar was giving ideas in the moment [*idehā-yi dar lahzeh midād*].

HK: I was asking Amir to play and I would start working at the same time, making the loops and putting them here and there. And he would come and listen and then go back and play again. But I was not working with my fingers [on the piano]. There were many, many layers of improvisation. …

AE: Which kept being added to …

HK: A very thick, dense structure, when you see it on the computer. But when you listen, you don't hear it. That's why we don't normally speak about it, how we constructed all these layers. But anyway, *golrizoon* has other meanings as well. One happens in the *zurkhāneh* when the *morshed* comes and the students throw flowers on his shoulders and hair. The other is at weddings when the bride comes, and you also have *golrizoon* for the deceased. And there is *golrizoon-e Kashān* at the time of rose water distilling [*golābgiri*] when there is a ceremony and they scatter flowers in the pool. And here's another thing, because we discussed how we define the titles that the *radif* bears, *golriz* is also the name of a *gusheh* in *Shur*.

LN: Is there a connection between *golriz* in the *radif* and this piece?

HK: Absolutely no connection. No reference to the figure melody at all. We just thought about the concept of *golriz* and what it is and what it should sound like. (16.7.11)

Re-imagining Musical Difference in Relation to Creative Practice

In using terms such as 'worked out' or 'pre-thought' improvisation' (Eslami, 26.11.10), Amir and Hooshyar are clearly seeking to bridge the divide between the 'improvisational' and the 'compositional'. On the one hand, their approach is highly compositional with the focus on exploring and expanding ideas initially discussed away from performance. Moreover, prior discussion means that less is 'left to chance' than in traditional improvisation where 'intuition' plays a more central role (Khayam, 26.11.10). There's also a cumulative process at work: analysing and discussing aspects of thematic material and structure *after* recording helped Amir and Hooshyar develop ideas for subsequent pieces (Eslami and Khayam 2010). At the same time, the music itself is presented as improvisational, as happening 'in the moment', '*dar lahzeh*', an expression regularly encountered in their discourses: once the initial discussions were over, Amir and Hooshyar headed straight for the recording room and what happened there often went in unexpected directions (Eslami and Khayam, 25.11.10). Amir in particular stressed the improvisational aspects of his contribution, 'What I performed in this work from my perspective is improvisation' (Shahr-e Ketāb seminar, Tehran, January 2011; see also Adak 2011). Similarly, the album liner notes frame the music primarily in terms of improvisation:

> *All of You* is in its core an improvisation. Some of the pieces have been performed and recorded only once with no edits or retakes and the rest use the technique of multilayer recording to achieve the desired effect. Sonorities heard are all of acoustic nature performed by the musicians and generated on their instruments.

Interestingly, this is all that the listener is given. In contrast to the copious post-publication discussion of intention and creative process in seminars and conferences, the album itself includes only this brief statement, the list of tracks (in Persian and English) and a photograph of the musicians and their instruments (see Figure 5.1).

Intriguingly, an aspect of performance which seems to be missing – one, moreover often taken to be a defining feature of improvisation – is the audience. In contrast to some of the discourses considered in Chapter 2, this is improvisation defined entirely from the perspective of production, with no input from the listener. No doubt this is symptomatic of the restrictions on live performance (including the complex process of obtaining a permit) faced by Iranian musicians over the past 30 years or so, as a result of which many have

Figure 5.1   Photograph of Amir Eslami and Hooshyar Khayam from the cover of their album *All of You* (Hermes Records, HER-059; reprinted with permission)

focused their energies on music-making and recording in private, rather than in public.[37] Amir discussed the advantages of studio versus live performance, noting factors which add to the stress of live performance in Iran, including last minute cancellations which musicians have come to expect:

> The atmosphere of a concert is very different from the isolation of the studio, especially home studios. Of course, in a concert there are stresses that affect everything. The player may forget part of the music, and generally the output of a concert is based on the atmosphere of the concert hall and the audience's mood, as well as the players', whilst in the recording studio the player has a free mind and is more relaxed. On the other hand, if everything goes well in a concert, this helps the musician to perform better. I think the concert is an active situation, whilst the studio is passive. Personally, I am influenced by the audience when I have a concert and I perform better than in rehearsals or recordings. (personal communication, October 2012)

As well as the separation of musicians from audience, it's also interesting to note the fragmented nature of the creative process itself, and the facilitating role of technology in this, for example, in '*Golrizoon*' where the musicians initially worked on their own, often improvisationally, subsequently assembling the resulting materials in a compositional manner.

---

[37]   At the time of writing, Amir and Hooshyar had performed together only twice in a live setting with an audience, both in the UK: at the Performance Studies Network Conference, University Cambridge, 15 July 2011; and at the Vortex Jazz Club, north London, 18 July 2011. Outside this particular collaboration, however, both are active performers with many years of live performance experience.

The ways in which Amir and Hooshyar have sought to bridge the composition-improvisation divide takes us back to some of the earlier discourses reported in Chapter 2 – for example, Mirza Hossein Qoli's statement that 'what I compose is what I play' (During 1987b:34) – before the influence of Western thought and the arrival of notation, and eventually trained composers using it, consolidated the emerging binary between the creative spheres of composition in performance and composition in notation. In January 2011, Hermes organized a discussion seminar at the Shahr-e Ketāb bookshop in Tehran which generated much interest and was attended by many involved in the local arts scene.[38] The panel comprised Amir and Hooshyar, together with Hermes director, Ramin Sadighi, and music critic, composer and lecturer Kiavash Sahebnassagh. Panel members discussed the album and answered questions from the audience. One of the central points of discussion was around the definition of, and the need to re-define (or at least refine our understanding of) 'improvisation' and its relationship with 'composition'. As Sadighi observed:

> Many people will ask, for example, when Mr Alizadeh and Pejman Hadadi go on stage, are they really improvising – only? We know that they will have already decided to work, for example in the mode [*māyeh*] of *Navā*. At least the starting point is agreed. It isn't that they just go on stage and see whatever happens. It is possible to philosophize about this and talk about inspiration coming from the heavens, and so on, but it isn't like that. We know that artists draw from what they have learnt and what is around them, and make decisions about what to play. It is after the initial decisions are made that they can give themselves some freedom … so I want to ask what kind of improvisation is this that the *nei* has been over-dubbed 12 times, for example [referring to '*Khiyāl*']? This is not improvisation. This is Mr Amir Eslami who has gone into the studio and played a line 12 times and these have been put on top of one another. In no way can we count this as improvisation.

Hooshyar responded:

> I think it's possible to define these words in a different way [from the past], particularly improvisation [*bedāheh*] … Until a certain point, we could separate these and say 'this is in the genre of improvisation' and 'this is in the genre of composition [*āhangsāzi*]', and these are separate from one another. But it's a very difficult thing to do, and not correct … is it because it happens in the moment that we call it improvised? Or if it doesn't happen in the moment and gets written down on paper, we call it composition? This separation that has taken shape in our minds through our musical education: that improvisation is a thing that you play and you don't write, and composition is something that you write and maybe gets played later, and you have to practise it. If you don't practise it, it isn't composition. This way of thinking has changed somewhat. It can be improvisation and it can be composition as well.

Contributing to the discussion, Sahebnassagh suggested that one might think not only in terms of *bedāheh-navāzi*, but also *bedāheh-andishi* ('improvisational thinking') – 'where two people working together make an agreement [*qarār*] and define an aim [*maqsad*] beforehand, for example to make these pieces in the space [*fazā*] of *Dashti* and with a hint [*sāyeh*, lit.: 'shadow'] of *Navā*' – and *bedāheh-nevisi* ('improvisational writing'), again suggesting a move away from simple binaries. What the discussion at this seminar shows is that some musicians today are thinking about creative practice in a much more nuanced and reflective way, questioning the categories which have long underpinned discourses around creative practice (and which I found so problematic in relation to my earlier work) and re-imagining musical difference in ways that blur the accepted boundaries.

Another point of discussion concerned the relationship between musicians and audience, the extent to which performers' creative freedom should be bound by audience expectations, and by the same token, the freedom of listeners to experience and interpret the music on their own terms. This was expressed by Sahebnassagh as follows: 'what these two improvisers have dared to do is to take us out of the circle of

---

[38]   The session took place on 22 January 2011, as part of an ongoing series of public seminars organized by Hermes in conjunction with Shahr-e Ketāb. I am grateful to Amir Eslami for making available to me a DVD recording of the seminar. All quotations presented here are translated from Persian by myself. See also a report of the seminar published in the national newspaper *Hamshahri* (Adak 2011).

obligation to a modal space and create a third space [*fazā-ye sevvom*]³⁹ where we as listeners can experience the music without any intermediary [*bedooneh vāseteh*]', implying a democratizing flattening of the musical hierarchy represented by specialist knowledge of the tradition and which previously served to pre-define listeners' engagement with it. Here, the only starting point is the pure sonic experience.

Concluding Thoughts: Towards a New Wave?

All of You has been well received in Iran among the relatively small specialist audience for the kinds of recordings produced by Hermes. In June 2011, only six months after publication, it was amongst the five best-selling Hermes albums. But what does this music tell us about the possible future direction of creative practice in Iranian music? I have chosen to write about music which is somewhat on the periphery because, whilst by no means representative of the mainstream of *radif*-based classical music performance today, it is indicative of a trend, a small but growing number of musicians exploring and extending the contemporary musical language. Asked how they would describe their music, Hooshyar explained:

> We are part of a new generation of contemporary performer-composers. Just two members of it. There are other groups who follow the same sort of trend. We are just part of that new trend. (16.7.11)

But he stressed that tradition is still important:

> Our generation still believes in the authenticity of the musical heritage and all that has come down to us from past masters. And so we take it as our responsibility to study the *radif* and different performance practices, but also to have in mind the study of rural music, and music from other parts of Iran such as Turkish music, Armenian music, and so on. (26.10.11)

Perhaps pre-empting inevitable criticism from purists, Amir and Hooshyar have felt the need to defend their music as a valid form of Iranian musical expression: 'What is absolutely clear from the beginning to the end of this album [*sar-tā-sar-e in albom*] is its *Iranian* musical identity, which even with the use of piano, is very obvious' (Eslami and Khayam 2011). Again, Hooshyar accorded the instrument agency here, describing how, after his earlier unsuccessful attempts at learning Iranian instruments, 'the piano showed me how to enter a new sound world; it showed me how Iranian an instrument it is' (Shahr-e Ketāb Seminar, Tehran, January 2011). In relation to national identity, Hooshyar described the:

> Quest for authenticity, by which I mean a quest for identity. I try to identify myself with my music and whatever I am as a Persian with all the heritage, but also as a modern person who wears jeans and Adidas shoes. So, identity doesn't have to mean just *radif* in the music of Iran. (26.11.10)

Seeking to reclaim the notion of 'tradition', he continued:

> For some people, modernity represents a threat to tradition; but there is another way of looking at it and saying 'no, in fact, modernity means we should pursue our traditions and inherit them again'. Our modernity is in this; our identity is in this. (ibid.)

In discussion, Hooshyar explained that his strumming on the piano was inspired by the various long-necked lutes of Iran, particularly regional instruments such as the *dotār* of Khorasan (Iran's most northeasterly province); and also the now obsolete harp, *chang*, which can be seen in ancient iconography.

---

³⁹   It isn't clear whether Sahebnassagh is familiar with the work of Homi Bhabha (1994), but the term certainly has resonances with Bhabha's use of the same expression to indicate the unsettling of 'colonial binarisms in a unstable semiotic "third space"' (Stokes 2003:104). In the context of the current discussion, therefore, this term would seem very apposite.

At various points in conversation, Amir and Hooshyar drew parallels between their music and the movement known as '*she'r-e now*' ('the new poetry'), which began in the 1920s and sought to break away from the strict regularity of rhyme and meter in classical Persian poetry. Now, 'for the first time, this is happening in music' (Khayam 26.11.10), which has long been over-shadowed by poetry, not least because of religious prohibitions and the fact that music has often sheltered under the respectability afforded by poetry.[40] Hooshyar went further, suggesting that the term *mowj-e now* might be applied to this new music movement:

> This stream of thought, this stream of energy is going towards somewhere that maybe in 10 or 15 years we can categorize it and give it a name, say this is now the new wave [*mowj-e now*] of music, as much as it was the new wave of poetry. (ibid.)

In part, the impetus for this 'new wave' comes from a reaction against the hitherto largely unquestioned authority of the *radif*. Amir, for instance, reported a certain resistance among his students to memorizing the *radif*:

> Young musicians today who have access to the internet, to satellite and who listen to all kinds of music, they are looking for new things. They are good musicians but they don't understand why they have to learn *radif*. I tell my students 'I don't insist that you memorize it, but if you want to improvise, it means you have a sound source [*mabnā-ye sowti*] on the basis of which to say something'. The *radif* is just one of the sources of Iranian art, like poetry, like painting, like anything that gives you the possibility to think beyond to other things [*fekr koni barāyeh chiz-e digeh-yi*]. But after so many years of being told what to do, today's generation is no longer prepared to memorize 239 *gushehs* to become an improviser. It just isn't important to them. (Eslami, 26.11.10)

Amir explained this in part as an attempt to break away from the culture of moralizing prevalent for so long in the Iranian classical tradition, as described in Chapter 3; indeed, one might draw parallels with the fate of canonical thinking elsewhere, as noted by Samson for Western classical music: 'in a postmodern age, an age determined to expose the ideological and political character of all discourses, the authority of the canon as a measurement of quality in some absolute sense has proved increasingly difficult to sustain' (2001:7). Beyond this, there would seem to be a need among these young musicians, operating in an increasingly global environment, to create music over which they feel a sense of ownership and through which to foreground alternative visions of 'Iranian-ness' which depend less on essentialized notions of cultural difference and instead explore more fluid identities which transcend cultural boundaries. In discussion with Amir and Hooshyar, one gets a strong sense of a deliberate disregard of – even transgression against – ideological conventions and constraints. Compared with previous generations of musicians, 'we've seen more and we've heard more. So, these prejudices [of musical purists] haven't had much impact on us. In fact, we've witnessed the breaking down of these various ideological approaches' (Khayam, 26.11.10). Clearly, there is no attempt in their music to be 'authentic', unless one takes authenticity to mean being true to oneself (the 'personal authenticity' discussed by Kivy 1995:108, see Chapter 3). As Hooshyar explained, referring to the period when work on *All of You* started and what was happening in Iran at the time:

> This album started from honesty, from telling the truth. There was never a point where I lied or Amir lied. There is no lying in this album, for neither of us. And ultimately this honesty started from really bad feelings; and maybe [pause] it's possible to say that it has finished with a good feeling. (26.11.10)

Hooshyar regularly invoked the idea of a musical 'quest', a quest for 'authenticity', for 'identity' and, ultimately, a 'quest for beauty' (26.11.10), a form of musical expression where aesthetics overrides ideology, and where compositional choices and strategies ultimately depend on 'reasons of the ear' (Kivy 1995:xi). One might also consider these trends in light of observations by Fayaz that in the absence of many other forms of music in the public arena (most obviously popular music) in the years following the 1979 Revolution,

---

[40]   The pioneer of *she'r-e now* was Nima Youshij (1896–1960). He was followed by a series of poets, notably Ahmad Shamlu (1925–2000) who in the 1950s established what came to be known as '*she'r-e sepid*' ('white poetry').

classical music became burdened with fulfilling a range of social needs, and moreover was only able to survive by aligning itself closely with notions of tradition:

> Throughout all the years [following 1979] when the existence of music as a whole in society was disputed, it was *musiqi-ye sonnati* alone which for various reasons was able in a shaky way to be the symbol of the life of music in society (53) ... But everyone realised sooner or later that *musiqi-ye sonnati* cannot be the complete answer to the needs of music in society. (1999:54)

Thus, it is hardly surprising that musicians are now exploring new forms of expression that challenge traditional boundaries.

A particularly noticeable aspect of Amir and Hooshyar's work is their presentation of a carefully crafted narrative about the music: whether in interviews, or in seminars and conference presentations, the story they tell is arguably as much a performance of the self (after Goffman 1959) as their music is. These artists are intensely aware of the importance of this meta-performance and actively seek out opportunities to 'perform', perhaps because they are also conscious that their boundary-breaking work may not stand on its own terms, that audiences may need help in understanding it in a way that was unnecessary for their predecessors. Perhaps such narratives are also a means by which musicians can exercise control over alternative interpretations, including those of musicologists. The following observation by Bithell is highly pertinent to the case of Amir and Hooshyar, who without doubt:

> ... have a vested interest in how they are represented by outsiders (ourselves included): they are often actively engaged in the construction of their own self-representation with which our representations might conflict ... those variously referred to as 'folk', 'ethnic' or 'roots' musicians are increasingly talking and writing about their own 'traditions' (via press releases, festival brochures, web sites and the like). (2003:70–71)

By talking to me, Amir and Hooshyar hope that their views and intentions are communicated widely and 'authentically'. Increasingly, it matters to musicians how they are received and represented on the 'global stage'.

*   *   *

The purpose of this final chapter has been to offer a postlude which looks to the future direction of creative performance in Iranian music and at how the ideas, discourses and practice of musical creativity are changing. There are clearly many continuities with traditional practice, not least in the compositional nature of the music. What is new is the explicit articulation of compositional intent, the development of an intellectual-analytical approach to performance and a more sophisticated understanding of, and attempt to explore, the relationship between the compositional and the improvisational which brings us back to the issues discussed in Chapter 1 where this journey began. My hope is that the journey has brought us one small step closer to understanding the creative impulse that makes us human.

Appendix A
List of Performances and *Radif*s under Study

Each of the performances and *radif*s analysed in this study is listed below with details of internal sectioning, including the progression and length of:

1. the main modal sections (on the left-hand side)
2. individual *gusheh*s and their internal sectioning.

Where relevant, the progression of modal movement in measured sections, such as *pishdarāmad*s and *reng*s, is indicated in brackets, using the following abbreviations: d = *darāmad*, z = *zābol*, mu = *muyeh*, mo = *mokhālef*, maq = *maqlub*, n.ma = *naqmeh-ye maqlub*, s.mu = *shekasteh muyeh*, hes = *hesār*, and haz = *hazeen*.

Where there is more than one performer, the instrument(s)/voice in each section is indicated. '*Eshāreh*' indicates a brief allusion to a *gusheh* (or *dastgāh*) in the context of another.

Also listed for each performances and *radif* are the musician(s), date and place of recording/publication, and publisher (where known). It should be noted that commercial recordings in Iran are notoriously poorly documented, and such details were not always available. In the case of re-releases, it is common for original details to be omitted; moreover, many good recordings circulate informally, often without supplementary information. As much information as possible has been provided for each recording.

Performance 1 (48'39")

Chavosh no. 9 (part of a series), performed by Gorooh-e Sheydā. Recording of a live concert in Tehran, July 1977. Commercial cassette published by Kanoon-e Honari va Fekri-ye Chāvosh, 1977.

Abdol Naqi Afsharnia (*nei*)
Ali Akbar Shekarchi (*kamāncheh*)
Mohammad Reza Lotfi (*tār*)
Mohammad Reza Shajarian (male voice)
Pashang Kamkar (*santur*)
Zeidollah Tului (*tār*)
Bijan Kamkar (*tombak*)
Mira Esmail Sedqi Asa (*'ud*)
Darvish Reza Monazami (*kamāncheh*)

Broad modal area	*Gusheh*	Length of section
darāmad (9'09")	*pishdarāmad* (ensemble) (d, mu, mo, n.ma, d)	5'54"
	darāmad (*tār/santur*)	3'15"
zābol	*kereshmeh-ye zābol* (*tār*)	0'54"
darāmad (6'21")	continuation of *darāmad* (*tār/santur*)	0'46"
	zang-e shotor (*zarbi-ye darāmad*) (ensemble) (d, *eshāreh* to mu)	2'38"
	darāmad continues (voice/*tār*)	2'57"
zābol	*zābol* (voice/*tār*) (voice/*kamāncheh* at end)	1'59"
muyeh	*muyeh* (voice/*kamāncheh*)	1'29"
mokhālef	*mokhālef* (voice/*kamāncheh*)	0'54"
muyeh (1'19")	*muyeh* (*kamāncheh*)	0'37"
	shekasteh muyeh (voice/*kamāncheh*)	0'42"
darāmad	*forud* (voice/*kamāncheh*)	0'13"
muyeh	*shekasteh muyeh* (*kamāncheh/tār*)	0'25"
darāmad	*forud* (*kamāncheh/tār*)	0'31"
maqlub	*maqlub* (voice/*tār*)	0'08"
mokhālef (6'07")	*mokhālef* (voice/*tār*)	0'18"
	chāhārmezrāb-e mokhālef (mo, *eshāreh* to *masnavi*) (*tār/nei/tombak*)	2'16"
	mokhālef continues (*tār*, voice/*nei*, *nei/tār*)	3'33"
maqlub	*mokhālef be maqlub* (voice/*tār*)	0'32"
mokhālef (3'45")	*mokhālef* continues (voice/*tār*)	0'53"
	masnavi-ye mokhālef (voice/*nei*, *nei/tār*)	1'21"
	mokhālef continues (voice/*nei*, voice/*tār*)	1'31"
hesār	*hesār* (voice/*tār*)	0'36"
darāmad	*hodi va pahlavi* (voice/*tār*)	1'28"

Broad modal area	*Gusheh*	Length of section
maqlub	*maqlub* (voice/*tār*)	0′16″
mokhālef	*mokhālef* continues (voice/*tār*)	0′18″
muyeh	*shekasteh muyeh* (voice/*tār*)	0′13″
darāmad	*forud* (voice/*tār*)	0′20″
mokhālef	*mokhālef* continues (*tār*)	0′19″
muyeh	*shekasteh muyeh* (*tār*)	0′26″
darāmad (10′57″)	*forud* (*tār*)	0′15″
	tasnif (voice and ensemble) (d, z, mu, mo, d)	8′11″
	reng (ensemble) (d, mu, mo, d)	2′31″

Performance 2 (30'45")

Hossein Alizadeh (*tār*). Recording of a concert given at Leighton House, London, 21.2.1986.

Broad modal area	*Gusheh*	Length of section
darāmad (5'30")	*pishdarāmad* (d, mu, z, d)	5'07"
	darāmad	0'23"
zābol	*zābol*	0'31"
darāmad (3'35")	*darāmad*	0'34"
	zarbi-ye darāmad	0'26"
	darāmad continues	1'13"
	zarbi-ye darāmad	1'12"
	darāmad continues	0'10"
zābol (4'59")	*zābol*	0'07"
	zarbi-ye zābol	4'17"
	zābol continues (includes *eshāreh* to *muyeh*)	0'35"
muyeh (3'09")	*muyeh*	1'45"
	zarbi-ye muyeh	1'24"
mokhālef (8'19")	*mokhālef*	0'39"
	slow *zarbi* based on *masnavi*, then on *mokhālef* (includes *eshāreh* to *naghmeh-ye maqlub*)	1'20" 2'37"
	chāhārmezrāb-e mokhālef, then based on *naghmeh-ye maqlub*, then on *mokhālef* again	0'46" 1'24" 0'55"
	mokhālef continues	0'38"
darāmad (4'42")	*forud* (with short sections of *zarbi-ye darāmad*)	0'51"
	hodi (*va pahlavi*)	0'15"
	forud	0'33"
	hejrān, piece in *darāmad* mode (includes *eshāreh* to *mokhālef*)	3'03"

Performance 3 (15′53″)

Abol Hassan Saba (*setār*). Informal performance recorded in Iran in the 1950s.

Broad modal area	*Gusheh*	Length of section
darāmad (2′27″)	*darāmad*	0′30″
	chāhārmezrāb-e darāmad	1′39″
	darāmad continues	0′18″
zābol (3′46″)	*kereshmeh-ye zābol*	0′30″
	zābol continues	1′27″
	chāhārmezrāb-e zābol	0′37″
	zābol continues	0′08″
	kereshmeh-ye zābol	0′21″
	zābol continues	0′43″
muyeh (2′06″)	*muyeh*	1′17″
	shekasteh muyeh	0′49″
mokhālef (3′51″)	*mokhālef*	1′05″
	kereshmeh-ye mokhālef	0′25″
	mokhālef continues (includes *eshāreh* to *maqlub*)	1′33″
	naghmeh-ye maqlub	0′38″
	mokhālef continues	0′10″
muyeh	*shekasteh muyeh*	0′16″
darāmad	*forud*	0′09″
maqlub	*maqlub*	0′47″
mokhālef (1′39″)	*mokhālef* continues	0′05″
	hazeen	0′24″
	masnavi-ye mokhālef	1′10″
darāmad	*forud*	0′52″

Performance 4 (9'34")

Ahmad Ebadi (*setār*). From *Ostādān-e Musiqi-ye Sonnati-ye Iran* (*Masters of Iranian Traditional Music*) series, SARTMS, no. 5, on the Āhang-e Ruz label. Recorded and published in Iran as a 33rpm LP disc; re-released on cassette after 1979 in the United States by Soundex Enterprises Inc. (ARCT 226). No date given.

Broad modal area	*Gusheh*	Length of section
darāmad (2'59")	*darāmad*	0'57"
	chāhārmezrāb-e darāmad	0'55"
	darāmad continues	1'07"
zābol (1'36")	*zābol*	0'11"
	chāhārmezrāb-e zābol (including *eshāreh* to *muyeh*)	1'00"
	zābol continues	0'25"
muyeh (1'14")	*muyeh*	0'30"
	chāhārmezrāb-e muyeh	0'11"
	muyeh continues	0'33"
darāmad	*hodi va pahlavi*	0'47"
muyeh	*muyeh*	0'31"
mokhālef (2'06")	*mokhālef*	0'02"
	chāhārmezrāb-e mokhālef	0'49"
	mokhālef continues	0'22"
	naghmeh-ye maqlub	0'38"
	mokhālef continues	0'15"
darāmad	*forud*	0'21"

Performance 5 (22'07")

Zeidollah Tului (*tār*). Recording of a concert given in London, 1987. Venue unknown.

Broad modal area	*Gusheh*	Length of section
darāmad (9'31")	*darāmad*	1'25"
	slow *zarbi* in the *darāmad* mode (d, z, mu, mo, hes, return to d after each section)	4'00"
	darāmad continues	1'12"
	chāhārmezrāb-e darāmad (brief *eshāreh*s to *mokhālef* and *hesār*)	2'19"
	darāmad continues	0'35"
zābol (3'02")	*zābol*	1'04"
	chāhārmezrāb-e zābol	1'13"
	zābol continues	0'45"
darāmad (2'56")	*zang-e shotor* (*chāhārmezrāb-e darāmad*) (*eshāreh*s to other *gusheh*s)	2'48"
	forud	0'08"
mokhālef (3'28")	*mokhālef* (includes *eshāreh* to *hazeen*)	0'59"
	masnavi-ye mokhālef	0'55"
	naghmeh-ye maqlub	0'23"
	mokhālef continues	0'44"
	eshāreh to *hazeen*	0'27"
muyeh	*muyeh*	0'25"
mokhālef	*chāhārmezrāb-e mokhālef*	0'24"
hesār	*hesār*	0'11"
darāmad	*forud*	0'27"
	reng (starts like *zang-e shotor*, but is varied, with *eshāreh*s to other *gusheh*s)	1'43"

Performance 6 (36'21")

Reza Shafeian (*santur*). Recording of a performance broadcast by BBC Radio 3, c.1987.

Broad modal area	*Gusheh*	Length of section
darāmad (10'42")	*darāmad*	0'49"
	kereshmeh-ye darāmad	0'32"
	darāmad continues	1'23"
	pishdarāmad (*chāhārmezrāb-e sangeen*) (d, z, mu, mo, d)	3'33"
	darāmad continues	1'07"
	chāhārmezrāb-e darāmad (d, z, mo, d)	3'18"
zābol (7'27")	*zābol*	2'14"
	chāhārmezrāb-e zābol	2'08"
	zābol continues (*eshāreh*s to *muyeh* and *mokhālef* at end)	3'05"
mokhālef (11'55")	*mokhālef*	1'52"
	chāhārmezrāb-e mokhālef (mo, maq, mo)	2'21"
	masnavi-ye mokhālef	1'50"
	mokhālef continues	0'43"
	naghmeh-ye maqlub	0'45"
	mokhālef continues	2'37"
	qeteh-ye zarbi-ye mokhālef (in the rhythm of *kereshmeh*; *eshāreh* to *maqlub*)	1'15"
	mokhālef continues	0'32"
hesār	*hesār*	0'24"
muyeh (1'21")	*muyeh*	0'31"
	shekasteh muyeh	0'50"
darāmad (4'32")	*forud*	0'44"
	hodi va pahlavi	1'08"
	forud	1'14"
	qeteh-ye zarbi az Saba (d)	1'26"

Performance 7 (27'26")

Mohammad Reza Lotfi (*tār*); Mohammad Reza Shajarian (male voice); with the orchestra of National Iranian Radio and Television, conducted by Farhad Fakhroldini. *Golhā-ye Tāzeh*, no. 147; commercial recording of a programme originally broadcast by Iranian Radio in the 1970s.

Broad modal area	*Gusheh*	Length of section
darāmad (11'49")	*pishdarāmad* (ensemble) (*eshārehs* to *mokhālef*)	1'05"
	tasnif (ensemble/voice) (d, mu, mo, d)	5'56"
	darāmad (*tār*)	1'03"
	chāhārmezrāb-e darāmad (*tār*)	1'39"
	darāmad continues (voice/*tār*)	2'06"
zābol	*zābol* (voice/*tār*)	2'52"
muyeh (3'43")	*muyeh* (voice/*tār*)	1'03"
	kereshmeh-ye muyeh (*tār*)	0'22"
	muyeh (*tār*)	0'28"
	shekasteh muyeh (voice/*tār*)	0'53"
	kereshmeh ye muyeh (*tār*)	0'44"
darāmad	*forud* (*tār*)	0'13"
mokhālef	*mokhālef* (voice/*tār*)	1'38"
muyeh	*shekasteh muyeh* (voice/*tār*)	0'22"
darāmad (7'02")	*forud* (voice/*tār*)	1'02"
	tasnif (ensemble/voice) (d, mu, mo, d)	6'00"

Performance 8 (10'54")

Asghar Bahari (*kamāncheh*). From *Ostādān-e Musiqi-ye Sonnati-ye Iran* (*Masters of Iranian Traditional Music*) series, SARTMS, no. 12, on the Āhang-e Ruz label. Recorded and published in Iran as a 33rpm LP disc; re-released on cassette after 1979 in the United States by Soundex Enterprises Inc. No date given.

Broad modal area	*Gusheh*	Length of section
darāmad (2'59")	*darāmad*	0'24"
	pishdarāmad (d, mu, mo, d)	1'31"
	darāmad continues	1'04"
zābol	*zābol*	1'10"
muyeh	*muyeh*	0'52"
mokhālef (2'38")	*mokhālef*	1'31"
	slow *zarbi* in *mokhālef*	1'07"
hesār	*hesār*	0'52"
mokhālef	*eshāreh* to *hazeen*	0'20"
darāmad	*forud*	0'08"
zābol	*zābol*	0'44"
hesār	*eshāreh* to *hesār*	0'09"
darāmad	*forud*	1'02"

Performance 9 (54'40")

Reza Shafeian (*santur*); Nasser Mehravar (*tombak*). Recording of a concert given in Germany c.1987. Venue unknown.

Broad modal area	*Gusheh*	Length of section
darāmad (19'56")	*pishdarāmad* (z, mu, mo, maq, d)	6'52"
	darāmad	3'08"
	chāhārmezrāb-e darāmad	5'53"
	darāmad continues	4'03"
zābol	*zābol* (*eshāreh* to *hazeen* in *forud*)	4'10"
darāmad (3'49")	*reng-e darāmad*	0'50"
	tombak solo	3'49"
mokhālef (13'40")	*chāhārmezrāb-e mokhālef* (includes *eshāreh* to *maqlub*)	(1'31") (5'46") 7'17"
	mokhālef	2'15"
	masnavi	0'59"
	mokhālef continues	2'18"
	naqmeh-ye maqlub	0'33"
	eshāreh to *hazeen*	0'18"
maqlub (1'37")	*kereshmeh-ye maqlub*	0'25"
	maqlub continues	1'12"
hesār	*eshāreh* to *hesār*	0'18"
darāmad	*forud*	0'17"
muyeh	*shekasteh muyeh*	0'20"
darāmad (6'44")	*forud*	0'47"
	qeteh-ye zarbi dar darāmad (d, mo, d)	1'28"
	tasnif (instrumental) (d, mu, mo, s.mu, d)	2'32"
	reng (d, mo, d)	1'57"
	tombak solo	2'59"

Performance 10 (14'40")

Lotfollah Majd (*tār*). From *Ostādān-e Musiqi-ye Sonnati-ye Iran* (*Masters of Iranian Traditional Music*) series, SARTMS, no. 8, on the Āhang-e Ruz label. Recorded and published in Iran as a 33rpm LP disc; re-released on cassette after 1979 in the United States by Soundex Enterprises Inc. No date given.

Broad modal area	*Gusheh*	Length of section
darāmad (8'40")	*darāmad*	0'39"
	chāhārmezrāb-e darāmad (d, z, mu, d)	4'36"
	darāmad continues	3'25"
zābol (1'06")	*zābol*	1'06"
mokhālef (3'02")	*mokhālef*	1'17"
	(section based on) *masnavi*	0'37"
	mokhālef continues	1'08"
muyeh	*shekasteh muyeh*	0'16"
darāmad	*forud*	1'36"

Performance 11 (18'32")

Akbar Golpayegani (male voice); Nur Ali Borumand (*tār*). From *A Musical Anthology of the Orient, Iran I*, Bärenreiter Musicaphon BM30L 2004; recorded in Iran; published in Germany, early 1960s (33rpm LP disc).

Broad modal area	*Gusheh*	Length of section
darāmad (4'26")	*darāmad* (*tār*)	0'08"
	chāhārmezrāb-e darāmad (*tār*) (d)	1'21"
	darāmad (voice/*tār*) continues	2'57"
zābol (3'47")	*zābol* (voice/*tār*)	2'48"
	qeteh-ye zarbi-ye zābol (*tār*)	0'37"
	zābol continues (*tār*)	0'22"
muyeh	*muyeh* (voice/*tār*)	1'40"
mokhālef (5'10")	*mokhālef* (voice/*tār*) (includes short *zarbi*)	2'59"
	kereshmeh-ye mokhālef (*tār*)	0'46"
	mokhālef continues (voice/*tār*) (includes short *eshāreh* to *maqlub*)	1'25"
maqlub	*maqlub* (voice/*tār*)	0'29"
hesār	*hesār* (voice/*tār*)	1'29"
darāmad (1'31")	*forud* (voice/*tār*)	0'41"
	reng (d)	0'50"

Performance 12 (17'00")

Hossein Malek (*santur*). From *A Musical Anthology of the Orient, Iran II*, Bärenreiter Musicaphon BM30L 2005; recorded in Iran; published in Germany, early 1960s (33rpm LP disc).

Broad modal area	*Gusheh*	Length of section
zābol	*zābol*	1'28"
darāmad	*chāhārmezrāb-e darāmad* (d, z, d)	1'44"
zābol (4'20")	*zābol*	1'38"
	zarbi-ye zābol	1'22"
	zābol continues	1'20"
muyeh (2'40")	*muyeh*	1'19"
	zarbi-ye muyeh	0'53"
	muyeh continues	0'28"
mokhālef (6'48")	*mokhālef*	0'26"
	chāhārmezrāb-e mokhālef	0'49"
	mokhālef continues (includes *eshāreh* to *hazeen*)	1'15"
	naqmeh-ye maqlub	1'19"
	mokhālef continues	1'15"
	hazeen	0'25"
	mokhālef continues	0'11"
	chāhārmezrāb-e mokhālef	0'58"
	mokhālef continues	0'10"

Performance 13 (14'51")

Farhang Sharif (*tār*); Hossein Tehrani (*tombak*). Unpublished recording, Iran, c.1970.

Broad modal area	*Gusheh*	Length of section
darāmad (7'40")	*darāmad*	2'19"
	chāhārmezrāb-e darāmad (d, z, mu, mo, hes, *eshāreh* to n.maq, d)	3'49"
	darāmad continues	1'32"
muyeh (1'29")	*muyeh*	0'35"
	shekasteh muyeh	0'54"
zābol	*zābol*	1'06"
mokhālef	*mokhālef* (includes short measured sections)	3'08"
hesār	*hesār*	0'09"
darāmad	*forud*	0'31"
muyeh	*shekasteh muyeh*	0'19"
darāmad	*forud*	0'29"

Performance 14 (23′45″)

From Āhang-e Ruz SARLP 22; LP disc recorded and published in Iran before 1979.

Jalil Shahnaz (*tār*)
Asghar Bahari (*kamāncheh*)
Abdol Vahab Shahidi (male voice; *'ud*)
Faramarz Payvar (*santur*)
Hassan Nahid (*nei*)
Rahmatollah Badii (violin)
Hossein Tehrani (*tombak*)
Shojaaldin Lashkarlou (violin)
Fereidoon Zarinbal (viola)

Broad modal area	Gusheh	Length of section
darāmad (11′41″)	*pishdarāmad* (ensemble) (d, mu, d)	3′27″
	darāmad (*tār*)	1′10″
	chāhārmezrāb-e darāmad (*tār*) (d, mu, mo, d)	2′42″
	darāmad continues (voice/*tār*)	4′22″
muyeh	*muyeh* (voice/*kamāncheh*)	2′10″
mokhālef	*mokhālef* (voice/*kamāncheh*)	2′18″
muyeh	*shekasteh muyeh* (voice/*tār*)	0′31″
darāmad (7′05″)	*forud* (voice/*tār*)	1′13″
	tasnif (voice/ensemble) (d, mu, mo, s.mu, d)	5′31″
	reng (ensemble) (d)	0′21″

Performance 15 (26'35")

Pashang Kamkar (*santur*); Jamshid Andalibi (*nei*); Arjang Kamkar (*tombak*). From a commercial cassette, recorded and published in Iran by Sherkat-e Ruh Afza, c.1987.

(All sections played by *nei* and *santur* together/alternating unless stated otherwise.)

Broad modal area	*Gusheh*	Length of section
darāmad (10'15")	*pishdarāmad* (d, mu, z mo, d)	6'01"
	darāmad	4'14"
zābol	*kereshmeh-ye zābol*	0'25"
darāmad	*darāmad* continues	0'36"
zābol	*zābol*	1'44"
darāmad	slow *zarbi* in *darāmad* (d, mu, d)	2'02"
muyeh	*muyeh*	1'55"
mokhālef (3'54")	*mokhālef* (*santur*)	0'29"
	chāhārmezrāb-e mokhālef (mo, maq, mo)	2'49"
	mokhālef continues	0'13"
	hazeen	0'23"
maqlub	*maqlub* (*nei*)	0'25"
mokhālef	*masnavi-ye mokhālef*	1'27"
darāmad	*forud* (*santur*)	0'16"
mokhālef	*hazeen*	0'30"
darāmad (3'06")	*hodi va pahlavi*	1'20"
	zarbi in the rhythm of *rajaz* (d, mu, mo, d)	1'46"

Performance 16 (22′24″)

Parviz Meshkatian (*santur*); Nasser Farhangfar (*tombak*). From a commercial cassette, recorded and published in Iran c.1984–5. Publisher unknown.

Broad modal area	*Gusheh*	Length of section
darāmad (10′03″)	*pishdarāmad* (d, z, mu, mo, maq, mu, d)	5′41″
	darāmad	1′06″
	naqmeh	1′30″
	zarbi-ye darāmad (based on *kereshmeh*) (d)	1′07″
	darāmad continues	0′39″
zābol	*zābol* (includes a section of *bastenegār*)	1′45″
mokhālef (5′38″)	*mokhālef*	0′40″
	chāhārmezrāb-e mokhālef (mo, maq, mo)	2′46″
	mokhālef continues	2′12″
maqlub	(*mokhālef be*) *maqlub*	0′28″
mokhālef (0′58″)	slow *zarbi* in the mode of *mokhālef* (includes *eshāreh* to *naqmeh-ye maqlub*)	0′29″
	hazeen	0′29″
muyeh	*eshāreh* to *muyeh*	0′16″
darāmad (3′16″)	*forud*	0′24″
	chāhārmezrāb-e darāmad (d, z, mu, mo, d)	2′52″

Performance 17 (22'24")

From *Iran: Musique Persane*. OCORA 57. Recorded in Tehran, 1979. Published in Paris, 1984 (33rpm LP disc).

Jalil Shahnaz (*tār*)
Abdol Vahab Shahidi (male voice; *'ud*)
Faramarz Payvar (*santur*)
Hassan Nahid (*nei*)
Hossein Tehrani (*tombak*)
Asghar Bahari (*kamāncheh*)

Broad modal area	Gusheh	Length of section
darāmad (8'33")	*pishdarāmad* (ensemble) (d)	0'58"
	darāmad (*tār*)	0'42"
	chāhārmezrāb-e darāmad (*tār/tombak*) (d)	1'44"
	darāmad continues (voice/*tār*)	5'09"
zābol	*zābol* (voice/*nei*)	1'14"
muyeh	*muyeh* (voice/*nei*/*santur*)	2'03"
mokhālef	*mokhālef* (voice/*santur*)	2'59"
muyeh	*shekasteh muyeh* (voice/*santur*)	0'34"
darāmad (7'01")	*forud* (*santur*)	0'39"
	tasnif (voice/ensemble) (d, mu, mo, s.mu, d)	6'00"
	reng (ensemble) (d)	0'22"

Performance 18 (28'15")

Faramarz Payvar (*santur*). Recording of a performance given at the School of Oriental and African Studies (London), c.1966 (made available courtesy of Professor Owen Wright).

Broad modal area	*Gusheh*	Length of section
darāmad (13'47")	*pishdarāmad* (d, mu, mo, d)	4'46"
	chāhārmezrāb-e darāmad (d)	1'24"
	darāmad	1'24"
	zarbi based on *pishzanguleh*	1'56"
	darāmad continues	2'32"
	zarbi-ye darāmad	0'45"
	darāmad continues	1'00"
zābol (4'10")	*zābol*	0'19"
	chāhārmezrāb-e zābol	0'56"
	zābol continues	1'00"
	chāhārmezrāb-e zābol	0'20"
	zābol continues	1'35"
muyeh	*muyeh*	1'31"
mokhālef (4'02")	*mokhālef*	0'12"
	chāhārmezrāb-e mokhālef	1'07"
	mokhālef continues	1'18"
	kereshmeh-ye mokhālef	0'30"
	naqmeh-ye maqlub	0'25"
	mokhālef continues	0'30"
maqlub	(*mokhālef be*) *maqlub*	0'37"
mokhālef (3'15")	*naqmeh-ye maqlub*	1'25"
	masnavi (-e mokhālef)	1'50"
darāmad	*forud*	0'53"

Performance 20 (24'09")

Mahmud Mahmudi Khonsari (male voice); Ahmad Ebadi (*setār*); Habibollah Badii (violin). *Barg-e Sabz*, no. 165. Commercial recording of a programme originally broadcast by Iranian Radio in the 1970s. Re-released in the United States in 1987 by Caspian Inc. (518).

Broad modal area	*Gusheh*	Length of section
darāmad (8'13")	*darāmad* (*setār*)	2'34"
	zarbi-ye darāmad (*setār*)	2'20"
	darāmad continues (*setār*)	1'10"
	recited poetry	0'26"
	chāhārmezrāb-e darāmad (violin)	2'09"
zābol	*zābol* (voice/violin)	2'03"
muyeh	*muyeh* (voice/violin)	3'34"
mokhālef (8'09")	*chāhārmezrāb-e mokhālef* (violin)	1'24"
	mokhālef continues (voice/violin) (includes *eshāreh* to *masnavi*)	2'43"
	naqmeh-ye maqlub (violin)	0'11"
	mokhālef continues (voice/violin)	3'51"
hesār	*hesār* (voice/violin)	0'48"
darāmad	*forud* (voice/violin)	0'22"
muyeh	*shekasteh muyeh* (voice/violin)	0'24"
darāmad	*forud* (voice/violin)	0'36"

Performance 22 (14′38″)

Hossein Malek (*santur*). From *Ostādān-e Musiqi-ye Sonnati-ye Iran* (*Masters of Iranian Traditional Music*) series, SARTMS, no. 10, on the Āhang-e Ruz label. Recorded and published in Iran before 1979 as a 33rpm LP disc; re-released on cassette in the United States in 1984 by C&G Audio &Video Recording and Duplicating Inc. (380)

Broad modal area	*Gusheh*	Length of section
darāmad (6′34″)	*darāmad*	1′25″
	chāhārmezrāb-e darāmad (*santur/tombak*) (based on *zang-e shotor*)	5′07″
	darāmad continues	0′11″
zābol (2′46″)	*zābol*	2′00″
	chāhārmezrāb-e zābol	0′19″
	kereshmeh-ye zābol	0′24″
	zābol continues	0′03″
muyeh	*muyeh*	1′55″
mokhālef (2′41″)	*mokhālef* (includes *eshāreh* to *masnavi*)	0′59
	masnavi (*-e mokhālef*)	0′20″
	mokhālef continues	0′59″
	hazeen	0′15′
	eshāreh to *naqmeh-ye maqlub*	0′08″
darāmad	*forud*	0′33″

Performance 23 (25'28")

Jean During (*setār*); Zia Mir Abdolbaghi (*tombak*). Recording of a concert given at Leighton House, London, 29.10.1983.

Broad modal area	*Gusheh*	Length of section
darāmad (5'25")	*darāmad*	1'33"
	zang-e shotor (*chāhārmezrāb-e darāmad*) (with *zarb*)	2'02"
	darāmad continues	1'50"
zābol (4'26")	*zābol* (includes short section from *kereshmeh-ye muyeh* from Borumand's *radif*)	1'37"
	kereshmeh-ye zābol	1'06"
	zābol continues	0'36"
	bastenegār	1'07"
hozān	*hozān* (leading to *darāmad forud*)	0'21"
hesār	*hesār*	2'02"
hozān	*hozān*	0'09"
darāmad	*forud*	0'40"
mokhālef (5'47")	*mokhālef*	0'43"
	zarbi-ye mokhālef (mo, maq, d, mo)	2'27"
	mokhālef continues	1'35"
	naqmeh-ye maqlub	0'26"
	zarbi-ye mokhālef	0'28"
	forud-e mokhālef	0'08"
muyeh	*muyeh* (*eshāreh* in *forud*)	0'14"
darāmad (6'24")	*forud*	0'27"
	hodi va pahlavi	1'04"
	rajaz	0'34"
	forud	0'22"
	reng-e delgoshā (d, z, mu, mo, haz, d)	3'57"

Performance 24 (21'14")

Daruiouche [spelt Dāryush just on this publication] Safvate (*setār*). From a recording published by the Center for Traditional and Spiritual Music of the East, New York (no date given).

Broad modal area	*Gusheh*	Length of section
darāmad (12'35")	*darāmad*	0'21"
	chāhārmezrāb (based on *zang-e shotor*) (d, z, mu, mo, d)	1'27"
	darāmad continues	1'10"
	kereshmeh-ye darāmad	0'32"
	darāmad continues	0'38"
	chāhārmezrāb-e darāmad (*bahārmast*) (d, mu, mo, n.maq, d)	2'12"
	darāmad continues	1'01"
	kereshmeh-ye darāmad	0'48"
	darāmad continues	0'48"
	pishzanguleh	1'12"
	zanguleh	0'23
	darāmad continues	0'27"
	zarbi-ye darāmad (slow)	0'40"
	darāmad continues	0'56"
zābol (3'57")	*zābol*	0'40"
	kereshmeh-ye zābol	0'57"
	zābol continues	0'16"
	zarbi-ye zābol (includes *eshāreh* to *hesār*)	1'09"
	bastenegār	0'55"
mokhālef (2'11")	*mokhālef*	0'18"
	naqmeh-ye maqlub	0'30"
	mokhālef continues	0'16"
	zarbi-ye mokhālef	0'18"
	mokhālef continues	0'11"
	masnavi	0'33"
	mokhālef continues	0'05"
darāmad (2'31")	*forud*	0'19"
	reng-e delgoshā (d, mu, s.mu, d)	2'12"

Performance 25 (16'20")

Nur Ali Borumand (*tār*). Recording made in Urbana, Illinois, by Bruno Nettl and Stephen Blum, May 1967 (made available courtesy of Professor Nettl).

Broad modal area	*Gusheh*	Length of section
darāmad (7'33")	*pishdarāmad* (d, mu, z, mo, d)	5'23"
	chāhārmezrāb (d)	1'12"
	darāmad	0'58"
zābol	*zābol*	1'12"
mokhālef (1'37")	*mokhālef*	0'48"
	naqmeh-ye maqlub	0'23"
	mokhālef continues	0'26"
muyeh	*shekasteh muyeh*	0'14"
darāmad (5'44")	*forud*	0'11"
	tasnif (instrumental) (d, mu, mo, d)	2'40"
	reng (d, mu, mo, maq, d)	2'53"

Performance 26 (10'08")

Nur Ali Borumand (*tār*). Recording made in Urbana, Illinois, by Bruno Nettl and Stephen Blum, May 1967 (made available courtesy of Professor Nettl).

Broad modal area	*Gusheh*	Length of section
darāmad	*darāmad*	2'18"
zābol	*zābol*	1'08"
muyeh	*muyeh*	1'26"
mokhālef (1'43")	*mokhālef*	0'39"
	kereshmeh-ye mokhālef	0'41"
	mokhālef continues	0'23"
darāmad	*forud*	0'21"
mokhālef	*tasnif-e mokhālef* (mo, mu, mo)	2'03"
darāmad	*reng* (d, mu, d)	1'09"

Performance 27 (27'06")

Mohammad Reza Shajarian (male voice); Faramarz Payvar (*santur*). From a cassette recorded and published by Moasseseh-ye Honari va Farhangi-ye Māhur, Iran, 1980 (distributed outside Iran by the Farabi Cultural Institute, Finland).

(Sections 1–14 are voice and *santur* together/alternating unless otherwise stated.)

Broad modal area	*Gusheh*	Length of section
darāmad (10'22")	*pishdarāmad* (ensemble) (d, mu, mo, d)	3'25"
	darāmad	6'57"
zābol (5'00")	*zābol*	1'45"
	chāhārmezrāb-e zābol (*santur*)	1'27"
	zābol continues	1'48"
muyeh	*muyeh*	2'57"
mokhālef	*mokhālef*	4'00"
maqlub	(*mokhālef be*) *maqlub*	0'18"
mokhālef	*mokhālef* continues	1'16"
muyeh	*muyeh* (in *forud*)	0'25"
hesār	*hesār*	0'11"
darāmad	*forud*	0'27"
hesār	*hesār* (*santur*)	0'11"
darāmad (1'59")	*forud* (*santur*)	0'31"
	reng (ensemble) (d, mu, mo, d)	1'28"

Performance 29 (21'28")

From *Āsāri az Darvish Khān*. Cassette recorded and published in Iran before 1979. Publisher unknown.

Faramarz Payvar (*santur*)
Rahmatollah Badii (violin)
Hooshang Zarif (*tār*)
Hassan Nahid (*nei*)
Mohammad Esmaili (*tombak*)

Broad modal area	Gusheh	Length of section
darāmad (7'49")	*pishdarāmad*	5'09"
	darāmad (kamāncheh)	2'40"
zābol	*zābol (kamāncheh)*	2'33"
muyeh	*muyeh (kamāncheh)*	2'21"
mokhālef (5'01")	*chāhārmezrāb-e mokhālef (santur)*	3'00"
	mokhālef (santur)	0'35"
	naqmeh-ye maqlub (santur)	0'42"
	mokhālef continues (santur)	0'44"
hesār	*eshāreh to hesār (santur)*	0'17"
mokhālef	*mokhālef continues (santur)*	0'55"
hesār	*hesār (santur)*	0'10"
darāmad (2'22")	*forud* in Segāh (santur)	0'40"
	reng (ensemble) (d, mu, mo, hes, d)	1'42"

Radif 1 (19'09")

The *radif* of Mirza Abdollah in the version of Nur Ali Borumand (*tār*), recorded in 1972 by the National Iranian Radio and Television Organization. A version of this *radif*, with transcriptions by Jean During (accompanied by sound recording) was published in 1991 (During 1991a).

(Timings do not include spoken sections.)

Broad modal area	*Gusheh*	Length of section
darāmad (2'13")	*chāhārmezrāb* (d)	0'44"
	darāmad	0'17"
	naqmeh	1'01"
	kereshmeh	0'11"
muyeh	*kereshmeh bā muyeh*	2'36"
zābol (1'49")	*zābol*	0'56"
	bastenegār	0'53"
muyeh	*muyeh*	1'01"
mokhālef (3'55")	*mokhālef*	1'53"
	hāji hassani	1'00"
	bastenegār	1'02"
maqlub	*maqlub*	0'18"
mokhālef (1'35")	*naqmeh-ye maqlub*	1'07"
	hazeen	0'28"
muyeh	*muyeh*	0'23"
shur (2'31")	*rohāb*	0'54"
	masihi	0'29"
	shāh khatāi	0'41"
	takht-e tāqedis (*yā takht-e kāvus*)	0'27"
darāmad	*reng-e delgoshā* (d, z, mu, mo, mu, d)	2'48"

Radif 2 (14'59")

Vocal *radif* (*radif-e āvāzi*) of Mahmud Karimi, recorded for the Iranian government in the mid-1970s and published in 1978, together with transcriptions by Mohammad Taghi Massoudieh (Massoudieh 1989[1978]).

Broad modal area	*Gusheh*	Length of section
darāmad (3'09")	*darāmad*	0'46"
	darāmad now-e digar	2'23"
zābol	*zābol*	1'19"
muyeh (2'59")	*muyeh*	1'30"
	shekasteh muyeh	1'29"
hesār	*hesār*	1'48"
mokhālef	*mokhālef*	1'15"
maqlub	*(mokhālef be) maqlub* (*eshāreh* to *shekasteh muyeh* towards the end)	1'25"
darāmad	*hodi va pahlavi*	1'31"
mokhālef	*masnavi-ye mokhālef*	1'33"

Radif 3 (31'30")

Published in 1976 as a set of 10 long-playing (33rpm) discs by Kānoon-e Parvaresh-e Fekri-ye Koodakān va Nowjavānān (Institute for the Intellectual Development of Children and Young Adults) under the supervision of Kambeez Roshanravan. Āhang-e Ruz (label) 2001–2010. The musicians are as follows:

Mohammad Reza Shajarian (male voice)
Esmail Tehrani (*santur*)
Hooshang Zarif (*tār*)
Mehrbanu Tofeegh (*setār*)
Rahmatollah Badii (*kamāncheh*)
Kamal Sameh (*nei*)
Mohammad Delnavazi (*'ud*)
Kazem Alami (*tār*)
Davood Vaseghi (*tombak*)

(Timings do not include spoken sections.)

Broad modal area	Gusheh	Length of section
	The scale of *Segāh*, played on *santur*	0'06"
darāmad	1. *darāmad* (*tār*)	0'57"
zābol	2. *zābol* (*setār*)	0'34"
darāmad	3. *pishzanguleh, zanguleh* (*tār*)	0'59" (0'25") (0'34")
muyeh	4. *muyeh* (*setār*)	0'44"
darāmad	5–10 (*setār*) 5. *darāmad*	0'32"
	6. *kereshmeh*	0'43"
	7. *zanguleh*	0'26"
zābol	8. *zābol*	0'30"
muyeh	9. *muyeh*	0'30"
darāmad	10. *forud*	0'14"
mokhālef	11. *mokhālef* (*santur*)	1'37"
	12–13 (voice/*kamāncheh*)	
mokhālef	12. *mokhālef*	4'57"
darāmad	13. *forud*	1'15"
maqlub	14. *maqlub* (*santur*)	0'39"
hozān	15–19 (*santur*) 15. *hozān*	0'38"
mokhālef	16. *mokhālef*	1'10"
	17. *chāhārmezrāb-e mokhālef* (mo, maq, mo)	1'55"
	18. *hazeen*	0'41"
darāmad	19. *forud*	0'29"

Broad modal area	*Gusheh*	Length of section
darāmad	20. *pishdarāmad* (ensemble) (d)	3'57"
darāmad	21. *darāmad* (*kamāncheh*)	1'33"
darāmad	22. *chāhārmezrāb-e darāmad* (*tār*)	1'16"
mokhālef	23. *mokhālef* (*nei*)	1'26"
darāmad	24. *reng* (ensemble) (based on *pishzanguleh* at the beginning)	2'11"
	25–27 (*setār*)	
darāmad	25. *darāmad*	0'34"
mokhālef	26. *mokhālef*	0'35"
darāmad	27. *bargasht be Segāh* (*forud*) (includes movement to other *dastgāhs*: *Afshāri* and *Māhur*)	0'22"

Radif 4 (34'30")

The *radif* of Mussa Ma'rufi published in 1963 (Barkeshli and Ma'rufi 1963).

A recording of *dastgāh Segāh* from this *radif* played on *tār* by Soleyman Ruhafza (probably dating from 1959–60), and with an introduction by Ma'rufi, was made available to the author courtesy of Professor Bruno Nettl (original copies provided by the University of Tehran, late 1960s). Although this recording has since been published by Mahoor Institute of Culture and Art, the present study uses the 1959/60 recording.

(Timings do not include spoken sections.)

Broad modal area	Gusheh	Length of section
darāmad (8'45")	*mogaddameh*	0'46"
	darāmad-avval (first *darāmad*)	0'53"
	darāmad-dovvom (second *darāmad*)	1'11"
	darāmad-sevvom (third *darāmad*)	1'15"
	kereshmeh	1'16"
	pishzanguleh	0'21"
	zanguleh	0'45"
	zang-e shotor	2'18"
zābol (3'15")	*zābol*	0'33"
	qesmat-e dovvom-e zābol (second section of *zābol*)	0'46"
	bastenegār	1'23"
	zanguleh	0'33"
muyeh (2'21")	*panjeh muyeh*	0'07"
	āvāz-e muyeh	0'42"
	forud-e muyeh	0'14"
	qesmat-e dovvom-e muyeh	1'18"
hesār (4'29")	*hesār*	0'43"
	qesmat-e dovvom-e hesār	0'35"
	zanguleh	0'46"
	qesmat-e sevvom-e hesār	1'17"
	kereshmeh	0'32"
	forud-e hesār	0'36"
hozān	*hozān*	0'37"
mokhālef to *darāmad*	*pas hesār*	0'51"
mokhālef	*maarbad*	0'15"
mokhālef (4'48")	*mokhālef*	1'05"
	qesmat-e dovvom-e mokhālef	0'47"
	qesmat-e sevvom-e mokhālef	0'37"
	hāji hassani	0'36"

Broad modal area	*Gusheh*	Length of section
	bastenegār	1′03″
maqlub	*maqlub*	0′38″
mokhālef (4′46″)	*naqmeh-ye maqlub*	1′23″
	dobeiti	1′24″
	par-e parastu	1′04″
	hazeen	0′55″
hozān	*hozān*	0′23″
muyeh	*muyeh*	1′24″
darāmad	*reng-e delgoshā* (d, z, d, mu, mo, mu, mo, d)	2′38″

Other Versions Referred To

Dastgāh Segāh

Performance 19 Mehdi Khaledi (violin); H. Hamedian (*tombak*). From *Ostādān-e Musiqi-ye Sonnati-ye Iran* (*Masters of Iranian Traditional Music*) series, SARTMS, no. 21, on the Āhang-e Ruz label. Recorded and published in Iran as a 33rpm long playing disc; re-released on cassette in the United States in 1984 by C&G Audio & Video Recording and Duplicating Inc. (C&G Inc.376)

Performance 21 Mohammad Reza Shajarian (male voice); Ahmad Ebadi (*setār*). *Mokhālef-e Segāh*. Recorded in Iran before 1979; re-released on cassette in the USA by C&G Inc. (SXC 486) in the early 1980s.

Performance 28 Golhā-ye Tāzeh, no. 107 ('*Hodi va Pahlavi*'). Commercial cassette recording of a programme originally broadcast by Iranian Radio in the 1970s. Mohammad Reza Shajarian (male voice); Hooshang Zarif (*tār*); Hassan Nahid (*nei*); Faramarz Payvar (*santur*); Rahmatollah Badii (violin); Mohammad Esmaili (*tombak*)

Radif 5 The first book of Abol Hassan Saba's violin *radif*: *Dowreh-ye Avval-e Violon*, c.1967 (originally published in the 1950s).

Radif 6 The second book of Abol Hassan Saba's violin *radif*: *Dowreh-ye Dovvom-e Violon*, c.1967 (originally published in the 1950s).

Dastgāh Māhur

Performance 30 Hossein Alizadeh (*tār*). Recording of a concert at Leighton House, London, 21.2.1986.

Performance 31 From *Ney Nāvā*. Hossein Alizadeh (*tār*). Published in Iran, c.1984, by Sazman-e Entesharati va Farhangi-ye Ebtekar.

Performance 32 Golhā-ye Tāzeh, no. 77 ('*Porkon Piāleh Rā*'). Mohammad Reza Shajarian (male voice); Habibollah Badii (violin); with the Orchestra of National Iranian Radio and Television, conducted by Fereidoon Sha'bazian. Commercial recording of a programme originally broadcast by Iranian Radio in the 1970s.

Performance 33 From *Tradition Classique de L'Iran. Le Tār*, Harmonia Mundi HM1031. Dariush Talai (*tār*); Jamshid Shemirani (*tombak*). Recorded in France, 1979; published in France, 1980 (33rpm LP disc).

Radif 7 *Māhur* from the *radif* of Mirza Abdollah, played on *santur* by Pashang Kamkar. Commercial cassette recorded and published in Iran in 1983 by Sherkat-e Ruhafzā.

Musicians Performing as Soloists in the Analysed Performances and *Radif*s

Afsharnia, Abdol Naqi (b.1951)	*nei*	performance 1
Alizadeh, Hossein (b.1951)	*tār*	performances 2, 30, 31
Andalibi, Jamshid (b.1956)	*nei*	performance 15
Badii, Rahmatollah (b.1936)	*kamāncheh*	performance 28; *radif* 3
Badii, Habibollah (1932–1991)	violin	performances 20, 32
Bahari, Asghar (1905–1995)	*kamāncheh*	performances 8, 14
Borumand, Nur Ali (1906–1978)	*tār*	performances 11, 25, 26; *radif* 1
During, Jean (b.1947)	*setār*	performance 23
Ebadi, Ahmad (1907–1994)	*setār*	performances 4, 20, 21
Golpayegani, Akbar (b.1934)	male voice	performance 11
Kamkar, Pashang (b.1951)	*santur*	performances 1, 15; *radif* 7
Karimi, Mahmoud (1927–1984)	male voice	*radif* 2
Khaledi, Mehdi (1919–1990)	violin	performance 19
Mahmudi Khonsari, Mahmud (1934–1987)	male voice	performance 20
Lotfi, Mohammad Reza (1947-2014)	*tār, setār*	performances 1, 7, 32
Majd, Lotfollah (1917–1978)	*tār*	performance 10
Malek, Hossein (1925–2008)	*santur*	performance 12, 22
Meshkatian, Parviz (1955–2009)	*santur*	performance 16
Nahid, Hassan (b.1943)	*nei*	performances 17, 28
Payvar, Faramarz (1932–2009)	*santur*	performances 17, 18, 27, 29
Ruhafza, Soleyman (1907–1980)	*tār*	*radif* 4
Saba, Abol Hassan (1902–1957)	*setār*	performance 3
Safvate, Dariouche (b.1928)	*setār*	performance 24
Sameh, Kamal (dates not known)	*nei*	*radif* 3
Shafeian, Reza (b.1941)	*santur*	performances 6, 9
Shahidi, Abold Vahab (b.1921)	male voice, *'ud*	performances 14, 17
Shahnaz, Jalil (b.1921)	*tār*	performances 14, 17
Shajarian, Mohammad Reza (b.1940)	male voice	performances 1, 7, 21, 27, 28, 32; *radif* 3
Sharif, Farhang (b.1931)	*tār*	performance 13
Shekarchi, Ali Akbar (b.1949)	*kamāncheh*	performance 1
Talai, Daruish (b.1953)	*tār, setār*	performance 33
Tehrani, Esmail (b.1948)	*santur*	*radif* 3
Tofeegh, Mehrbanu (b.1946)	*setār*	*radif* 3
Tului, Zeidollah (dates not known)	*tār*	performance 5
Zarif, Hooshang (b.1938)	*tār*	performance 28; *radif* 3

Appendix B
Note on Musical Transcriptions in Chapter 4

The transcriptions in Chapter 4 use an adapted form of five-line staff notation, the aim being to offer a visual representation as close as possible to the aural experience. Unmetered sections are transcribed without note stems and bar-lines, and phrase markings are used to indicate approximate lengths of sustained pitches. In regularly metered sections, notes are stemmed but not beamed (since this would create note groupings aligned with Western music theory which are not necessarily appropriate to Iranian music). Note stems are occasionally used in short metered sections within largely unmetered *gushehs*.

In metered sections, time signatures are given in parentheses and divisions of pulse are indicated using half rather than full bar-lines. It should be noted that time signatures are often simply suggestive of the predominant pulse; there are many examples of uneven bars, or sections with a 4-beat pulse which shift to 5 beats for a single bar, for instance.

'Key signatures' are not set out in conventional order, but in order of ascent, for example:

Iranian classical musicians often employ a light drone, most notably on stringed instruments and usually on the lowest sounding string(s). Where there is one, the drone has usually been transcribed but is occasionally omitted.

For ease of comparison, all of the examples are notated in the treble stave and with e-*koron* as the *shāhed* of the *darāmad* of *Segāh* (or c as the *shāhed* of the *darāmad* of *Māhur*). The actual starting pitch is indicated in square brackets. Thus, where the actual starting pitch is in the area of a-*koron*/ab/a♮, the transcription is either (approximately) a 5th higher or a 4th lower than sounded pitch. The decision to notate higher or lower than pitch was generally determined by the range of the music, and where it would lie comfortably on the stave.

The following symbols were also used in the transcriptions (some following conventional five-line staff notation symbols):

pitch is slightly sharp $^{(↑)}$ or flat $^{(↓)}$

an arrow beneath the stave indicates that the music is accelerating (→) or slowing down (←)

koron, approximately quarter-tone flat (for example, a-*koron* lies between a♮ and ab).

riz or tremolo: the only instance where note stems are used in unmetered sections.

Where two notes an octave apart are played tremolo, the following is used: . However, if the tremolo is *between* these pitches, the following is used:

(a)
(b)

phrase markings are used to indicate (a) approximate lengths of sustained pitches; (b) note groupings; occasionally (c) longer phrase sections.

a slightly extended note may be indicated using a dot.

accented note.

8ve

or

8ve

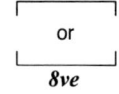

above/below a section indicates that the music sounds an octave higher/lower.

dorāb, an ornamental pattern, often heard at the beginning of phrases, particularly on *tār* and *setār*.

a slide between two pitches in which the individual pitches are not clearly discernable.

mālesh, heard occasionally on lute-type instruments, where the musician rotates the finger of the left hand on the vibrating string; the result is rather like an exaggerated vibrato.

(●) or

a faint pitch may be indicated in parentheses.

pauses between phrases are indicated with an apostrophe.

< >

significant changes of volume are indicated using conventional 'Western' symbols.

Bibliography

Abt, Lawrence E. and Stanley Rosner (1970) *The Creative Experience*. New York: Grossman Publishers.

Adak, Saeed (2011) 'Report from the 5th Shahr-e Ketāb Critical Music Seminar', *Hamshahri Online*, Monday 31 January 2011. http://www.hamshahrionline.ir/news-127158.aspx (accessed 12.9.12).

Adlington, Robert and Sophie Fuller (2005) 'Editorial', *Twentieth-Century Music* 2(1):3–5.

Agawu, Kofi (1992) 'Representing African Music', *Critical Inquiry* 18:245–66.

— (2003) *Representing African Music: Postcolonial Notes, Queries, Positions*. New York and London: Routledge.

Ahmad, Aijaz (1992) *In Theory: Nations, Classes, Literatures*. London: Verso.

Aiello, Rita (1984) 'Music and Language: Parallels and Contrasts', in *Musical Perceptions*, ed. Rita Aiello and John A. Sloboda. pp. 40–60. New York: Oxford University Press.

Aitchison, Jean (1987) *Linguistics*. London: Hodder and Stoughton, Teach Yourself Books.

— (1989) *The Articulate Mammal: An Introduction to Psycholinguistics*, 3rd edition. London: Unwin Hyman.

Alizadeh, Hossein (1992) *Radif-navāzi: Dastgāh-e Musiqi-ye Sonnati-e Iran – Radif-e Mirza Abdollah be Ravāyat-e Ostād Nur Ali Borumand. Setār H.Alizadeh* [*Radif-playing: The Traditional Dastgāh Music of Iran – Radif of Mirza Abdollah in the Version of Ostād Nur Ali Borumand. Setār H.Alizadeh*]. Tehran: Moasseseh-ye Mahur.

— (1998) 'Negāhi Gozarā be Amoozesh-e Musiqi dar Iran' ['A Brief Survey of Music Education in Iran'], *Mahoor Music Quarterly* 1:73–83.

— (2004) 'Yād-dāshti az Hossein Alizadeh' ['A Note by Hossein Alizadeh'], *Mahoor Music Quarterly* 23:215–16.

Allen, Mathew Harp (2007) 'Standardize, Classicize, and Nationalize: The Scientific Work of the Music Academy of Madras, 1930–521', in *Performing Pasts: Reinventing the Arts in Modern South India*, ed. Indira Viswanathan Peterson and Davesh Soneji. pp. 93–132. Oxford and New Delhi: Oxford University Press.

Ansari, Ali (2003) *The History of Modern Iran Since 1921: The Pahlavis and After*. London: Longman, Pearson Education.

Asadi, Hooman (2001) 'Az Maqām tā Dastgāh' ['From Maqām to Dastgāh'], *Mahoor Music Quarterly* 11:59–75.

— (2004) 'Bonyād-hā-ye Nazari-ye Musiqi-ye Kelāssik-e Iran: Dastgāh be Onvān-e Majmooeh-ye Chand-modi' ['Theoretical Foundations of Persian Classical Music: Dastgāh as a Multi-Modal Cycle'], *Mahoor Music Quarterly* 22:43–56.

Attali, Jacques (1985 [1977]) *Noise: The Political Economy of Music* (translated by Brian Massumi). Minneapolis, MN, University of Minnesota Press.

Ayako, Tatsumura (1980) 'Performance of Persian Classical Vocal Music', in *Musical Voices of Asia: Report of Asian Traditional Performing Arts 1978*, ed. Richard Emmert and Minegishi Yuki. pp. 83–99. Tokyo: Heibonsha Limited Publishers.

Azadehfar, Mohammad Reza (2006) *Rhythmic Structure in Iranian Music*. Tehran: University of Art.

Babiracki, Carol M. and Bruno Nettl (1987) 'Internal Interrelationships in Persian Classical Music: The Dastgah of Shur in Eighteen Radifs', *Asian Music* 19(1):46–98.

Bailey, Derek (1980) *Improvisation: Its Nature and Practice in Music*, 1st edition. Ashbourne: Moorland Publishing.

Baily, John (1977) 'Movement Patterns in Playing the Herati Dutar', in *The Anthropology of the Body*, ed. John Blacking. pp. 275–330. London: Academic Press.

— (1985) 'Music Structure and Human Movement', in *Musical Structure and Cognition*, ed. P. Howell, I. Cross and R. West. pp. 237–58. London: Academic Press.

— (1988) *Music of Afghanistan: Professional Musicians in the City of Herat*. Cambridge: Cambridge University Press.

— (1989) 'Principles of Rhythmic Improvisation for the Afghan Rubab', *Bulletin of the International Council for Traditional Music (UK Chapter)* 22:3–16 (originally published as 'Principes d'improvisation rythmique dans le jeu du Rebab d'Afghanistan', in *L'Improvisation dans les musiques de tradition orale*. 1987. ed. B. Lortat-Jacob. pp. 177–88. Paris: Selaf).

— (1991) 'Some Cognitive Aspects of Motor Planning in Musical Performance', *Psychologica Belgica* 31(2):147–62.

— (1992) 'Music Performance, Motor Structure, and Cognitive Models', in *European Studies in Ethnomusicology: Historical Developments and Recent Trends. Selected Papers Presented at the VIIth European Seminar in Ethnomusicology, Berlin, October 1–6, 1990*, ed. M.P. Baumann, A. Simon and U. Wegner. pp. 142–58. Wilhelmshaven: Florian Noetzel Verlag.

— (1994) 'The Role of Music in the Creation of an Afghan National Identity, 1923–73', in *Music, Ethnicity and Identity: The Musical Construction of Place*, ed. Martin Stokes. pp. 45–60. Oxford: Berg.

Baily, John and Peter Driver (1992) 'Spatio-Motor Thinking in Playing Folk Blues Guitar', *The World of Music* 34(3):57–71.

Barkeshli, Mehdi and Musa Ma'rufi (1963) *Radif-e Musiqi-e Iran* [*The Traditional Art Music of Iran*]. Teheran: The Fine Arts Organisation.

Barry, Phillips (1961) 'The Part of the Folk Singer in the Making of Folk Balladry', in *The Critics and the Ballad*, ed. MacEdward Leach and Tristram P. Coffin. pp. 59–76. Carbondale, IL: Southern Illinois University Press.

Bartók, Béla (1931) *Hungarian Folk Music*. London: Oxford University Press.

Battesti, T. (1969) 'La Musique traditionelle iranienne: aspects socio-historiques', *Objets et mondes* 9:317–40.

Beale, Charles (2005) 'Jazz Education', in *The Oxford Companion to Jazz*, ed. Bill Kirchner. pp. 756–65. Oxford: Oxford University Press.

Bearman, C.J. (2002) 'Cecil Sharp in Somerset: Some Reflections on the Work of David Harker', *Folklore* 113(1):11–34.

Becker, Judith and Alton Becker (1979) 'A Grammar of the Musical Genre Srepegan', *Journal of Music Theory* 23(1):1–43 (reprinted in *Asian Music*. 1983. 14(1):30–73).

— (1983) 'A Reconsideration in the Form of a Dialogue', *Asian Music* 14(1):9–16.

Bee, Darlene and Vida Chenoweth (1971) 'Comparative-Generative Models of a New Guinea Melodic Structure', *American Anthropologist* 73:773–82.

Beeman, William O. (1976) 'You Can Take the Music out of the Country, But …: The Dynamics of Change in Iranian Musical Tradition', *Asian Music* 7(2):6–19.

Behroozi, Shapour (1988) *Chehreh-hā-ye Musiqi-ye Iran* [*Profiles of Iranian Musicians*]. Volume 1. Tehran: Ketab Sara.

Bellman, Jonathan (1998) *The Exotic in Western Music*. Boston, MA: Northeastern University Press.

Benson, Bruce (2003) *The Improvisation of Musical Dialogue: A Phenomenology of Music*. Cambridge: Cambridge University Press.

Bergeron, Katherine and Philip V. Bohlman (eds) (1992) *Disciplining Music: Musicology and Its Canons*. Chicago, IL: University of Chicago Press.

Berkowitz, Aaron L. (2010) *The Improvising Mind: Cognition and Creativity in the Musical Moment*. New York: Oxford University Press.

Berkowitz, Aaron L. and Daniel Ansari (2008) 'Generation of Novel Motor Sequences: The Neural Correlates of Musical Improvisation', *NeuroImage* 41:535–43.

— (2010) 'Expertise-related Deactivation of the Right Temporoparietal Junction During Musical Improvisation', *NeuroImage* 49:712–19.

Berliner, Paul (1978) *The Soul of Mbira*. Chicago, IL: University of Chicago Press.

— (1994) *Thinking in Jazz: The Infinite Art of Improvisation*. Chicago, IL: University of Chicago Press.

Bhabha, Homi K. (1994) *The Location of Culture*. London and New York: Routledge.

Bhunnoo, Seth Ayyaz (2013) 'In the Midst of it All Something Is Stirring: The Biopsychosocial Condition of Listening', in *On Listening*, ed. Angus Carlyle and Cathy Lane. pp. 207–12. London: Research Group for Artists Publications.

Bigenho, Michelle (2002) *Sounding Indigenous: Authenticity in Bolivian Music Performance*. New York: Palgrave Macmillan.

Bithell, Caroline (2003) 'On the Playing Fields of the World (and Corsica): Politics, Power, Passion and Polyphony', *British Journal of Ethnomusicology* 12(1):67–95.

Blacking, John (1961) 'Patterns of Nsenga Kalimba music', *African Music* 2(4):26–43.

— (1967) *Venda Children's Songs: A Study in Ethnomusicological Analysis*. Johannesburg: Witwatersrand University Press.

— (1969) 'The Value of Music in Human Experience', *Yearbook of the International Folk Music Council* 1:33–71.

— (1970) *Process and Product in Human Society*. Inaugural Lecture Delivered 13 September 1967. Johannesburg: Witwatersrand University Press.

— (1971a) 'Deep and Surface Structures in Venda Music', *Journal of the International Folk Music Council* 3:92–108.

— (1971b) 'Towards a Theory of Musical Competence', in *Man: Anthropological Essays Presented to O.F. Raum*, ed. E.J. De Jager. pp. 19–34. Cape Town: Struik.

— (1973) *How Musical Is Man?* Seattle, WA: University of Washington Press.

— (1984) 'What Languages Do Musical Grammars Describe?', in *Musical Grammars and Computer Analysis*, ed. B. Baroni and L. Callegari. pp. 363–70. Florence: Leo S. Olschki.

— (1987) *'A Commonsense View of All Music': Reflections on Percy Grainger's Contribution to Ethnomusicology and Music Education*. Cambridge: Cambridge University Press.

— (1989) 'Challenging the Myth of "Ethnic" Music: First Performances of a New Song in an African Oral Tradition, 1961", *Yearbook for Traditional Music* 21:17–24.

Blum, Stephen (1998) 'Recognizing Improvisation', in *In the Course of Performance: Studies in the World of Musical Improvisation*, ed. Bruno Nettl with Melinda Russell. pp. 27–45. Chicago, IL: University of Chicago Press.

— (2001) 'Composition', *The New Grove Dictionary of Music and Musicians*, ed. Stanley Sadie. Volume 6: 186–201. London: Macmillan.

— (2009) 'Representations of Music Making', in *Musical Improvisation: Art, Education, and Society*, ed. Gabriel Solis and Bruno Nettl. pp. 239–62. Urbana and Chicago, IL: University of Illinois Press.

Boden, Margaret (1990) *The Creative Mind: Myths and Mechanisms*. London: George Weidenfeld and Nicolson.

Bohlman, Philip V. (1988) *The Study of Folk Music in the Modern World*. Bloomington, IN: Indiana University Press.

— (1993) 'Musicology as a Political Act', *The Journal of Musicology* 4:411–36.

Boilès, Charles (1967) 'Tepehua Thought-Song: A Case of Semantic Signalling', *Ethnomusicology* 11:267–92.

Boorman, Stanley (1999) 'The Musical Text', in *Rethinking Music*, ed. Nicholas Cook and Mark Everist. pp. 403–23. Oxford: Oxford University Press.

Born, Georgina (2005) 'On Musical Mediation: Ontology, Technology and Creativity', *Twentieth-Century Music* 2(1):7–36.

Born, Georgina and David Hesmondhalgh (eds) (2000a) *Western Music and Its Others: Difference, Representation, and Appropriation in Music*. Berkeley, CA: University of California Press.

— (2000b) 'Introduction: On Difference, Representation, and Appropriation in Music', in *Western Music and Its Others: Difference, Representation, and Appropriation in Music*, ed. Georgina Born and David Hesmondhalgh. pp. 1–58. Berkeley, CA: University of California Press.

Brăiloiu, Constantin (1984) *Problems of Ethnomusicology* (edited and translated by A.L. Lloyd). Cambridge University Press.

Brett, Philip, Elizabeth Wood and Gary C. Thomas (eds) (1994) *Queering the Pitch: The New Gay and Lesbian Musicology*. New York and London: Routledge.

Bright, William (1963) 'Language and Music: Areas for Cooperation', *Ethnomusicology* 7:26–32.

Brown, Steven (2000) 'The "Musilanguage" Model of Music Evolution', in *The Origins of Music*, ed. Nils L. Wallin, Björn Merker and Steven Brown, pp. 271–300. Cambridge, MA: The MIT Press.

Brown, Steven, Michael J. Martinez and Lawrence M. Parsons (2006) 'Music and Language Side by Side in the Brain: A PET Study of Generating Melodies and Sentences', *European Journal of Neuroscience* 23:2791–803.

Butt, John (2002) *Playing with History: The Historical Approach to Musical Performance*. Cambridge: Cambridge University Press.

Caron, Nelly and Dariouche Safvate (1966) *Iran: Les Traditions musicales*. Paris: Buchet/Chastel.

Caton, Margaret L. (1983) 'The Classical "Tasnif": A Genre of Persian Vocal Music' (2 volumes). PhD Dissertation. University of California, Los Angeles.

Chanan, Michael (1994) *Musica Practica: The Social Practice of Western Music from Gregorian Chant to Postmodernism*. London and New York: Verso.

— (1999) *From Handel to Hendrix: The Composer in the Public Sphere*. London and New York: Verso.

Chehabi, Houchang, E. (1990) *Iranian Politics and Religious Modernism: The Liberation Movement of Iran under the Shah and Khomeini*. Ithaca, NY: Cornell University Press.

— (1999) 'From Revolutionary *Tasnif* to Patriotic *Sorud*: Music and Nation-Building in Pre-World War II Iran', *Iran* 37:143–54.

Chomsky, Noam (1957) *Syntactic Structures*. The Hague: Mouton.

— (1965) *Aspects of a Theory of Syntax*. Cambridge, MA: The MIT Press.

— (1972) *Language and Mind*, enlarged edition. New York: Harcourt Brace Jovanovich.

— (1980) *Rules and Representations*. Oxford: Basil Blackwell.

— (1986) *Knowledge of Language: Its Nature, Origin and Use*. New York: Praeger.

Christensen, Dieter (1991) 'Erich M. von Hornbostel, Carl Stumpf, and the Institutionalization of Comparative Musicology', in *Comparative Musicology and Anthropology of Music: Essays on the History of Ethnomusicology*, ed. Bruno Nettl and Philip V. Bohlman. pp. 201–9. Chicago, IL: University of Chicago Press.

Clayton, Martin (2003) 'Comparing Music, Comparing Musicology', in *The Cultural Study of Music*, ed. Martin Clayton, Trevor Herbert and Richard Middleton. pp. 57–68. New York and London: Routledge.

Clayton, Martin and Bennett Zon (eds) (2007) *Music and Orientalism in the British Empire, 1780s–1940s: Portrayal of the East*. Farnham: Ashgate.

Clifford, James (1988) *The Predicament of Culture: Twentieth-Century Ethnography, Literature and Art*. Cambridge, MA: Harvard University Press.

Colles, H.C. (1954) 'EXTEMPORIZATION or IMPROVISATION', in *Grove's Dictionary of Music and Musicians*, 5th edition, ed. Eric Blom. Volume 2: 991–3. London: Macmillan.

Collins, Dave (ed.) (2012) *The Act of Musical Composition: Studies in the Creative Process*. Farnham: Ashgate.

Cook, Nicholas (1990) *Music, Imagination, and Culture*. Oxford: Clarendon Press.

— (1998) *Music: A Very Short Introduction*. Oxford: Oxford University Press.

Cook, Nicholas and Mark Everist (eds) (1999) *Rethinking Music*. Oxford: Oxford University Press.

Csikszentmihalyi, Mihalyi (1988) 'Society, Culture, and Person: A Systems View of Creativity', in *The Nature of Creativity: Contemporary Psychological Perspectives*, ed. R.J. Sternberg. pp. 325–39. Cambridge: Cambridge University Press.

— (1990) *Flow: The Psychology of Optimal Experience*. New York: Harper and Row.

Danielson, Virginia (1997) *The Voice of Egypt: Umm Kulthūm, Arabic Song, and Egyptian Society in the Twentieth Century*. Chicago, IL: University of Chicago Press.

Darvishi, Mohammad Reza (1995) *Negāh be Qarb. Bahsi dar Ta'sir-e Musiqi-ye Qarb bar Musiqi-ye Irani* [Translated as *Westward Look: A Discussion of the Impact of Western Music on the Iranian Music*]. Tehran: Mahoor Institute of Culture and Art.

Davis, Ruth (1997) 'Cultural Policy and the Tunisian Ma'luf: Redefining a Tradition', *Ethnomusicology* 41(1):1–21.

Dawkins, Richard (1976) *The Selfish Gene*. New York: Oxford University Press.

Derrida, Jacques (1972) *Positions*. Chicago, IL: University of Chicago Press.

Donnan, Hastings and Martin Stokes (2002) 'Interpreting Interpretations of Islam', in *Interpreting Islam*, ed. Hastings Donnan. pp. 1–19. London: Sage.

Downes, Stephen (2007) 'Cultural Affiliations and National Filiations: Textuality and History in Edward Said's "Secular Criticism" and Szymanowski's Poetics of "Paneuropeanism"', in *Karol Szymanowski w Perspectywie Kultury Muzycznej Przeszłości i Współczesności*, ed. Zbigniew Skowron. pp. 93–104. Krakow: Musica Iagellonica.

Drabkin, William (1980) 'Motif', *The New Grove Dictionary of Music and Musicians*, ed. Stanley Sadie. Volume 12: 648. London: Macmillan.

Durbin, Mridula Adenwala (1971) 'Transformational Models Applied to Musical Analysis: Theoretical Possibilities', *Ethnomusicology* 15:353–62.

During, Jean (1975) 'Elements spirituels dans la musique traditionelle iranienne contemporaire', *Sophia Perennis* 1(2):129–54.

— (1977) 'The Imaginal Dimension and Art of Iran', *The World of Music* 19(3/4):24–44.

— (1984a) *La Musique iranienne. Tradition et evolution*. Paris: Editions Recherche sur les Civilisations.

— (1984b) 'La Musique traditionelle iranienne en 1983', *Asian Music* 15(2):11–31.

— (1987a) 'Le Jeu des relations sociales: éléments d'une problematique', in *L'Improvisation dans les musiques de tradition orale*, ed. B. Lortat-Jacob. pp. 17–23. Paris: Selaf.

— (1987b) 'Le Point de vue du musicien: improvisation et communication', in *L'Improvisation dans les musiques de tradition orale*, ed. B. Lortat-Jacob. pp. 33–4. Paris: Selaf.

— (1987c) 'L'Improvisation dans la musique d'art iranienne', in *L'Improvisation dans les musiques de tradition orale*, ed. B. Lortat-Jacob. pp. 135–41. Paris: Selaf.

— (1989) *Musique et mystique dans les traditions de l'Iran*. Paris: Institut Français de Recherche en Iran.

— (1991a) *Le Repertoire-modele de la musique iranienne. Radif de tar et de setar de Mirza Abdollah, version de Nur 'Ali Borumand* (avec la Collaboration de Pirouz Sayar). Tehran: Editions Soroush.

— (1994) *Quelque chose se passe. Le Sens de la tradition dans l'orient musical*. Lagrasse: Editions Verdier.

—, with Zia Mirabdolbaghi and Dariush Safvat (1991b) *The Art of Persian Music*. Washington, DC: Mage Publishers.

Dyson, Kathy (2006) 'Learning Jazz Improvisation'. PhD Thesis. University of Sheffield.

Eftekhari, Mohammad (1999) 'Neshān-e Picasso; Dars-hā-ye Ostād Shajarian; Khāneh-ye Musiqi' ['The Picasso Medallion; Some Lessons from Maestro Shajarian; The House of Music'], *Mahoor Music Quarterly* 5:139–47.

El-Shawan, Salwa (1987) 'Aspects de l'improvisation dans la musique arabe d'Egypte', in *L'Improvisation dans les musiques de tradition orale*, ed. B. Lortat-Jacob. pp. 151–7. Paris: Selaf.

Erlmann, Veit (1996) *Nightsong: Performance, Power and Practice in South Africa*. Chicago, IL: University of Chicago Press.

Eslami, Amir and Hooshyar Khayam (2010) 'New Improvisation in Iranian Music', paper presented at the Middle East and Central Asia Music Forum, Institute of Musical Research, University of London, November 2010.

— (2011) 'A New Approach to Improvisation in Persian Music', lecture-recital presented at the Performance Studies Network International Conference, University of Cambridge, July 2011.

Everist, Mark (1996) 'Meyebeer's *Il Crociato in Egitto: Mélodrame*, Opera, Orientalism', *Cambridge Opera Journal* 8:215–50.

Falk, Dean (2000) 'Hominid Brain Evolution and the Origins of Music', in *The Origins of Music*, ed. Nils L. Wallin, Björn Merker and Steven Brown. pp. 197–216. Cambridge, MA: The MIT Press.

Farhat, Hormoz (1965) 'The Dastgah Concept in Persian Music'. PhD Dissertation. University of California, Los Angeles.

— (1980a) 'The Evolution of Performance Style and the Contemporary Dastgah "Suite" in Persian Music', paper presented at the 1980 Annual Meeting of the Society for Ethnomusicology, Bloomington, Indiana.

— (1980b) 'Iran: I. Art Music', *The New Grove Dictionary of Music and Musicians*, ed. Stanley Sadie. Volume 9: 292–300. London: Macmillan.

— (1990) *The Dastgah Concept in Persian Music*. Cambridge: Cambridge University Press.

Farhi, Farideh (1990) *States and Urban-based Revolutions: Iran and Nicaragua*. Urbana, IL: University of Illinois Press.

Fayaz, Mohammad Reza (1998) 'Bāzkhooni-ye Esālat' ['A Look at the Notion of Originality in Iranian Music'], *Mahoor Music Quarterly* 1:93–112.
— (1999) 'Dood-e In Ātash' ['The Smoke of this Fire'], *Mahoor Music Quarterly* 5:49–56.
Feld, Steven (1974) 'Linguistic Models in Ethnomusicology', *Ethnomusicology* 18:197–217.
— (1984) 'Communication, Music, and Speech about Music', *Yearbook for Traditional Music* 16:1–18.
Feldman, Walter (1996) *Music of the Ottoman Court: Makam, Composition and the Early Ottoman Instrumental Repertoire*. Berlin: VWB.
Ferand, Ernst (1938) *Die Improvisation in der Musik*. Zurich: Rhein-Verlag.
— (1961) *Improvisation in Nine Centuries of Western Music: An Anthology with an Historical Introduction*. Köln: Arno Volk Verlag.
Finnegan, Ruth (1977) *Oral Poetry: Its Nature, Significance and Social Context*. Cambridge: Cambridge University Press.
Foley, John Miles (1988) *The Theory of Oral Composition: History and Methodology*. Bloomington, IN: Indiana University Press.
Forsat al-Dowleh Shirazi, Sayyed Mirza Moḥammad (1903) *Bohur al-Alhan* [*Meters of Melodies*]. Shiraz: n.p. (revised edition Bombay 1913; reprinted 1966, Tehran: Forughi Press).
Fossum, David (2010) 'The Ahal School: Turkmen Dutar and the Individual'. MA Thesis. Wesleyan University.
— (2012) 'Musical Canons in Ethnomusicology: The Case of Turkmen Instrumental Music', paper presented at the Musical Geographies of Central Asia Conference, Institute of Musical Research (Middle East and Central Asia Music Forum), University of London, May 2012.
Garfias, Robert (1990) 'An Ethnomusicologist's Thoughts on the Processes of Language and Music Acquisition', in *Music and Child Development: Proceedings of the 1987 Denver Conference, The Biology of Music Making*, ed. Frank Wilson and Franz Roehmann. pp. 100–105. St Louis, MO: MMB Music.
Geertz, Clifford (1973) *The Interpretation of Cultures*. New York: Basic Books.
Gerson-Kiwi, Edith (1963) *The Persian Doctrine of Dastga-Composition: A Phenomenological Study in Music Modes*. Tel-Aviv: Israel Music Institute.
Ghader, Sarmad (1999) 'Bedāheh va Shirin Navazi' [translated as 'Improvisation and Certain Techniques'], *Mahoor Music Quarterly* 5:133–6.
Ghaneifard, Erfan (ed.) (2003) *Soroosh-e Mardom. Andisheh va Aqāyed-e Mohammad Reza Shajarian dar bāreh-ye Āvāz va Honar-e Musiqi* [*Angel of the People: The Thoughts and Views of Mohammad Reza Shajarian about Singing and the Art of Music*]. Tehran: Dadar Press.
Ghiselm, B. (ed.) (1952) *The Creative Process*. New York: Mentor.
Gjerdingen, Robert O. (2007) *Music in the Galant Style*. New York: Oxford University Press.
Godøy, Rolf and Marc Leman (eds) (2010) *Musical Gestures: Sound, Movement, and Meaning*. New York: Routledge.
Goehr, Lydia (1992) *The Imaginary Museum of Musical Works: An Essay in the Philosophy of Music*. Oxford: Clarendon Press.
— (2012) 'The Agon of Improvising – On Broken Strings', paper presented at the conference Perspectives on Musical Improvisation, University of Oxford, September 2012.
Goertzen, Valerie Woodring (1998) 'Setting the Stage: Clara Schumann's Preludes', in *In the Course of Performance: Studies in the World of Musical Improvisation*, ed. Bruno Nettl with Melinda Russell. pp. 237–60. Chicago, IL: University of Chicago Press.
Goffman, Erving (1959) *The Presentation of Self in Everyday Life*. Edinburgh: University of Edinburgh Social Sciences Research Centre.
Grenier, Line (1989) 'From "Diversity" to "Difference": The Case of Socio-Cultural Studies of Music', *New Formations* 9:125–42.
Grenier, Line and Jocelyne Guilbault (1990) '"Authority" Revisited: The "Other" in Anthropology and Popular Music Studies', *Ethnomusicology* 34(3):381–97.
Gronow, Pekka (1981) 'The Record Industry Comes to the Orient', *Ethnomusicology* 25:251–84.
Grunfeld, Frederic V. (1969) *The Art and Times of the Guitar: An Illustrated History of Guitars and Guitarists*. London: Collier Macmillan.
Guildford, J.P. (1950) 'Creativity', *American Psychologist* 5:444–54.

Hall, Stuart (1992) 'The West and the Rest: Discourse and Power', in *Formations of Modernity*, ed. Stuart Hall and Bram Gieben. pp. 275–331. Cambridge: Polity Press.

Halliday, Fred (1993) '"Orientalism" and Its Critics', *British Journal of Middle Eastern Studies* 20(2):145–63.

— (1996) *Islam and the Myth of Confrontation: Religion and Politics in the Middle East*. London: I.B. Tauris.

Harker, Dave (1972) 'Cecil Sharp in Somerset: Some Conclusions', *Folk Music Journal* 2(3):220–40.

Harris, Rachel (2008) *The Making of a Musical Canon in Chinese Central Asia: The Uyghur Twelve Muqam*. Farnham: Ashgate.

Harwood, Dane (1976) 'Universals in Music: A Perspective from Cognitive Psychology', *Ethnomusicology* 20(3):521–33.

Hatten, Robert S. (2009) 'Opening the Museum Window: Improvisation and Its Inscribed Values in Canonic Works by Chopin and Schumann', in *Musical Improvisation: Art, Education, and Society*, ed. Gabriel Solis and Bruno Nettl. pp. 281–95. Urbana and Chicago, IL: University of Illinois Press.

Hawkes, Terrence (1977) *Structuralism and Semiotics*. London: Routledge.

Hayward, Philip (ed.) (1999) *Widening the Horizon: Exoticism in Post-War Popular Music*. Bloomington, IN: Indiana University Press.

Head, Matthew (2000) *Orientalism, Masquerade and Mozart's Turkish Head*. London: Royal Musical Association.

Hedayat, Mehdi Qoli (1928) *Majma ol-Advar* [*Collection from the Eras*]. Tehran: n.p.

Heinze, Shirley J. and Morris Isaac Stein (1960) *Creativity and the Individual*. Chicago, IL: Free Press.

Henley, Jennie (2013) 'Response to "Pedagogy, Practice, and Embodied Creativity in Hindustani Music" by Dard Neuman', part of a roundtable on Embodied Creativity in Hindustani Music. South Asia Music and Dance Forum, Institute of Musical Research, University of London, February 2013.

Herndon, Marcia (1993) 'Insiders, Outsiders: Knowing Our Limits, Limiting Our Knowing', *The World of Music* 35(1):63–80.

Herndon, Marcia and Roger Brunyate (eds) (1976) *Proceedings from the Symposium on Form in Performance, Hard-Core Ethnography*. Austin, TX: Office of the College of Fine Arts, The University of Texas.

Herndon, Marcia and Norma McLeod (1979) *Music as Culture*. Norwood: Norwood Editions.

Herzog, George (1950) 'Song: Folk Song and the Music of Folk Song', in *Funk and Wagnalls Standard Dictionary of Folklore, Mythology and Legend*, ed. Maria Leach. Volume 2: 1032–50. New York: Funk and Wagnalls.

Hood, Mantle (1975) 'Improvisation in the Stratified Ensembles of Southeast Asia', *Selected Reports in Ethnomusicology* 2:25–33.

Howard, Keith (1991) 'John Blacking: An Interview', *Ethnomusicology* 35(1):55–76.

— (2006) *Preserving Korean Music: Intangible Cultural Properties as Icons of Identity*. Farnham: Ashgate.

Hughes, David (1988) 'Deep Structure and Surface Structure in Javanese Music: A Grammar of Gendhing Lampah', *Ethnomusicology* 32:23–74.

— (1991) 'Grammars of Non-Western Musics: A Selective Survey', in *Representing Musical Structure*, ed. Peter Howell, Ian Cross and Robert West. pp. 327–62. London: Academic Press.

Ingold, Timothy and Elizabeth Hallam (2007) *Creativity and Cultural Improvisation*. Oxford: Berg.

Iyer, Vijay (2002) 'Embodied Mind, Situated Cognition, and Expressive Microtiming in African-American Music', *Music Perception* 19(3):387–414.

Jamali, Bahram (2004) 'Olgooi Barāyeh Amoozesh-e Bedāheh-navāzi dar Musiqi-ye Irāni' ['A Framework for Teaching Improvisation in Iranian Music']. MA Thesis. Tehran Art University.

Jan, Steven (2007) *The Memetics of Music: A Neo-Darwinian View of Musical Structure and Culture*. Farnham: Ashgate.

Johnson-Laird, Philip (1988) 'Freedom and Constraint in Creativity', in *The Nature of Creativity: Contemporary Psychological Perspectives*, ed. R.J. Sternberg. pp. 202–19. Cambridge: Cambridge University Press.

— (1991) 'Jazz Improvisation: A Theory at the Computational Level', in *Representing Musical Structure*, ed. Peter Howell, Ian Cross and Robert West. pp. 291–326. London: Academic Press.

Jones, Laura Jafran (1971) 'The Persian Santur: A Description of the Instrument Together with Analysis of the Four Dastgah'. MA Dissertation. University of Washington.

Joneydi, Fereydoun (1982) *Zamineh-ye Shenākht-e Musiqi-ye Irāni* [*The Basis for Understanding Iranian Music*]. Tehran: Entesharat-e Part.

Kashani-Sabet, Firoozeh (1999) *Frontier Fictions: Shaping the Iranian Nation, 1804–1946*. Princeton, NJ: Princeton University Press.

Katouzian, Homa (2003) *Iranian History and Politics: The Dialectic of State and Society*. London: Routledge Curzon.

Keddie, Nikki (1981) *Roots of Revolution: An Interpretive History of Modern Iran*. New Haven, CT: Yale University Press.

Keller, Peter. E. and Martina Rieger (2009) 'Editorial: Special Issue – Musical Movement and Synchronization', *Music Perception* 26(5):397–400.

Kertész Wilkinson, Irén (1989) 'Communal versus Individual Composition in Hungarian Folk Music Research', *Bulletin of the International Council for Traditional Music (UK Chapter)* 24:4–17.

Khaleqi, Ruhollah (1982) *Nazari be Musiqi* [*A View of Music*], 2nd edition. Volume 1. Tehran: Safi Ali Shah Publishers (1st ed. 1938).

— (1983a) *Nazari be Musiqi* [*A View of Music*], 2nd edition. Volume 2. Tehran: Safi Ali Shah Publishers (1st ed. 1938).

— (1983b) *Sargozasht-e Musiqi-ye Iran* [*A History of Iranian Music*], 2nd edition. Volume 1. Tehran: Safi Ali Shah Publishers (1st ed. 1954).

— (1983c) *Sargozasht-e Musiqi-ye Iran* [*A History of Iranian Music*], 2nd edition. Volume 2. Tehran: Safi Ali Shah Publishers (1st ed. 1956).

Khatschi, Khatschi (1962) *Der Dastgah*. Regensburg: Bosse.

— (1967) 'Das Intervallbildungsprinzip des Persichen Dastgah Shur', *Jahrbuch für Musikalische Völks – und Volkerunde* 3:70–84.

Khazrai, Babak (2009) 'Estelāh-e Musiqi-ye Kelāssik-e Irani' [Translated as 'Persian Classical Music: A Discussion on Terminology'], *Mahoor Music Quarterly* 42:163–79.

Kiani, Majid (1987) *Radif-e Mirza Abdollah: Haft Dastgāh-e Musiqi-ye Iran* [*The Radif of Mirza Abdollah: The Seven Dastgāhs of Iranian Music*]. Tehran: Iran Seda (Parvaneh).

— (2004) 'Goftogoo bā Majid Kiani (Goftogoo-gar Aynollah Mosayyebzadeh)' ['Interview with Majid Kiāni (Interviewer: Aynollāh Mosayyebzādeh)'], *Mahoor Musical Quarterly* 22:149–58.

Kinderman, William (2009) 'Improvisation in Beethoven's Creative Process', in *Musical Improvisation: Art, Education, and Society*, ed. Gabriel Solis and Bruno Nettl. pp. 296–312. Urbana and Chicago, IL: University of Illinois Press.

Kinnear, Michael S. (2000) *The Gramophone Company's Persian Recordings, 1899 to 1934: A Complete Numerical Catalogue, by Matrix Serials, of Persian Recordings Made from 1899 to 1934 by the Gramophone Company, Limited, Together with a Supplement of Recordings Made by Columbia Gramophone Company Ltd., from 1928 to 1934*. Heidelberg, Vic.: Bajakhana.

Kippen, James (1985) 'The Dialectical Approach: A Methodology for the Analysis of Tabla Music', *Bulletin of the International Council for Traditional Music (UK Chapter)* 12:4–12.

— (1988a) *The Tabla of Lucknow: A Cultural Analysis of a Musical Tradition*. Cambridge: Cambridge University Press.

— (1988b) 'Computers, Fieldwork, and the Problem of Ethnomusicological Analysis', *Bulletin of the International Council for Traditional Music (UK Chapter)* 20:20–35.

— (1990) 'In Memoriam. John Blacking (1928–1990): A Personal Obituary', *Ethnomusicology* 34(2):263–70.

Kippen, James and Bernard Bel (1992) 'Bol Processor Grammars', in *Understanding Music with AI: Perspectives on Music Cognition*, ed. M. Balaban, K. Ebcioglu and O. Laske. pp. 366–401. Menlo Park, CA: AAAI Press.

Kivy, Peter (1995) *Authenticities: Philosophical Reflections on Musical Performance*. Ithaca, NY and London: Cornell University Press.

Klitz, Brian and Norma Cherlin (1971) 'Musical Acculturation in Iran', *Iranian Studies* 4:157–66.

Koestler, Arthur (1964) *The Act of Creation*. London: Arkana.

Koskoff, Ellen (1982) 'The Music-Network: A Model for the Organisation of Music Concepts', *Ethnomusicology* 26:353–70.

Kramer, Laurence (1995) *Classical Music and Postmodern Knowledge*. Berkeley, CA: University of California Press.

Kubik, Gerhard (1994) *Theory of African Music*. Wilhelmshaven: Florian Noetzel Verlag.

Kuckertz, Josef (1992) 'Der persische Awaz-e Afshiri in Darbietungen des Setar-Spielers Ahmad Rahmanipur, Teheran', in *Regionale maqam-Traditionen in Geschichte und Gegenwalt. Materialien der 2. Arbeitstagung der Study Group 'maqam' beim International Council for Traditional Music, 1992*, ed. J. Elsner and G. Jahnichen, part 2, pp. 345–54. Berlin.

Kuper, Adam (1999) *Culture: The Anthropologists' Account*. Cambridge, MA: Harvard University Press.

Larson, Steve (2005) 'Composition versus Improvisation', *Journal of Music Theory* 49(2):241–75.

Leman, Marc (2007) *Embodied Music Cognition and Mediation Technology*. Cambridge, MA: The MIT Press.

Lerdahl, Fred (1988) 'Cognitive Constraints on Compositional Systems', in *Generative Processes in Music: The Psychology of Performance, Improvisation, and Composition*, ed. J.A. Sloboda. pp. 231–59. Oxford: Clarendon Press.

Lerdahl, Fred and Ray Jackendorff (1981) 'Generative Music Theory and Its Relation to Psychology', *Journal of Music Theory* 25(1):45–90.

— (1983) *A Generative Theory of Tonal Music*. Cambridge, MA: The MIT Press.

Lévi-Strauss, Claude (1969) *The Raw and the Cooked*. New York: Harper & Row.

— (1972) *Structural Anthropology*. Harmondsworth: Penguin Books.

Levin, Robert (2009) 'Improvising Mozart', in *Musical Improvisation: Art, Education, and Society*, ed. Gabriel Solis and Bruno Nettl. pp. 143–9. Urbana and Chicago, IL: University of Illinois Press.

Levman, Bryan G. (1992) 'The Genesis of Music and Language', *Ethnomusicology* 36(2):147–70.

Lewis, C.S. (1989 [1955]) *The Magician's Nephew*. London: Lions/Collins.

Lindblom, Björn and Johan Sundberg (1970) 'Towards a Generative Theory of Melody', *Svensk Tidskrift for Musikforskning* 52:71–88.

Lindley, Mark (1980) 'Composition', *The New Grove Dictionary of Music and Musicians*, ed. S. Sadie. Volume 4: 599–602. London: Macmillan.

Lloyd, A.L. (1967) *Folk Song in England*. London: Lawrence and Wishart.

Locke, Ralph (1991) 'Constructing the Oriental "Other": Saint-Saëns's Samson et Dalila', *Cambridge Opera Journal* 3:261–302.

— (1993) 'Reflections on Orientalism in Opera and Musical Theater', *Opera Quarterly* 10(1):48–64.

— (2011) *Musical Exoticism: Images and Reflections*. Cambridge: Cambridge University Press.

Lord, Albert (1960) *The Singer of Tales*. Cambridge, MA: Harvard University Press.

Lortat-Jacob, Bernard (ed.) (1987a) *L'Improvisation dans les musiques de tradition orale*. Paris: Selaf.

— (1987b) 'Improvisation: Le Modèle et ses Réalisations', in *L'Improvisation dans les Musiques de Tradition Orale*, ed. Bernard Lortat-Jacob. pp. 45–59. Paris: Selaf.

Lotfi, Mohammad Reza (1976) *Musique vocale de l'Iran: radif du maître Abdollah Davami*. Tehran: n.p.

Lowenfield, V. (1952) *The Nature of Creative Activity*. London: Routledge and Kegan Paul.

Loza, Stephen (1999) *Tito Puente and the Making of Latin Music*. Urbana, IL: University of Illinois Press.

Lucas (Riordan), Ann E. (2010) 'Music and Modernity in Iran: The Radif Revisited'. MA Thesis, University of California, Los Angeles.

— (2014) 'The Creation of Iranian Music in the Age of Steam and Print, c.1880–1914', in *Global Muslims in the Age of Steam and Print, 1850–1930*, ed. James Gelvin and Nile Green. pp. 143–57. Berkeley, CA: University of California Press.

Lyons, John (1981) *Language, Meaning and Context*. London: Fontana Press.

McClary, Susan (1985) 'Afterword: The Politics of Silence and Sound', in *Noise: The Political Economy of Music*, by Jacques Attali (translated by Brian Massumi). pp. 149–58. Minneapolis, MN: University of Minnesota Press.

Mackenzie, Ian (2000) 'Improvisation, Creativity, and Formulaic Language', *Journal of Aesthetics and Art Criticism* 58(2):173–9.

Mansfield, R.S. and T.V. Busse (1981) *The Psychology of Creativity and Discovery*. Chicago, IL: Nelson-Hall.

Mansuri, P. and H. Shirvani (1977) *Fa'āliyat-hā-ye Honari dar Panjāh Sāl Shāhānshāhi-ye Pahlavi (Namāyesh, Musiqi, Operā, Raqs)* [*Artistic Activities in Fifty Years of the Pahlavi Monarchy (Theatre, Music, Opera, Dance)*]. Tehran: Ministry of Arts and Culture.

Martin, Vanessa (2000) *Creating an Islamic State: Khomeini and the Making of a New Iran*. London: I.B. Tauris.

Ma'rufi, Mussa (1964) 'Radif-e Musiqi-ye Iran' ['The Radif of Iranian Music'], *Iran Music Magazine* 130 (January):5–6, 27.

Massoudieh, Mohammad Taghi (1968) *Āwāz-e Šur: Zur Melodiebildung in der persichen Kunstmusik* [*Āvāz-e Shur: Melodic Construction in Persian Art Music*]. Regensburg: Gustav Bosse Verlag.

— (1973) 'Tradition und Wandel in der persichen Musik des 19. Jahrhunderts', in *Musikkulturen Asiens, Afrikas und Ozeaniens im 19. Jahrhundert*, ed. R. Günther. pp. 73–94. Regensburg: Bosse.

— (1988/1367) *Musiqi-ye Mazhabi-ye Iran. Jeld-e Avval: Musiqiy-e Ta'ziyeh* [*Religious Music in Iran. Volume 1: Music of the Ta'ziyeh*]. Tehran: Soroush Publishers.

— (1989 [1978]) *Radif vocal de la musique traditionelle de l'Iran: version de Mahmud-e Karimi*, 4th edition. Tehran: Editions Sorouche (originally published in 1978 by the Iranian Ministry of Arts and Culture).

Mattax Moersch, Charlotte (2009) 'Keyboard Improvisation in the Baroque Period', in *Musical Improvisation: Art, Education, and Society*, ed. Gabriel Solis and Bruno Nettl. pp. 150–70. Urbana and Chicago, IL: University of Illinois Press.

— (1991) *Feminine Endings: Music, Gender and Sexuality*. Minneapolis, MN: University of Minnesota Press.

— (1992) *Georges Bizet: Carmen*. Cambridge: Cambridge University Press.

May, Rollo (1975) *The Courage to Create*. New York: Norton.

Merriam, Alan (1964) *The Anthropology of Music*. Evanston, IL: Northwestern University Press.

Miller, Lloyd Clifton (1999) *Music and Song in Persia: The Art of Avaz*. Richmond: Curzon Press.

Minow, Marta (1990) *Making All the Difference: Inclusion, Exclusion and American Law*. Ithaca, NY: Cornell University Press.

Mitchell, Timothy J. (ed.) (2000) *Questions of Modernity*. Minneapolis, MN: University of Minnesota Press.

Mithen, Steven (2006) *The Singing Neanderthals: The Origins of Music, Language, Mind, and Body*. Cambridge, MA: Harvard University Press.

Modir, Hafez (1986a) 'Model and Style in Classical Iranian Music: The Performance Practice of Mahmoud Zoufonoun'. MA Thesis. University of California, Los Angeles.

— (1986b) 'Research Models in Ethnomusicology Applied to the Radif Phenomenon in Iranian Classical Music', *Pacific Review of Ethnomusicology* 3:63–78.

Mohammadi, Mohsen (2001) 'Zayli bar Maqāleh-ye "Az Maqām tā Dastgāh"' ['A Postscript to "From Maqām to Dastgāh"'], *Mahoor Music Quarterly* 12:41–60.

— (2006) 'The Emergence of Dastgah in Persian Music, c. 1500–1925'. MA Thesis. University of Tehran.

— (2011). 'Persian Records by the Lindström Company: Triangle of Political Relationships, Local Agents and Recording Company', in *The Lindström Project: Contributions to the History of the Record Industry. Beiträge zur Geschichte der Schallplattenindustrie*, ed. P. Gronow and C. Hofer. pp. 121–8. Wien: Gesellschaft für Historische Tonträger.

Monelle, Raymond (1992) *Linguistics and Semiotics in Music*. London: Harwood Academic Publishers.

Monson, Ingrid (1996) *Saying Something: Jazz Improvisation and Interaction*. Chicago, IL: University of Chicago Press.

— (1998) 'Oh Freedom: George Russell, John Coltrane, and Modal Jazz', in *In the Course of Performance: Studies in the World of Musical Improvisation*, ed. Bruno Nettl with Melinda Russell. pp. 149–68. Chicago, IL: University of Chicago Press.

— (2009) 'Jazz as Political and Musical Practice', in *Musical Improvisation: Art, Education, and Society*, ed. Gabriel Solis and Bruno Nettl. pp. 21–37. Urbana and Chicago, IL: University of Illinois Press.

Moran, Nikki (2013) 'Music, Bodies and Relationships: An Ethnographic Contribution to Embodied Cognition Studies', *Psychology of Music* 41(1):5–17.

Movahed, Azin (2003/4) 'Religious Supremacy, Anti-Imperialist Nationhood and Persian Musicology after the 1979 Revolution', *Asian Music* 35(1):85–113.

Myers, Helen (1992) 'Ethnomusicology', in *Ethnomusicology: An Introduction*, ed. Helen Myers. pp. 3–18. London: Macmillan.

Napier, John James (2006) 'Novelty that Must be Subtle: Continuity, Innovation and "Improvisation" in North Indian Music', *Critical Studies in Improvisation* 1(3).

Nash, Denison (1961) 'The Role of the Composer', *Ethnomusicology* 5:81–94, 187–201.

Nattiez, Jean-Jacques (1973) 'Linguistics: A New Approach for Musical Analysis', *International Review of the Aesthetics and Sociology of Music* 4(1):51–68.

— (1983) 'Some Aspects of Inuit Vocal Games', *Ethnomusicology* 27(3):457–75.

Nettl, Bruno (1954) 'Notes on Musical Composition in Primitive Culture', *Anthropological Quarterly* 27(3):81–90.

— (1956) *Music in Primitive Culture*. Cambridge, MA: Harvard University Press.

— (1958) 'Some Linguistic Approaches to Musical Analysis', *The Journal of the International Folk Music Council* 10:37–41.

— (1972) 'Notes on Persian Classical Music of Today: The Performance of the Hesar Section as Part of Dastgah Chahargah', *Orbis Musicae* 1:175–92.

—(1974a) 'Aspects of Form in the Instrumental Performance of the Persian Avaz', *Ethnomusicology* 18:405–14.

— (1974b) 'Nour-Ali Bouroumand, a Twentieth Century Master of Persian Music', *Studia Instrumentorum Musicae Popularis* 3:167–71.

— (1974c) 'Thoughts on Improvisation: A Comparative Approach', *The Musical Quarterly* 60(1):1–19.

— (1975) 'The Role of Music in Culture: Iran, a Recently Developed Nation', in *Contemporary Music and Music Cultures*, ed. C. Hamm, B. Nettl and R. Byrnside. pp. 71–100. Englewood Cliffs, NJ: Prentice-Hall.

— (1978) 'Persian Classical Music in Tehran: The Process of Change', in *Eight Urban Musical Cultures: Tradition and Change*, ed. B. Nettl. pp. 146–76. Urbana, IL: University of Illinois Press.

— (1980) 'Musical Values and Social Values: Symbols in Iran', *Asian Music* 12(1):129–48.

— (1981) 'Comments on the Persian Radif', in *Music East and West: Essays in Honour of Walter Kaufmann*, ed. T. Noblitt. pp. 111–21. New York: Pendragon Press.

— (1983) *The Study of Ethnomusicology: Twenty-nine Issues and Concepts*. Urbana, IL: University of Illinois Press.

— (1985) *The Western Impact on World Music: Change, Adaptation, and Survival*. New York: Schirmer Books.

— (1987) *The Radif of Persian Music: Studies of Structure and Cultural Context*. Champaign, IL: Elephant and Cat.

— (ed.) (1991) *The World of Music: New Perspectives on Improvisation*, 33(3).

— (1995) 'Foreword', in *Music, Culture, and Experience: Selected Papers of John Blacking*, ed. Reginald Byron. pp. vii–x. Chicago, IL: University of Chicago Press.

— (1998) 'Introduction: An Art Neglected in Scholarship', in *In the Course of Performance: Studies in the World of Musical Improvisation*, ed. Bruno Nettl with Melinda Russell. pp. 1–23. Chicago, IL: University of Chicago Press.

— (2005) *The Study of Ethnomusicology: Thirty-one Issues and Concepts*, 2nd edition. Urbana and Chicago, IL: University of Illinois Press.

— (2009) 'On Learning the Radif and Improvisation in Iran', in *Musical Improvisation: Art, Education, and Society*, ed. Gabriel Solis and Bruno Nettl. pp. 185–99. Urbana and Chicago, IL: University of Illinois Press.

— (2012) 'Contemplating the Concept of Improvisation and Its History in Scholarship', paper presented at the 2012 Annual Meeting of the Society for Ethnomusicology as part of a joint SEM/AMS/SMT roundtable on 'Improvisation: Object of Study and Critical Paradigm', New Orleans, November 2012.

Nettl, Bruno et al. (2001) 'Improvisation', *The New Grove Dictionary of Music and Musicians*, 2nd edition, ed. Stanley Sadie. Volume 12: 94–133. London: Macmillan.

Nettl, Bruno, with Bela Foltin Jr. (1972) *Daramad of Chahargah: A Study in the Performance Practice of Persian Music*. Detroit Monographs in Musicology, no. 2. Detroit, MI: Harmonie Park Press.

Nettl, Bruno and Ronald Riddle (1973) 'Taqsim Nahawand: A Study of Sixteen Performances by Jihad Racy', *Yearbook of the International Folk Music Council* 5:11–50.

Nettl, Bruno, with Melinda Russell (eds) (1998) *In the Course of Performance: Studies in the World of Musical Improvisation*. Chicago, IL: University of Chicago Press.

Neuman, Daniel (1990) *The Life of Music in North India: The Organization of an Artistic Tradition*, 2nd edition. Chicago, IL: University of Chicago Press.

Neuman, Dard (2012) 'Pedagogy, Practice, and Embodied Creativity in Hindustani Music', *Ethnomusicology* 56(3):426–9.

Nooshin, Laudan (1996) 'The Processes of Creation and Re-creation in Persian Classical Music'. PhD Thesis. University of London, Goldsmiths' College.

— (1998) 'The Song of the Nightingale: Processes of Improvisation in *Dastgah Segah* (Iranian Classical Music)', *British Journal of Ethnomusicology* 7:69–116.

— (2001) 'Alizadeh, Hossein', *The New Grove Dictionary of Music and Musicians*, ed. S. Sadie. Volume 1: 376–7. London: Macmillan.

— (2003) 'Improvisation as "Other": Creativity, Knowledge and Power – The Case of Iranian Classical Music', *Journal of the Royal Musical Association* 128:242–96.

— (2005a) 'Subversion and Counter-subversion: Power, Control and Meaning in the New Iranian Pop Music', in *Music, Power and Politics*, ed. Annie J. Randall. pp. 231–72. New York and London: Routledge.

— (2005b) 'Underground, Overground: Rock Music and Youth Discourses in Iran', *Iranian Studies* (Special Issue: Music and Society in Iran) 38(3):463–94.

— (2009a) 'Prelude: Power and the Play of Music', in *Music and the Play of Power in the Middle East, North Africa and Central Asia*, ed. Laudan Nooshin. pp. 1–13. Farnham: Ashgate.

— (2009b) '"Tomorrow Is Ours": Re-imagining Nation, Performing Youth in the New Iranian Pop Music', in *Music and the Play of Power in the Middle East, North Africa and Central Asia*, ed. Laudan Nooshin. pp. 245–68. Farnham: Ashgate.

— (2013) 'Two Revivalist Moments in Iranian Classical Music', in *The Oxford Handbook of Music Revival*, ed. Caroline Bithell and Juniper Hill. pp. 277–99. Oxford: Oxford University Press.

— (2015) 'Jazz and Its Social Meanings in Iran: From Cultural Colonialism to the Universal', in *Jazz Worlds/ World Jazz*, ed. Philip V. Bohlman, Goffredo Plastino and Travis Jackson. Chicago, IL: University of Chicago Press.

Ogger, Thomas (1987) *Maqam Segah/Sikah. Vergleich der Kunstmusik des Irak und des Iran Anhand Eines Maqam Modells*. Hamburg: Verlag der Musikalienhandlung Karl Dieter Wagner.

Olley, Jacob (2010) 'Improvisation in Historical and Regional Perspective: Comparing Performance Practice and Modal Structure in Turkish and Persian Classical Music'. BMus Dissertation. University of London, School of Oriental and African Studies.

Ong, Walter (1982) *Orality and Literacy: The Technologizing of the Word*. London: Methuen & Co. (2nd ed. 2002).

Parisa (Fatemeh Va'ezi) (1985/1364) 'Shiveh-ye Kār va Tadris-e Ostād Karimi' ['Ostād Karimi's Methods of Working and Teaching'], in *Yādnāmeh-ye Ostād Mahmud Karimi* [*Remembrance of Ostād Mahmud Karimi*]. pp. 77–82. Tehran: n.p.

Parry, Hubert (1954) 'Composition', in *Grove's Dictionary of Music and Musicians*, 5th edition, ed. Eric Blom. Volume 2: 388–9. London: Macmillan.

Parsa, Misagh (1989) *Social Origins of the Iranian Revolution*. New Brunswick, NJ: Rutgers University Press.

Patel, Aniruddh D. (2003) 'Language, Music, Syntax and the Brain', *Nature Neuroscience* 6:674–81.

— (2008) *Music, Language, and the Brain*. New York: Oxford University Press.

Patel, Aniruddh D., Meredith Wong, Jessica Foxton, Aliette Lochy and Isabelle Peretz (2008) 'Speech Intonation Perception Deficits in Musical Tone Deafness (Congenital Amusia)', *Music Perception* 25(4):357–68.

Payvar, Faramarz (1961) *Dastur-e Santur* [*Santur Manual*]. Tehran: Ferdowsi Press.

Pelinski, Ramon (1984) 'A Generative Grammar of Personal Eskimo Songs', in *Musical Grammars and Computer Analysis*, ed. M. Baroni and L. Callegari. pp. 273–86. Florence: Leo S. Olschki.

Peretz, Isabelle (2006) 'The Nature of Music from a Biological Perspective', *Cognition* 100(1):1–32.

Porter, Dennis (1983) 'Orientalism and Its Problems', in *Colonial Discourse and Post-Colonial Theory: A Reader*, ed. Patrick Williams and Laura Chrisman. pp. 150–61. New York: Columbia University Press.

Porter, James (1991) 'Muddying the Crystal Spring: From Idealism and Realism to Marxism in the Study of English and American Folk Song', in *Comparative Musicology and Anthropology of Music: Essays on the History of Ethnomusicology*, ed. Bruno Nettl and Philip V. Bohlman. pp. 113–30. Chicago, IL: University of Chicago Press.

Powers, Harold (1980a) 'Classical Music, Cultural Roots, and Colonial Rule: An Indic Musicologist Looks at the Muslim World', *Asian Music* 12(1):5–39.

— (1980b) 'Language Models and Musical Analysis', *Ethnomusicology* 24:1–60.

— (1980c) 'Mode', *The New Grove Dictionary of Music and Musicians*, ed. S. Sadie. Volume 12: 376–450. London: Macmillan.

— (1989) 'International Segah and Its Nominal Equivalents in Central Asia and Kashmir', in *Maqam, Raga, Zeilenmelodik. Konzeptionen und Prinzipien der Musikproduction. Materialien der 1. Arbeitstagung der Study Group 'Maqam' beim International Council for Traditional Music vom 28. Juni bis 2. Juli 1988 in Berlin*, ed. Jürgen Elsner. pp. 40–85. Berlin.

Pressing, Jeff (1988) 'Improvisation: Methods and Models', in *Generative Processes in Music: The Psychology of Performance, Improvisation and Composition*, ed. J.A. Sloboda. pp. 129–78. Oxford: Clarendon Press.

— (1998) 'Psychological Constraints on Improvisational Expertise and Communication', in *In the Course of Performance: Studies in the World of Musical Improvisation*, ed. Bruno Nettl with Melinda Russell. pp. 47–68. Chicago, IL: University of Chicago Press.

Prociuk, P. (1981) 'The Deep Structure of Ukrainian Hardship Songs', *Yearbook for Traditional Music* 13:82–96.

Qureshi, Regula Burckardt (1987) 'Music, Sound and Contextual Input: A Performance Model for Musical Analysis', *Ethnomusicology* 31:56–86.

— (1999) 'Other Musicologies: Exploring Issues and Confronting Practice in India', in *Rethinking Music*, ed. Nicholas Cook and Mark Everist. pp. 311–15. Oxford: Oxford University Press.

Racy, Ali Jihad (2009) 'Why Do They Improvise? Reflections on Meaning and Experience', in *Musical Improvisation: Art, Education, and Society*, ed. Gabriel Solis and Bruno Nettl. pp. 313–22. Urbana and Chicago, IL: University of Illinois Press.

Radano, Ronald and Philip V. Bohlman (eds) (2000) *Music and the Racial Imagination*. Chicago, IL: University of Chicago Press.

Rasmussen, Ann K. (2009) 'The Juncture between Creation and Re-Creation among Indonesian Reciters of the Qu'ran', in *Musical Improvisation: Art, Education, and Society*, ed. Gabriel Solis and Bruno Nettl. pp. 72–89. Urbana and Chicago, IL: University of Illinois Press.

Rees, Helen (2009) 'Introduction: Writing Lives in Chinese Music', in *Lives in Chinese Music*, ed. Helen Rees. pp. 1–30. Urbana and Chicago, IL: University of Illinois Press.

Reti, Rudolph (1961) *The Thematic Process in Music*. London: Faber and Faber.

Rice, Timothy (1987) 'Toward the Remodelling of Ethnomusicology', *Ethnomusicology* 31:469–88.

— (2003) 'Time, Place, and Metaphor in Musical Experience and Ethnography', *Ethnomusicology* 47(2):151–79.

Rink, John (1993) 'Schenker and Improvisation', *Journal of Music Theory* 37(1):1–54.

— (2001) 'The Legacy of Improvisation in Chopin', in *Muzyka w kontekscie kultury*, ed. Małgorzata Janicka-Słysz, Teresa Malecka and Krzysztof Szwajgier. pp. 78–89. Cracow: Akademia Muzyczne.

Rosaldo, Renato (1989) 'Imperialist Nostalgia', *Representations* 26:107–22.

Rose, Simon and Raymond MacDonald (2012) 'Improvisation as Real-time Composition', in *The Act of Musical Composition: Studies in the Creative Process*, ed. Dave Collins. pp. 187–214. Farnham: Ashgate.

Rosenberg, Neil V. (1993) 'Introduction', in *Transforming Traditions: Folk Music Revivals Examined*, ed. Neil V. Rosenberg. pp. 1–25. Urbana, IL: University of Illinois Press.

Rubin, David C. (1995) *Memory in Oral Traditions: The Cognitive Psychology of Epic, Ballads, and Counting-Out Rhymes*. New York: Oxford University Press.

Rycroft, David (1961/2) 'The Guitar Improvisations of Mwenda Jean Bosco', *African Music* 2(4):81–98; 3(1):86–102.

Saba, Abol Hassan (c.1965) *Dowreh-ye Avval, Dovvom, Sevvom va Chāhārom-e Santur* [*First, Second, Third and Fourth Santur Course*]. Tehran: n.p. (originally published in the 1950s).

— (c.1967) *Dowreh-ye Avval, Dovvom va Sevvom-e Violon* [*First, Second and Third Violin Course*]. Tehran: n.p. (originally published in the 1950s).

— (c.1970) *Dowreh-ye Avval-e Tār va Setār* [*First Tār and Setār Course*]. Tehran: n.p. (originally published in the 1950s).

Sadeghi, Manuchehr (1971) 'Improvisation in Nonrhythmic Solo Instrumental Contemporary Persian Art Music'. MA Thesis. California State College, Los Angeles.

Sadie, Stanley (ed.) (1980) 'Improvisation', *The New Grove Dictionary of Music and Musicians*, ed. Stanley Sadie. Volume 9: 31–56. London: Macmillan.

Sadighi, Ramin and Sohrab Mahdavi (2009) 'The Song Does Not Remain the Same', *Middle East Research and Information Project*, 12 March 2009. http://www.merip.org/mero/mero031209 (accessed 12.11.12).

Said, Edward W. (1978) *Orientalism*. London: Routledge and Kegan Paul.

— (1991) *Musical Elaborations*. New York: Columbia University Press.

— (1993) *Culture and Imperialism*. London: Vintage.

Samson, Jim (2001) 'Canon (iii)', *The New Grove Dictionary of Music and Musicians*, 2nd edition, ed. Stanley Sadie. Volume 5: 6–7. London: Macmillan.

Sanyal, Ritwik and D. Richard Widdess (2004) *Dhrupad: Tradition and Performance in Indian Music*. Aldershot: Ashgate.

Sarami, Jahanshah (1990) 'Borumand, Hāfez va Ostād-e Musiqi' ['Borumand, Guardian and Master of Music'], *Adineh* 43/44:50–52.

Sarkoohi, Faraj (1989) 'Goftogoo bā Hossein Alizadeh' ['Interview with Hossein Alizadeh'], *Adineh* 39:33–9.

Schoenberg, Arnold (1967) *Fundamentals of Musical Composition*, ed. G. Strang with L. Stein. London: Faber.

Schofield, Katherine Butler (2010) 'Reviving the Golden Age Again: "Classicization", Hindustani Music, and the Mughals', *Ethnomusicology* 45(3):484–517.

Scholes, Percy A. (1970) 'Motif', in *The Oxford Companion to Music*, 10th edition, ed. John Owen Ward. p. 661. Oxford: Oxford University Press.

Seeger, Anthony (1991) 'Styles of Musical Ethnography', in *Comparative Musicology and Anthropology of Music: Essays on the History of Ethnomusicology*, ed. Bruno Nettl and Philip V. Bohlman. pp. 342–55. Chicago, IL: University of Chicago Press.

Seeger, Charles (1969) 'On the Formational Apparatus of the Music Compositional Process', *Ethnomusicology* 13(2):230–47.

— (1977) 'The Music Compositional Process as a Function in a Nest of Functions and in Itself a Nest of Functions', in *Studies in Musicology 1935–1975*. pp. 139–67. Berkeley, CA: University of California Press.

Sepanta, Sassan (1959) 'Segāh', *Iran Music Magazine* 7(6):9, 14.

— (1964) 'Naqdi be Radif-e Musiqi-ye Irān az Enteshārāt-e Honar-hā-ye Zibā' ['A Critique of Radif-e Musiqi-e Iran, published by the Ministry of Fine Arts'], *Iran Music Magazine* 131 (February):4–6, 28–9.

— (1987/1366) *Tarikh-e Tahavvol-e Zabt-e Musiqi dar Iran* [*A History of Sound Recording in Iran*]. Esfahan: Entesharat-e Nima.

Sha'bani, Aziz (1973) *Shenāsāi-ye Musiqi-ye Iran: Osool-e Nazari-ye Musiqi-ye Iran* [*Understanding Iranian Music: The Theoretical Principles of Iranian Music*]. Volume 3. Shiraz: Edareh-ye Kol-e Farhang o Honar-e Fars.

Shahrnazdar, Mohsen (1998/99) 'Jāygāh-e Barkhi Mafāhim va Vājehā-ye Musiqi-ye Irani' [translated as 'Some Concepts and Words in Iranian Music'], *Mahoor Music Quarterly* 1:149–59; 4:147–53.

— (2004a) *Goftogoo bā Dariush Talai dar bāreh-ye Musiqi-ye Irani* [*Conversations with Dariush Talai about Iranian Music*]. Tehran: Nashr-e Ney.

— (2004b) *Goftogoo bā Hossein Alizadeh dar bāreh-ye Musiqi-ye Irani* [*Conversations with Hossein Alizadeh about Iranian Music*]. Tehran: Nashr-e Ney.

Shelemay, Kay Kaufmann (2001) *Soundscapes: Exploring Music in a Changing World*. New York: W.W. Norton.

Sherman, Bernard D. (2003) 'Speaking Mozart's Lingo: Robert Levin on Mozart and Improvisation', in *Inside Early Music: Conversations with Performers*, 2nd edition. pp. 315–38. Oxford and New York: Oxford University Press.

Simms, Rob and Amir Koushkani (2012a) *The Art of Avaz and Mohammad Reza Shajarian: Foundations and Contexts*. Lanham, MD: Lexington Books.

— (2012b) *Mohammad Reza Shajarian's Avaz in Iran and Beyond, 1979–2010*. Lanham, MD: Lexington Books.

Singleton, Brian (1997) 'Introduction: The Pursuit of Otherness for the Investigation of Self', *Theatre Research International* 22(2):93–7.

Slawek, Stephen (2009) 'Hindustani Sitar and Jazz Guitar Music: A Foray into Comparative Improvology', in *Musical Improvisation: Art, Education, and Society*, ed. Gabriel Solis and Bruno Nettl. pp. 200–220. Urbana and Chicago, IL: University of Illinois Press.

Sloboda, John A. (1982) 'Music Performance', in *The Psychology of Music*, ed. D. Deutsch. pp. 479–96. London: Academic Press.

Smith, Gregory (1991) 'In Quest of a New Perspective on Improvised Jazz: A View from the Balkans', *The World of Music* 33(3):29–52.

Smith, Paul (ed.) (1959) *Creativity*. New York: Hastings House.

Snyder, Bob (2000) *Music and Memory: An Introduction*. Cambridge, MA: The MIT Press.

Solie, Ruth (1993) 'Introduction', in *Musicology and Difference: Gender and Sexuality in Musical Scholarship*, ed. Ruth Solie. pp. 1–20. Berkeley, CA: University of California Press.

Solis, Gabriel (2009) 'Introduction', in *Musical Improvisation: Art, Education, and Society*, ed. Gabriel Solis and Bruno Nettl. pp. 1–17. Urbana and Chicago, IL: University of Illinois Press.

Solis, Gabriel and Bruno Nettl (eds) (2009) *Musical Improvisation: Art, Education, and Society*. Urbana and Chicago, IL: University of Illinois Press.

Solomon, Thomas (2012) 'Where Is the Postcolonial in Ethnomusicology?', in *Ethnomusicology in East Africa: Perspectives from Uganda and Beyond*, ed. Sylvia Nannyonga-Tamusuza and Thomas Solomon. pp. 216–51. Kampala: Fountain Publishers.

Sorrell, Neil and Ram Narayan (1980) *Indian Music in Performance: A Practical Introduction*. Manchester: Manchester University Press.

Sternberg, Robert J. (ed.) (1988) *The Nature of Creativity: Contemporary Psychological Perspectives*. Cambridge: Cambridge University Press.

Stock, Jonathan (1996) *Musical Creativity in Twentieth-Century China: Abing, His Music, and Its Changing Meanings*. Eastman Studies in Music. Rochester, NY: University of Rochester Press.

— (2001) 'Toward an Ethnomusicology of the Individual, Or Biographical Writing in Ethnomusicology', *World of Music* 43(1):5–19.

Stokes, Martin (1992) *The Arabesk Debate: Music and Musicians in Modern Turkey*. Oxford: Clarendon Press.

— (2000) 'East, West, Arabesk', in *Western Music and Its Others: Difference, Representation, and Appropriation in Music*, ed. Georgina Born and David Hesmondhalgh. pp. 213–33. Berkeley, CA: University of California Press.

— (2001) 'Ethnomusicology, §IV: Contemporary Theoretical Issues', *The New Grove Dictionary of Music and Musicians*, 2nd edition, ed. Stanley Sadie. Volume 8: 386–403. London: Macmillan.

— (2002) 'Silver Sounds in the Inner Citadel? Reflections on Musicology and Islam', in *Interpreting Islam*, ed. Hastings Donnan. pp. 167–89. London: Sage.

— (2003) 'Postcolonialism', in *The Continuum Encyclopaedia of Popular Music of the World*, ed. J. Shepherd, D. Horn, P. Oliver and P. Wicke. Volume 1: 103–6. New York: Continuum.

Stolz, Benjamin and Richard Shannon (1976) *Oral Literature and the Formula*. Ann Arbor, MI: Center for the Coordination of Ancient and Modern Studies, The University of Michigan.

Sudnow, David (1978) *Ways of the Hand: The Organisation of Improvised Conduct*. Cambridge, MA: Harvard University Press.

Sumits, William (2011) 'The Evolution of the Maqām Tradition in Central Asia: From the Theory of 12 Maqām to the Practice of Shashmaqām'. PhD Thesis. University of London, School of Oriental and African Studies.

Summerfield, J.D. and L. Thatcher (eds) (1964) *The Creative Mind and Method*. New York: Russell and Russell.

Tabar, Hassan (2005) *Les Transformations de la musique iranienne au début du XXe siècle (1898–1940). Les Premiers enregistrements en Iran*. Paris: L'Harmattan.

Talai, Dariouche (1997) *Radif-e Mirza Abdollah*. Tehran: n.p.

— (2000) *Traditional Persian Art Music: The Radif of Mirza Abdollah*. Costa Mesa: Mazda Publishers.

Taruskin, Richard (1992) '"Entoiling the Falconet": Russian Musical Orientalism in Context', *Cambridge Opera Journal* 4:253–80.

— (1995) *Text and Act: Essays on Music and Performance*. Oxford: Oxford University Press.

Taylor, Irving (1959) 'The Nature of the Creative Process', in *Creativity: An Examination of the Creative Process*, ed. Paul Smith. pp. 51–82. New York: Hastings House.

Taylor-Jay, Claire (2009) '"I Am Blessed with Fruit": Masculinity, Androgyny and Creativity in Early 20th-Century German Music', in *Masculinity and Western Musical Practice*, ed. Ian Biddle and Kirsten Gibson. pp. 183–208. Farnham: Ashgate.

Temperley, Nicholas (2009) 'Preluding at the Piano', in *Musical Improvisation: Art, Education, and Society*, ed. Gabriel Solis and Bruno Nettl. pp. 323–41. Urbana and Chicago, IL: University of Illinois Press.

Tenzer, Michael (2000) *Gamelan Gong Kebyar: The Art of Twentieth-Century Balinese Music*. Chicago, IL: University of Chicago Press.

Toynbee, Jason (2003) 'Music, Culture, and Creativity', in *The Cultural Study of Music: A Critical Introduction*, ed. Martin Clayton, Trevor Herbert and Richard Middleton. pp. 102–12. Routledge: New York.

Tracey, Andrew (1961) 'The Mbira Music of Jege A. Tapera', *African Music Society Journal* 2(4):44–63.

Treitler, Leo (1974) 'Homer and Gregory: The Transmission of Epic Poetry and Plainchant', *The Musical Quarterly* 60(3):333–72.

— (1991) 'Medieval Improvisation', *The World of Music* 33(3):66–91.

— (1993) 'Gender and Other Dualities of Music History', in *Musicology and Difference: Gender and Sexuality in Musical Scholarship*, ed. Ruth Solie. pp. 23–45. Berkeley, CA: University of California Press.

— (2007) *With Voice and Pen: Coming to Know Medieval Song and How It Was Made*. Oxford and New York: Oxford University Press.

Tsuge, Gen'ichi (1974) 'Avaz: A Study of the Rhythmic Aspects in Classical Iranian Music'. PhD Dissertation. Wesleyan University.

Turino, Thomas (2009) 'Formulas and Improvisation in Participatory Practice', in *Musical Improvisation: Art, Education, and Society*, ed. Gabriel Solis and Bruno Nettl. pp. 103–16. Urbana and Chicago, IL: University of Illinois Press.

Vaziri, Ali Naqi (1913) *Dastur-e Tār* [*Tār Manual*]. Berlin: n.p. (reprinted in Iran).

— (1933) *Dastur-e Violon* [*Violin Manual*]. Tehran: n.p.

— (1936) *Nouvelle méthode de tar*. Tehran: n.p.

Vernon, P.E. (ed.) (1970) *Creativity: Selected Readings*. Harmondsworth: Penguin Books.

Vetter, Roger (2004) 'A Square Peg in a Round Hole: Teaching Javanese Gamelan in the Ensemble Paradigm of the Academy', in *Performing Ethnomusicology: Teaching and Representation in World Music Ensembles*, ed. Ted Solís. pp. 115–25. Berkeley, CA: University of California Press.

Wachsmann, Klaus (1982) 'The Changeability of Musical Experience', *Ethnomusicology* 26(2):197–215.

Walker, Alan (1962) *A Study in Musical Analysis*. London: Barrie and Rockliff.

Weidman, Amanda J. (2006) *Singing the Classical: Voicing the Modern. The Postcolonial Politics of Music in South India*. Durham, NC and London: Duke University Press.

Weisberg, Robert (1986) *Creativity and Other Myths*. New York: W.H. Freeman.

Widdess, D. Richard (1994) 'Involving the Performers in Transcription and Analysis: A Collaborative Approach to Dhrupad', *Ethnomusicology* 38(1):59–79.

— (2011) 'Dynamics of Melodic Discourse in Indian Music: Budhaditya Mukherjee's Alāp in Rāg Pūriyā-Kalyān', in *Analytical and Cross-Cultural Studies in World Music*, ed. Michael Tenzer and John Roeder. pp. 187–24. New York: Oxford University Press.

Wilkens, Eckart (1967) *Künstler und Amateure im persichen Santurspiel. Studien zum Gestaltungswermögen in der iranischen Musik*. Regensburg: Bosse.

Williams, Alastair (2000) 'Musicology and Postmodernism', *Music Analysis* 19(3):385–407.

— (2001) *Constructing Musicology*. Farnham: Ashgate.

Wilson, Charles (2004) 'György Ligeti and the Rhetoric of Autonomy', *Twentieth-Century Music* 1:5–28.

Winograd, Terry (1968) 'Linguistics and the Computer Analysis of Tonal Harmony', *Journal of Music Theory* 12:2–49.

Wray, Alison (2002) *Formulaic Language and the Lexicon*. Cambridge: Cambridge University Press.

— (2008) *Formulaic Language: Pushing the Boundaries*. New York: Oxford University Press.

Wright, Owen (1978) *The Modal System of Arab and Persian Music A.D. 1250–1300*. Oxford: Oxford University Press.

— (1994) 'Segah: An Historical Outline', in *Regionale Maqam-Traditionen in Geschichte und Gegenwalt. Materialien der 2. Arbeitstagung der Study Group 'Maqam' beim International Council for Traditional Music, 1992*, ed. J. Elsner and G. Jahnichen. Part 2. pp. 480–509. Berlin.

— (2001) 'Arab Music. I. Art Music. 1. Introduction', *The New Grove Dictionary of Music and Musicians*, 2nd edition, ed. Stanley Sadie. Volume 1: 797–8. London: Macmillan.

— (2009) *Touraj Kiaras and Persian Classical Music: An Analytical Perspective*. Farnham: Ashgate.

Wyver, John (producer) (1990) 'Signs of Life', transcript of a programme in the BBC series *Horizon*, broadcast 11 June 1990.

Zadeh, Chloe (2012) 'Formulas and the Building Blocks of *Thumrī* Style: A Study in "Improvised" Music', *Analytical Approaches to World Music Journal* 2(1):1–48.

Zolfonoun, Jalal (1980) 'Characteristics of Iranian Classical Music', in *Musical Voices of Asia: Report of 'Asian Traditional Performing Arts 1978'*, ed. Richard Emmert and Minegishi Yuki. pp. 29–31. Tokyo: Heibonsha Limited Publishers.

— (2001) *The Analysis of Persian Music: Based on Darvish Khan's Works and Its Comparison with Radif in Iranian Music*. Tehran: Hastan Press.

Zonis, Ella (1964) 'Review of *La Musique traditionelle de l'Iran* by M. Ma'rufi and M. Berkeshli', *Ethnomusicology* 8:303–10.

— (1965) 'Contemporary Art Music in Persia', *The Musical Quarterly* 51(4):636–48.

— (1973) *Persian Classical Music: An Introduction*. Cambridge, MA: Harvard University Press.

Index